T0075150

Data Analytics in the AWS Cloud

Building a Data Platform for BI and Predictive Analytics on AWS

Joe Minichino

WILEY

Copyright © 2023 by John Wiley & Sons, Inc. All rights reserved.

Published by John Wiley & Sons, Inc., Hoboken, New Jersey.

Published simultaneously in Canada and the United Kingdom.

ISBN: 978-1-119-90924-8

ISBN: 978-1-119-90926-2 (ebk.)

ISBN: 978-1-119-90925-5 (ebk.)

No part of this publication may be reproduced, stored in a retrieval system, or transmitted in any form or by any means, electronic, mechanical, photocopying, recording, scanning, or otherwise, except as permitted under Section 107 or 108 of the 1976 United States Copyright Act, without either the prior written permission of the Publisher, or authorization through payment of the appropriate per-copy fee to the Copyright Clearance Center, Inc., 222 Rosewood Drive, Danvers, MA 01923, (978) 750-8400, fax (978) 750-4470, or on the web at www.copyright.com. Requests to the Publisher for permission should be addressed to the Permissions Department, John Wiley & Sons, Inc., 111 River Street, Hoboken, NJ 07030, (201) 748-6011, fax (201) 748-6008, or online at www.wiley.com/go/permission.

Trademarks: WILEY and the Wiley logo are trademarks or registered trademarks of John Wiley & Sons, Inc. and/or its affiliates, in the United States and other countries, and may not be used without written permission. AWS is a registered trademark of Amazon Technologies, Inc. All other trademarks are the property of their respective owners. John Wiley & Sons, Inc. is not associated with any product or vendor mentioned in this book.

Limit of Liability/Disclaimer of Warranty: While the publisher and author have used their best efforts in preparing this book, they make no representations or warranties with respect to the accuracy or completeness of the contents of this book and specifically disclaim any implied warranties of merchantability or fitness for a particular purpose. No warranty may be created or extended by sales representatives or written sales materials. The advice and strategies contained herein may not be suitable for your situation. You should consult with a professional where appropriate. Further, readers should be aware that websites listed in this work may have changed or disappeared between when this work was written and when it is read. Neither the publisher nor author shall be liable for any loss of profit or any other commercial damages, including but not limited to special, incidental, consequential, or other damages.

For general information on our other products and services or for technical support, please contact our Customer Care Department within the United States at (800) 762-2974, outside the United States at (317) 572-3993 or fax (317) 572-4002.

If you believe you've found a mistake in this book, please bring it to our attention by emailing our reader support team at wileysupport@wiley.com with the subject line "Possible Book Errata Submission."

Wiley also publishes its books in a variety of electronic formats. Some content that appears in print may not be available in electronic formats. For more information about Wiley products, visit our web site at www.wiley.com.

Library of Congress Control Number: 2023931100

Cover image: © deepagopi2011/Adobe Stock

Cover design: Wiley

SKY10045081_032823

About the Author

Gionata "Joe" Minichino is a software engineer with nearly 20 years of experience. Joe has focused on a number of areas of engineering, specializing in data, data architecture, machine learning, and artificial intelligence, in particular in the field of computer vision, and has written a number of books and courses on the subject. Joe is also the author of a popular open source project called LokiJS, an in-memory database written in JavaScript. After working in the mobile, healthcare, advertising, and energy industries, Joe now works as a data architect at Teamwork.com, a project management SaaS company in Cork, Ireland. Outside of work Joe's passions are ancient and medieval history, heavy metal music, and fantasy literature.

About the Technical Editor

Chris Johnson is a Solutions Architect at Amazon Web Services (AWS). In his role, Chris works with customers on a day-to-day basis, translating their business needs into technical architectures and engagements that help those customers to achieve the outcomes they want leveraging the cloud. His tenure in AWS is more than seven years; he has a background in solutions architecture, support, and datacenter operations spanning more than 25 years.

Acknowledgments

I would like to acknowledge my life partner, Rowena, and our daughters, Livia and Siabhra, for all the unconditional love and support.

I also would like to acknowledge Peter Coppinger, Dan Mackey, and everyone at Teamwork.com for graciously supporting me in the writing of this book, and for creating an environment in which people can thrive personally and professionally.

I would also like to thank everyone at Wiley for their support, and Chris Johnson for his impeccable work on the technical review.

Contents at a Glance

Contents

Introduction

Welcome to your journey to AWS-powered cloud-based analytics!

If you need to build data lakes, import pipelines, or perform large-scale analytics and then display them with state-of-the-art visualization tools, all through the AWS ecosystem, then you are in the right place.

I will spare you an introduction on how we live in a connected world where businesses thrive on data-driven decisions based on powerful analytics. Instead, I will open by saying that this book is for people who need to build a data platform to turn their organization into a data-driven one, or who need to improve their current architectures in the real world. This book may help you gain the knowledge to pass an AWS certification exam, but this is most definitely not its only aim.

I will be covering a number of tools provided by AWS for building a data lake and analytics pipeline, but I will cover these tools insofar as they are applicable to data lakes and analytics, and I will deliberately omit features that are not relevant or particularly important. This is not a comprehensive guide to such tools—it's a guide to the features of those tools that are relevant to our topic.

It is my personal opinion that analytics, be they in the form of looking back at the past (business intelligence [BI]) or trying to predict the future (data science and predictive analytics), are the key to success.

You may think marketing is a key to success. It is, but only when your analytics direct your marketing efforts in the right direction, to the right customers, with the right approach for those customers.

You may think pricing, product features, and customer support are keys. They are, but only when your analytics reveal the correct prices and the right features to strengthen customer retention and success, and your support team possesses the necessary skills to adequately satisfy your customers' requests and complaints.

That is why you need analytics.

Even in the extremely unlikely case that your data all resides in one data store, you are probably keeping it in a relational database that's there to back your customer-facing applications. Traditional RDBs are not made for large-scale[1] storage and analysis, and I have seen very few cases of storing the entire history of records of an RDB in the RDB itself.

So you need a massively scalable storage solution with a query engine that can deal with different data sources and formats, and you probably need a lot of preparation and clean-up before your data can be used for large-scale analysis.

You need a data lake.

What Is a Data Lake?

A *data lake* is a centralized repository of structured, semi-structured, and unstructured data, upon which you can run insightful analytics. This is my ultra-short version of the definition.

While in the past we referred to a data lake strictly as the facility where all of our data was stored, nowadays the definition has extended to include all of the possible data stores that can be linked to the centralized data storage, in a kind of hybrid data lake that comprises flat-file storage, data warehouses, and operational data stores.

When You Do Not Need a Data Lake

If all your data resides in a single data store, you're not interested in analyzing it, or the size and velocity of your data are such that you can afford to record the entire history of all your records in the same data store and perform your analysis there without impacting customer-facing services, then you do not need a data lake. I'll confess I never came across such a scenario. So, unless you are running some kind of micro and very particular business that does not benefit from analysis, most likely you will want to have a data lake in place and an analytics pipeline powering your decisions.

When Do You Need Analytics?

Really, always.

---

[1] Everything is relative, but generally speaking if you tried to store all the versions of all the records in a large RDBS you would put the database itself under unnecessary pressure, *and* you would be doing so at the higher cost of the I/O optimized storage that databases use in AWS (read about I/O provision), rather than utilizing a cheap storage facility that scales to virtually infinite size, like S3.

When Do You Need a Data Lake for Analytics?

Almost always, and they are generally cheap solutions to maintain. In this book we will explore ways to store and analyze vast quantities of data for very little money.

How About an Analytics Team?

One of the most common mistakes companies make is to put analysts to work before they have data engineers in place. If you do that, you are only going to cause these effects in order:

- Your analysts will waste their time trying to either work around engineering problems or worse, try their hand at data engineering themselves.

- Your analysts will get frustrated, as most of their time will be spent procuring, transforming, and cleaning the data instead of analyzing it.

- Your analysts will produce analyses, but they are not likely to set up automation for the data engineering side of the work, meaning they will spend hours rerunning data acquisition, filtering, cleaning, and transforming rather than analyzing.

- Your analysts will leave for a company that has an analytics team in place that includes both data analysts and data engineers.

So just skip that part and do things the right way. Get a vision for your analytics, put data engineers in place, and then analysts to work who can dedicate 100 percent of their time to analyzing data and nothing else. We will explore designing and setting up a data analytics team in Chapter 2, "The Path to Analytics: Setting Up a Data and Analytics Team."

The Data Platform

In this book, I will guide you through the extensive but extremely interesting and rewarding journey of creating a data platform that will allow you to produce analytics of all kinds: look at the past and visualize it through business intelligence and BI tools and predict the future with intelligent forecasting and machine learning models, producing metrics and the likelihood of events happening.

We will do so in a scalable, extensible way that will grant your organization the kind of agility needed for fast turnaround on analytics requests and to deal with changes in real time by building a platform that is centered around the best technologies for the task at hand with the correct resources in place to accomplish such tasks.

The End of the Beginning

I hope you enjoy this book, which is the fruit of my many years of experience collected in the "battlefield" of work. Hopefully you will gain knowledge and insights that will help you in your job and personal projects, and you may reduce or altogether skip some of the common issues and problems I have encountered throughout the years.

Data Analytics in the AWS Cloud

AWS Data Lakes and Analytics Technology Overview

In the introduction I explained why you need analytics. Really powerful analytics require large amounts of data. The *large* here is relative to the context of your business or task, but the bottom line is that you should produce analytics based on a comprehensive dataset rather than a small (and inaccurate) sample of the entire body of data you possess.

Why AWS?

But first let's address our choice of cloud computing provider. As of this writing (early 2022) there are a number of cloud computing providers, with three competitors leading the race: Amazon Web Services (AWS), Google Cloud Platform (GCP), and Microsoft Azure. I recommend AWS as your provider of choice, and I'll tell you why.

The answer for me lies in the fact that analytics is a vast realm of computing spanning numerous technologies and areas of technology: business analysis, data engineering, data analytics, data science, data storage (including transactional databases, data lakes, and warehouses), data mining/crawling, data cataloging, data governance and strategy, security, visualization, business intelligence, and reporting.

Although AWS may not win out on some of the costs of running services and has to cover some ground to catch up to its competitors in terms of user interface/user experience (UI/UX), it remains the only cloud provider that has a solid and stable solution for each area of the business, all seamlessly integrated through the AWS ecosystem.

It is true that other cloud providers are ideal for some use cases and that leveraging their strength in certain areas (for example, GCP tends to be very developer-friendly) can make for easy and cost-effective solutions. However, when it comes to running an entire business on it, AWS is the clear winner.

Also, AWS encourages businesses to use their resources in an optimal fashion by providing a free tier of operation, which means that for each tool you use there will be a certain amount of usage below a specified threshold provided for free. Free-tier examples are 1 million AWS Lambda invocations per month, or 750 hours of small Relational Database Service (RDS) databases.

As far as this book's use case, which is setting up and delivering large-scale analytics, AWS is clearly the leader in the field at this time.

What Does a Data Lake Look Like in AWS?

For the most part, you will be dealing with Amazon Simple Storage Service (S3), with which you should be familiar, but if you aren't, fear not, because we've got you covered in the next chapters.

S3 is the storage facility of choice for the following reasons:

- It can hold a virtually infinite amount of data.
- It is inexpensive, and you can adopt storage solutions that make it up to 50 times cheaper.
- It is seamlessly integrated with all data and analytics-related tools in AWS, from tools like Kinesis that store data in S3 to tools like Athena that query the data in it.
- Data can be protected through access permissions, it can be encrypted in a variety of ways, or it can be made publicly accessible.

There are other solutions for storage in AWS, but aside from one that has some use cases (the EMR File System, or EMRFS), you should rely on S3. Note that EMRFS is actually based on S3, too. Other storage solutions like Amazon Elastic Block Store (EBS) are not ideal for data lake and analytics purposes, and since I discourage their use in this context, I will not cover them in the book.

Analytics on AWS

If you log into the AWS console, you will see the following products listed under the Analytics heading:

- Athena
- EMR
- CloudSearch
- Kinesis
- QuickSight
- Data Pipeline
- AWS Data Exchange
- AWS Glue
- AWS Lake Formation
- MSK

The main actors in the realm of analytics in the context of big data and data lakes are undoubtedly S3, Athena, and Kinesis.

EMR is useful for data preparation/transformation, and the output is generally data that is made available to Athena and QuickSight.

Other tools, like AWS Glue and Lake Formation, are not less important (Glue in particular is vital to the creation and maintenance of an analytics pipeline), but they are not directly generating or performing analytics. MSK is AWS's fully managed version of Kafka, and we will take a quick look at it, but we will generally favor Kinesis (as it performs a similar role in the stack).

Opting for MSK or plain Kafka comes down to cost and performance choices.

CloudSearch is a search engine for websites, and therefore is of limited interest to us in this context.

In addition, SageMaker can be a nice addition if you want to power your analytics with predictive models or any other machine learning/artificial intelligence (ML/AI) task.

Skills Required to Build and Maintain an AWS Analytics Pipeline

First of all, you need familiarity with AWS tools. You will gain that familiarity through this book. For anything that goes beyond the creation of resources through the AWS console, you will need general AWS Sysops skills. Other skills you'll need include the following:

- Knowledge of AWS Identity and Access Management (IAM) is necessary to understand the permissions requirements for each task.
- DevOps skills are required if you want to automate the creation and destruction of resources using CloudFormation or Terraform (or any other infrastructure-as-code tool).
- SQL skills are needed to write Athena queries, and basic database administrator (DBA) skills to understand Athena data types and schemas.
- Data analysis and data science skills are required for SageMaker models.
- Basic business understanding of charts and graphs are required to create QuickSight visualizations.

CHAPTER

2

The Path to Analytics: Setting Up a Data and Analytics Team

Creating analytics, especially in a large organization, can be a monumental effort, and a business needs to be prepared to invest time and resources, which will all repay the company manifold by enabling data-driven decisions. The people who will make this shift toward data-driven decision making are your Data and Analytics team, sometimes referred to as Data Analytics team or even simply as Data team (although this latest version tends to confuse people, as it may seem related to database administration). This book will refer to the Data and Analytics team as the *DA team*.

Although the focus of this book is architectural patterns and designs that will help you turn your organization into a data-driven one, a high-level overview of the skills and people you will need to make this happen is necessary.

> **NOTE** Funny anecdote: At Teamwork, our DA team is referred to with the funny-sounding name DANDA, because we create resources on AWS with the identifier *D&A*, but because AWS has a habit of converting some characters into full text, *&* became *AND*. Needless to say, it stuck, and since then we have been known as *DANDA*.

The Data Vision

The first step in delivering analytics is to create a data vision, a statement for your business as a whole. This can be a simple quote that works as a compass for all the projects your DA team will work on.

A vision does not have to be immutable. However, you should only change it if it is somehow only applicable to certain conditions or periods of time and those conditions have been satisfied or that time has passed.

A vision is the North Star of your data journey. It should always be a factor when you're making decisions about what kind of work to carry out or how to prioritize a current backlog. An example of a data vision is "to create a unified analytics facility that enables business management to slice and dice data at will."

Support

It's important to create the vision, and it's also vital for the vision to have the support of all the involved stakeholders. Management will be responsible for allocating resources to the DA team, so these managers need to be behind the vision and the team's ability to carry it out. You should have a vision statement ready and submit it to management, or have management create it in the first place.

I won't linger any further on this topic because this book is more of a technical nature than a business one, but be sure not to skip this vital step.

> **REDUCTIO AD ABSURDUM: HOW *NOT* TO GO ABOUT CREATING ANALYTICS**
>
> Before diving into the steps for creating analytics, allow me to give you some friendly advice on how you should *not* go about it. I will do so by recounting a fictional yet all too common story of failure by businesses and companies.
>
> Data Undriven Inc. is a successful company with hundreds of employees, but it's in dire need of analytics to reverse some worrying revenue trends. The leadership team recognizes the need for a far more accurate kind of analytics than what they currently have available, since it appears the company is unable to pinpoint exactly what side of the business is hemorrhaging money. Gemma, a member of the leadership team, decides to start a project to create analytics for the company, which will find its ultimate manifestation in a dashboard illustrating all sorts of useful metrics. Gemma thinks Bob is a great Python/SQL data analyst and tasks Bob with the creation of reports. The ideas are good, but data for these reports resides in various data sources. This data is unsuitable for analysis because it is sparse and inaccurate, some integrity is broken, there are holes due to temporary system failures, and the DBA team has been hit with large and unsustainable queries run against their live transactional databases, which are meant to serve data to customers, not to be reported on.

Bob collects the data from all the sources and after weeks of wrangling, cleaning, filtering, and general massaging of the data, produces analytics to Gemma in the form of a spreadsheet with graphs in it.

Gemma is happy with the result, although she notices some incongruence with the expected figures. She asks Bob to automate this analysis into a dashboard that managers can consult and that will contain up-to-date information.

Bob is in a state of panic, looking up how to automate his analytics scripts, while also trying to understand why his numbers do not match Gemma's expectations—not to mention the fact that his Python program takes between 3 and 4 hours to run every time, so the development cycle is horrendously slow.

The following weeks are a harrowing story of misunderstandings, failed attempts at automations, frustration, degraded database performance, with the ultimate result that Gemma has no analytics and Bob has quit his job to join a DA team elsewhere.

What is the moral of the story? Do *not* put any analyst to work before you have a data engineer in place. This cannot be stated strongly enough. Resist the temptation to want analytics *now*. Go about it the right way. Set up a DA team, even if it's small and you suffer from resource constraints in the beginning, and let analysts come into the picture when the data is ready for analytics and not before. Let's see what kind of skills and roles you should rely on to create a successful DA team and achieve analytics even at scale.

DA Team Roles

There are two groups of roles for a DA team: the early stages and the mature stage. The definitions for these are not strict and vary from business to business. Make sure core roles are covered before advancing to more niche and specialized ones.

Early Stage Roles

By "early stage roles" we refer to a set of roles that will constitute the nucleus of your nascent DA team and that will help the team grow. At the very beginning, it is to be expected that the people involved will have to exercise some flexibility and open-mindedness in terms of the scope and authority of their roles, because the priority is to build the foundation for a data platform. So a team lead will most likely be hands-on, actively contributing to engineering, and the same can be said of the data architect, whereas data engineers will have to perform a lot of work in the realms of data platform engineering to enable the construction and monitoring of pipelines.

Team Lead

Your DA team should have, at least at the beginning, strong leadership in the form of a team lead. This is a person who is clearly technically proficient in the realm of analytics and is able to create tasks and delegate them to the right people, oversee the technical work that's being carried out, and act as a liaison between management and the DA team.

Analytics is a vast domain that has more business implications than other strictly technical areas (like feature development, for example), and yet the technical aspects can be incredibly challenging, normally requiring engineers with years of experience to carry out the work. For this reason, it is good to have a person spearheading the work in terms of workflow and methodology to avoid early-stage fragmentation, discrepancies, and general disruption of the work due to lack of cohesion within the team. The team can potentially evolve into something more of a flat-hierarchy unit later on, when every member is working with similar methods and practices that can be—at that later point—questioned and changed.

Data Architect

A data architect is a fundamental figure for a DA team and one the team cannot do without. Even if you don't elect someone to be officially recognized as the architect in the team, it is advisable to elect the most experienced and architecturally minded engineer to the role of supervisor of all the architectures designed and implemented by the DA team. Ideally the architect is a full-time role, not only designing pipeline architectures but also completing work on the technology adoption front, which is a hefty and delicate task at the same time.

Deciding whether you should adopt a serverless architecture over an Airflow- or Hadoop-based one is something that requires careful attention. Elements such as in-house skills and maintenance costs are also involved in the decision-making process.

The business can—especially under resource constraints—decide to combine the architect and team lead roles. I suggest making the data architect/team lead a full-time role before the analytics demand volume in the company becomes too large to be handled by a single team lead or data architect.

Data Engineer

Every DA team should have a data engineering (DE) subteam, which is the beating heart of data analytics. Data engineers are responsible for implementing systems that move, transform, and catalog data in order to render the data suitable for analytics.

In the context of analytics powered by AWS, data engineers nowadays are necessarily multifaceted engineers with skills spanning various areas of technology. They are cloud computing engineers, DevOps engineers, and database/ data lake/data warehouse experts, and they are knowledgeable in continuous integration/continuous deployment (CI/CD).

You will find that most DEs have particular strengths and interests, so it would be wise to create a team of DEs with some diversity of skills. Cross-functionality can be built over time; it's much more important to start with people who, on top of the classic extract, transform, load (ETL) work, can also complete infrastructure work, CI/CD pipelines, and general DevOps.

At its core, the Data Engineer's job is to perform ETL operations. They can be of varied natures, dealing with different sources of data and targeting various data stores, and they can perform some kind of transformation, like flattening/ unnesting, filtering, and computing values. Ultimately, the broad description of the work is to *extract* (data from a source), *transform* (the data that was extracted), and *load* (the transformed data into a target store).

You can view all the rest of the tasks as ancillary tasks to this fundamental operation.

Data Analyst

Another classic subteam of a DA team is the Data Analysts team. The team consists of a number of data analysts who are responsible for the exploratory and investigative work that identifies trends and patterns through the use of statistical models and provides management with metrics and numbers that help decision making. At the early stages of a DA team, data analysts may also cover the role of business intelligence developers, responsible for visualizing data in the form of reports and dashboards, using descriptive analytics to give an easy-to-understand view of what happened in the business in the past.

Maturity Stage Roles

When the team's workflow is established, it is a good idea to better define the scope of each role and include figures responsible for specialist areas of expertise, such as data science or cloud and data platform engineering, and let every member of the team focus on the areas they are best suited for.

Data Scientist

A data scientist (DS) is the ultimate data "nerd" and responsible for work in the realm of predictive and prescriptive analytics. A DS usually analyzes a dataset and, through the use of machine-learning (ML) techniques, is able to produce various predictive models, such as regression models that produce the likelihood of a certain outcome given certain conditions (for example, the likelihood of a prospective customer to convert from a trial user to a paying user). The DS may also produce forecasting models that use modern algorithms to predict the trend of a certain metric (such as revenue of the business), or even simply group records in clusters based on some of the records' features.

A data scientist's work is to investigate and resolve complex challenges that often involve a number of unknowns, and to identify patterns and trends not immediately evident to the human eye (or mind). An ideally structured centralized DA team will have a Data Science subteam at some point. The common ratio found in the industry is to have one DS for every four data analysts, but this is by no means a hard-and-fast rule. If the business is heavily involved in statistical models, or it leverages machine-learning predictions as a main feature of its product(s), then it may have more data scientists than data analysts.

Cloud Engineer

If your team has such a large volume of work that a single dedicated engineer responsible for maintaining infrastructure is justified, then having a cloud engineer is a good idea. I strongly encourage DEs to get familiar with infrastructure and "own" the resources that their code leverages/creates/consumes. So a cloud engineer would be a subject matter expert who is responsible for the domain and who oversees the cloud engineering work that DEs are already performing as part of their tasks, as well as completing work of their own. These kinds of engineers, in an AWS context, will be taking care of aspects such as the following:

- Networking (VPCs, VPN access, subnets, and so on)
- Security (encryption, parameter stores and secrets vault, security groups for applications, as well as role/user permission management with IAM)
- Tools like CloudFormation (or similar ones such as Terraform) for writing and maintaining infrastructure

Business Intelligence (BI) Developer

Once your DA team is mature enough, you will probably want to restrict the scope of the data analysts' work to exploration and investigation and leave the visualization and reporting to developers who are specialized in the use of business intelligence (BI) tools (such as Amazon QuickSight, Power BI, or Tableau) and who can more easily and quickly report their findings to stakeholders.

Machine Learning Engineer

A machine learning engineer (MLE) is a close relative of the DE, specialized in ML-focused operations, such as the setup and maintenance of ML-oriented pipelines, including their development and deployment, and the creation and maintenance of specialized data stores (such as feature stores) exclusively aimed at the production of ML models. Since the tools used in ML engineering differ from classic DE tools and are more niche, they require a high level of understanding of ML processes. A person working as an MLE is normally a DE with an interest in data science, or a data scientist who can double as a DE and who has found their ideal place as an MLE.

The practice of automating the training and deployment of ML models is called MLOps, or machine learning operations.

Business Analyst

A business analyst (BA) is the ideal point of contact between a technical team and the business/management. The main task of a BA is to gather requirements from the business and turn these requirements into tasks that the technical personnel can execute. I consider a BA a maturity stage role, because in the beginning this is work that the DA team lead should be able to complete, albeit at not as high a standard as a BA proper.

Niche Roles

Other roles that you might consider including in your DA team, depending on the nature of the business and the size/resources of the team itself, are as follows:

AI Developer   All too often anything ML related is also referred to as artificial intelligence (AI). Although there are various schools of thought and endless debates on the subject, I agree with Microsoft in summarizing the matter like so: machine learning is how a system develops intelligence, whereas AI is the intelligence itself that allows a computer to perform a task on its own and makes independent decisions. In this respect ML is a subset of AI and a gear in a larger intelligent machine. If your business has a need for someone who is responsible for developing algorithms aimed at resolving an analytics problem, then an AI developer is what you need.

TechOps / DevOps Engineer   If your team is sizable, and the workload on the CI/CD and cloud infrastructure side is too much for DEs to tackle on top of their main function (creating pipelines), then you might want to have dedicated TechOps/DevOps personnel for the DA team.

MLOps Engineer   This is a subset role of the greater DevOps specialty, a DevOps engineer who specializes in CI/CD and infrastructure dedicated to putting ML models into production.

Analytics Flow at a Process Level

There are many ways to design the process to request and complete analytics in a business. However, I've found the following to be generally applicable to most businesses:

1. A stakeholder formulates a request, a business question that needs answering.

2. The BA (or team lead at early stages) translates this into a technical task for a data analyst.

3. The data analyst conducts some investigation and exploration, leading to a conclusion. The data analyst identifies the portion of their work that can be automated to produce up-to-date insights and designs a spec (if a BI developer is available, they will do this last part).

4. A DE picks up the spec, then designs and implements an ETL job/pipeline that will produce a dataset and store it in the suitable target database.

5. The BI developer utilizes the data made available by the DE at step 4 and visualizes it or creates reports from it.

6. The BA reviews the outcome with the stakeholder for final approval and sign-off.

Workflow Methodology

There are many available software development methodologies for managing the team's workload and achieving a satisfactory level of productivity and velocity. The methodology adopted by your team will greatly depend on the skills you have on your team and even the personalities of the various team members. However, I've found a number of common traits throughout the years:

- Cloud engineering tends to be mostly planned work, such as enabling the team to create resources, setting up monitoring and alerting, creating CI/CD pipelines, and so on.

- Data analytics tends to be mostly reactive work, whereby a stakeholder asks for a certain piece of work and analysts pick it up.

- Data engineering is a mixed bag: on one hand, it is reactive insofar as it supports the work cascading from analysts and is destined to be used by BI developers; on the other hand, some tasks, such as developing utilities and tooling to help the team scale operations, is planned and would normally be associated with a traditional deadline for delivery.

- Data architects tend to have more planned work than reactive, but at the beginning of a DA team's life there may be a lot of real-time prioritization to be done.

So given these conditions, what software development methodology should you choose? Realistically it would be one of the many Agile methodologies available, but which one?

A good rule of thumb is as follows: if it's planned work, use Scrum; if it's reactive work, use Kanban. If in doubt, or you want to use one method for everyone, use Kanban.

Let me explain the reason for this guideline. Scrum's central concept for time estimation is user stories that can be scored. This is a very useful idea that enables teams to plan their sprints with just the right amount of work to be completed within that time frame. Planned work normally starts with specifications, and leadership/management will have an expectation for its completion. Therefore, planning the work ahead, and dividing it into small stories that can be estimated, will also produce a final time metric number that will work as the deadline.

In my opinion Scrum is more suited to this kind of work, as I find it more suited to feature-oriented development (as in most product teams).

Kanban, on the other hand, is an extremely versatile methodology meant to combine agility and flexibility with team velocity and productivity. When a team is constantly dealing with a flow of requests, how do you go about completing them? The key is in real-time prioritization, which in turn depends on breaking down tasks to the smallest possible unit.

Limits and constraints that I've found useful are as follows:

- No task should ever exceed 3 days of work, with 1 being ideal.
- There should never be more than one task per member in the In Progress column of your Kanban board.
- There should never be more than one task per member in the Review/Demo column of your board.
- Encourage cooperation by setting a "work in progress" limit that is less than twice the number of team members, so at least one task must have more than one person assigned to it. For example, if you only want this constraint to be applied to one task, you could set the WIP limit at

$$(2 \times \text{number of team members}) - 1$$

Also, I strongly encourage code-based work to require the approval of at least one other team member before any one code contribution is merged into the codebase. This is true for DEs and data analysts alike.

Applying these constraints, you will immediately notice that if an urgent task lands in the team's backlog (the "drop what you're doing" kind of task), you should always be at most three days away from being able to assign the task and have it completed.

And aside from those business-critical anomalies that require immediate attention (which, by the way, should never be the case in a DA team since they are rarely a customer-facing team), real-time prioritization and management of the backlog is relatively easy, especially in the realms of data analytics and BI, where demands for investigations and reports are an ever-flowing stream.

In conclusion, Kanban is a versatile methodology, suitable for real-time prioritization that can be applied to the whole team. If you have subteams only completing planned work, they could be more optimally managed with Scrum.

The DA Team Mantra: "Automate Everything"

If there is one thing I wish readers would learn from my experience, it's the vital importance of automation. If you are dealing with terabytes of data across several data sources, vast data lakes and data warehouses, countless ETL pipelines, dashboards, and tables to catalog in metadata stores, you cannot expect to maintain the operation manually. Neither should you aspire to. On the contrary, you should strive to achieve complete automation where the data lake practically maintains itself.

Here is a list of aspects of the work that are better managed through automation:

Infrastructure Creation, Update, and Destruction   There are many tools to accomplish this. The main infrastructure-as-code solutions available are CloudFormation, Terraform, and AWS CDK (the latter two utilize CloudFormation under the hood but are easier to write and maintain).

Data Cataloging   As data flows into your data lake, new partitions and new tables are better discovered automatically. The umbrella tool AWS Glue covers this part of your automation by scanning newly deposited data with so-called *crawlers*.

Pipeline Execution   AWS EventBridge allows pipelines to execute on particular triggers; this may be simple schedules or more complex events such as the creation of a new object in storage.

Visualizations/Dashboard Update   AWS QuickSight bases its dashboards on datasets that can be set to have a refresh rate, so reports are always up to date.

Test and Deployment   You should treat data engineering and analytics the same way you would a product, by setting up a CI/CD pipeline that tests code and deploys it upon a successful code review following a pull request. The de facto standard for version control of the code is Git, although other solutions are available.

Monitoring and Alerting   Whatever your delivery system of choice is (a message in a chat application, an email, an SMS), be sure to automate monitoring and alerting so that you are immediately notified when something has gone wrong. Especially in data engineering, missing a day's worth of data can result in problems and a lot of hassle to backfill the information.

Analytics Models in the Wild: Centralized, Distributed, Center of Excellence

Finally, let's take a look at how the DA team may be placed within the organization and how it could interact with the other functions.

There are plenty of models available, but there are three models that are in a way the basic version of every other variation available: centralized, distributed, and center of excellence, or CoE (which is ideal for a hybrid structure).

Centralized

A centralized DA team is a place where all the analytics needs of an organization are satisfied. It not only means that every single piece of data engineering or analytics will be performed by the DA team, but it also means no data engineering, data analysis, or data science should happen outside of the DA team.

This may not be suitable for all organizations, but I do find that at least at the beginning of a business's transformation to data-driven, a centralized approach brings order and method to the chaos. Rogue initiatives outside of it only create duplication and fragmentation of work methodology, practices, and tools and may even produce results that conflict with similar work conducted within the DA team, which may result in poor buy-in from the business and slow down the production of analytics or question its accuracy. If you do not have analytics in your company, start with a centralized team.

If you do have analysts in your company because you made the very common mistake of putting analysts to work before data engineering was in place, bring your analysts into the DA team and transform what may be a community of practice into a structured team.

An early-stages DA team works mainly in three areas: architecture, engineering, and analysis. Data science may come soon after but not right away. For this reason, I believe an early-stages DA team and indeed a centralized DA team may have the structure shown in Figure 2.1.

It is important to note that, as specified earlier, the architect role can be covered by a team lead, but it is not the same thing. A competent person who can design resilient, maintainable, and extensible architectures is needed to review the work done by all the teams, but especially the data engineering team.

Later in the data journey, you may drift more toward a hub-and-spoke model. If so, your centralized team may in time become the core team of the center of excellence, which we will explore soon.

The main disadvantage of centralized teams in the long term is that they may produce slower lead times from request to analytics, as the analytics requests coming from the business will have to join a prioritized queue and there are no resources dedicated to each function.

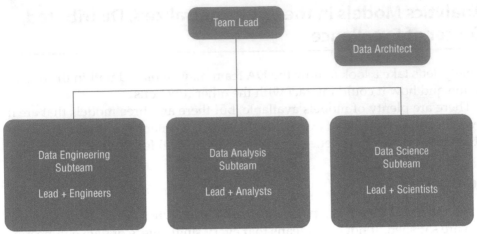

Figure 2.1: An example structure of an early-stages DA team

A main advantage of a centralized team is that it inherently encourages cross-functionality among the members of each subteam; therefore, if resources are not available or for some reason temporarily constrained, it means work can proceed (albeit at a slower pace) rather than coming to a grinding halt. So a centralized team has a certain degree of resilience.

Distributed

A distributed DA team is especially suitable for those organizations whose analytical needs are so large, and there is so much domain knowledge to be acquired by the people carrying out engineering and analysis work, that it is faster and more productive to split the team out. The main advantage of distributed teams is the quicker turnaround. If Finance is in need of a piece of analytics, they don't need to share resources with Marketing. The Finance DA team will swiftly produce the analytics requested without having to go to a centralized team and share resources with the entire business.

But there are drawbacks. Inevitably, teams will drift apart and develop practices and adopt methodologies that in time are going to diverge, especially given the different domains of work, and transferring resources or regulating analytics at the business level may become very challenging.

Distributed teams may have a structure that internally is similar to the centralized team but on a smaller scale.

Center of Excellence

There is a third model, which combines the benefits of centralized and distributed models: the center of excellence. This model requires a high level of data maturity in the business, because it involves a great deal of agility while remaining regulated, and it addresses domain knowledge, quick iterations, and data governance.

Instead of aggregating all of the DA resources into one team, you form a center of excellence containing the people with high-value skills and experience. From this center of excellence, you can regulate activity and establish a rhythm to analytics production. You can also review work carried out in the distributed units and establish communities of practice to contain the drift between the various functions.

A center of excellence is at the core of a hub-and-spoke model where the central unit (the *hub*) is responsible for overseeing and regulating activities, as well as performing tasks that are to be considered business-wide or business-critical (for example, managing and regulating access to the business's centralized data lake). The *spokes* are units (teams) embedded within the various functions that can perform work at a higher pace while having their activity reviewed and approved by the people in the center of excellence.

As mentioned, this model suits businesses and organizations that are far down the road of analytics, and it is one model that allows quick iterations on producing insights and analytics while limiting fragmentation and duplication of work.

Summary

In this chapter we discussed the formation of a DA team, which is a vital prerequisite for the successful creation and maintenance of a data platform in any organization. While not all organizations are the same, the general advice is to start with an embryonic unit with a strong leadership, and gradually and iteratively add specialist roles to your growing team.

Working on AWS

AWS is an incredibly vast ecosystem of tools and components, and—especially if you are not familiar with it—learning to work with it may seem like a daunting task.

Therefore, it seems only fitting that we should take a look at the basics of how to work in an AWS environment and build your understanding of cloud computing and engineering.

Since you are reading this book to implement analytics on AWS, it would seem logical that you are already using AWS for other parts of your business. Therefore, we will take a quick look at initial steps (sign-up and user creation), but we will dive into deeper detail on the subsequent steps. We will discuss the following:

- Accessing AWS
- Managing users
- Interacting with AWS through the Web Console
- Interacting with the command line
- Interacting with AWS CloudShell
- Creating virtual private clouds to secure your resources
- Managing roles and policies with IAM
- Using CloudFormation to manage infrastructure

Accessing AWS

First things first: you need to access AWS. To do this, you will need to create an AWS account, with credentials that will grant you root access. The URL to create an AWS account (and for subsequent sign-ins) is `https://aws.amazon.com`.

Once in, you will be prompted with the Console Home screen (shown in Figure 3.1), which gives you a high-level overview of the status of your account's health and billing.

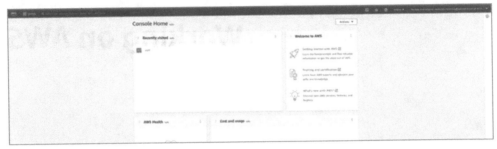

Figure 3.1: The Console Home screen

Root in this case means a special kind of super-admin account that allows you to perform all kinds of operations in AWS. You should *never* use this level of access for your day-to-day work tasks.

Instead, once you have registered in AWS, the first thing you should do is create a user that you will be using to start actual work. You must have your billing and payment details set up to be able to proceed. So begin by clicking the drop-down menu at the top left of the screen under your login details, then selecting "Billing Dashboard."

Type **IAM** in the search bar at the top left, select Users, and create a new user. Since the newly created user will be an administrator, you want to grant administrator privileges to it. To do this, follow these steps:

1. Click the Add User button.

2. Enter **Administrator** as the username.

3. Select the option AWS Management Console Access, then select Custom Password and enter it.

4. Optionally select the option that forces the user to change their password at first sign-in.

5. Click Next: Permissions.

6. Under Set Permissions, select Add User To Group.

7. Click Create Group and name that group **Administrators**.

8. Choose Filter Policies and select AWS Managed – Job Function.

9. In the policies list, choose AdministratorAccess, then click Create Group.

At this point you will be returned to the user creation screen. Refresh the list of groups and select Administrators, then click Next: Tags to add optional metadata. We will explore tags a little later in this chapter.

Clicking Next: Review will give you a summary of the user you are about to create. If you're satisfied with the settings, click Create User. With this user, you can log into the AWS console and start working on your resources.

Everything Is a Resource

In AWS, everything is a resource. A server and a user both have resource identifiers, and this enables security with a very fine granularity. You can create users who have access to only one resource and who cannot access anything else in the system. Such identifiers are called Amazon Resource Names (ARNs), and they are used to reference entities and resources in your AWS account, or even in external AWS accounts.

ARNs have a specific format, which follows this pattern:

```
arn:partition:service:region:account-id:resource-id
arn:partition:service:region:account-id:resource-type/resource-id
arn:partition:service:region:account-id:resource-type:resource-id
```

Remember that the region of a resource is very important, because it indicates in which data center your resource is physically located. Ideally you want resources interacting with each other to be geographically close to each other, especially if user facing, to limit latency.

Considering that for most regions (except for China, for example) the partition value is *aws*, you can derive the ARN of a resource by knowing its `resource-id`. For example, deploying an EC2 instance (a virtual server) in the us-east-1 region with the ID *myserver*, and assuming a (bogus) account ID of 111111111, the resource would have the ARN

```
arn:aws:ec2:us-east-1:111111111:instance/myserver
```

where *instance* is the `resource-type` and *myserver* its `resource-id`.

S3: An Important Exception

S3 is a global service and therefore the region and account ID are not specified. This means that the name for your S3 buckets has to be unique globally, not just in your account—a bit like your username for a certain application or website has to be. However, S3 buckets are indeed—like every other resource—physically located in a data center, and for that reason you need to specify the region in which you are going to locate the bucket when creating it.

If you deposit a file in the `reports` bucket in S3 with the filename (or "key" in S3 jargon) `january.csv`, then the ARN for that resource would be

```
arn:aws:s3:::reports/january.csv
```

Notice the absence of region and account ID in the ARN.

Buckets are region based, so while their availability is global, interacting with them might be subject to regional constraints. For example, some services that deliver data to S3 can only do so in buckets that are based in the same region as the service.

IAM: Policies, Roles, and Users

When working with analytics, but in general with AWS, it is vital to understand how to manage users, roles, and policies. Even in the unlikely case that you don't want to implement any security measures in your AWS account, you will still have to deal with the default security system that AWS imposes on you and your resources, and the only way to get anything working (and working properly) in AWS is through a good understanding of identity access management (IAM).

If you start to create a resource that uses another resource, and try to run some kind of task with it, it will not work, because by default no resource has permission to interact with anything outside of itself.

Let's examine the three basic concepts of policies, roles, and users.

Policies

Policies are sets of permissions grouped under a common name. For example, the policy that grants full read, write, and administrative access to S3 is called AmazonS3FullAccess and it's automatically created when you sign up for an AWS account.

A policy is defined in JSON and consists of one or more statements allowing (or denying/disallowing) some kind of action to a resource. Here's the structure of a policy:

```
{
  "Statement":[{
    "Effect":"effect",
    "Action":"action",
    "Resource":"arn",
    "Condition":{
```

```
    "condition":{
      "key":"value"
      }
    }
   }
  }
 ]
}
```

Let's look at the components of each statement:

Effect   Allows or denies the use of a resource.

Action   The single permission or set of permissions (you can use the wildcard * to grant the whole set of permissions) being affected by the statement.

Resource   The resource (referenced by its ARN) affected by the statement. It can be a single ARN or a wildcard representing all resources.

Condition   An optional condition that needs to be met for the policy to be applied, such as the time of day or the IP range from which a request is coming.

Let's look at an example. Suppose you want to allow read and write access to objects in an S3 bucket, so you write the following policy:

```
{
    "Version": "2012-10-17",
    "Statement": [
        {
            "Sid": "ListObjectsInBucket",
            "Effect": "Allow",
            "Action": ["s3:ListBucket"],
            "Resource": ["arn:aws:s3:::bucket-name"]
        },
        {

            "Sid": "AllObjectActions",
            "Effect": "Allow",
            "Action": "s3:*Object",
            "Resource": ["arn:aws:s3:::bucket-name/*"]
        }
    ]
}
```

Note that the version attribute never changes—it just specifies the API policy structure version. You can simply copy it and paste it in all your policy documents.

The sid attribute is an arbitrary identifier to help you understand what the statement does. This is helpful when AWS throws errors referring to policies, because it gives you a reference to the problematic policy statement. Note that you can change the SID to whatever you want, but it must be unique within that policy document.

The `Action` attribute in the second statement contains a wildcard at the beginning of the second portion of the action identifier. This means that all actions ending in `Object` will be affected by the policy. In our case, these are the S3 actions `GetObject`, `DeleteObject`, and `PutObject`. If you wanted to apply the action to all `Get`-type actions, you'd write `s3:Get*`.

Note that the first statement only lists the bucket name. That's because the policy applied on it can only list objects contained in the bucket. However, the second statement uses `/*` because it explicitly refers to all the objects contained in the bucket. The first statement applies to the bucket and the second to its objects.

There are several types of IAM policies:

- Identity-based policies
- Resource-based policies
- Permission boundaries
- Organization service control protocols
- Access control lists (ACLs)
- Session policies

Since we are going to focus throughout this book on those aspects of AWS that are particularly relevant to creating and managing analytics, we will concentrate on the first two types of policy, which are by far the most common.

Identity-Based Policies

Identity-based policies are policies attached to an identity that grant permissions to that identity. Identities in AWS IAM are users, roles, and user groups.

There are two kinds of identity-based policies in AWS: managed and inline. Managed policies are policies that are created as resources and can be attached to other IAM identities. For example, say you want to create a user who will be writing data to S3 buckets. You could create a policy called S3WriteOnly and attach it to that user. This is indeed a common case for ETL and "stitching" services, which are given permission to write data into S3 buckets but are not allowed to read or delete. Such a policy, created as a resource (i.e., it has an ARN) and reusable with other identities, is defined as *managed*.

Inline policies are policies that are defined "inline" within the IAM resource itself, which means the policy can only be edited "inline." The only use case for inline policies is a strict one-to-one relationship between the IAM resource and its policy. They do not have an ARN, as they are "properties"—so to speak—of an identity and therefore cannot be reused.

I have not come across a scenario where an inline policy is better than a managed one.

Resource-Based Policies

Resource-based policies work exactly like the mirror image of an identity-based policy. Instead of granting an identity the ability to do something with resources, you attach a policy to a resource allowing a specific principal to access that resource. An example is attaching a resource-based policy to an S3 bucket. A principal can be an AWS account (and its root user), an IAM user or role, an AWS service (such as S3 or EC2), and sessions. A typical S3-based use case is to allow access to a bucket only for a specific principal, like an IAM user.

It's important to understand these concepts because they will be an integral part of life on AWS. I guarantee you that after the initial learning curve (which is neither too long nor too steep), these concepts will become second nature to you.

Roles

Next is the concept of a *role*. A role is an IAM entity to which you can attach policies. How does this differ from a user? The answer is in the concept behind roles and users. Users are most likely (but not necessarily) physical people interacting with AWS. Roles are more like execution profiles that are used to perform work on AWS. A user can assume a role, for example, inheriting the policies attached to that role.

Think of an AWS Lambda function, for example. This is a computing resource that can be triggered in several ways, say with a schedule or a system/API event. When this function performs its work, it will do so with the permissions associated with the role that is assigned to the execution of the function. If this Lambda needs to access S3, then the execution role for that function will need the appropriate S3 policy attached to it.

Users and User Groups

The last type of IAM entity is the *user* (and user groups). A user is the right kind of entity for completing tasks such as creating and configuring resources, rather than executing work or consuming services, which is done through roles. The big difference here is that users can create credentials (consisting of an access key and a secret key) that will enable access to the AWS account through either a terminal (with the AWS CLI tool) or the Web Console.

Users are better managed in user groups, since micromanaging permissions on an individual level is a less maintainable and less secure way than attributing permissions to groups and adding users to them. As you might have already guessed, the way you assign permissions to user groups is by attaching policies to them.

Summarizing IAM

This overview of IAM was specifically focused on enabling your analytics work on AWS, and as you will soon discover, the default security levels in AWS are such that nothing works unless you grant it permission to do so. Therefore, it is of vital importance for your work to understand the basic concepts of identity access management in AWS, specifically policies, users, and roles.

Here are some general considerations:

- Think of policies as the atom of security in AWS. Policies are a nice way to organize permissions, and they can be attached to roles or users.

- You should have one role for similar kinds of work. For example, if you have two EC2 servers that perform different workloads but end up writing to the same S3 bucket after querying the same DynamoDB table, you can create two policies (an S3 and a DynamoDB) and a single role with which to execute both workloads.

- You create users for real people, or for entities that need "programmatic" access to your AWS account, such as AWS-based services in other AWS accounts, so you can create a resource-based policy allowing the external user to interact with the resource.

Working with the Web Console

You might have found it unusual or illogical for us to describe IAM even before you've seen a basic interaction with the Web Console, but the reason for that is extremely simple: if you don't grant yourself privileges to do something, you won't be able to do anything at all in AWS. At this stage, you know how to create an administrative user and how to grant permissions to users and roles through policies, so you can begin doing more than create identities and start some actual work.

The Web Console (shown in Figure 3.2) gives you a simple and intuitive way to create resources with a point-and-click interface. Especially in the beginning, while you familiarize yourself with the AWS ecosystem, it is the easiest way to start performing work. Once logged in, you can click Services and all AWS tools and services will be listed, grouped by category. You can also search for a particular service in the search bar.

As you can see, several categories are listed, with Analytics the very top group. Let's take a look at what is included in the Analytics family of AWS Services:

- Athena
- Managed Search Service

- AWS Data Exchange
- Data Pipeline
- EMR
- Amazon FinSpace
- AWS Glue
- AWS Glue DataBrew
- Kinesis
- AWS Lake Formation
- MSK
- Amazon OpenSearch Service (successor to Amazon Elasticsearch Service)
- QuickSight
- Amazon Redshift

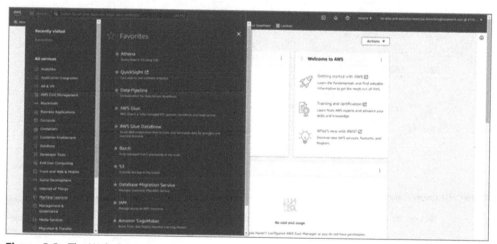

Figure 3.2: The Web Console

We will be taking a much closer look at all of these services later on, but for now we will focus on getting used to working with the Web Console. To do so, we will perform a simple operation in the console that will work as a template for other ways to accomplish the same goal but using alternative methods.

CREATING A NoSQL DATABASE TABLE USING AMAZON DynamoDB THROUGH THE AWS CONSOLE

DynamoDB is a key-value NoSQL database solution developed by AWS. We will explore DynamoDB extensively, but for now all you need to know is that you can create tables in which you have to specify a partition key and a sort key. Your records may contain many more fields than these two, but DynamoDB does not need any schema definition for them. In AWS jargon, DynamoDB is an *abstracted service*, which means you only worry about the data you want to put into it—AWS will take care of provisioning and updating the underlying infrastructure.

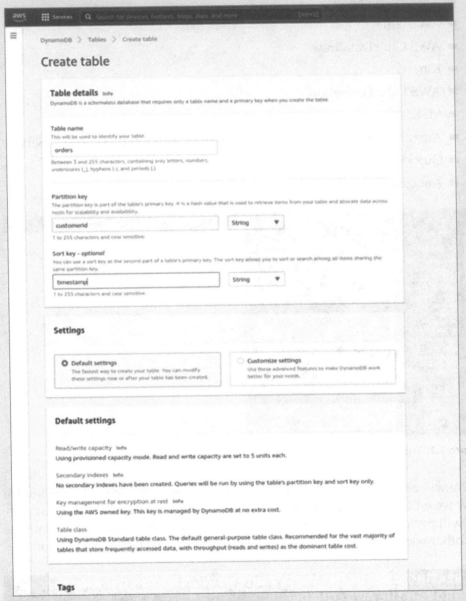

Figure 3.3: DynamoDB table creation form

Let's create an `orders` table (see Figure 3.3) in which the partition key is the `customerID` and the sort key is the timestamp of the order placement.

When you leave every setting at its default value, creating the table is as simple as clicking Create Table at the bottom of the form. The table creation is near instantaneous, and you will be brought to a summary screen showing the newly created resource.

Since, as mentioned, this book is not a thorough guide to AWS as much as it is focused on creating analytics on AWS, I do not think there is much more that you need to know about interacting with the Web Console. Like any other web application or website, it's mostly forms with required and optional fields. AWS tends to make creating resources easy by proposing default values that suit most use cases, but you can always choose to customize settings for more advanced or personalized configurations.

Creating a table on DynamoDB is a simple enough task that lends itself perfectly to being illustrated with other techniques, such as the command-line (AWS CLI and CloudShell) or CloudFormation.

The AWS Command-Line Interface

Working with the command line is the preferred way of doing things for a number of reasons:

- It is much faster than interacting with web pages which, compared to issuing a command, is a lot slower.
- Despite the learning curve of having to memorize all the options, it represents an amazingly effective tool to learn all the available options in each tool provided by AWS.
- It is the way you would interact with AWS from other machines, such as servers that do not have a desktop environment, so you may as well be doing so on your computer.
- It becomes easy to translate from CloudFormation to a command, and vice versa.

The AWS command-line interface needs to be installed and configured to work as desired, so let's see how to do that first.

Installing AWS CLI

The AWS CLI tool is a Python-based tool that allows you to interact with your AWS account from your terminal window. You'll find instructions on how to do so on your operating system at https://docs.aws.amazon.com/cli/latest/userguide/getting-started-install.html. The page covers the three operating systems, Linux, macOS, and Windows, which we will explore in detail. If you are on FreeBSD, running `pkg add awscli` will suffice.

Linux Installation

On Linux, download the file indicated in the installation page, unzip the downloaded archive, then—within the extracted folder— run the installation script, a file called `install`. As of this writing, the whole process looks like this:

```
curl "https://awscli.amazonaws.com/awscli-exe-linux-x86_64.zip" -o
"awscliv2.zip"
unzip awscliv2.zip
sudo ./aws/install
```

Note that you need administrative privileges to install the tool.

macOS Installation

On a Mac, you have the option to install with a graphic installer or with the command line. In the terminal you can choose to install for the currently logged-in user or for all users. The installer for macOS is at `https://awscli.amazonaws.com/AWSCLIV2.pkg`. Once it's downloaded, you can install it for the current user without issue, or you can choose to install for all users by creating the following *symlinks* (which require sudo access):

```
sudo ln -s /folder/installed/aws-cli/aws /usr/local/bin/aws
sudo ln -s /folder/installed/aws-cli/aws_completer /usr/local/bin/
aws_completer
```

where `/folder/installed/` represents the installation folder you selected in the graphic installer.

If instead you choose to use the command line for all users, you can use the following script:

```
curl "https://awscli.amazonaws.com/AWSCLIV2.pkg" -o "AWSCLIV2.pkg"
sudo installer -pkg AWSCLIV2.pkg -target /
```

which downloads the installer in the current folder, saving the file with the name `AWSCLIV2.pkg`. Then you run the installer tool with administrative privileges so that all users on the machine can use the AWS CLI tool.

Should you opt to install the AWS CLI tool for the currently logged-in user *only*, then the second command (`sudo installer ...`) will be replaced with

```
installer -pkg AWSCLIV2.pkg \
          -target CurrentUserHomeDirectory \
          -applyChoiceChangesXML choices.xml
```

where *choices.xml* is an XML file that specifies where the tool should be installed, like so:

```
<?xml version="1.0" encoding="UTF-8"?>
<!DOCTYPE plist PUBLIC "-//Apple//DTD PLIST 1.0//EN"
"http://www.apple.com/DTDs/PropertyList-1.0.dtd">
<plist version="1.0">
  <array>
    <dict>
      <key>choiceAttribute</key>
      <string>customLocation</string>
      <key>attributeSetting</key>
      <string>/Users/myusername</string>
      <key>choiceIdentifier</key>
      <string>default</string>
    </dict>
  </array>
</plist>
```

Be sure to replace */Users/myusername* with your own home directory. At this point, whatever method you chose, you can run

```
> which aws
```

and

```
> aws -version
```

to verify that the tool exists and confirm the version installed.

Windows

On Windows, download the installer at `https://awscli.amazonaws.com/AWSCLIV2.msi` and then either run it or, from the command prompt, run:

```
> msiexec.exe /i https://awscli.amazonaws.com/AWSCLIV2.msi
```

On Windows you should be able to run the command

```
> aws -version
```

to check which version of the tool is installed. As of this writing, the tool is at version 2.4.18.

Configuring AWS CLI

Now that you have the AWS CLI tool installed, you need to provide configuration details so that it can connect and work with your AWS account. First let's explore the parameters that need to be configured, then how to do it.

When trying to access your AWS account from the command line, you will need the following at the very minimum:

- An access key
- A secret key
- A region parameter
- An output format parameter

You can also have profiles on your local machine. This enables you to use the AWS CLI tool against different AWS accounts (or against the same account but using a different user with different permissions) by specifying the profile option. Each profile needs the four components outlined above.

When you create a user, there are no credentials automatically created to allow programmatic access to AWS. These credentials need to be created in turn. To do so, click your account name in the navigation bar, and select My Security Credentials. If you are in a corporate account and accessing through a role, you can go to IAM ⇨ Users and select the user you want to create credentials for. Select Continue To Security Credentials if you see a warning, and then expand the Access Keys section of the page. There you can select Create New Access Key if the option is available. If it's not, that means you have exceeded the maximum number of access key credentials. So you'll need to delete an old one first, but assuming this is your first time performing this operation, you should not encounter this limitation.

Access keys are only displayed once, and you cannot retrieve them later. Your only option in case you lost an access key is to create a new pair and delete the one you lost the credentials for.

Once the access key has been created, you have two options:

- You can choose Show Access Key and copy and paste the details in a secured file on your computer.
- You can choose Download Key File, which will trigger the download of a file named `rootkey.csv`, which contains the access key ID and secret key for the access key. Save this file somewhere safe.

As AWS strongly recommends, delete the access key when you don't need it anymore, or at least mark it as inactive so that it cannot be used.

Access Key ID and Secret Access Key are long alphanumeric strings that work as secret codes for you to be able to access AWS from the command line or even from programs/applications you develop. The AWS documentation has a nice example of what they look like:

```
Access key ID: AKIAIOSFODNN7EXAMPLE
Secret access key: wJalrXUtnFEMI/K7MDENG/bPxRfiCYEXAMPLEKEY
```

At this point, you are ready to configure AWS CLI. The easiest way to do so is by typing the following in your terminal:

```
> aws configure
```

This will prompt you with Access Key ID, Secret Access Key, Region, and Output Format interactive options. Enter your newly created credentials for the first two fields. For the region, choose the region you will be operating in. The default region in AWS is us-east-1, but I chose eu-west-1 as I am based in Ireland. For the output format you can adopt the default (JSON) or another format you prefer. JSON is machine readable, which is good for automation.

A Note on Region

It is always better to have resources in the same locality as you are operating for a number of reasons, from time zones to regulations (especially in the EU) to pricing consistency and even latency. Different governments have different guidelines and regulations for privacy, and moving data around different regions might be subjected to inspection/audit and will have to comply with local rules, especially for personally identifiable information (PII). Europe in particular is very strict on GDPR (General Data Protection Regulations), and you will be saving yourself a number of headaches if you simply work in the region that is as close to your work base as possible.

Each resource you create and the data you put into it will be created in the region you are working on at that moment, which you can check at the top-right corner of the Web Console. Some resources allow you to replicate the data to other regions, but this is something you have to explicitly configure.

Setting Individual Parameters

Once you are done with the configuration, you might want to return to a particular setting, in case you need to change it or you realize you made a mistake. This is as simple as typing

```
> aws configure set <parameter name> <parameter value>
```

For example, if you want to change the region setting of your configuration, use this:

```
> aws configure set region eu-west-1
```

Using Profiles and Configuration Files

Once AWS CLI is configured, it will store the settings in two files in a directory called .aws in your home directory. On Linux, my home directory is /home/joe, so the files will be in `/home/joe/.aws/`. These files are called `credentials` and `config` and they use the TOML syntax for configuration, whereby sections of the file are wrapped in square brackets—[]—followed by key-value pairs with the key name on the left side of an equal sign and the key value on the right side. Strings can be wrapped in double quotes, and arrays are supported through the use of square brackets.

Here is where profiles come into play. You can think of profiles as named configuration sets. For example, you can store access key IDs and secret keys for multiple AWS accounts in a single file—you just need to take care to name such profiles.

By default when you configure AWS CLI, the tool creates a default profile named `default` with its relative access key ID and secret key just under it in the `credentials` file, and the region and output format in the `config` file.

Let's explore these files in detail.

The *credentials* File

In this file you can store sensitive information, what you would actually call credentials. Nothing should go in this file other than your security credentials. If you have configured your AWS CLI tool, you can open the `~/.aws/credentials` file and it will look similar to this:

```
[default]
aws_access_key_id = ACCESSKEYHERE
aws_secret_access_key = secretaccesskeyhere
```

To illustrate the idea of multiple profiles, let's assume I have a default profile that I use for work and another profile connecting to a separate AWS account that I use for a personal side project called *sidegig*. My `credentials` file would look something like this:

```
[default]
aws_access_key_id = ACCESSKEYHERE
aws_secret_access_key = secretaccesskeyhere

[sidegig]
aws_access_key_id = SIDEGIGACCESSKEYHERE
aws_secret_access_key = sidegigsecretaccesskeyhere
```

The *config* File

If you have the AWS CLI tool configured, you will find that the information about region and output format are not contained in the `credentials` file (as they are not credentials per se) but in the `config` file.

So the `config` file contents would look similar to this:

```
[default]
region = eu-west-1
output = json
```

Again, should I want to specify different settings for the `sidegig` profile, I could do so by declaring them in another profile:

```
[default]
region = eu-west-1
output = json

[sidegig]
region = us-east-1
output = json
```

And that's it. There is nothing preventing you from storing normal settings in the `credentials` file, and if you have an overlap (e.g., you have re-declared the output format in `credentials` and `config`) whatever is contained in `credentials` will take precedence.

Viewing Configuration Values Individually

You can use the `aws configure` command to view values as well as setting them. If you want to check what value you have set for the region, you would enter

```
> aws configure get region
```

Now that you are familiar with the idea of profiles, you can specify the profile you want to configure and view by using the `profile` flag (in this example, assume I have created a `joe_work` profile):

```
> aws configure set region eu-west-1 –profile joe_work
```

and then

```
> aws configure get region –profile joe_work
```

Import Configuration

AWS CLI also supports import credentials from a CSV file, a common use case since the credentials can be downloaded in CSV format. The command is

```
> aws configure import –csv file://credentials.csv
```

assuming a `credentials.csv` file exists in your current directory. Optionally you can pass a `--skip-invalid` flag to skip invalid entries.

Once you have imported or configured your profiles, you can view them by typing `aws configure list` (which will list the location of each profile setting) or simply view a list of configured profiles with `aws configure list-profiles`.

Using Environment Variables or Command-Line Options

You don't necessarily have to use files to store your configuration—you can use environment variables or command-line options. These options are suited to particular scenarios—for example, you could store access credentials in a Secrets Manager and pass these values as environment variables to a virtual server that's executing some work and needs AWS access. The environment variable names are as follows:

```
AWS_ACCESS_KEY_ID
AWS_SECRET_ACCESS_KEY
AWS_DEFAULT_REGION
AWS_DEFAULT_OUTPUT
```

If you try any operation with AWS CLI and these environment variables are set in your terminal, then all should work just the same as if you were using a `credentials` and a `config` file.

Command-line options are very handy, as they allow you to address a particular profile or region when issuing the command. You saw an example earlier of command-line options in action when setting a parameter using `aws configure set` with the `--profile` flag. For example, if you want to try to invoke a Lambda function in a particular profile, you'd use this:

```
> aws lambda invoke myFunction –profile joe_work –region eu-east-1
```

Final Notes on Configuration

There are more options to the configuration tool, but this is not an in-depth guide on configuring the tool but more of an overview of the necessary details to proceed to your analytics work. Nevertheless, I suggest you take a look at the full documentation for the configuration of the AWS CLI tool at `https://docs.aws.amazon.com/cli/latest/userguide/cli-chap-configure.html`.

Using the AWS CLI

Now that your environment is configured, you can start using the AWS CLI tool, but before we dig deep into the intricacies of the CLI tool, allow me to share some advice: In the following section you will learn how to create, configure, edit, and delete resources through the CLI and how to perform operations on AWS resources, which is vital knowledge you need to acquire to deliver analytics at scale. However, you should strive to obtain complete automation of your infrastructure, including the creation and configuration of resources, and the industry standard is to do so through infrastructure as code (IaC), with tools such as CloudFormation, Terraform, or other similar technologies. Learning how to use the CLI will help you with the writing of CloudFormation templates or Terraform files, and it will allow you to run ad hoc operations. But it is not how you should build and maintain your production infrastructure, which should instead be written and deployed with IaC tools. IaC tools are exceptionally powerful in that they allow you to do even more than what the Web Console allows.

Let's run the `help` command to understand AWS CLI a little better:

```
> aws help
```

This command will output the following:

```
NAME
        aws -

DESCRIPTION
        The  AWS  Command  Line  Interface is a unified tool to manage
your AWS
        services.

SYNOPSIS
            aws [options] <command> <subcommand> [parameters]
```

There's obviously much more following this initial output, but we will focus on this for the moment. As you can see, there are a precise number of required and optional parts to each command:

- The `aws` part is constant.

- The `[options]` part is optional and can include any or all of the available options, which are flags prefixed by a double hash, `--`. The documentation shows all of them in detail; here are some examples:

  - `--debug (boolean)`: If you include the `--debug true` option, the command will run in debug mode.

  - `--endpoint-url (string)`: If you specify an alternative URL, the command will run against this endpoint instead of the default. This is handy when locally testing code or applications targeting a locally running service as opposed to the cloud ones—for example, an instance of DynamoDB running on your local machine instead of targeting the cloud (production) one.

  - And so on. . .

- The `<command>` part is mandatory and is one of the services listed at the end of the chapter.

- The `<subcommand>` part is also mandatory, and it represents the operation you want to perform on the service you inserted in the `<command>` part.

- The `[parameters]` part is theoretically optional because not all subcommands require options, but in reality the vast majority of subcommands do. They vary greatly from command to command.

CREATING A DynamoDB TABLE WITH THE AWS CLI

Following the previous command structure, you can now guess a good part of the command you will be typing to create a table on DynamoDB. You know `aws` is constant, you know (or can guess) the service is `dynamodb`, and you know that the action is the creation of a table. You know that AWS subcommands use a dash, `-`, to separate words, so most likely the subcommand is `create-table`. Let's run the help for this command to see if you have it right, and if you do, what parameters you need to specify to successfully create the table:

```
> aws dynamodb create-table help
```

This outputs the following:

```
        --attribute-definitions <value>
        --table-name <value>
        --key-schema <value>
        [--local-secondary-indexes <value>]
        [--global-secondary-indexes <value>]
        [--billing-mode <value>]
        [--provisioned-throughput <value>]
        [--stream-specification <value>]
        [--sse-specification <value>]
        [--tags <value>]
        [--table-class <value>]
        [--cli-input-json | --cli-input-yaml]
        [--generate-cli-skeleton <value>]
```

This means our guess was correct. The required parameters for this command are the attribute definitions, and the table name and the key schema are illustrated in the parallel example task with the Web Console.

Now, let's replicate the task by creating an `orders` table. If you recall, earlier you specified a `customerId` string field that worked as a partitioning key (`HASH`) and a timestamp string field that worked as a sort key (`RANGE`). We're not quite ready to look at DynamoDB in detail yet, so let's restrict ourselves to the required options to make this command work.

The command will be as follows:

```
> aws dynamodb create-table \
  -table-name orders
```

```
   -attribute-definitions AttributeName=customerId,AttributeType=S
AttributeName=timestamp, AttributeType=S \
   -key-schema AttributeName=customerId,KeyType=HASH AttributeName=
timestamp, KeyType=RANGE \
   -billing-mode PAY_PER_REQUEST
```

Using Skeletons and File Inputs

The previous example illustrates how to create a table in DynamoDB with the AWS CLI tool, which is great. However, it is entirely unrealistic for a cloud engineer dealing with several dozens of resource types (EC2 instances, S3 buckets and objects, tables, Lambda functions, etc.) to be able to memorize all of the options of a subcommand—it's near to impossible unless you possess a photographic memory.

For this reason, the AWS CLI tool provides a handy feature called *skeletons*. Notice the last two optional parameters in the `dynamodb create-table` command:

```
[--cli-input-json | --cli-input-yaml]
[--generate-cli-skeleton <value>]
```

If you pass the `generate-cli-skeleton` option to a command, the command itself will not run. Instead, it will generate a skeleton with all the options that the issued command takes. You can generate the skeleton in JSON or YAML, and you can then save it in a file.

This is where the other option, `[--cli-input-json | --cli-input-yaml]`, comes into play: you can run your command and specify the file you just saved as input for your command rather than typing all the options manually in the command at the risk of mistyping and making mistakes. This is certainly a far more controlled and precise process, especially for those commands that take a lot of optional parameters.

Let's see the workflow in action. First, we generate the skeleton; I like YAML because it's a superset of JSON but it's less verbose and relies on indentation, which I find elegant. And because it's a superset of JSON, if you find some particular structures difficult to express in YAML, you can simply put them in their JSON format and the YAML parser will work just fine. CloudFormation, the framework for infrastructure management in AWS, supports both JSON and YAML, but in my (anecdotal) experience, YAML is more commonly used.

So let's create a YAML skeleton by using the `input-yaml` value for the `--generate-cli-skeleton` option. Leaving it empty or using `input` would generate JSON instead.

Let's also specify a file, which I'm going to name `dynamodb_create-table`
`.yaml`, to take the generated skeleton. Here's the command:

```
> aws dynamodb create-table --generate-cli-skeleton yaml-input >
dynamodb_create-table.yaml
```

The resulting file will have the following content:

```
AttributeDefinitions:  # [REQUIRED] An array of attributes that describe
the key schema for the table and indexes.
- AttributeName: ''  # [REQUIRED] A name for the attribute.
  AttributeType: S # [REQUIRED] The data type for the attribute, where.
Valid values are: S, N, B.
TableName: '' # [REQUIRED] The name of the table to create.
KeySchema: # [REQUIRED] Specifies the attributes that make up the
primary key for a table or an index.
- AttributeName: ''  # [REQUIRED] The name of a key attribute.
  KeyType: RANGE # [REQUIRED] The role that this key attribute will
assume. Valid values are: HASH, RANGE.
LocalSecondaryIndexes: # One or more local secondary indexes (the
maximum is 5) to be created on the table.
- IndexName: ''  # [REQUIRED] The name of the local secondary index.
  KeySchema: # [REQUIRED] The complete key schema for the local
secondary index, consisting of one or more pairs of attribute names and
key types.
  - AttributeName: ''  # [REQUIRED] The name of a key attribute.
    KeyType: HASH # [REQUIRED] The role that this key attribute will
assume. Valid values are: HASH, RANGE.
  Projection: # [REQUIRED] Represents attributes that are copied
(projected) from the table into the local secondary index.
    ProjectionType: KEYS_ONLY  # The set of attributes that are
projected into the index. Valid values are: ALL, KEYS_ONLY, INCLUDE.
    NonKeyAttributes: # Represents the non-key attribute names which
will be projected into the index.
    - ''
GlobalSecondaryIndexes: # One or more global secondary indexes (the
maximum is 20) to be created on the table.
- IndexName: ''  # [REQUIRED] The name of the global secondary index.
  KeySchema: # [REQUIRED] The complete key schema for a global secondary
index, which consists of one or more pairs of attribute names and
key types.
  - AttributeName: ''  # [REQUIRED] The name of a key attribute.
    KeyType: RANGE # [REQUIRED] The role that this key attribute will
assume. Valid values are: HASH, RANGE.
  Projection: # [REQUIRED] Represents attributes that are copied
(projected) from the table into the global secondary index.
    ProjectionType: KEYS_ONLY  # The set of attributes that are
projected into the index. Valid values are: ALL, KEYS_ONLY, INCLUDE.
    NonKeyAttributes: # Represents the non-key attribute names which
will be projected into the index.
    - ''
```

```
ProvisionedThroughput: # Represents the provisioned throughput
settings for the specified global secondary index.
    ReadCapacityUnits: 0  # [REQUIRED] The maximum number of strongly
consistent reads consumed per second before DynamoDB returns a
ThrottlingException.
    WriteCapacityUnits: 0 # [REQUIRED] The maximum number of writes
consumed per second before DynamoDB returns a ThrottlingException.
BillingMode: PAY_PER_REQUEST # Controls how you are charged for read
and write throughput and how you manage capacity. Valid values are:
PROVISIONED, PAY_PER_REQUEST.
ProvisionedThroughput: # Represents the provisioned throughput settings
for a specified table or index.
    ReadCapacityUnits: 0  # [REQUIRED] The maximum number of strongly
consistent reads consumed per second before DynamoDB returns a
ThrottlingException.
    WriteCapacityUnits: 0 # [REQUIRED] The maximum number of writes
consumed per second before DynamoDB returns a ThrottlingException.
StreamSpecification: # The settings for DynamoDB Streams on the table.
    StreamEnabled: true  # [REQUIRED] Indicates whether DynamoDB Streams
is enabled (true) or disabled (false) on the table.
    StreamViewType: NEW_AND_OLD_IMAGES #  When an item in the table is
modified, StreamViewType determines what information is written to the
stream for this table. Valid values are: NEW_IMAGE, OLD_IMAGE, NEW_AND_
OLD_IMAGES, KEYS_ONLY.
SSESpecification: # Represents the settings used to enable server-side
encryption.
    Enabled: true  # Indicates whether server-side encryption is done
using an Amazon Web Services managed key or an Amazon Web Services
owned key.
    SSEType: AES256 # Server-side encryption type. Valid values are:
AES256, KMS.
    KMSMasterKeyId: '' # The KMS key that should be used for the KMS
encryption.
Tags: # A list of key-value pairs to label the table.
- Key: ''  # [REQUIRED] The key of the tag.
    Value: '' # [REQUIRED] The value of the tag.
TableClass: STANDARD_INFREQUENT_ACCESS # The table class of the new
table. Valid values are: STANDARD, STANDARD_INFREQUENT_ACCESS.
```

Another advantage of YAML over JSON is that YAML supports comments, which in this case is very useful. The equivalent operation using JSON produces the same template but in JSON format and without comments:

```
{
    "AttributeDefinitions": [
        {
            "AttributeName": "",
            "AttributeType": "B"
        }
    ],
```

```
        "TableName": "",
        "KeySchema": [
            {
                "AttributeName": "",
                "KeyType": "HASH"
            }
        ],
        "LocalSecondaryIndexes": [
            {
                "IndexName": "",
                "KeySchema": [
                    {
                        "AttributeName": "",
                        "KeyType": "HASH"
                    }
                ],
                "Projection": {
                    "ProjectionType": "ALL",
                    "NonKeyAttributes": [
                        ""
                    ]
                }
            }
        ],
        "GlobalSecondaryIndexes": [
            {
                "IndexName": "",
                "KeySchema": [
                    {
                        "AttributeName": "",
                        "KeyType": "RANGE"
                    }
                ],
                "Projection": {
                    "ProjectionType": "KEYS_ONLY",
                    "NonKeyAttributes": [
                        ""
                    ]
                },
                "ProvisionedThroughput": {
                    "ReadCapacityUnits": 0,
                    "WriteCapacityUnits": 0
                }
            }
        ],
        "BillingMode": "PAY_PER_REQUEST",
        "ProvisionedThroughput": {
            "ReadCapacityUnits": 0,
            "WriteCapacityUnits": 0
        },
```

```json
    "StreamSpecification": {
        "StreamEnabled": true,
        "StreamViewType": "KEYS_ONLY"
    },
    "SSESpecification": {
        "Enabled": true,
        "SSEType": "AES256",
        "KMSMasterKeyId": ""
    },
    "Tags": [
        {
            "Key": "",
            "Value": ""
        }
    ],
    "TableClass": "STANDARD_INFREQUENT_ACCESS"
}
```

At this point, you can edit the file with your desired values and run the `create-table` command, taking an input from a file instead of passing parameters manually. For the JSON version:

```
> aws dynamodb create-table –cli-input-json dynamodb_create-table.json
```

And YAML:

```
> aws dynamodb create-table –cli-input-yaml dynamodb_create-table.yaml
```

You should prefer this approach for a number of reasons, not the least of which is the fact that you can aggregate all your resource creation input templates in a version control system like Git and share these resources collaboratively.

Cleaning Up!

These resources were created as a working example of how to interact with AWS, but they might incur costs. So it is important to clean up afterward unless you are going to use the resources in your workloads (in which case, congratulations!). My guess is that we can delete a table with the `delete-table` subcommand of `dynamodb`, so let's check `help` to see if we have it right:

```
> aws dynamodb delete-table help
```

It appears we were right, and the only required parameter is `--table-name` (unless of course you are going to use a skeleton file for it, which is entirely feasible!).

Since I named my example table `orders`, all I need to do is to specify `orders` for the `--table-name` parameter:

```
> aws dynamodb delete-table –table-name orders
```

And the output will look like this:

```
{
        "TableDescription": {
            "TableStatus": "DELETING",
            "TableSizeBytes": 0,
            "ItemCount": 0,
            "TableName": "orders",
            "ProvisionedThroughput": {
                "NumberOfDecreasesToday": 0,
                "WriteCapacityUnits": 5,
                "ReadCapacityUnits": 5
            }
        }
}
```

And there you have it! We installed and configured the AWS CLI, then created and destroyed resources with it.

As highlighted earlier in the chapter, the best practice is through IaC tools, so that cleaning up all the resources created for the exercise can be done with a single command.

Infrastructure-as-Code: CloudFormation and Terraform

I will happily pay the price of being accused of repetitiveness, but I feel I should once more reiterate that IaC is the way to manage your infrastructure correctly and at scale. We made a couple of brief mentions of CloudFormation and Terraform, so let's go deeper into these infrastructure management tools.

CloudFormation

The last way to interact with AWS, specifically with regard to infrastructure management (rather than workload execution) is by using infrastructure-as-code (IaC) solutions. AWS does this through CloudFormation, and CloudFormation is also used under the hood by a similar tool called Terraform.

Since this book focuses on analytics, Big Data, and large-scale workloads, it should be obvious that you should not attempt to manually manage anything at all in your infrastructure. Automation should be as close to 100 percent as possible. For this reason, it is better to think of infrastructure as ephemeral, a set of resources that can be set up, put to work, and optionally torn down and destroyed. This life cycle can also be automated and scheduled.

CloudFormation is a simple tool that executes configuration files called *templates*. These templates are nothing more than JSON or YAML, whichever you prefer to work with. Like the AWS CLI, each resource has multiple parameters to be configured, which can be hard to memorize. But the good thing is that the generated skeleton of a command is very similar to the CloudFormation template needed to create the resource in question.

Let's look at an example template, an S3 bucket:

```yaml
Type: AWS::S3::Bucket
Properties:
  AccelerateConfiguration:
    AccelerateConfiguration
  AccessControl: String
  AnalyticsConfigurations:
    - AnalyticsConfiguration
  BucketEncryption:
    BucketEncryption
  BucketName: String
  CorsConfiguration:
    CorsConfiguration
  IntelligentTieringConfigurations:
    - IntelligentTieringConfiguration
  InventoryConfigurations:
    - InventoryConfiguration
  LifecycleConfiguration:
    LifecycleConfiguration
  LoggingConfiguration:
    LoggingConfiguration
  MetricsConfigurations:
    - MetricsConfiguration
  NotificationConfiguration:
    NotificationConfiguration
  ObjectLockConfiguration:
    ObjectLockConfiguration
  ObjectLockEnabled: Boolean
  OwnershipControls:
    OwnershipControls
  PublicAccessBlockConfiguration:
    PublicAccessBlockConfiguration
  ReplicationConfiguration:
    ReplicationConfiguration
  Tags:
    - Tag
  VersioningConfiguration:
    VersioningConfiguration
  WebsiteConfiguration:
    WebsiteConfiguration
```

As you can see, it's just YAML.

As usual, as for the AWS CLI, not all the properties are required. Some have default values, and some don't necessarily have to be specified or configured. Effectively, an S3 bucket will only require the bucket name to be created (in fact to be precise, not even that—CloudFormation will create a unique ID and use that for the bucket name). So how do we take the previous template and create a bucket from it using CloudFormation?

It depends on the context: on your machine, you can use the Web Console, the `cloudformation` command of the AWS CLI; in an application, you would use the AWS SDK for whatever programming language you are using to write your code.

We will explore all approaches, but for now let's focus on the command-line approach.

CloudFormation Stacks

A *stack* is the group of AWS resources created by the deployment of a CloudFormation template. You can add resources to a stack, remove from it, and when you're done you can delete the stack itself, knowing everything that was contained in the stack will be deleted, which is important to make sure you don't have lingering resources uselessly costing your business.

Since CloudFormation's basic unit is the stack, we can assume that when we go to create resources from a template, we will be creating a stack, and therefore following the normal AWS CLI conventions. The subcommand will probably be `create-stack`. So we can guess the command to create a stack will be

```
> aws cloudformation create-stack
```

Now, since you learned about skeletons, we are not going to dig into every single option but simply generate the skeleton input for it:

```
> aws cloudformation create-stack –generate-cli-skeleton yaml-input
```

Of the template generated by that command, I retain only a few options:

```
StackName: 'test-bucket-stack'  # [REQUIRED] The name that's associated
with the stack.
TemplateBody: file://test-bucket.yaml # Location of file containing the
template body.
Capabilities: # In some cases, you must explicitly acknowledge that your
stack template contains certain capabilities in order for CloudFormation
to create the stack.
- CAPABILITY_IAM
OnFailure: ROLLBACK # Determines what action will be taken if stack
creation fails. Valid values are: DO_NOTHING, ROLLBACK, DELETE.
```

Now we can go and create the YAML file that contains the definition of the S3 bucket and save it at `test-bucket.yaml`, which we specified in the previous skeleton file.

The YAML file for the S3 bucket is as follows:

```
Resources:
  MyTestBucket:
```

```
Type: AWS::S3::Bucket
Properties:
  BucketName: "joes-test-bucket-123456"
```

This gives us a chance to look into a CloudFormation template and how to define resources in it.

CloudFormation Template Anatomy

Let's take the template anatomy from the documentation at `https://docs .aws.amazon.com/AWSCloudFormation/latest/UserGuide/template-anatomy .html` and examine it:

```
AWSTemplateFormatVersion: "version date"

Description:
  String

Metadata:
  template metadata

Parameters:
  set of parameters

Rules:
  set of rules

Mappings:
  set of mappings

Conditions:
  set of conditions

Transform:
  set of transforms

Resources:
  set of resources

Outputs:
  set of outputs
```

The template version at the top is a reference for CloudFormation validation. You would want to leave it either empty (defaulting to the current version) or the latest version, which as of this writing is `2010-09-09`.

The `Description` property is optional, and it describes the template itself. It's certainly advisable to put a description of a template if you are working in a collaborative setting, which is most likely the case if you are setting up analytics in AWS.

The `Metadata` property is also optional, and it contains details about the template. You can, for example, provide further details about groups of resources that are going to be created in the template. These are machine readable so that CloudFormation can retrieve and display this data.

The `Parameters` property is an optional list of parameters you may want to define in your template. These are usually values that are then reused within resource definition. The main uses of parameters are as follows:

- To create references to a specific value that may repeat itself in the template, rather than typing the value multiple times. This saves you from making typos and also allows you to rerun a template, changing the parameter value, which will change everywhere in the template this parameter is referenced. Consider it a template variable.

- To enable overriding of those parameters. You can only override parameters you defined and referenced in a resource, so you need to define them before they can be overridden. A classic use case is injecting environment variables in services, where in the template itself you would make the value of the environment variable be that of a parameter, and you override the default parameter value by passing it to CloudFormation.

- You may need input from the user, such as their CostCenter code. This allows one CloudFormation template to support many deployments, with dynamic values added to the resources created, declared by the user when they run the CloudFormation template.

Later in the book (Chapter 6, "Processing Data"), I'll show you how to use Secret Manager and resolve values in the template through SSM parameters.

The `Rules` property, also optional, is there to let you control conditionally the management of resources based on conditions that you specify. The rule functions available are as follows:

Fn::And

Fn::Contains

Fn::EachMemberEquals

Fn::EachMemberIn

Fn::Equals

Fn::Not

Fn::Or

Fn::RefAll

```
Fn::ValueOf

Fn::ValueOfAll
```

This is fairly advanced use of CloudFormation templates, and I believe you should use rules only as a last resort mechanism. Nevertheless, we will explore some use cases later on.

The `Mappings` optional property is similar to the `Parameters` value, but instead of flat key-value pairs you can define maps with the following structure (YAML):

```
MyMap:
    Key1:
        SubKey1: Value1
        SubKey2: Value2
```

These can then be referenced in the template with the CloudFormation function `Fn::FindInMap`.

The `Conditions` property is optional, and it lets you define named conditions, a bit like defining a function, which you can then reference in the template as a condition for a resource. It can be very useful to create switches based on the environment you are deploying your resources to, such as production or staging, so that resource management behaves differently according to what environment the template is applied to.

The `Transform` property, also optional, specifies macros to process a Cloud-Formation template. I will confess I never had a use case where a macro was necessary or the preferred way of accomplishing the task.

Now on to the principal (and very much required) section of the template, the `Resources`. Here you will define the resources you intend to manage (that is, create, update, or destroy). There are hundreds of types of resources, with all sorts of custom properties only applicable to a single resource in particular. However, the structure is always the same:

```
Resource:
  NameOfResource:
    Type: String
    Properties:
      All other properties here...
```

Let's go back to our S3 bucket example:

```
Resources:
  MyTestBucket:
    Type: AWS::S3::Bucket
    Properties:
      BucketName: "joes-test-bucket-123456"
```

Now let's destructure it to understand its components and see how we can extend it and improve it. First of all, though not required, we should have a version declaration at the top, which we now know has to specify a date; the latest version is dated `2010-09-09`:

```
AWSTemplateFormatVersion: "2010-09-09"
```

Second, we have a `Resources` section, which declares our resources. You are probably familiar with YAML, but if you aren't, just know that indenting text means that the section you are about to declare is a property of the section above it. In this case `MyTestBucket` is what we named the resource, and it's a property of `Resources`. `MyTestBucket` is just an identifier; you could call it whatever you want (as long as it's a unique name in the YAML). The proper term for the resource name is `Logical ID`.

There is no mandatory order to specify properties of a resource, but it is good practice to always start with `Type` since it gives us context with regard to the rest of the properties we are going to declare. If you didn't declare the resource type first and started with some obscure property, you would not know how to put the value of that property in context. So we specify `Type` as one of the available CloudFormation resource types. Resource types follow the convention `service-provider::service-name::data-type-name`—in our case, `AWS::S3::Bucket`. The full list of resources is available at `https://docs.aws .amazon.com/AWSCloudFormation/latest/UserGuide/aws-template-resource-type-ref.html`.

For example, if you look at the Amazon S3 resource types available, you will find the following list:

`AWS::S3::AccessPoint`

`AWS::S3::Bucket`

`AWS::S3::BucketPolicy`

`AWS::S3::MultiRegionAccessPoint`

`AWS::S3::MultiRegionAccessPointPolicy`

`AWS::S3::StorageLens`

After the resource type, we specify the resource properties, and the first step is always to add a `Properties` field; this is where all the resource properties will go. Even in a scenario as simple as an S3 bucket, the bucket name will go under `Properties`.

So far, you have seen where to declare resources and how to declare them by specifying `Logical ID`, `Type`, and `Properties`.

However, we can do better than simply typing the name of the bucket—`BucketName`—we can make this value dynamic, which may be overridden by passing a manual parameter. To accomplish this, we add a section to our template called `Parameters` (as you've seen earlier) and move the bucket name in the

`Parameters` section, and then reference that value in the `BucketName` property of our S3 bucket, like so:

```
AWSTemplateFormatVersion: "2010-09-09"

Parameters:
  MyBucketName:
    Type: String
    Default: "joes-test-bucket-123456"
Resources:
  MyTestBucket:
    Type: AWS::S3::Bucket
    Properties:
      BucketName: !Ref MyBucketName
```

Much better already. Note the `!Ref` function added after `BucketName`, which tells CloudFormation to reference the value of whatever object in the template has the ID `MyBucketName`. This change now allows us to only specify the value of this parameter once and have it reference in the template as many times as we want. It enables us to override the parameter value through the AWS CLI tool by passing the flag `--parameter-overrides` to the `cloudformation` command.

Let's take it a step further and address the complexity of having to deploy different resources (or differently named resources) according to the environment we are working in (such as production, staging, or development). We can do this in a number of ways, and you can determine the best way to accomplish it on a use case basis.

The first approach is to use the `!Sub` function of `cloudformation`, which interpolates values into another value. In this case, we would do the following:

```
BucketName: !Sub "joes-test-bucket-${Env}"
```

assuming `Env` is a parameter you declared at the top of the file like so:

```
Parameters:
  Env:
    Type: String
    Default: production
    AllowedValues:
      - prod
      - test
```

which would result in your bucket being named `joes-test-bucket-production`. Note that you can restrict the values that can be assigned to a parameter by specifying that the `AllowedValues` be a precise list of values rather than arbitrary.

Another approach is to use maps, which can be variable and declared in the property itself or a map in the `Mappings` section:

```
Mappings:
  Environments:
    prod: "productionbucket"
    Test: "stagingbucket"
Resources:
  MyTestBucket:
    Type: AWS::S3::Bucket
    Properties:
      BucketName: !FindInMap [Environments, !Ref Env]
```

Since `Env` can only be `prod` or `test`, there will be a corresponding value in the `Environments` mapping, which in turn corresponds to a string value.

There are many more ways of constructing values in CloudFormation, and I invite you to explore them all, especially commonly used functions such as `Fn::Join` and `Fn::Sub` as well as common conditional constructs such as `!If`.

CloudFormation Changesets

As part of the life cycle of your infrastructure management, you will definitely come across the need to update an existing stack, whether it is to add or remove resources or update the configuration of existing resources. This is done through the `deploy` subcommand of the `cloudformation` command of the AWS CLI tool.

Changesets are the representation of what changes are going to be implemented on your stack. It is always a good idea to examine the changeset before applying changes to a stack so that you can verify that the changes that will be applied to your infrastructure are in fact the desired outcome of your change. You'll want to make sure that you don't accidentally delete anything, because more often than not your resources will have interdependencies and deleting one means another one stops working, or at the very least it stops working properly.

Generating a changeset is easy, and it is done by passing the `--no-execute-changeset` flag. Let's look at an example. We'll update our bucket template to enable versioning on it. Versioning is a feature whereby the uploading of an object with the same key as an existing object will cause an overwrite, but previous versions of the same object will be kept and remain accessible, as opposed to being bluntly overwritten.

The changes we need to make to our original simple template are as follows:

```
Resources:
  MyTestBucket:
    Type: AWS::S3::Bucket
    Properties:
```

```
BucketName: "joes-test-bucket-123456"
VersioningConfiguration:
  Status: Enabled
```

To generate a changeset, we run the `deploy` command of `cloudformation` with the aforementioned flag:

```
> aws cloudformation deploy –no-execute-changeset –stack-name mystack
-template-file bucket-template.yaml
```

where `mystack` is whatever stack identifier you used in the first place and `bucket-template.yaml` is the file where you saved the YAML of the bucket creation template.

This will output the following:

```
Waiting for changeset to be created..
Changeset created successfully. Run the following command to review
changes:
aws cloudformation describe-change-set --change-set-name
 arn:aws:cloudformation:eu-west-1:972520707061:changeSet/awscli-
cloudformation-
package-deploy-1646496270/9b256632-2db0-47a7-927a-0804b798c991
```

We are given the complete command to run the inspection of the changeset; therefore, we copy and paste that in our terminal, run it, and get the following output:

```
$ aws cloudformation describe-change-set --change-set-name
 arn:aws:cloudformation:eu-west-1:972520707061:changeSet/awscli-
cloudformation-
package-deploy-1646496270/9b256632-2db0-47a7-927a-0804b798c991
{
    "Changes": [
        {
            "Type": "Resource",
            "ResourceChange": {
                "Action": "Modify",
                "LogicalResourceId": "MyTestBucket",
                "PhysicalResourceId": "joes-test-bucket-123456",
                "ResourceType": "AWS::S3::Bucket",
                "Replacement": "False",
                "Scope": [
                    "Properties"
                ],
                "Details": [
                    {
                        "Target": {
```

```
                                  "Attribute": "Properties",
                                  "Name": "VersioningConfiguration",
                                  "RequiresRecreation": "Never"
                              },
                              "Evaluation": "Static",
                              "ChangeSource": "DirectModification"
                          }
                      ]
                  }
              }
          }
      ],
      "ChangeSetName": "awscli-cloudformation-package-deploy-1646496270",
      "ChangeSetId": "arn:aws:cloudformation:eu-west-1:972520707061
:changeSet/awscli-cloudformation-package-deploy-1646496270/9b256632-2db0
-47a7-927a-0804b798c991",
      "StackId": "arn:aws:cloudformation:eu-west-1:972520707061:stack/
test-bucket-stack/84f352f0-9bce-11ec-8cfd-0ad3ae919137",
      "StackName": "test-bucket-stack",
      "Description": "Created by AWS CLI at 2022-03-05T16:04:30.623993
UTC",
      "Parameters": null,
      "CreationTime": "2022-03-05T16:04:31.051000+00:00",
      "ExecutionStatus": "AVAILABLE",
      "Status": "CREATE_COMPLETE",
      "StatusReason": null,
      "NotificationARNs": [],
      "RollbackConfiguration": {},
      "Capabilities": [],
      "Tags": null,
      "ParentChangeSetId": null,
      "IncludeNestedStacks": false,
      "RootChangeSetId": null
  }
```

Despite its verbosity, this changeset is very simple to understand. Head straight to the Changes section of the JSON output and look at the array of changes that are going to be applied to your stack. You will notice one change, of type modify, to the bucket with the exact physical resource ID we are addressing. Down in the details section you will notice that the property being addressed by the change is VersioningConfiguration and that this kind of change never requires a re-creation of the resource ("RequiresRecreation": "Never").

We're flying. All we need to do is rerun the initial deploy command without the --no-execute-change flag.

Note that the modify change type is important because it means the resource will be modified and not replaced. It is important, especially in production, to know if a resource will be modified or replaced, as it may break resources that are dependent on the targeted resource.

```
$ aws cloudformation deploy --template-file test-bucket.yaml --stack-name
test-bucket-stack

Waiting for changeset to be created..
Waiting for stack create/update to complete
Successfully created/updated stack - test-bucket-stack
```

And we're done. Our bucket now supports versioning, as our trusty console tells us in Figure 3.4.

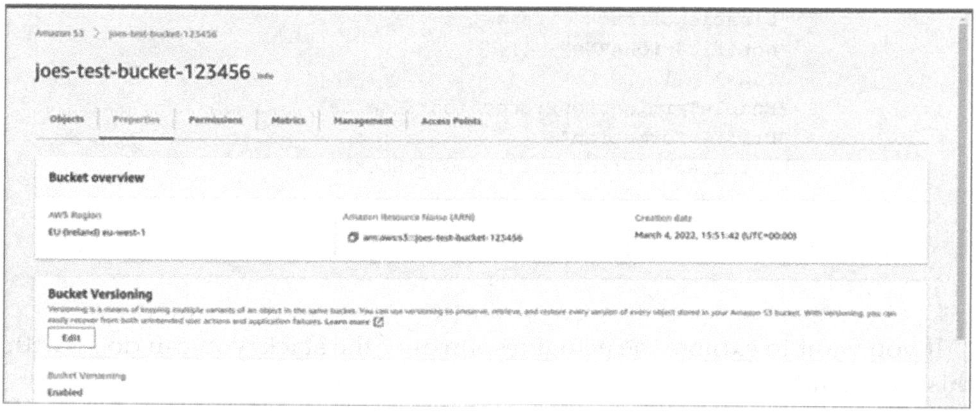

Figure 3.4: Verifying the changes to the bucket in the Web Console

Note that you can save a changeset with

```
$ aws cloudformation create-change-set –stack-name mystackname
–template-body mytemplatefile.(json|yaml)
```
and execute it at a later time with

```
$ aws cloudformation execute-change-set –change-set-name mychangeset
–stack-name mystackname
```

Getting Stack Information

Once your stack is up, you may want to explore its state. My first guess at this command was wrong, in that I thought `describe-stack` would do it. I was close, but the command is

```
$ aws cloudformation describe-stacks –stackname test-bucket-stack
```

Obviously, replace *stackname* with the actual stack you are working on. The output produced is as follows:

```
{
    "Stacks": [
        {
```

```
        "StackId": "arn:aws:cloudformation:eu-
west-1:972520707061:stack/test-bucket-stack/163b9720-9d3e-11ec-a92e-
0232ccd641b7",
        "StackName": "test-bucket-stack",
        "ChangeSetId": "arn:aws:cloudformation:eu-west-1:97252070
7061:changeSet/awscli-cloudformation-package-deploy-1646565047/8af52ad3-
1d7a-45e6-9eef-941b8563f0c0",
        "CreationTime": "2022-03-06T11:10:52.872000+00:00",
        "LastUpdatedTime": "2022-03-06T11:10:58.202000+00:00",
        "RollbackConfiguration": {},
        "StackStatus": "CREATE_COMPLETE",
        "DisableRollback": false,
        "NotificationARNs": [],
        "Tags": [],
        "EnableTerminationProtection": false,
        "DriftInformation": {
            "StackDriftStatus": "NOT_CHECKED"
        }
      }
    ]
}
```

If you want to explore the actual resources of the stack, you can do so with
this command:

```
$ aws cloudformation list-stack-resources –stack-name test-bucket-stack
```

which produces a list of resources like so:

```
{
    "StackResourceSummaries": [
        {
            "LogicalResourceId": "MyTestBucket",
            "PhysicalResourceId": "joes-test-bucket-123456",
            "ResourceType": "AWS::S3::Bucket",
            "LastUpdatedTimestamp": "2022-03-06T11:11:23.658000+00:00",
            "ResourceStatus": "CREATE_COMPLETE",
            "DriftInformation": {
                "StackResourceDriftStatus": "NOT_CHECKED"
            }
        }
    ]
}
```

As expected, our stack contains an S3 bucket with the correct name.

Cleaning Up Again

Cleaning up, as we mentioned earlier in the book, is a very important operation. There are many reasons for cleaning up your resources, primarily cost and that it's a good practice to keep the number of resources that are active to a minimum, which limits the number of alerts you may receive and the monitoring of those unnecessary resources.

CloudFormation naturally can take care of deleting resources by deleting a stack. Remember that resources are grouped in stacks, and deleting a stack means deleting all the resources contained in that stack. This might sound dramatic, but it is actually good practice to do so. In well-designed architectures, you limit the coupling and the interdependencies between resources and services to the lowest possible level. Therefore, you should think of your next application written to run on AWS as much as possible as its own self-contained unit, with this unit being the stack, and if your application does not need to run all the time you can simply tear it down.

My advice is that you should always strive to reach the position of having ephemeral architectures. You spin them up when you need them, you tear them down when you don't.

How do we delete a stack? Let's keep up our guessing game. We know the cloudformation service of the aws command is going to take care of it. My guess is that the action is going to be called delete-stack, so let's run the help on this command to see if I have it right:

```
$ aws cloudformation delete-stack help
```

As expected, the command is right, and two parameters jump out at the top of the help output:

```
--stack-name (string)
    The name or the unique stack ID that's associated with the stack.

--retain-resources (list)
    For  stacks  in  the DELETE_FAILED state, a list of resource logical
    IDs that are associated with the resources you want to retain.  Dur-
    ing  deletion,  CloudFormation  deletes the stack but doesn't delete
    the retained resources.

    Retaining resources is useful when you can't delete a resource, such
    as a non-empty S3 bucket, but you want to delete the stack.

(string)
```

The --stack-name is obvious—we need to specify which stack we are going to delete. The next option is --retain-resources, and as help tells us, in case the deletion of the stack fails, we can specify a list of resources that we may want to retain.

> **NOTE**   You cannot try to delete a stack and retain some of its resources. The `--retain-resources` flag only works on stacks that are in the `DELETE_FAILED` state.

Let's go ahead and delete the stack:

```
$ aws cloudformation delete-stack –stack-name test-bucket-stack
```

CloudFormation Conclusions

Our overview of CloudFormation stops here because in the context of producing analytics we only focus on those features of the AWS tools that are useful to the job at hand. However, as you may have gathered at this point, CloudFormation is a powerful tool with lots of useful features. But not to worry: throughout our journey to producing analytics at scale we will be making extensive use of CloudFormation, exploring some of those more advanced features as they become relevant to our work.

Terraform

Terraform is the main alternative to CloudFormation, and it can be used alternatively to CloudFormation or alongside it. Terraform has its pros and its cons. First of all, Terraform's main advantage is that it supports multiple cloud providers. Should you decide (or be in a position) to have some of your resources located outside of AWS (for example, on Google Cloud Provider or Microsoft Azure), you would not be able to manage the resources on other cloud providers with CloudFormation, which exclusively targets AWS.

Second, when you use Terraform for AWS work, under the hood the work will be done with CloudFormation, so Terraform very much works as an abstraction layer.

With these considerations out of the way, why and when would you use Terraform over CloudFormation for AWS work? Let's explore a few reasons.

Coding Style

If you are into declarative configuration files, Terraform is the tool for you. Terraform uses a programming language called HCL, which is similar to JSON and YAML. So picking it up with only JSON/YAML experience should take a matter of hours. Resources are defined with a syntax that is intuitive, and

I personally found that Terraform files work well as self-explanatory infra-structure manifest files. CloudFormation by nature is a lot more "nested" as a templating engine and less readable.

For example, the Terraform equivalent of the creation of a bucket would look like this:

```
resource "aws_s3_bucket" "joesbucket" {
  bucket = "joes-test-bucket-123456"

  tags = {
    Name        = "Stack"
    Environment = "test-bucket-stack"
  }
}

resource "aws_s3_bucket_acl" "example" {
  bucket = aws_s3_bucket.joesbucket.id
  acl    = "private"
}
```

I added an `acl` declaration for the bucket to show how a resource is referenced in another, precisely through the `aws_s3_bucket.joesbucket.id` syntax, which dynamically referenced the bucket created in the `aws_s3_bucket` statement.

As you can see, using Terraform is very easy and intuitive.

Modularity

With Terraform, you can create your modules, which can contain multiple resources and, once executed, return values that can then be referenced in other Terraform modules, or the main file (called `main.tf` usually). This allows great flexibility in teams, especially those with complex needs where a fairly complex section of the architecture can be automated and isolated into a unit and reused at will by being modularized.

Limitations

Terraform does not have a couple of the limitations that CloudFormation has: a template can exceed the CloudFormation size of 51,000 bytes, and it can have more than the maximum of 60 dynamic parameters that is imposed by CloudFormation.

In either case (and other limitations that may arise), AWS will suggest you separate your resources into smaller templates, and I can't help but agree that—in anything, not just cloud infrastructure management or analytics—if a piece of work is exceedingly large, you are possibly putting more than you should into it.

> **NOTE**   The Unix philosophy of sticking to one thing and doing it very well always proves right in software engineering.

Terraform vs. CloudFormation

Both Terraform and CloudFormation have advantages and disadvantages. If you are entirely tied to AWS, then your only reason to choose Terraform would be that you like the language and the modularity aspects. If you are not entirely tied to AWS, you will be faced with the dilemma of using similar CloudFormation tools for other cloud providers, leading to fragmentation and inconsistency.

Either way, I strongly suggest you use infrastructure-as-code solutions for your work, and when it comes to building a data platform on AWS to support large-scale analytics, you would do well to adopt one.

Infrastructure-as-Code: CDK, Pulumi, Cloudcraft, and Other Solutions

Let's take a brief look at some alternative solutions to the aforementioned IaC tools, which may offer different approaches that suit different use cases.

AWS CDK

Many tools are available on the market (and in the open source community) to resolve the question of infrastructure management. One such solution, produced by AWS, is Cloud Development Kit (CDK). This particular SDK produced by AWS allows you to write infrastructure management code in your preferred programming language. The concept might sound a bit exotic, so what is it all about?

There are a number of reasons why you would choose something like CDK. In my experience, the most enticing reasons to make such a move are as follows:

- You don't know "a priori" what the architecture will be. There may be complex use cases where architecture is determined by input parameters and particular (and variable) conditions. Therefore, you are left with the choice of creating CloudFormation templates for every scenario possible, or creating your infrastructure "programmatically," executing conditional statements in an imperative fashion, rather than through a large and complex CloudFormation template full of rules, mappings, and conditions.

- You don't have dedicated DevOps or infrastructure engineers and are delegating the creation of your infrastructure to coders coming from different backgrounds. You might deem the learning curve for these engineers to be too steep and instead let them use their favorite programming language to accomplish a task as complex as infrastructure management by means of writing a program they are well used to doing.

A CDK program looks like this:

```
import * as s3 from '@aws-cdk/aws-s3';
import * as cdk from '@aws-cdk/core';

export class S3BucketExampleStack extends cdk.Stack {
  constructor(scope: cdk.App, id: string, props?: cdk.StackProps) {
    super(scope, id, props);

    const s3Bucket = new s3.Bucket(this, 'joes-test-bucket-123456')
  }
}
```

NOTE A full GitHub repository of examples is available here: `https://github` `.com/aws-samples/aws-cdk-examples.`

If you are someone with years of experience in software engineering and programming, this certainly feels familiar. Not only that, but challenges such as conditional execution or string interpolation feel easier in CDK than they do in CloudFormation:

```
import * as s3 from '@aws-cdk/aws-s3';
import * as cdk from '@aws-cdk/core';

export class S3BucketExampleStack extends cdk.Stack {
  constructor(scope: cdk.App, id: string, props?: cdk.StackProps) {
    super(scope, id, props);
    const { stage } = props;
    if (stage === 'dev') {
      const s3temp = new s3.Bucket(this, 'testbucketoftempresults');
    }
    const bucketName = `joes-test-bucket-${stage}`
    const s3Bucket = new s3.Bucket(this, bucketName)
  }
}
```

This all looks very good, and it certainly has its applications. Why would you stick to CloudFormation instead of writing all your infrastructure with the CDK then?

For starters, I think of CloudFormation templates as the manifest of a cargo shipment: I can see what is in it, I tend to avoid conditional executions, but if they exist, I can determine the potential resources created by any such conditions. Second, using the CDK means you have to deploy this code in a standard application/service fashion. You need to set up the boilerplate for it, set up CI/CD for it, maintain it, monitor it, and take the risk that if you have a bug in your code (outside of the infrastructure management statements) the resulting infrastructure might be wrong or not there at all.

So, while I applaud the initiative and I can see how this may have its uses, I'd tread very carefully in the direction of CDK or CDK-like tools, such as Pulumi.

Pulumi

Pulumi, however, does have an edge over CDK, in the same way as Terraform has an edge over CloudFormation when it comes to multicloud support. Additionally, Pulumi supports setting up infrastructure for Kubernetes clusters, which is impressive in a world that is moving toward container-based runtimes and deployments for applications.

Cloudcraft

Cloudcraft is a tool that has evolved from a simple cloud architecture diagrams web application into a cost prediction tool that, given a certain diagram, will produce Terraform files for its instantiation, which is impressive. I tend to write my infrastructure files from scratch so as to familiarize myself with the language, resources, and general ecosystem, but if you want a handy solution that feeds three birds with one fava bean, then look no further than Cloudcraft. It is my default tool of choice for diagrams, which I use in articles posted on the web, such as my post on data engineering based on serverless and Golang, available at `https://engineroom.teamwork.com/the-go-serverless-data-engineering-revolution-at-teamwork-golang-aws-f2fd3cb1f563`. The architecture diagram shown in Figure 3.5 and that appears in the article shows off Cloudcraft's output.

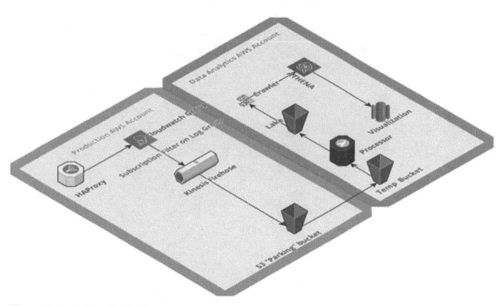

Figure 3.5: A Cloudcraft diagram

Infrastructure Management Conclusions

At this point you should be familiar with AWS basics, with how you create an account; create users and roles with the right permissions; create resources with the Web Console, with the AWS CLI tool, or with CloudFormation; as well as alternative solutions that work well on AWS, such as Terraform, Pulumi, or Cloudcraft.

From this point on, we can start becoming more focused on the specific aspects of building a data platform for analytics, starting with how we store data and with what AWS tools.

Serverless Computing and Data Engineering

Since the advent of AWS Lambda in late 2014, serverless computing has gained a tremendous amount of momentum and revolutionized the way we do cloud computing.

Let's first see what serverless computing is and what use cases it fits, and then explore how it is applied to the world of data engineering and analytics.

> **SERVERLESS, ONLY BY NAME**
>
> Clearly, any piece of software needs a computer to run on, and when this computer is not a personal workstation but rather serves or processes data within a wider system, it is a server. Serverless does not mean "without servers" as much as it means "no need to manage servers." I question how misleading this nomenclature is, but that's what we have, and we will stick with it. "Manageless servers" sounds horrible anyway.

Serverless vs. Fully Managed

There is an important distinction to be made. *Serverless* tends to represent all those tools made available by cloud providers, chiefly AWS in our case, where the developer does not have to manage the servers required to run your code or application. For example, AWS Lambda's pricing is a factor of the memory size allocated to execute work, the execution time (which has a time limit of

15 minutes) and the number of so-called "invocations," which is substantially executions.

The idea is to produce a piece of code without worrying about the boilerplate code (for web apps, for example) and focusing only on executing the task, and then deploying that code as a stand-alone unit that can be executed at will.

If you have ever developed backend web applications or APIs, you will be familiar with the idea of using a framework that simplifies and automates the setup and management of endpoints or the handling of web requests. With Lambdas you can forget about all of that. You can still use frameworks such as Express in Node.js or Echo in Golang, but this would be entirely optional and down to stylistic preferences or to use certain features of the framework. None of it is necessary for your code to work. And in fact, by and large AWS Lambda web endpoints do not make use of frameworks.

A classic example in the analytics domain is a Lambda function triggered by an object being deposited on S3; it processes that object and stores the output somewhere else.

In between "invocations" you don't pay for Lambda functions. If a function is never invoked, it will cost you nothing.

This is the main difference with fully managed computing. A fully managed tool like AWS MSK (Managed Kafka), for example, is up and running all the time and it has costs, but you do not have to provision servers or configure them. You only need to create streams, producers, and consumers; you don't have to worry about the cluster resources or applications, such as Zookeeper, which is in charge of keeping the cluster healthy. However, since MSK is running all the time, you will pay for the hours it is active, as well as other charges (such as bandwidth and storage), even if you were to transmit no data on it.

AWS Serverless Technologies

AWS has released a number of serverless technologies through the years since the advent of AWS Lambda, which was historically the first.

The most common serverless tools available are as follows:

- **AWS Lambda:** Serverless computing
- **AWS Fargate:** Long-running container-based jobs
- **AWS DynamoDB:** Serverless NoSQL database service hosted by AWS that's fully managed
- **Amazon Aurora:** Serverless relational databases
- **Amazon SNS:** Serverless notification system that allows communication between AWS resources

- **Amazon SQS:** Serverless Queue Service for message queueing in software systems

- **AWS CloudWatch:** Serverless logs

- **Amazon QuickSight:** Serverless business intelligence, reporting, and dashboards

- **AWS Step Functions:** Serverless compute workflows

- **Amazon API Gateway:** Serverless API Gateway for mapping resources to URLs and configuring access

- **Amazon Cognito:** Serverless authentication, authorization, and user management for both web and mobile apps

Some of these technologies (e.g., Aurora) are only partially relevant to analytics, but we will explore all of them, some more in depth than others.

AWS Lambda

There are many advantages to using serverless computing, and Lambdas in particular. Besides the obvious (scalability and no operational overheads), there are a few more. Let's take a look at the general pros and cons of Lambdas, and then see how they apply in the context of the building and deployment of a data platform.

Pricing Model

A single Lambda charge is a function of the instance type used to compute (specifically the memory size) and the duration of the execution. As of early 2023, these are the prices in the us-east-1 region:

Memory (MB) Price per 1ms

128 $0.0000000021

512 $0.0000000083

1024 $0.0000000167

1536 $0.0000000250

2048 $0.0000000333

3072 $0.0000000500

4096 $0.0000000667

5120 $0.0000000833

6144 $0.0000001000

7168 $0.0000001167

8192 $0.0000001333

9216 $0.0000001500

10240 $0.0000001667

As you can see, the more memory you allocate, the more expensive it is to run the Lambda. The way I simplify the configuration of Lambdas in my mind is by picturing a gauge, as shown in Figure 4.1.

Cheap, but at OOM risk ⟵ ⟶ No OOM risk, but expensive

Figure 4.1: Configuration of Lambdas

Clearly, there is a perfect configuration for each of your Lambdas, but configuration is not the only thing you can do. For example, optimizing your code for faster execution has a measurable impact on the billing; when possible, we have adopted developing Lambdas in Go for those tasks where Go has proven orders of magnitude faster than Python. Another cost-saving measure we applied was to issue a query in Athena without waiting for its result but rather exiting the code as soon as the query was running successfully and picking up the query result through events. Also keep in mind that adding memory to a Lambda also adds more CPU, in terms of both overall compute capacity and the ability to take advantage of many threads within your compute function.

Depending on what your task is, there are many ways to make the best of the Lambda pricing model. However, there is a point at which you may want to consider a different solution to optimize cost. An on-demand pricing option is great because the single charge for a Lambda execution is ridiculously cheap, but if you have steady traffic, with clear patterns and generally deprived of bursts, you may find that the same application running on EC2 instances or an EKS (Kubernetes) cluster will cost less, even accounting for the operational overheads involved.

Laser Focus on Code

First, Lambdas are laser-focused on the code that executes a task—no boiler-plate, no frameworks, no initialization of sorts. You write code that performs a particular task and deploy it. In this respect, they save your team the headaches of maintaining a large codebase and familiarizing themselves with frameworks and tools (other than the chosen programming language for the development of the task). Clearly it means that a change applied to one Lambda is not going to affect the code in another Lambda, which is a common problem in monolithic applications.

Moreover, Lambdas don't impose particular technologies or programming languages, so you can choose to write every single function with the programming language that best fits the task at hand, a luxury you can rarely (or never?) afford when you write a monolithic application.

The Lambda Paradigm Shift

Second, Lambdas have a time execution limit that is configurable up to a maximum of 15 minutes. This may sound like a limitation (it certainly is in certain situations), but it's also a paradigm shift.

All too often, developers tend to relax into the languages and tools they know, and use them in the way they have learned to use them in their professional experience. Don't get me wrong—there is nothing inherently wrong with this approach. But there is certainly scope for improvement and advancement, and if you were given AWS Lambdas as your only tool for the deployment of code and told that no matter what, you cannot have a single workload execution go beyond a 15-minute limit, what would you do? This is where Lambda functions are revolutionary; let's take a look at a real-life example that clarifies the challenges, but also the opportunities, offered by AWS Lambdas.

As part of a team of developers working in the energy industry, I was tasked with the retrieval of the history of several energy product prices for the purpose of storing into a data warehouse. The high-level overview of the task was trivial: retrieve CSV files, store the product ID, the product name, the price, and the date of that price in a Redshift cluster, so analysts could subsequently concentrate on creating forecasting models based on the variations of prices through time. I was not even asked to take care of the forecasting part, simply the retrieval and storage. The files containing the prices were stored on an old-fashioned FTP server, and each file was quite large.

Here is where the people in charge of the FTP server threw a spanner in the works of our Lambda-based infrastructure: the FTP server allowed only one file download per FTP client at a time. Since there were thousands of files and their retrieval had to be sequential, we were entirely sure a single Lambda could not retrieve all the files on time before it would inevitably time out.

We devised a number of solutions for storing state (such as marking how many files we had downloaded and resuming file download with a subsequent Lambda). These solutions may well have worked, but we were not satisfied with them, and not only because they made such a trivial task a long task to execute but also because the design seemed very flimsy. We feared we'd end up with a lot of failed executions and missing files.

The eureka moment came when we thought of the ability of a Lambda to execute any kind of AWS operation, including invoking another Lambda—or thousands for that matter.

So we redesigned the system like so: we had an "invoker" Lambda, which generated an array of dates (going as far back in time as we were interested in doing), and this invoker Lambda then "spawned" a Lambda per date, which in turn created an FTP client and downloaded the single file for the date. The result was that thousands of Lambdas were spawned simultaneously and performed their work in a few seconds, and so our system replaced an old three-hour job with a six-second one.

This is the paradigm shift I am trying to illustrate: basing your applications on Lambdas implies a move toward the destructuring and decomposition of tasks into smaller workload units that can be chained and orchestrated through appropriate means, such as Lambdas themselves, Step Functions, wiring systems such as AWS SNS or SQS, or streaming applications such as Kinesis. There is no denying code developed in this way is healthier and more resilient. If you are used to monoliths that feel a bit like a game of Jenga, where modifying something means the whole thing may come crumbling down, then Lambdas are a refreshingly novel way to develop applications.

Very often our code tends to do a lot, and Lambda prevents this by design. In fact, it is aptly named like those inline expression functions that we may find in languages supporting functional programming. And that is the way you should think of your Lambda functions: do one thing and do it well, and quickly.

In the context of data engineering, Lambdas are a bold and courageous choice, but there are multiple instances where they find their place and save you and your team a whole lot of headaches, from cluster maintenance to scalability.

Virtually Infinite Scalability

AWS manages scalability for you. You have to configure your Lambdas so that they can execute your workloads effectively, and that is all you are asked to worry about. AWS will take care of bursts, upscaling on demand, and downscaling accordingly. In any case, you are not charged for AWS running to keep your Lambdas running—only for when they execute.

Scalability can be a major pain point. It's difficult to react to traffic and demand to scale up your resources, and it's just as challenging to detect when the bursts are over or the traffic tide has died down. It's therefore safe to scale down again (or choose to take the hit on the billing if you don't), but AWS Lambdas save you from this major operational headache.

Geographical Distribution

A feature of Lambda called Lambda@Edge allows you to reduce latency by deploying Lambda functions in the various AWS regions located around the world so that users can have their response time reduced by interacting with

Lambda functions that are as close as possible geographically. More recently, AWS announced CloudFront Functions. Here, rather than executing in regional edge caches, these functions execute at the very edge of their content delivery network (CDN). CloudFront Functions is a new serverless scripting platform that allows you to run lightweight JavaScript code at the 218+ CloudFront edge locations at approximately one sixth of the price of Lambda@Edge.

A Lambda Hello World

Let's look at a few example implementations, including some very common use cases. First, let's produce the Hello World equivalent of a Lambda function, and we'll do so using Node.js.

The best way is to start with a blueprint, so in your AWS Web Console, navigate to Lambda and then choose Create Function. In the Create Function dialog box, you can choose from several available templates. You can author a Lambda from scratch or use one of hundreds of blueprints already available, covering all sorts of scenarios in different programming languages. Node.js and Python are the most popular, but there are plenty of blueprints for all sorts of languages.

Select the Blueprint option and then type **hello world** in the search bar. You should be able to see a Node.js hello-world blueprint available for selection, as shown in Figure 4.2.

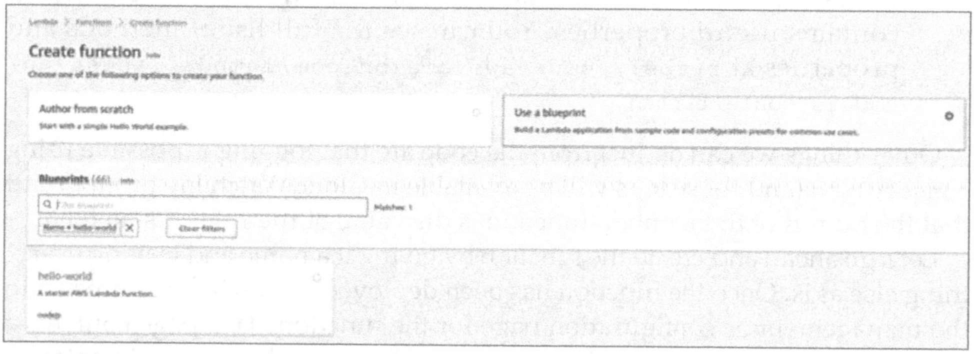

Figure 4.2: Node.js hello-world blueprint

Select the hello-world template and click the Configure button at the bottom right of the page. Aside from basic details such as the function name and the execution role (you should always create a new role for the Lambda and incrementally add policies to enable the function to interact with other AWS resources), the focus of our attention goes to the function code.

The basic template contains the following code:

```
console.log('Loading function');

exports.handler = async (event, context) => {
    //console.log('Received event:', JSON.stringify(event, null, 2));
    console.log('value1 =', event.key1);
    console.log('value2 =', event.key2);
    console.log('value3 =', event.key3);
    return event.key1;  // Echo back the first key value
    // throw new Error('Something went wrong');
};
```

As you can see, it doesn't do much—it simply returns the key1 property of the event object. However, this little snippet is already giving us some information about how Lambdas work:

- Code is executed in the handler function of the exports object.

- The handler is marked as async, which means we can perform await operations in the handler code, if we so wish, as the runtime is Node.js 12.x.

- The parameters passed are an event and a context. The event object changes structure according to the kind of event that triggered a Lambda invocation, while context is an optional but also fixed kind of event, which contains useful properties. You can see the full list of methods and properties at https://docs.aws.amazon.com/lambda/latest/dg/nodejs-context.html.

Other things we can deduct from the code are that logging is possible using console.log (and those logs will be available in CloudWatch log groups) and that the output of the Lambda function is the value of the return statement.

Let's go ahead and create the function by giving it a name and leaving everything else as is. Once the function has been deployed, you will be redirected to the management or configuration page for the function. This page contains a rudimentary code editor in which you can conduct some basic experimentation at a code level. Interestingly, the editor lets you create different event objects to test the Lambda, so let's do that. Click the Test drop-down to configure a test event, which I unsurprisingly called test and inserted the following JSON in the body of the event:

```
{
    "author": "joe minichino",
    "title": "Data Analytics in the AWS Cloud",
    "publisher": "Wiley"
}
```

We want to see the Lambda logging this information, so we need to change the code to reflect this. Instead of `key1`, `key2`, and `key3`, we will use `author`, `title`, and `publisher`, like so:

```
console.log('Loading function');

exports.handler = async (event, context) => {
    console.log('Received event:', JSON.stringify(event, null, 2));
    console.log('author =', event.author);
    console.log('title =', event.title);
    console.log('publisher =', event.publisher);
    return event.author;  // Echo back the first key value
    // throw new Error('Something went wrong');
};
```

Now click Deploy to deploy the changes and then click the Test button to see the Lambda executed. The output is the following:

```
A function update is still in progress so the invocation went to the previously
deployed code and configuration.

Test Event Name
test

Response
"joe minichino"

Function Logs
START RequestId: f0913a37-ea61-433e-806d-9d71f013daef Version: $LATEST
2022-05-31T15:00:28.519Z        undefined       INFO        Loading function
2022-05-31T15:00:28.525Z        f0913a37-ea61-433e-806d-9d71f013daef
INFO        Received event: {
   "author": "joe minichino",
   "title": "Data Analytics in the AWS Cloud",
   "publisher": "Wiley"
}
2022-05-31T15:00:28.528Z        f0913a37-ea61-433e-806d-9d71f013daef
INFO        author = joe minichino
2022-05-31T15:00:28.529Z        f0913a37-ea61-433e-806d-9d71f013daef
INFO        title = Data Analytics in the AWS Cloud
2022-05-31T15:00:28.529Z        f0913a37-ea61-433e-806d-9d71f013daef
INFO        publisher = Wiley
END RequestId: f0913a37-ea61-433e-806d-9d71f013daef
REPORT RequestId: f0913a37-ea61-433e-806d-9d71f013daef        Duration:
6.44 ms      Billed Duration: 7 ms      Memory Size: 128 MB      Max Memory
Used: 54 MB       Init Duration: 226.24 ms

Request ID
f0913a37-ea61-433e-806d-9d71f013daef
```

Although the code is very simple, executing it is a very important milestone toward your understanding of Lambdas, since adding complexity to the code is nothing more than what you probably do in traditional monolithic applications or web applications.

Go ahead and augment this function with a `log` statement that shows the structure of the `context` object, too. That way, you can explore all the metadata and context properties available in it.

Lambda Configuration

Configuring a Lambda function is not complicated, but to obtain the best performance at the cheapest price, you must do it carefully. Fortunately, AWS released a tool called Compute Optimizer that, since December 2020, also includes Lambda Functions, so you can work out the best configuration for your Lambda.

Runtime

Choosing the right runtime is a good first step toward optimal performance. Sometimes you won't have a choice, or sometimes the choice is constrained by the skillset available in house, so you will likely fall on a runtime that is a default choice for all the work you normally carry out in traditional development. For example, if you perform all your work in Java and all your developers are versed primarily in Java, then even simply from a maintenance point of view it's not worth the effort to research a better-performing runtime for the task at hand. However, performance differences exist, and when you forecast executing a single Lambda function millions of times per month or even per day, those drops of performance that you squeeze out of your code and function may have a real monetary impact on your monthly AWS bill.

In my own experience, I've found, for example, that Go is a language that yields exceptional performance in tasks involving concurrency, completing a task up to 30 times faster than Python. In conclusion, where you can afford flexibility in terms of skills, you may want to run benchmarks on which runtime gives the best performance on the same task; it won't just perform better, it will save you money.

Runtimes available as of this writing are several versions of Node.js, Python, Go, C#, Java, Ruby, and PowerShell. These capabilities are provided through native runtime support, as well as any runtime you choose when you create a function defined as a container image. Here you choose a runtime and the Linux distribution when you create the container image.

Container-Based Lambdas

In recent times, Lambda started to offer support for container images. This is a revolutionary step in that it allows developers to build their own runtime and system images, containing all sorts of "baked in" libraries and dependencies, configurations, and whatever else is needed for a program to run correctly. This may be the case for a development house working with less common languages such as Rust or Haskell, or for programs that require high levels of optimization.

That said, working with containers is easy and extremely developer friendly (containers revolutionized portability of applications). It is now commonplace to develop applications in languages for which there exist Lambda runtimes and yet opt for the container-based version of the same. For example, you may want to develop an application in Python, and you may require a legacy version of the runtime that's not offered by Lambda (anymore), or you are simply far more comfortable with developing your code and packaging it as a container image that can be deployed and executed by Lambda. This image also has the enormous advantage of being reusable in other contexts (such as a Kubernetes cluster).

For those not entirely familiar with container technology, the AWS Serverless Application Model (SAM) has made the entire process of developing and deploying functions very easy. We will take an in-depth look at it further into the chapter.

Architectures

Two architectures are available in AWS Lambda:

- **arm64:** 64-bit ARM architecture, for the AWS Graviton2 processor
- **x86_64:** 64-bit x86 architecture, for x86-based processors

The official documentation states that compute-intensive workloads such as video encoding or high-performance computing are better deployed on arm64. Better performance means cheaper execution. By and large, all your applications should run without a problem on either architecture, but AWS also has a guide for operating the migration from x86_64 to arm64 here: `https://docs.aws`
`.amazon.com/lambda/latest/dg/foundation-arch.html#foundation-arch-`
`steps`.

Memory

How much memory you allocate to a Lambda determines the amount of information a function can process at any one time. AWS cleverly couples the amount of memory allocated with the CPU power allocated for the Lambda, so you only need to worry about the `memory` parameter. AWS will allocate a proportionately powerful CPU to process that amount of information.

Recently, Lambda's maximum memory was upgraded to 10 GB. This means that typical batch or extract, transform, load (ETL) jobs previously difficult to perform with Lambdas are now perfectly feasible. Clearly, allocating memory requires an a priori knowledge of the amount of information you are going to receive, and it is always advisable to err on the side of caution, lest your function run out of memory, causing it to fail.

On top of the AWS Compute Optimizer, AWS offers a tool called AWS Lambda Power Tuning, developed by Italian software engineer and AWS expert Alex Casalboni. The tool, available on GitHub at `https://github.com/alexcasalboni/aws-lambda-power-tuning`, allows you to find the sweet spot of highest performance for the lowest cost, and I highly recommend you check it out.

Networking

By default, Lambda functions are not deployed within a virtual private cloud (VPC), which is a "logically isolated" section of the AWS cloud, effectively making resources within the VPC inaccessible from the outside world. If you need your Lambda functions to work within the security of a VPC, then you will need to correctly configure networking parameters, such as the VPC ID, subnets, and security groups. When you are trying to deploy a Lambda in a VPC and find that execution fails due to permission errors, you should investigate whether networking is correctly configured.

Execution Role

Lambdas normally interact with other resources on AWS; the function itself is executed by an IAM role, so you need to ensure this execution role has all the necessary permissions (and preferably not more than what is absolutely necessary) to access these resources. For example, if your Lambda is triggered by an S3 event and needs to read content of an S3 object, the execution role will require S3 Read Access. If as part of the workload it then writes to an S3 bucket, it will also need S3 Write Access, and so on.

I recommend only using wildcards (e.g., `s3:*`) when you are debugging permissions that may impede the correct execution of a Lambda function. Once you identify and correct the issue, always restrict the permissions to improve security.

Environment Variables

You can make your Lambda function code retrieve values from environment variables. This approach enhances flexibility and promotes code reutilization, in compliance with the Twelve-Factor App standard, highly regarded as a best-in-class methodology for application deployment and maintenance, as illustrated here: `https://12factor.net/config`. Configuration should reside in the environment, and specifically in environment variables. The benefits of this approach became even more apparent with the advent of containers since the values of environment variables can be specified in the Dockerfile (or similar build file) used to create system images. As your use cases grow in complexity, you can leverage Lambda layers to package libraries and dependencies into your functions, so that you can even reuse code across functions and reduce the size of the uploads necessary for deployment.

AWS EventBridge

EventBridge is an event bus that allows users to publish events and react to them within the AWS ecosystem. EventBridge is the glue of all applications based on AWS, and it allows complete decoupling between application components and services.

AWS Fargate

Fargate is a serverless tool that allows the deployment of containerized applications. Since you only pay for what you use, it is well suited for compute workloads that exceed the maximum execution time limits of a Lambda (15 minutes), and whose invocation can be triggered by any event published on AWS EventBridge. Fargate is based on ECR (Elastic Container Registry, AWS's equivalent of Docker Hub) and EKS (Elastic Kubernetes Service), which is AWS's fully managed Kubernetes alternative.

AWS DynamoDB

We already peeked at DynamoDB earlier in the book and explored the concepts of table, provisioning read and write capacity units, partitioning, and sorting with HASH and RANGE keys. Aside from granting single-digit-millisecond response times at any scale, DynamoDB is an ideal store for serverless stack applications because you don't have to manage scaling.

AWS SNS

SNS (Simple Notification Service) is a handy tool for emitting events that contain a body that can be used for triggering the execution of compute workloads enriched with meaningful data and context contained in the event itself. An example is a Lambda that processes an S3 object and then publishes an SNS event, which other resources can pick up and use. We will illustrate its usage later on to link the completion of a step in a workflow to the triggering of another.

Amazon SQS

SQS (Simple Queue Service) is a serverless system that allows messages to be sent in a queue for processing. It allows a much higher throughput and scalability than SNS, and it allows processing in order if you use a FIFO (first in, first out) queue. In this respect SQS is more of an alternative to systems such as RabbitMQ, but SQS clients have to perform "polling" to receive new messages. While it gets a mention, SQS is not widely used in AWS-powered data engineering since there are more effective ways to transport information between resources.

AWS CloudWatch

CloudWatch is a complex tool that allows you to collect data, monitor and analyze resources, and take action, based on the information received. CloudWatch is the default logging system in AWS and a very good one at that. Logs from AWS resources by default are stored into a log group in CloudWatch, where you can inspect and debug applications. CloudWatch gives you the ability to create dashboards that display metrics for your resources so that you can monitor the health of your systems. It also provides a feature called Insights, which is a simple and effective query language for filtering logs and finding relevant entries.

CloudWatch has a retention period that comes at a price; the longer you retain logs, the more you pay for it. CloudWatch is indeed easy to use but at the same time quite a vast system. We will explore how to inspect logs later in this chapter in the "AWS SAM" section.

Amazon QuickSight

QuickSight is a serverless, intuitive, and powerful business intelligence (BI) and reporting solution that allows you to create beautiful-looking dashboards. The main advantage of QuickSight is its seamless integration with any data source based on AWS, including the ability to augment a dataset with machine learning (ML) predictions provided by a model deployed on Amazon SageMaker, as well as a powerful feature called Insights, which allows you to visualize ML-powered forecasts and anomaly detection on your datasets.

AWS Step Functions

Step Functions is a workflow management engine that allows composable functions with conditional executions and iterations to orchestrate two or more resources. It's a powerful solution in the same domain as tools like Apache Airflow.

Amazon API Gateway

API Gateway is a tool that allows you to map resources deployed on AWS to URLs with a very granular configuration. Using API Gateway, you can associate a path to a Lambda function and configure how requests and responses are processed and the authorization needed to access those resources.

Amazon Cognito

Cognito is a useful service that allows you to implement authorization without code. It is especially useful for integrating with identity providers such as Google, Apple, and Facebook. With Cognito, you can manage and monitor user logins, sessions, and access to resources.

AWS Serverless Application Model (SAM)

The advent of serverless was revolutionary. Not only did it resolve many headaches in terms of operational overheads (it dramatically reduced the need for specialized in-house skills in the realm of SysOps and DevOps), but it also represented a massive cost save (because regardless of how expensive some resources are to execute, you only pay for what you use). And since AWS offers a free tier of usage, developers and upcoming businesses could suddenly find it affordable to deploy an application only focusing on the code/business logic and forget about managing servers, with the serenity of knowing that if nobody used their product, then it would incur little to no cost to them. In this respect, serverless has multiplied by several orders of magnitude the ease with which a business can be set up and consequently scaled, with costs that should be proportional to the generated revenue.

AWS went a step further and developed SAM (Serverless Application Model), which is a framework that allows you to create a template with AWS's infrastructure solution (CloudFormation) containing all the resources needed by your application, which can be deployed with a single command.

But what, exactly, can you do with SAM? In short, you can create an application whose logic runs on Lambda functions that can connect to other resources in AWS. You need to specify all the resources needed by your application, and they will all be associated to a single CloudFormation stack. You can make incremental changes to the stack, and you can deploy, update, and destroy it with a single command.

Ephemeral Infrastructure

I love the workflow that SAM offers because it encourages ephemeral infrastructure, and the idea that when you are done with an application you can tear it down, but you can also reinstantiate it at will. I find that very elegant and clean. In fact, SAM has some design aspects that may represent a bit of a constraint at times, but ultimately the idea behind it is:

- You do not meddle with existing resources.
- You create as many resources as you need for your application from scratch.
- You destroy them when you are finished.

In the context of data engineering, I have successfully used SAM to create and deploy stand-alone pipelines for workloads executed by one or more Lambda functions writing to S3 or databases, after having received data from a query or a third-party API.

Let's take a closer look at SAM first, and then we'll create a pipeline to perform a typical and mundane data import job to be executed on a daily basis.

AWS SAM Installation

First of all, SAM is a command tool (`aws-sam-cli`) that requires installation on the machine you are going to execute it on. This could be your workstation or even a server running the SAM commands to "spin up" some infrastructure. The documentation for installing the SAM CLI tool is available here: `https://docs` `.aws.amazon.com/serverless-application-model/latest/developerguide/` `serverless-sam-cli-install.html`.

As usual, installation for macOS, Windows, and Linux differs. However, in all three cases the actual command tool is a single executable file that needs to reside somewhere in your machine where it can be found and executed by the operating system.

> **NOTE** At some point, you will (most likely) deploy functions or resources that are containerized, and in fact you will probably favor containerized solutions in the long run, as they are more maintainable and portable. This means you will have to have Docker installed. Installation instructions for Docker are available at `https://docs` `.docker.com/get-docker`.

Configuration

Configuring SAM is just the same as configuring the AWS CLI tool. You can store your credentials in a credentials file and configurations in a config file.

Each project will require configuration. You do so by supplying parameters interactively when running an `aws-sam-cli` command or through a configuration file in the project. We will explore these two options later in the chapter in the next section, "Creating Your First AWS SAM Project."

Creating Your First AWS SAM Project

Now that you have the SAM CLI tool installed, we can go ahead and create a project that we will call `hello-sam`. To begin, launch your favorite terminal and move to a directory of your choice (which will be the parent directory for the directory of your project). Then run the following:

```
> sam init
```

You will be prompted with a question:

```
Which template source would you like to use?
        1 - AWS Quick Start Templates
        2 - Custom Template Location
```

Since you have not yet learned how to author templates, choose existing AWS Quick Start Templates by typing **1**.

The tool will check a special GitHub repository where templates are stored and then offer you a choice of eight quick-start templates:

```
Cloning from https://github.com/aws/aws-sam-cli-app-templates

Choose an AWS Quick Start application template
        1 - Hello World Example
        2 - Multi-step workflow
        3 - Serverless API
        4 - Scheduled task
        5 - Standalone function
        6 - Data processing
        7 - Infrastructure event management
        8 - Machine Learning
```

For now, you just want to familiarize yourself with SAM, so choose `1 - Hello World Example`.

At this point, you will be asked to specify the runtime and package type for your SAM application. The default choices are Node.js and Zip (meaning your application will be a zipped file uploaded to AWS before deployment). However, we will go an acceptably small step further and decline the default choice by typing **N** and checking the list of runtimes and package types available:

```
Use the most popular runtime and package type? (Nodejs and zip) [y/N]: N
Which runtime would you like to use?
        1 - dotnet5.0
        2 - dotnetcore3.1
        3 - go1.x
        4 - java11
        5 - java8.al2
        6 - java8
        7 - nodejs14.x
        8 - nodejs12.x
        9 - python3.9
       10 - python3.8
       11 - python3.7
       12 - python3.6
       13 - ruby2.7
```

Let's indeed use the latest Node.js runtime available (as of this writing it's nodejs14.x) and type **7**. Should this vary by the time you are running this command, simply choose your preferred runtime.

After this we must choose the package type:

```
What package type would you like to use?
        1 - Zip
        2 - Image
```

As I mentioned, the Zip option means your application will be a zipped bundle, uploaded to S3 and from there deployed to Lambda. However, there is a second option, Image, which allows you to deploy your Lambda code as a Docker image to be stored in AWS's own container image registry, ECR (Elastic Container Registry).

I've used Zip in very few cases. Creating a container image, uniquely tagged for every deployment, means that your image repository is also an artifact registry, which effectively stores all the versions of the application you've ever deployed.

That said, you can continue this tutorial even choosing the Zip option, since the deployment mechanism is identical. In fact, it will be simpler as you won't have to create a registry in ECR for your Docker images.

Go ahead and choose your package type:

```
Package type: 2

Based on your selections, the only dependency manager available is npm.
We will proceed copying the template using npm.

Project name [sam-app]: hello-sam
```

At this point, the tool will create the skeleton of the application in the directory you specified in the project name (`hello-sam`), which will be created for you.

```
Project name [sam-app]: hello-sam


-----------------------
Generating application:
-----------------------
Name: hello-sam
Base Image: amazon/nodejs14.x-base
Architectures: x86_64
Dependency Manager: npm
Output Directory: .
Next steps can be found in the README file at ./hello-sam/README.md


Commands you can use next
=========================
[*] Create pipeline: cd hello-sam && sam pipeline init --bootstrap
[*] Test Function in the Cloud: sam sync --stack-name {stack-name} --watch
```

Great; our first SAM application has been created. Let's peek at its structure:

```
$ ls hello-sam/
events  hello-world  README.md  template.yaml
```

Application Structure

`Events` and `hello-world` are folders containing sample events to test your Lambda function and the Lambda function code, respectively. But let's first focus on the most important file in the entire project: `template.yaml`. This is a YAML file that should be very familiar to anybody with experience with CloudFormation. In fact, some resources have special configuration parameters only available in SAM, but writing plain CloudFormation is perfectly fine. CloudFormation documentation is available at this address: `https://docs.aws.amazon.com/AWSCloudFormation/latest/UserGuide/Welcome.html`.

Regardless of your prior experience with CloudFormation, let's explore the file structure:

```
$ cat template.yaml
AWSTemplateFormatVersion: '2010-09-09'
Transform: AWS::Serverless-2016-10-31
Description: >
  hello-sam

  Sample SAM Template for hello-sam
```

```
# More info about Globals: https://github.com/awslabs/serverless-
application-model/blob/master/docs/globals.rst
Globals:
  Function:
    Timeout: 3


Resources:
  HelloWorldFunction:
    Type: AWS::Serverless::Function
    Properties:
      PackageType: Image
      Architectures:
        - x86_64
      Events:
        HelloWorld:
          Type: Api
          Properties:
            Path: /hello
            Method: get
    Metadata:
      DockerTag: nodejs14.x-v1
      DockerContext: ./hello-world
      Dockerfile: Dockerfile


Outputs:
  # ServerlessRestApi is an implicit API created out of Events key under
Serverless::Function
  # Find out more about other implicit resources you can reference
within SAM
  # https://github.com/awslabs/serverless-application-model/blob/master/
docs/internals/generated_resources.rst#api
  HelloWorldApi:
    Description: "API Gateway endpoint URL for Prod stage for Hello
World function"
    Value: !Sub "https://${ServerlessRestApi}.execute-
api.${AWS::Region}.amazonaws.com/Prod/hello/"
  HelloWorldFunction:
    Description: "Hello World Lambda Function ARN"
    Value: !GetAtt HelloWorldFunction.Arn
  HelloWorldFunctionIamRole:
    Description: "Implicit IAM Role created for Hello World function"
    Value: !GetAtt HelloWorldFunctionRole.Arn
```

The first property is `AWSTemplateFormatVersion`, which defines the version of CloudFormation templates being used. The specifications used are dated 2010-09-09, and they are the most recent as of this writing.

The `Description` property is a text field describing what your application does. Feel free to edit this with a more meaningful description of the application you are developing.

The next section is `Globals`. This section has the particularly useful role of specifying parameters for certain resources that are to be used as default. For example, it contains a `Function` property (which refers to Lambda functions), whose `Timeout` field is set to `3`. This means, "unless I specify otherwise, all of the Lambdas in this file will have a timeout of three seconds."

The `Globals` section is very useful when there are several resources of the same type contained in the template, so you can omit those properties specified in `Globals` unless you need to override the `Globals` value. For example, if you specified a timeout of three seconds for all your Lambda functions, but you need a particular Lambda (which we will call `MyFunctionWithALongerTimeout`) to have a 60-second timeout, then you can specify:

```
MyFunctionWithALongerTimeout:
  Properties:
    Timeout: 60
```

The `Resources` property is the "meat" of the template file. It's where you specify all the resources needed by your application.

In this Hello World example, we are only creating an echo Lambda that responds to an `HttpApi` event with a `hello-world` kind of response.

Each resource is specified like so:

1. The logical ID of the resource (the human-readable "name" of it)

2. The type of the resource (the kind of AWS resource)

3. The properties of the resource (which is itself a map containing all sorts of variable configuration parameters that are specific to the resource type specified at 2)

4. The `Metadata` property, which is specific to the type of resource, and in our case goes to specify Docker information

SAM Resource Types

SAM was developed with the idea of making development and deployment of serverless applications much faster than traditional ways of accomplishing the same task. For this reason, there is a special set of resources available in SAM that are not available in normal CloudFormation:

- `AWS::Serverless::Api`

- `AWS::Serverless::Application`

- `AWS::Serverless::Function`

- `AWS::Serverless::HttpApi`

- `AWS::Serverless::LayerVersion`

- `AWS::Serverless::SimpleTable`

- `AWS::Serverless::StateMachine`

Note that they look very similar to other normally available resource types you may be used to in CloudFormation, However, the "Serverless" service does not exist in CloudFormation but only in SAM. For example, Lambda functions in plain CloudFormation are defined as `AWS::Lambda::Function` instead of `AWS::Serverless::Function`.

This set of special SAM resources is intended for creating a serverless application using `Application` as the root object for all your Lambda functions, `StateMachine` as a workflow/orchestrator, `SimpleTable` for database storage using DynamoDB, and `Api` and `HttpApi` for API configuration and mapping. The simplest web applications don't need much more than this.

In this respect, SAM works as an introduction to the wider CloudFormation tool. This is not an exhaustive list of resources, and writing resources with standard CloudFormation types is just fine. But you can dip your toe into serverless using SAM-specific resources and then evolve into much more complex stacks but with the agility that SAM grants you through its one-command build/deployment.

SAM Lambda Template

Let's inspect the Lambda template SAM created for us. First of all, its logical ID is `HelloWorldFunction`. You can use the logical ID of a resource as a reference in other parts of the template, so it's important to name your resources meaningfully and uniquely (failing to do this will result in an error at deployment time). Immediately below we have the type of the resource, in our case `AWS::Serverless::Function`.

The `Properties` map contains a few fields of interest:

- `Architectures` specifies the types of architectures on which the function should run, so bear in mind our earlier cost and performance considerations on x86_64 and arm64.

- The `PackageType` field indicates we are going to package the function as a container image by specifying `Image` as the value.

- The `Events` property specifies a list of events coming from EventBridge that can trigger an execution of the function in question.

You can consider each of the events in this section as a nested `Event` object following the same structure as parent resources under the `Resources` field: each `Event` will have a logical ID, a type, and properties. In our case, our function can be invoked by an event identified with the name `HelloWorld`, of Type `Api` (which is a web request), which is mapped to the `/hello` path and the `GET HTTP` method.

Obviously, a web request is not the only way to trigger a Lambda. In fact, you'll find an extensive list of events that can cause an execution here: `https://docs.aws.amazon.com/serverless-application-model/latest/developerguide/sam-property-function-eventsource.html`.

Here are the some of the event types (the list is always growing):

- S3
- SNS
- Kinesis
- DynamoDB
- SQS
- Api
- Schedule
- CloudWatchEvent
- EventBridgeRule
- CloudWatchLogs
- IoTRule
- AlexaSkill
- Cognito
- HttpApi
- MSK
- MQ
- SelfManagedKafka

For each of these services, there are a number of events that can be configured to trigger the function execution. A common example is to configure the `s3:putObject` event on an S3 bucket to trigger a Lambda. You would do this to immediately process new objects that are deposited into the configured S3 bucket. A common scenario is creating thumbnails for uploaded images, so you would trigger a Lambda execution as soon as an image is uploaded to S3, process the image to create a smaller version of it, and store it in a different location.

Again, these are SAM-specific events, handy shortcuts for the more verbose CloudFormation "proper" equivalent. In a well-formed CloudFormation event, it would be good practice to declare the event as a separate resource and reference it in the Function ⇨ Properties ⇨ Events field.

All of the function properties available in a SAM function are documented here: `https://docs.aws.amazon.com/serverless-application-model/latest/developerguide/sam-resource-function.html`.

!! Recursive Lambda Invocation !!

Note that the thumbnail example is not coincidental, but a way to introduce you to an infinite cycle of Lambda executions that may result in unwanted costs: the recursive Lambda invocation.

Let's assume you have a function `CreateThumbnail` configured to process newly uploaded images that are uploaded to S3 into a bucket called `myimages`. Also assume that the `CreateThumbnail` function is invoked so it goes to create a 100×100 pixel version of the original image, and then stores it in the `myimages` bucket, too.

S3 will emit an `s3:putObject` event for the original image, but also for the new thumbnail image. That means the `CreateThumbnail` function will be invoked again, and it will create a new thumbnail image from the newly created thumbnail, causing another `CreateThumbnail` invocation, and so on, forever. Your bucket will be filled with infinite copies of thumbnails, and you will be paying the price of each function invocation, which can be hefty.

Naturally, the first step is to prevent this from happening at all, making sure that the target of your functions is different from the source, so as not to trigger this infinite cycle. But not to worry; AWS does also offer a mechanism to trip this cycle up and stop the panic, specifically, as cited in AWS documentation. If you trigger a recursive invocation loop accidentally, you can click the Throttle button in the Lambda console to scale the function concurrency down to zero and break the recursion cycle.

This article describes patterns that cause recursive invocations and the measures that can be taken to prevent this from happening: `https://aws.amazon.com/blogs/compute/avoiding-recursive-invocation-with-amazon-s3-and-aws-lambda`.

Function Metadata

With the big "recursive invocation" scare out of the way, let's continue our inspection of the function properties. The last field is `Metadata`. This is a field used by SAM to build, package, and deploy the function, and in our case it specifies Docker properties such as the path at which we find the function code to be copied into our container (property `DockerContext` with the value `./hello-world` indicating that the code resides in the `hello-world` subfolder), the tag to associate to the built image, and the location of the Dockerfile in `DockerContext`, which is—unsurprisingly—the file `Dockerfile`.

For those unfamiliar with Docker, a Dockerfile is much like a makefile for container images, where you specify the following:

- The base container image you are going to use to create the container
- The files you want to copy over to the container
- Preparatory commands such as installation of binaries and libraries
- The command to run once the container is up and running

Outputs

Outputs is the final section of our SAM template. Here you declare what values of the application deployment you want to output to your terminal. In our template that SAM generated, the output values are the URL of the API endpoint for our function, the ARN value of our function, and the ARN of the Lambda execution role.

Implicitly Generated Resources

At this point, you might be scratching your head, wondering where the Lambda execution role came from—and rightly so. You didn't have to declare one; SAM generated one for you. This is one of the benefits of SAM: some necessary operations such as creating IAM roles are automated so that you can focus on your application and not on the ancillary tasks needed to make the application run.

Beware, however, of the strictness of AWS permissions. If you want your Lambda function to interact with S3, you will still need the execution role to be granted the correct S3 permissions. But how do you do that if the role is implicitly generated for you? If you take a look at the function properties documentation (https://docs.aws.amazon.com/serverless-application-model/latest/developerguide/sam-resource-function.html), you will notice a Policies field. This field can take a YAML String, List, or Map.

If you specify a String corresponding to the ARN of a policy, it will attach the policy you specified. If you specify a list of ARNs, it will attach all the policies you specified. If you want to declare policies inline, you can create a map in which each object specifies a policy.

You can also create a combination of values, such as something like this:

```
Policies:
        - "arn:aws:iam::1234567890:policy/data-lambda-generic"
        - Statement:
          - Sid: SendRawEmail
            Effect: Allow
            Resource: "*"
            Action:
              - "ses:SendRawEmail"
```

As an alternative to letting SAM create the execution role augmented by the policies you specified, you can create an IAM role in your account, attaching all the policies you need for your Lambda to execute correctly and then specifying the ARN of the role in the Role field. This field supersedes the Policies field, so if you specify a role with which to execute your Lambda function, the Policies field will be ignored.

The full list of generated resources is available here: docs.aws.amazon.com/
serverless-application-model/latest/developerguide/sam-specification-
generated-resources-function.html.

Some of these resources stand out. For example:

When the Event property of an AWS::Serverless::Function *is set to*
Api, *but the* RestApiId *property is not specified, AWS SAM generates the*
AWS::ApiGateway::RestApi *AWS CloudFormation resource.*

Same for the HttpApi event type:

When the Event *property of an* AWS::Serverless::Function *is set to*
HttpApi, *but the* ApiId *property is not specified, AWS SAM generates the*
AWS::ApiGatewayV2::Api *AWS CloudFormation resource.*

And to confirm what we discussed earlier about the execution role:

When the Role *property of an* AWS::Serverless::Function *is not specified,*
AWS SAM generates an AWS::IAM::Role *AWS CloudFormation resource.*

The idea that some resources might be generated behind the scenes, especially given that some of them may bear a cost, is quite perplexing. However,
it all makes sense in SAM, primarily for three reasons:

- Serverless is by definition based on an on-demand pricing model. When
  you don't use something, you don't pay for it.
- You would need the implicitly created resources anyway; it's just up to
  you if you define them in the SAM template or let SAM do it for you.
  Nothing you don't need is created.
- SAM applications should be deployed to be used but destroyed when
  they are not used. All resources created by a SAM application belong to
  the same stack, and when the stack is deleted, all associated resources
  are, too.

Other Template Sections

A SAM template is really a CloudFormation template, and you may refer to
the previous chapter "Working with AWS," in the "CloudFormation" section
of the chapter to see what other main properties of the template are available,
such as Parameters and Mappings.

Lambda Code

Now let's dig into the nitty-gritty of the actual Lambda function code.

The `hello-world` folder contains all the code that's necessary to run the Lambda. Exploring the directory created by SAM, we see it contains the following files and folders:

```
$ ls -al hello-world/
total 28
drwxrwxr-x 3 joe joe 4096 Jun 11 14:49 .
drwxrwxr-x 4 joe joe 4096 Jun 11 14:49 ..
-rw-rw-r-- 1 joe joe 1046 Jun 11 14:49 app.js
-rw-rw-r-- 1 joe joe  341 Jun 11 14:49 Dockerfile
-rw-rw-r-- 1 joe joe    8 Jun 11 14:49 .npmignore
-rw-rw-r-- 1 joe joe  468 Jun 11 14:49 package.json
drwxrwxr-x 3 joe joe 4096 Jun 11 14:49 tests
```

We know the SAM template is delegating the building of the actual Lambda container to the Dockerfile contained in this folder. So let's see what the Dockerfile contains:

```
FROM public.ecr.aws/lambda/nodejs:14

COPY app.js package*.json ./

RUN npm install
# If you are building your code for production, instead include a
package-lock.json file on this directory and use:
# RUN npm ci --production

# Command can be overwritten by providing a different command in the
template directly.
CMD ["app.lambdaHandler"]
```

This Dockerfile is doing the following:

1. Creating a container based on the `public.ecr.aws/lambda/nodejs:14` image, which is the AWS Nodejs (v14) container image for Lambdas
2. Copying the `app.js` and `package.*.json` files to the root of the container
3. Running the command `npm install` to install all dependencies specified in `package.json`
4. Running the `app.lambdaHandler` command

This last command may seem a bit obscure, but when you peek at the `app.js` file you will notice it has a function, `lambdaHandler`, exported, which is the handler for this Lambda function:

```
// const axios = require('axios')
// const url = 'http://checkip.amazonaws.com/';
let response;

/**
 *
```

```
 * Event doc: https://docs.aws.amazon.com/apigateway/latest/developerguide/set-up-
lambda-proxy-integrations.html#api-gateway-simple-proxy-for-lambda-input-format
 * @param {Object} event - API Gateway Lambda Proxy Input Format
 *
 * Context doc: https://docs.aws.amazon.com/lambda/latest/dg/nodejs-
prog-model-context.html
 * @param {Object} context
 *
 * Return doc: https://docs.aws.amazon.com/apigateway/latest/
developerguide/set-up-lambda-proxy-integrations.html
 * @returns {Object} object - API Gateway Lambda Proxy Output Format
 *
 */
exports.lambdaHandler = async (event, context) => {
    try {
        // const ret = await axios(url);
        response = {
            'statusCode': 200,
            'body': JSON.stringify({
                message: 'hello world',
                // location: ret.data.trim()
            })
        }
    } catch (err) {
        console.log(err);
        return err;
    }

    return response
};
```

The generated code does nothing aside from returning a "hello world" message upon hitting the /hello path through a GET request. However, some lines are commented out to show where you would put a hypothetical call to another URL and return its response value.

Note that the default import mechanism is CommonJS, but you can easily switch to ES6 (using the import statements) by specifying the property

```
"type": "module"
```

in package.json.

Out of curiosity, let's take a look at package.json too:

```
{
  "name": "hello_world",
  "version": "1.0.0",
  "description": "hello world sample for NodeJS",
  "main": "app.js",
  "repository": "https://github.com/awslabs/aws-sam-
```

```
cli/tree/develop/samcli/local/init/templates/cookiecutter-aws-sam-hello-nodejs",
    "author": "SAM CLI",
    "license": "MIT",
    "dependencies": {
      "axios": "^0.21.1"
    },
    "scripts": {
      "test": "mocha tests/unit/"
    },
    "devDependencies": {
      "chai": "^4.2.0",
      "mocha": "^9.1.4"
    }
}
```

This is a straightforward `package.json` file containing a dependency for `axios` and `devDependencies` for `chai` and `mocha` for your unit tests, which are contained in the `tests` folder and can be executed by issuing `npm test` in your terminal.

At this point, we want to put SAM into action by building and deploying the application.

Building Your First SAM Application

To build the application, go to the root directory of the application (`hello-sam`) and run the command `sam build`. Here's the output of the `help` command for `sam build`:

```
$ sam build --help
Usage: sam build [OPTIONS] [RESOURCE_LOGICAL_ID]

  Use this command to build your AWS Lambda Functions source code to
  generate artifacts that target AWS Lambda's execution environment.

  Supported Resource Types
  ---------------------------
  1. AWS::Serverless::Function

  2. AWS::Lambda::Function

  Supported Runtimes
  ------------------
  1. Python 2.7, 3.6, 3.7, 3.8 3.9 using PIP

  2. Nodejs 14.x, 12.x, 10.x, 8.10, 6.10 using NPM

  3. Ruby 2.5 using Bundler

  4. Java 8, Java 11 using Gradle and Maven
```

```
5. Dotnetcore2.0 and 2.1 using Dotnet CLI (without --use-
container flag)

6. Go 1.x using Go Modules (without --use-container flag)

Examples
--------
To use this command, update your SAM template to specify the path
to your function's source code in the resource's Code or CodeUri property.

To build on your workstation, run this command in folder containing
SAM template. Built artifacts will be written to .aws-sam/build folder
$ sam build

To build inside a AWS Lambda like Docker container
$ sam build --use-container

To build with inline environment variables passed inside build containers
$ sam build --use-container --container-env-var Function.ENV_VAR=value
--container-env-var GLOBAL_ENV_VAR=value
```

`help` is telling us that we can build the Lambda function using the `build` command, and we have a few examples (the output contains more but they are unnecessary at this point) of how we can do so. As we said at the beginning of this exercise, we are going to build the Lambda function as a container, so we will need the `–use-container` flag for that.

Our `hello-world` Lambda does not use environment variables, so for this first build and deploy we are not going to specify any. However, you can see that specifying them is as simple as this:

```
"--container-env-var HelloWorldFunction.MY_ENV_VAR=some_value"
```

Let's move on to the build. If we use the simple `sam build` command, it will build all Lambdas declared in the template. Since we have only one, this would do in our case, but we can try building a single Lambda, which can be done with `sam build FUNCTION_LOGICAL_ID`, as specified in the help.

Since it's our first build, we will run without specifying any logical ID and simply add the `--use-container` flag:

```
$ sam build --use-container
Starting Build inside a container
Your template contains a resource with logical ID "ServerlessRestApi",
which is a reserved logical ID in AWS SAM. It could result in unexpected
behaviors and is not recommended.
Building codeuri: /home/joe/wileybook/hello-sam runtime: None metadata:
{'DockerTag':
```

```
'nodejs14.x-v1', 'DockerContext': '/home/joe/wileybook/hello-sam/hello-world',
'Dockerfile': 'Dockerfile'} architecture: x86_64 functions: ['HelloWorldFunction']
Building image for HelloWorldFunction function
Setting DockerBuildArgs: {} for HelloWorldFunction function
Step 1/4 : FROM public.ecr.aws/lambda/nodejs:14
 ---> 0463f52dca73
Step 2/4 : COPY app.js package*.json ./
 ---> Using cache
 ---> 837c85cb36f6
Step 3/4 : RUN npm install
 ---> Using cache
 ---> 64e33b3eeb8e
Step 4/4 : CMD ["app.lambdaHandler"]
 ---> Using cache
 ---> f62ec737650b
Successfully built f62ec737650b
Successfully tagged helloworldfunction:nodejs14.x-v1


Build Succeeded

Built Artifacts   : .aws-sam/build
Built Template    : .aws-sam/build/template.yaml

Commands you can use next
=========================
[*] Invoke Function: sam local invoke
[*] Test Function in the Cloud: sam sync --stack-name {stack-name} --watch
[*] Deploy: sam deploy --guided
```

The app is extremely simple, and it builds without issues. Now we have a
container image built and ready for use.

Note that we can actually run the image itself on our development machine:

```
$ docker run -d helloworldfunction:nodejs14.x-v1
514ffccc8102b3ea67f793542d569739432f12f55b174d0221cfc8e2c7f46bb1
$ docker ps -a
CONTAINER ID    IMAGE                              COMMAND               CREATED
STATUS                        PORTS        NAMES
514ffccc8102    helloworldfunction:nodejs14.x-v1   "/lambda-entrypoint.…"   5
seconds ago     Up 5 seconds                       condescending_einstein
```

This can be useful if you want to debug issues with mounting of volumes or
the copying of resources from inside the container. In addition, you may want
to install libraries or binaries and commit the image to an ECR repository so
that you can build future Lambda functions using your own custom images as
the base image (the one specified in the FROM directive in Dockerfile) as opposed
to AWS's public ones.

Testing the AWS SAM Application Locally

Among the advantages that SAM offers is the ability to test an application locally. This is where the `events` folder that we mentioned in the skeleton structure of the SAM application comes into play. SAM offers a command that allows you to test an application locally, specifying an event (a JSON file) that will be passed into the Lambda handler as the `event` argument. That way, you can simulate all of your scenarios.

The command for testing applications locally is `sam local`, which offers a number of useful subcommands:

```
$ sam local --help
Usage: sam local [OPTIONS] COMMAND [ARGS]...

  Run your Serverless application locally for quick development & testing


Options:
  -h, --help  Show this message and exit.

Commands:
  generate-event  You can use this command to generate sample payloads from...
  invoke          Invokes a local Lambda function once.
  start-api       Sets up a local endpoint you can use to test your API.
                  Supports hot-reloading so you don't need to restart this
                  service when you make changes to your function.

  start-lambda    Starts a local endpoint you can use to invoke your local
                  Lambda functions.
```

The `generate-event` subcommand helps you with the creation of sample events that replicate real events generated by various AWS services. For example, instead of guessing the structure of an event generated by a `s3:putObject` event, you can use the `sam local generate-event` command and choose the `s3` option to create the JSON file that simulates a S3 event. The `invoke` subcommand tests the invocation of a Lambda function supplied with a test event. The `start-api` subcommand starts a local API exposed through a port that you can use to test a local SAM API application, with the massive advantage that you can simply apply changes to your function without any need for restarting the API itself. Finally, the `start-lambda` subcommand starts a container running a Lambda that you can hit through a local endpoint.

Since our application is a simple echo, we will run it without events at first and see what the output is:

```
$ sam local invoke HelloWorldFunction
Invoking Container created from helloworldfunction:nodejs14.x-v1
Image was not found.
```

```
Removing rapid images for repo helloworldfunction
Building image................
Skip pulling image and use local one: helloworldfunction:rapid-1.38.0-x86_64.

START RequestId: 46186413-fd5b-4196-9b5e-a090ea650097 Version: $LATEST
{"statusCode":200,"body":"{\"message\":\"hello world\"}"}END RequestId:
46186413-fd5b-4196-9b5e-a090ea650097
REPORT RequestId: 46186413-fd5b-4196-9b5e-a090ea650097          Init
Duration: 0.12 ms         Duration: 127.61 ms         Billed Duration: 128
ms          Memory Size: 128 MB        Max Memory Used: 128 MB
```

This is what happened: SAM created a container using the image built through the `sam build` command, then ran the Lambda handler and sent the response of the Lambda to the terminal output.

Great! All works as expected.

Now we want to test using an event, so we will need to perform three steps:

1. Create an event with an arbitrary field in it to use in the output.

2. Change the function code to use that newly added field and include it in the response.

3. Rebuild the container image.

At that point, we will be able to invoke the function again, this time by specifying the event file to pass as an argument to the Lambda handler, and all should work as expected. So first let's create the event using the `generate-event` subcommand. Calling the help for the subcommand yields a list of services available for the `generate-event` subcommand:

```
Commands:
  alexa-skills-kit
  alexa-smart-home
  apigateway
  appsync
  batch
  cloudformation
  cloudfront
  cloudwatch
  codecommit
  codepipeline
  cognito
  config
  connect
  dynamodb
  kinesis
  lex
  rekognition
  s3
  sagemaker
```

```
ses
sns
sqs
stepfunctions
```

In our case, we want to use `apigateway` (since we are simulating a web request), so let's call the help on that option by running this:

```
$ sam local generate-event apigateway –help
```

The output gives us two possible options:

```
Commands:
  authorizer  Generates an Amazon API Gateway Authorizer Event
  aws-proxy   Generates an Amazon API Gateway AWS Proxy Event
```

We'll use the `aws-proxy` option:

```
$ sam local generate-event apigateway aws-proxy > events/aws-proxy.json
```

Note that the output of the command is the actual JSON content, so we save the output to a file in the `events` folder. If you open that file, you will notice that the first property is a `body` field with a random string associated with it. Let's change that to something more meaningful, like this:

```
"body": "hello SAM local!",
```

Now let's change our function code to use that field by changing the line where we output a simple `"hello world"` string to include the `body` field of the `event` object, like so:

```
message: 'we received: ' + event.body,
```

This syntax is not great, but it has the enormous advantage of being universal (there are a number of languages where string concatenation is done with a plus operator), so I hope the JavaScript nerds out there will forgive the lack of elegance in favor of the educational value.

Now we have to rebuild the container image by issuing `sam build –use-container` again, and then we can rerun the local invocation. But this time we'll supply the event we created:

```
$ sam local invoke HelloWorldFunction -e events/aws-proxy.json
Invoking Container created from helloworldfunction:nodejs14.x-v1
Building image................
Skip pulling image and use local one: helloworldfunction:rapid-1.3
8.0-x86_64.

START RequestId: 4305575c-a4f9-49f4-81fa-4a4e6dbceb9c Version: $LATEST
```

```
{"statusCode":200,"body":"{\"message\":\"we received: hello SAM
local!\"}"}END RequestId: 4305575c-a4f9-49f4-81fa-4a4e6dbceb9c
REPORT RequestId: 4305575c-a4f9-49f4-81fa-4a4e6dbceb9c          Init
Duration: 0.14 ms          Duration: 60.97 ms          Billed Duration: 61
ms          Memory Size: 128 MB          Max Memory Used: 128 MB
```

All went well—the output is exactly what we expected it to be. Upon inspection of the generated event, you will notice very familiar properties such as `pathParameters` and `queryStringParameters`, which are very common in API development. All are usable within the Lambda handler code by accessing those properties in the `event` object

```
event.pathParameters.bookId
```

if we were to hypothetically write a REST API where `{bookId}` is a path parameter.

Deployment

Deploying a SAM application is done with the `sam deploy` command. If issued like that, the terminal prompt will ask for deployment parameters such as the stack name and the repository for your container images. This is fine but also tedious to do if you are performing many deployments. Instead, let's create a deployment configuration file that will speed up operations.

AWS SAM lets you save the parameters you input manually to a `samconfig .toml` file, which I suggest you do unless you are already familiar with the framework and prefer to just create the configuration file from scratch. The guide to the configuration file is available here:

```
https://docs.aws.amazon.com/serverless-application-model/latest/
    developerguide/serverless-sam-cli-config.html
```

As mentioned, we need a registry for our container images. In our Hello World deployment example we will let SAM create it for us during deployment, but you may want to create a centralized repository for your containers. You can do so with ECR, AWS's equivalent of Docker Hub. To create a repository, go to ECR in the AWS Web Console and click the Create Repository button. You can make the repository public or private (depending on whether or not you want to share the container images in it). Once the repository is created, it will appear on the list. A very handy Copy ARN icon is next to the ARN of the newly created repository, so if you are ever going to deploy an application using a configuration file, make sure to use the ARN you just copied as the value for the `image_repository` key in `samconfig.toml`.

Now let's create a deployment configuration file. For the first time, I suggest you use `sam deploy -guided`, which will then give you the option to save your configuration to `samconfig.toml`. The output of the deployment is lengthy but of utmost importance, as it covers fundamental aspects of the deployment and release life cycle when working with serverless applications, so fasten your seatbelts.

First, we issue the command, and we supply parameters:

```
$ sam deploy --guided

Configuring SAM deploy
======================

        Looking for config file [samconfig.toml] :  Not found

        Setting default arguments for 'sam deploy'
        =========================================
        Stack Name [sam-app]: hello-world-stack
        AWS Region [eu-west-1]:
        #Shows you resources changes to be deployed and require a 'Y' to
initiate deploy
        Confirm changes before deploy [y/N]: N
        #SAM needs permission to be able to create roles to connect to
the resources in your template
        Allow SAM CLI IAM role creation [Y/n]: Y
        #Preserves the state of previously provisioned resources when an
operation fails
        Disable rollback [y/N]: N
        HelloWorldFunction may not have authorization defined, Is this
okay? [y/N]: y
        Save arguments to configuration file [Y/n]: Y
        SAM configuration file [samconfig.toml]:
        SAM configuration environment [default]:

        Looking for resources needed for deployment:
         Managed S3 bucket: aws-sam-cli-managed-default-
samclisourcebucket-1nq23i7aviy5t
         A different default S3 bucket can be set in samconfig.toml
         Image repositories: Not found.
         #Managed repositories will be deleted when their functions are
removed from the template and deployed
         Create managed ECR repositories for all functions? [Y/n]: Y
```

Some noteworthy choices here:

- I recommend not disabling rollbacks; if something goes wrong in the deployment, your application will still be online and working, as opposed to putting your entire stack in a broken state.

- Allow SAM to create IAM roles unless you absolutely know what you are doing and you have a requirement to disallow SAM from doing so.

■ Allow SAM to create the ECR repository, as it will keep the container images for all the Lambdas in your application in one central place and separate from container images of other applications. Isolation is always good.

I disabled the confirmation of changes before deployment because this application is extremely simple. If you are working with complex applications, you may wish to confirm the changes before they go live.

Note that I left the configuration filename and environment name at the default values, but you can change them to suit your preference. You can add as many environments (dev, staging, production, and so on) as you wish.

Lastly, be aware that an S3 bucket is created containing objects needed for the deployment of your application. When you destroy the application, the S3 bucket is also destroyed.

After allowing the creation of ECR repositories, SAM CLI starts uploading your container image, in a fashion that looks very familiar to anybody who has worked with Docker Hub before:

```
        Saved arguments to config file
        Running 'sam deploy' for future deployments will use the
parameters saved above.
        The above parameters can be changed by modifying samconfig.toml
        Learn more about samconfig.toml syntax at
        https://docs.aws.amazon.com/serverless-application-model/latest/
developerguide/serverless-sam-cli-config.html

7c97748c6753: Pushed
c44e6431d0d3: Pushed
87d21f86140f: Pushed
7041057703df: Pushed
1b1312f842d8: Pushed
cda6cbc1a28c: Pushed
8fafca045f49: Pushed
4f464b9377e3: Pushed
helloworldfunction-51e7b0386774-nodejs14.x-v1: digest:
sha256:08dc06cebb38543527aa7da308f53b0739be53f49fd640ed36005debcd625a79
size: 1998
```

At this point, your containers are uploaded to the newly created repository. SAM CLI then outputs a summary of the deployment options you specified:

```
        Deploying with following values
        ===============================
        Stack name                    : hello-world-stack
        Region                        : eu-west-1
        Confirm changeset             : False
        Disable rollback              : False
        Deployment image repository   :
```

```
                                                  {
                                                        "HelloWorldFunction":
"972520707061.dkr.ecr.eu-west-1.amazonaws.com/helloworldstackc2f19bde/
helloworldfunction19d43fc4repo"
                                                  }
        Deployment s3 bucket           : aws-sam-cli-managed-default-
samclisourcebucket-1nq23i7aviy5t
        Capabilities                   : ["CAPABILITY_IAM"]
        Parameter overrides            : {}
        Signing Profiles               : {}
```

We're all set. Actual deployment begins in two phases: the changeset creation and the changeset application. SAM uses CloudFormation, so the output will look very familiar to any CloudFormation user:

```
Initiating deployment
=====================
HelloWorldFunction may not have authorization defined.
Uploading to hello-world-stack/67a1a31b191a66700732a77a60f89a7b.template
1285 / 1285  (100.00%)

Waiting for changeset to be created..

CloudFormation stack changeset
-----------------------------------------------------------------------
-----------------------------------------------------------------------
-----------------------------------------------------------
Operation                                 LogicalResourceId
ResourceType                              Replacement
-----------------------------------------------------------------------
-----------------------------------------------------------------------
-----------------------------------------------------------
+ Add
HelloWorldFunctionHelloWorldPermissionProd      AWS::Lambda::Permission
N/A
+ Add                                     HelloWorldFunctionRole
AWS::IAM::Role                            N/A
+ Add                                     HelloWorldFunction
AWS::Lambda::Function                     N/A
+ Add
ServerlessRestApiDeployment47fc2d5f9d           AWS::ApiGateway::Deployment
N/A
+ Add                                     ServerlessRestApiProdStage
AWS::ApiGateway::Stage                    N/A
+ Add                                     ServerlessRestApi
AWS::ApiGateway::RestApi                  N/A
-----------------------------------------------------------------------
-----------------------------------------------------------------------
-----------------------------------------------------------
```

```
Changeset created successfully. arn:aws:cloudformation:eu-
west-1:972520707061:changeSet/samcli-deploy1655457062/08cf1762-68fe-
42d0-9da4-970c6be21fb2
```

This output specifies that all the resources listed are going to be added (that is, newly created) to the stack. On your screen, addition operations are colored in green, modifications in yellow, and deletions in red.

Now that SAM has computed the changeset, it applies it to the stack, as shown in Figure 4.3.

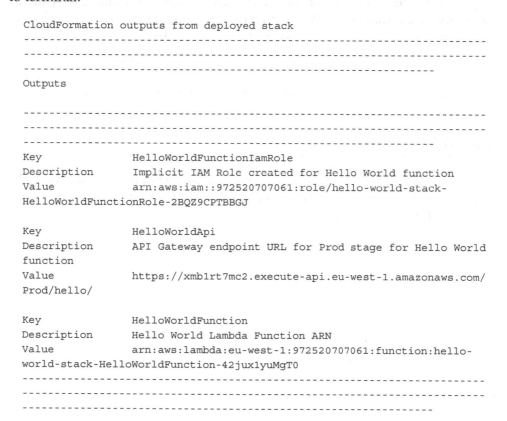

Figure 4.3: The changeset applied to the stack

After changes have been applied successfully, the output values are printed to terminal:

```
CloudFormation outputs from deployed stack
-------------------------------------------------------------------------
-------------------------------------------------------------------------
----------------------------------------------------------------------
Outputs

-------------------------------------------------------------------------
-------------------------------------------------------------------------
----------------------------------------------------------------------
Key           HelloWorldFunctionIamRole
Description   Implicit IAM Role created for Hello World function
Value         arn:aws:iam::972520707061:role/hello-world-stack-
HelloWorldFunctionRole-2BQZ9CPTBBGJ

Key           HelloWorldApi
Description   API Gateway endpoint URL for Prod stage for Hello World
function
Value         https://xmb1rt7mc2.execute-api.eu-west-1.amazonaws.com/
Prod/hello/

Key           HelloWorldFunction
Description   Hello World Lambda Function ARN
Value         arn:aws:lambda:eu-west-1:972520707061:function:hello-
world-stack-HelloWorldFunction-42jux1yuMgT0
-------------------------------------------------------------------------
-------------------------------------------------------------------------
----------------------------------------------------------------------
```

And that's it. Your application is live! You can now invoke it from the command line or go to the Web Console, as shown in Figure 4.4.

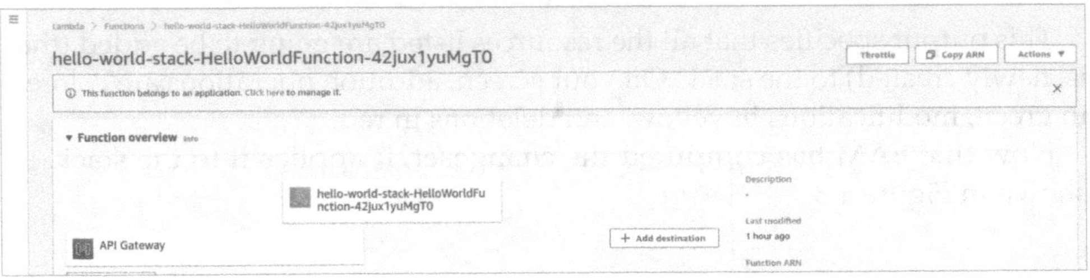

Figure 4.4: `HelloWorldFunction` invoked from the Web Console

As you can see, the `api` event is correctly configured. That means you can test the Lambda by hitting the endpoint listed in the outputs, or by clicking the Test button in the AWS Web Console, where you can also create a test event.

Your first SAM application is online!

Cleaning Up

It's very important to clean up so you don't litter your environment with test applications and don't incur unwanted costs. So as soon as you are done, you can delete the stack from your AWS account either by going to the CloudFormation page of the Web Console or by issuing this command:

```
aws cloudformation delete-stack --stack-name <STACK-NAME>
```

where `<STACK-NAME>` is the name of the stack in your `samconfig.toml`.

Summary

We have explored the idea of serverless computing and deployed our first SAM application. In the next chapter, we will apply our newfound knowledge to the world of data engineering.

Data Ingestion

In this chapter, we are going to take a look at a data lake architecture and specifically focus on the ingestion phase. We will explore several ingestion solutions focusing on serverless (Lambda, Fargate, Kinesis), fully managed (AppFlow), and self-managed (DMS). Please ensure to be familiar with storage technologies, and check out the additional content provided with this book to ensure the data you ingested is correctly stored. Storage: S3 Data Lake and Redshift Data Warehouse in this book is available for download at www.wiley .com/go/dataanalyticsintheawscloud.

Now that you are familiar with the concepts of serverless and Lambda functions, using the AWS SAM framework you can start applying your knowledge to data engineering.

On-demand pricing models are proving to be an ideal case for data engineering, as it is a world full of scheduled jobs and routines. Before the advent of serverless computing, required resources and servers had to be running all the time, although scheduled jobs were maybe running for a few hours each day.

Also, Lambda provides a very elegant and composable mechanism to create pipelines and orchestrated flows. Single compute workloads can now be decoupled and invoked through AWS EventBridge.

But there are plenty of serverless technologies that are nowadays standard practice in data engineering, so let's take a look at a classic data lake architecture in AWS. We'll then move on to some sample architectures that will cover most of the technologies you should be familiar with.

AWS Data Lake Architecture

It is no wonder that serverless computing is gaining so much popularity, and AWS has designed standard architectures to create and maintain data lakes based primarily (but not exclusively) on serverless technologies, like the diagram shown in Figure 5.1.

AWS's website has a whole section dedicated to serverless architectures, such as the Serverless Data Processing page at `https://aws.amazon.com/lambda/data-processing`. This page illustrates various use cases that can be implemented using serverless technologies such as Kinesis, Lambda, S3, and DynamoDB.

Let's take a closer look at the diagram in Figure 5.1 to understand it better.

Serverless Data Lake Architecture Structure

From the diagram you can identify six major areas of work within the serverless data lake architecture:

1. Ingestion
2. Storage and Processing
3. Cataloging, Governance, and Search
4. Security and Monitoring
5. Consumption

Let's explore each area and define its responsibilities and boundaries.

Ingestion

Ingestion is the part of the architecture responsible for acquiring data, and it can be done in multiple ways. In fact, this is the entry block of the architecture and the one that deals with the most disparate sources and methods of data acquisition—anything from server logs to web requests, passing through steps such as API imports, data export from transactional databases, direct uploads (especially with S3), or any form of data exchange. Our main concern at the ingestion phase is to ensure resilience and stability (to prevent data loss) and security (to prevent malicious uploads/imports).

Typically, the technologies involved in the ingestion phase are AWS DMS (Data Migration Service), Kinesis streams, long-running jobs on Fargate, web requests through Lambda, and more.

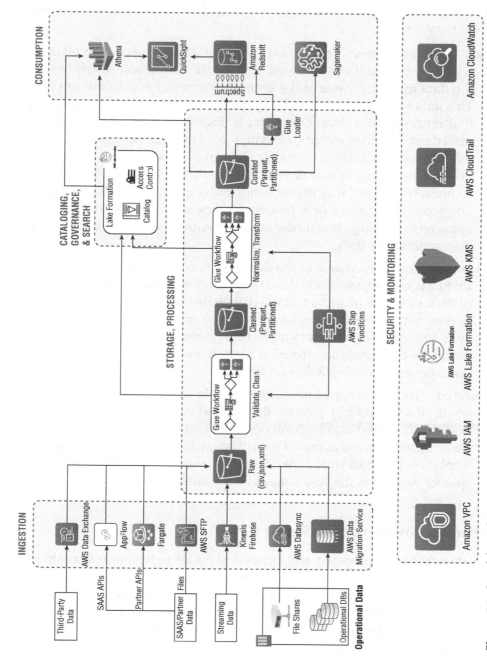

Figure 5.1: Data lake architecture

Storage and Processing

In this phase of work, we receive data and store it into our data lake. You will notice that there are three main types of storage (although there can be more, intermediary stages):

Raw   The raw area is where data lands in our data lake as it is received, in whatever format it was received. The format that is best suited to store the data in the raw area of the data lake is entirely up to the use case. This data should not be used for queries, so it is better left in the format that represents the data. For example, JSON is better for representing nested or embedded records, and you would not want to lose that kind of information by flattening your data right away. Also, it is a recommended practice, because you may develop new use cases for the data, requiring an entirely different way of processing the original raw data, and ideally you would only add a new processing pipeline to the existing ones, as opposed to creating a brand-new import pipeline because you prematurely manipulated the data.

Cleaned   The cleaned area of the data lake is where data is stored after a first ETL (extract, transform, load) pass. Data that landed in the raw area of the data lake is picked up, cleaned, flattened, and filtered (both in terms of relevant attributes and relevant records) and stored in a format more suited to the kind of work that needs to be performed on it at this point. Normally this data is best stored in Parquet, but there are instances where you may want to adopt other formats.

Curated   The curated area of the data lake is where datasets that are the result of a second ETL pass on the cleaned data are stored. In this second ETL step, you may perform operations such as data enrichment and denormalization, and augment your existing data with computed/derived attributes. This data will be the data used by analytical engines to perform queries or used as the base dataset for visualizations.

Cataloging, Governance, and Search

After data has been prepared and curated, it needs to be made available to data catalogs in AWS so that it can be accessed for querying. The first step is to define (or detect) the data's schema and structure, creating tables in a metadata store. Different catalogs exist to group different databases and tables. These catalogs are stored and managed by AWS Glue. On top of Glue, a product called LakeFormation can manage access to catalogs, databases, and tables for AWS users, effectively working as a governance tool through Glue abstraction.

Security and Monitoring

Perhaps the first and most important form of protection you should consider is that of creating resources within a virtual private cloud (VPC). By doing so, only resources within the VPC can access each other, and in fact you need to create VPC endpoints to enable VPC resources to access data in S3 since S3 buckets cannot be located in a VPC as of this writing.

> **NOTE** Data stores should always be placed within private subnets of your VPC, and VPC endpoints should be used for allowing access to such services from vetted locations outside of your VPC.

Internal and organizational security in the data lake is managed through the LakeFormation tool, but also through accurate and granular permission management offered by IAM roles and policies, and through activity inspection (which can be done with CloudTrail and CloudWatch).

Consumption

After data has been ingested, processed, cataloged, and made available to analytical engines, it can finally be consumed to produce insights, BI dashboards, and reports, and also used as training data for machine learning (ML) and AI models. This is where all the work you have dedicated to building a data platform delivers its value to a business.

To introduce the idea of how serverless and SAM can be used in data engineering, the next section illustrates a sample architecture and its implementation.

Sample Processing Architecture: Cataloging Images into DynamoDB

Let's explore a simple use case that will work as a sort of fundamental block to replicate many of the steps illustrated in the serverless data lake architecture diagram in Figure 5.1.

If you look closely at the Storage Processing block of the diagram, you will see three steps where some kind of processing happens after data has been deposited into an S3 bucket. Let's discuss how to trigger processing steps from S3.

Use Case Description

Let's assume you have an application that allows users to upload images to a storage facility. We'll also assume that you want each image's metadata to be stored in DynamoDB for querying purposes. The ideal way to build this with serverless technologies is as follows:

1. Use S3 as the initial storage layer.
2. Use a Lambda function that's triggered by an S3 event.
3. Use a DynamoDB table to store the image metadata.

To better organize, we will leverage S3 partitioning so that when each image is uploaded on S3, the object key will also contain metadata, such as what user uploaded the object and when.

SAM Application Creation

We'll create a new SAM application, which we'll call `image_catalog`, with our trusty `sam init` command, using the same options we used for the Hello World example in Chapter 4, "Serverless Computing and Data Engineering," including the use of a container image for the Lambda function. This will create the initial skeleton of the application. Next, we'll create the S3 bucket for the image uploads.

> **NOTE**   SAM is designed so that you have to declare the resource needed by the application in the application. You can interact with resources outside of your application without problem (such as querying an RDS database), but if this is the case, then these resources cannot be referenced in the template (aside from IAM policies and roles). If your Lambda is invoked by an event occurring on an S3 bucket, this bucket needs to be declared in the same template as the Lambda.

To create the bucket, we will first declare a parameter value with the bucket name and reuse it in the template. There might be only one occurrence, but it's good to know how to reuse parameters.

Let's add a `Parameters` section to our template and declare a `String` parameter called `BucketName` in it, like so:

```
Parameters:
  BucketName:
    Type: String
    Default: daitawscloud-example
```

Remember that S3 buckets need to have a unique name (in the world!) so a unique prefix works well to ensure that no other bucket created in AWS has the same name as yours does.

Now, under the `Resources` section, add the S3 bucket:

```
ImageBucket:
  Type: AWS::S3::Bucket
  Properties:
    Name: !Ref BucketName
```

We see the parameter reference in action through the CloudFormation function `!Ref`, which means that the bucket name will be set to `daitawscloud_example`.

Next, we'll add the DynamoDB table with a `PrimaryKey` called `id` and leave the default values for provisioning:

```
SampleTable:
    Type: AWS::Serverless::SimpleTable
    Properties:
      PrimaryKey:
        Name: id
        Type: String
      ProvisionedThroughput:
        ReadCapacityUnits: 2
        WriteCapacityUnits: 2
```

Now that we have a bucket and a DynamoDB table, let's move on to configuring our Lambda function.

First, we change its name and all its references (especially in `Outputs`). Rename the function `ImageCatalogFunction`.

Second, we change the `Timeout` parameter in `Globals` to `15` seconds just to make sure we do not exceed the execution limit.

S3-Triggered Lambda

Now, we have to configure the event that triggers the Lambda function. This is going to be an `s3:ObjectCreated:*` type event (refer to this page for all event types: `https://docs.aws.amazon.com/AmazonS3/latest/userguide/notification-how-to-event-types-and-destinations.html`).

Next, we'll replace the standard `Api` event in the Lambda function with an S3 event, structuring it as described here: `https://docs.aws.amazon.com/serverless-application-model/latest/developerguide/sam-property-function-s3.html`.

Let's go ahead and delete the previous event and create a new one. We'll call this `S3ObjectCreatedEvent`, and it looks like the following:

```
Events:
      S3ObjectCreated:
        Type: S3
        Properties:
          Bucket:
            Ref: ImageBucket
          Events: s3:ObjectCreated:*
          Filter:
            S3Key:
              Rules:
                - Name: suffix
                  Value: "png"
```

> **NOTE**   That you don't have to delete the old event, but we don't want to allow this Lambda to be triggered by an `Api` call, so we'll delete it. In real-life scenarios you can configure as many triggers as you need.

Let's go through the details of this event:

- It is an event of type `S3`, which refers to events occurring on AWS S3.
- It references the bucket we declared in our template through the `Ref` property of the `Bucket` field.
- The `Events` property accepts a `String` or a `List`. This is the single event type, or a list of event types, that will trigger the invocation.
- We use the `s3:ObjectCreated:*` event, which covers the `Put`, `Copy`, and `Post` variants of the `ObjectCreated` event.
- Lastly, I added an example filter. Let's assume we don't want to catalog all objects deposited in our bucket but only PNG-type images. We can do this by specifying a filter of type `S3Key` (which means that the filter rule will use the object key as its input parameter).

Under the `Rules` property of the filter, we can list rules that apply. There are two filters you can apply on an S3 key: `prefix` and `suffix`. With the prefix rule, you can specify that the event will only invoke the Lambda if the key starts with the value specified in `Value`. The suffix rule does the same but checking the key ends with the string specified in `Value`.

At this point, your `template.yaml` should look like this:

```
AWSTemplateFormatVersion: '2010-09-09'
Transform: AWS::Serverless-2016-10-31
Description: >
  image_catalog

  Sample SAM Template for image_catalog

Parameters:
  BucketName:
    Type: String
    Default: daitawscloud-example

# More info about Globals: https://github.com/awslabs/serverless-
application-model/blob/master/docs/globals.rst
Globals:
  Function:
    Timeout: 15

Resources:
  ImageBucket:
    Type: AWS::S3::Bucket
```

```
    Properties:
      BucketName: !Ref BucketName

  ImageCatalogFunction:
    Type: AWS::Serverless::Function
    Properties:
      PackageType: Image
      Architectures:
        - x86_64
      Events:
        S3ObjectCreated:
          Type: S3
          Properties:
            Bucket:
              Ref: ImageBucket
            Events: s3:ObjectCreated:*
            Filter:
              S3Key:
                Rules:
                  - Name: "suffix"
                    Value: "png"

    Metadata:
      DockerTag: nodejs14.x-v1
      DockerContext: ./imagecatalog
      Dockerfile: Dockerfile

Outputs:
  ImageCatalogFunction:
    Description: "Hello World Lambda Function ARN"
    Value: !GetAtt ImageCatalogFunction.Arn
```

Notice that I renamed the folder where the Lambda code is contained to
`imagecatalog`. Right now, the code of the Lambda itself does nothing, so let's
keep things simple at first and just output the event the Lambda receives once
invoked. We make a simple change to the Lambda function code to return the
bucket name and object key of the newly created S3 object:

```
let response;

export const lambdaHandler = async (event, context) => {
    try {
        const { s3 } = event.Records[0];
        const body = `Bucket: ${s3.bucket.name}, Key: ${s3.object.key}`;
        console.log(body);
        response = {
            'statusCode': 200,
            body,
        }
    } catch (err) {
```

```
            console.log(err);
            return err;
        }

        return response
    };
```

NOTE A quick note to remind Node.js users: you can switch from Common JS imports to ES6 by specifying

```
    ""type"": ""module""
```

in your package.json.

You might be wondering about the destructuring of the S3 event. Don't panic—we'll go through this very soon.

So now that the Lambda code is returning something of informative value, we can build the function, test it locally with a locally generated S3 test event, and then deploy this to AWS Lambda. As usual, we run sam build --use-container first, an operation with which you are now familiar.

Next, let's create the event. If you recall in the previous chapter, we can peruse the list of events available per service by calling the help on the generate-event <SERVICE_NAME> subcommand, in our case S3:

```
$ sam local generate-event s3 -h
Usage: sam local generate-event s3 [OPTIONS] COMMAND [ARGS]...

Options:
  -h, --help  Show this message and exit.

Commands:
  delete  Generates an Amazon S3 Delete Event
  put     Generates an Amazon S3 Put Event
```

We want to react to PUT events, so we call the help on PUT to see what further options are available:

```
$ sam local generate-event s3 put -h
Usage: sam local generate-event s3 put [OPTIONS]

Options:
  --region TEXT       Specify the region name you'd like, otherwise the
                      default = us-east-1

  --partition TEXT    Specify the partition name you'd like, otherwise the
                      default = aws

  --bucket TEXT       Specify the bucket name you'd like, otherwise the
                      default = example-bucket
```

```
--key TEXT          Specify the key name you'd like, otherwise the
                    default = test/key

--debug             Turn on debug logging to print debug message
                    generated by SAM CLI and display timestamps.

--config-file TEXT  The path and file name of the configuration file
                    containing default parameter values to use.
                    Its default value is 'samconfig.toml' in
                    project directory. For more information about
                    configuration files, see:
                    https://docs.aws.amazon.com/serverless-
                    application-model/latest/developerguide/
                    serverless-sam-cli-config.html.

--config-env TEXT   The environment name specifying the default
                    parameter values in the configuration file to
                    use. Its default value is 'default'. For more
                    information about configuration files, see:
                    https://docs.aws.amazon.com/serverless-application-
                    model/latest/developerguide/serverless-sam-cli-
                    config.html.

-h, --help          Show this message and exit.
```

We know the name of the bucket (`daitawscloud-example`), and we can specify our own made-up object key (`test.png`), so we will specify them when issuing the `generate-event` command.

If you were to run this `generate-command` after an initial deployment, you could augment your generated `samconfig.toml` with environment-specific parameters as specified in the help for the `--config-file` and `--config-env` descriptions.

Let's run it:

```
$ sam local generate-event s3 put --region eu-west-1 --key test.png
--bucket
 daitawscloud-example > events/s3put.json
```

Remember to pipe the output of the `generate-event` command into a file (in our case `events/s3put.json`):

```
$ cat events/s3put.json
{
  "Records": [
    {
      "eventVersion": "2.0",
      "eventSource": "aws:s3",
      "awsRegion": "eu-west-1",
      "eventTime": "1970-01-01T00:00:00.000Z",
```

```
      "eventName": "ObjectCreated:Put",
      "userIdentity": {
        "principalId": "EXAMPLE"
      },
      "requestParameters": {
        "sourceIPAddress": "127.0.0.1"
      },
      "responseElements": {
        "x-amz-request-id": "EXAMPLE123456789",
        "x-amz-id-2":
"EXAMPLE123/5678abcdefghijklambdaisawesome/mnopqrstuvwxyzABCDEFGH"
      },
      "s3": {
        "s3SchemaVersion": "1.0",
        "configurationId": "testConfigRule",
        "bucket": {
          "name": "daitawscloud-example",
          "ownerIdentity": {
            "principalId": "EXAMPLE"
          },
          "arn": "arn:aws:s3:::daitawscloud_example"
        },
        "object": {
          "key": "test.png",
          "size": 1024,
          "eTag": "0123456789abcdef0123456789abcdef",
          "sequencer": "0A1B2C3D4E5F678901"
        }
      }
    }
  ]
}
```

Now let's invoke the function locally using this event:

```
$ sam local invoke ImageCatalogFunction -e events/s3put.json
Invoking Container created from imagecatalogfunction:nodejs14.x-v1
Building image.................
Skip pulling image and use local one: imagecatalogfunction:
rapid-1.38.0-x86_64.

START RequestId: 189f3156-7947-4e68-bd16-472b4c9363b0 Version: $LATEST
{"statusCode":200,"body":"Bucket: daitawscloud-example, Key: test.png"}
END RequestId:
189f3156-7947-4e68-bd16-472b4c9363b0
REPORT RequestId: 189f3156-7947-4e68-bd16-472b4c9363b0          Init
Duration: 0.08 ms
Duration: 63.44 ms          Billed Duration: 64 ms          Memory Size: 128 MB
Max
Memory Used: 128 MB
```

Everything seems to be working as desired, so let's do a first deployment. If the theory holds, after we deploy the resources (which will involve SAM creating the S3 bucket for us) if we upload a PNG image in it, we should get an output similar to this one. Let's roll a guided deploy, leaving all the default options. The deploy should succeed, showing all the resources that were created, which should include an IAM role, a Lambda permission, a Lambda function, and an S3 bucket.

We can inspect the resources with the AWS CLI tool by calling the `describe-stack` option of `cloudformation`:

```
$ aws cloudformation describe-stack-resources --stack-name imagecatalog
{
    "StackResources": [
        {
            "StackName": "imagecatalog",
            "StackId": "arn:aws:cloudformation:eu-west-
1:972520707061:stack/imagecatalog/dd2c73e0-f0a9-11ec-9202-068308898ecf",
            "LogicalResourceId": "ImageBucket",
            "PhysicalResourceId": "daitawscloud-example",
            "ResourceType": "AWS::S3::Bucket",
            "Timestamp": "2022-06-20T15:03:15.366000+00:00",
            "ResourceStatus": "CREATE_COMPLETE",
            "DriftInformation": {
                "StackResourceDriftStatus": "NOT_CHECKED"
            }
        },
        {
            "StackName": "imagecatalog",
            "StackId": "arn:aws:cloudformation:eu-west-
1:972520707061:stack/imagecatalog/dd2c73e0-f0a9-11ec-9202-068308898ecf",
            "LogicalResourceId": "ImageCatalogFunction",
            "PhysicalResourceId": "imagecatalog-ImageCatalogFunction-
R4taYsgusLtj",
            "ResourceType": "AWS::Lambda::Function",
            "Timestamp": "2022-06-20T15:02:39.019000+00:00",
            "ResourceStatus": "CREATE_COMPLETE",
            "DriftInformation": {
                "StackResourceDriftStatus": "NOT_CHECKED"
            }
        },
        {
            "StackName": "imagecatalog",
            "StackId": "arn:aws:cloudformation:eu-west-
1:972520707061:stack/imagecatalog/dd2c73e0-f0a9-11ec-9202-068308898ecf",
            "LogicalResourceId": "ImageCatalogFunctionRole",
            "PhysicalResourceId":
"imagecatalog-ImageCatalogFunctionRole-1PA43REBRMBV",
            "ResourceType": "AWS::IAM::Role",
            "Timestamp": "2022-06-20T15:02:04.964000+00:00",
            "ResourceStatus": "CREATE_COMPLETE",
```

```
                    "DriftInformation": {
                        "StackResourceDriftStatus": "NOT_CHECKED"
                    }
            },
            {
                    "StackName": "imagecatalog",
                    "StackId": "arn:aws:cloudformation:eu-west-
        1:972520707061:stack/imagecatalog/dd2c73e0-f0a9-11ec-9202-068308898ecf",
                    "LogicalResourceId": "ImageCatalogFunctionS3ObjectCreated
        Permission",
                    "PhysicalResourceId": "imagecatalog-
        ImageCatalogFunctionS3ObjectCreatedPermission-XGL55035NO2P",
                    "ResourceType": "AWS::Lambda::Permission",
                    "Timestamp": "2022-06-20T15:02:51.464000+00:00",
                    "ResourceStatus": "CREATE_COMPLETE",
                    "DriftInformation": {
                        "StackResourceDriftStatus": "NOT_CHECKED"
                    }
            }
        ]
    }
```

It's all looking good. If everything works as it should, uploading a PNG image into our bucket should trigger a Lambda invocation. AWS SAM gives you the option to monitor logs for various resources, so let's tail the output of the Lambda and then upload an image to see if everything works as expected. Open a separate terminal session and issue this command:

```
$ sam logs --stack-name imagecatalog --name ImageCatalogFunction --tail
```

Now return to your original terminal, and upload an image using **aws s3 cp**, specifically:

```
aws s3 cp customreporting.png s3://daitawscloud-example/images/
```

In your logs terminal, you should see the Lambda being invoked, like so:

```
2022/06/20/[$LATEST]45c1c2f9c68e49fcb9d3e268f0f22973
2022-06-20T15:41:22.195000  2022-
06-20T15:41:22.191Z        e84a3e59-1f81-44b4-bf8e-32ae9dd64f31 INFO
Bucket:
daitawscloud-example, Key: images/customreporting.png
2022/06/20/[$LATEST]45c1c2f9c68e49fcb9d3e268f0f22973
2022-06-20T15:41:22.220000 END
RequestId: e84a3e59-1f81-44b4-bf8e-32ae9dd64f31
2022/06/20/[$LATEST]45c1c2f9c68e49fcb9d3e268f0f22973
2022-06-20T15:41:22.221000 REPORT
 RequestId: e84a3e59-1f81-44b4-bf8e-32ae9dd64f31        Duration: 29.79 ms
Billed Duration: 578 ms        Memory Size: 128 MB        Max Memory
Used: 55 MB
Init Duration: 547.69 ms
```

It worked! Note that it also executed correctly, retrieving the correct bucket and key for the object uploaded:

```
INFO        Bucket: daitawscloud-example, Key: images/
customreporting.png
```

Adding DynamoDB

Now for the last piece of the puzzle: we need to use the object key as the primary ID when we go to store a record into DynamoDB. First, we have to create the DynamoDB table in our template. SAM has a special `SimpleTable` resource, which makes the creation of a DynamoDB table extremely simple. Go ahead and add the following code to your template (under `Resources`):

```
ImagesTable:
    Type: AWS::Serverless::SimpleTable
    Properties:
      PrimaryKey:
        Name: id
        Type: String
      ProvisionedThroughput:
        ReadCapacityUnits: 2
        WriteCapacityUnits: 2
```

Now that a table is declared in our template, we also want to pass the table name as an environment variable into our Lambda code so that we can address the correct DynamoDB table. We also need to allow our Lambda function to interact with DynamoDB, so let's apply two simple changes under our Lambda function `Properties`:

```
Policies:
        # Give Create/Read/Update/Delete Permissions to the SampleTable
        - DynamoDBCrudPolicy:
            TableName: !Ref ImagesTable
    Environment:
      Variables:
        # Make table name accessible as environment variable from
function code during execution
        IMAGES_TABLE: !Ref ImagesTable
```

The first change allows the Lambda function to interact specifically with the DynamoDB table in the template. The second change creates an environment variable called `IMAGES_TABLE` populated with the table name through the `!Ref` CloudFormation function.

This covers the infrastructure side of our DynamoDB addition. Now we need to cover the code changes. Remember that if you change the code and are using container images to deploy, you need to rebuild the Lambda first by using `sam build --use-container`.

The first thing we need to do to use DynamoDB in our code is install the relevant library. So let's move into the Lambda code folder (`imagecatalog`) and run this:

```
$ npm install @aws-sdk/client-dynamodb  @aws-sdk/lib-dynamodb --save
```

I use `npm` for simplicity, but you can use whatever other package manager you prefer.

Now we need to include DynamoDB code in our Lambda, so let's modify our original Lambda function to the following:

```javascript
// Create clients and set shared const values outside of the handler.
Import { DynamoDBClient } from '@aws-sdk/client-dynamodb';
import { DynamoDBDocument } from '@aws-sdk/lib-dynamodb';

// Create a DocumentClient that represents the query to add an item
const client = new DynamoDBClient();
const docClient = DynamoDBDocument.from(client);
const tableName = process.env.IMAGES_TABLE;

export const lambdaHandler = async (event) => {
    let response;
    try {
        // const ret = await axios(url);
        const { s3 } = event.Records[0];
        const info = `Bucket: ${s3.bucket.name}, Key: ${s3.object.key}`;
        console.log('TABLENAME: ', tableName);
        console.log('OBJECT INFO: ', info);
        var params = {
            TableName: tableName,
            Item: { id: s3.object.key, ts: (new Date()).toUTCString() }
        };
        const body = await docClient.put(params);
        response = {
            'statusCode': 200,
            body,
        }
    } catch (err) {
        console.log(err);
        return err;
    }

    return response
};
```

Let's dissect this code a bit. The first line imports the `DynamoDBClient`, which allows all sorts of operations. This includes sending commands representing a document insertion. However, for simplicity it is better to import the `DocumentClient`, which has methods such as `put` to insert an item into the table.

There is no other advantage to using a `DocumentClient` over a normal `DBClient`, but I think it adds value in terms of simplicity and readability of the code.

After the initial creation of the `DBClient`, we create the `DocumentClient` here:

```
const docClient = DynamoDBDocument.from(client);
```

You will notice that the `DBClient` and `DocumentClient` are created outside of the Lambda handler; this may look a bit weird. However, this is done on purpose to leverage a feature of AWS Lambda called *execution context*.

Lambda Execution Context

Every Lambda is—simply put—a container running your image. Once a Lambda is invoked for the first time, a container is instantiated and it will remain running for some time. Therefore, all the code will be executed, but every subsequent Lambda invocation will only execute the handler code. This means that you can create resources such as database connections outside of the Lambda handler and save the Lambda time because it doesn't have to re-create those connections every time it is invoked. And that's exactly what we are doing here, by placing the creation of the `DBClient` and `DocumentClient` outside of the handler.

For functions that are invoked often, it is advisable to create shared resources across Lambda invocations outside of the handler itself.

Inserting into DynamoDB

Now that we have a client ready to insert documents, all that's left to do is to insert the item into DynamoDB. In our example, we want to perform a very simple operation, by using the object key as the `id` of the record and specifying a timestamp. This is in fact a classic usage of DynamoDB, whereby DynamoDB works as a metadata store for S3 objects and makes querying S3 objects very easy. We are augmenting our S3 object with a timestamp, but we could do a lot more. For example, we could have some ML model classifying the image and then storing the class of the image, or the objects detected within the image recorded in S3.

The sky's the limit, and what information you add into DynamoDB simply depends on what your use case is and what your search and query fields are.

Creating an item in DynamoDB is very simple:

```
var params = {
TableName: tableName,
Item: { id: s3.object.key, ts: (new Date()).toUTCString() }
};
```

And adding it to DynamoDB is also very simple:

```
const body = await docClient.put(params);
```

Note the `await` keyword. If we didn't include it, the execution of the code may reach the `return` statement of the Lambda, which means that if you wanted to return some kind of value from the insertion operation, you would not be able to. You need to force the code to wait for the operation to complete to do that. If you didn't, your insertion operation would still be performed, but you would not be able to check if it was successful. This is specific to Node.js, but other languages have similar features so keep this point in mind.

Time to deploy the function and trigger it. If the theory holds once more, once the function has been built and deployed, we should be able to trigger it by uploading an image into our bucket, we should see logs appearing in our terminal indication that the Lambda has been successfully triggered, and we should be able to see the DynamoDB item appearing in our table.

Let's first build and deploy the function, which you can do in a single command like this:

```
$ sam build --use-container && sam deploy --config-file samconfig.toml
```

After the resources have been created (DynamoDB table) or modified (Lambda function), we can trigger it:

```
$ aws s3 cp myimage.png s3://daitawscloud-example/images/test_
dynamo2.png
```

Let's switch to the logs terminal. The command is `sam logs`, for example:

```
$ sam logs --stack-name imagecatalog --name ImageCatalogFunction --tail
```

Now observe the output:

```
2022/06/22/[$LATEST]a460f1a003b04f61b5bfd51bd410e687
2022-06-22T14:05:55.238000
2022-06-22T14:05:55.237Z        2ba3fb1b-7717-4a6c-b22d-296d70f577a6
INFO
        TABLENAME:  imagecatalog-ImagesTable-1VE6QDFPON4MO
2022/06/22/[$LATEST]a460f1a003b04f61b5bfd51bd410e687
2022-06-22T14:05:55.238000
2022-06-22T14:05:55.237Z        2ba3fb1b-7717-4a6c-b22d-296d70f577a6
INFO
        OBJECT INFO:  Bucket: daitawscloud-example, Key: images/test_
dynamo2.png
2022/06/22/[$LATEST]a460f1a003b04f61b5bfd51bd410e687
2022-06-22T14:05:55.721000 END RequestId:
2ba3fb1b-7717-4a6c-b22d-296d70f577a6
2022/06/22/[$LATEST]a460f1a003b04f61b5bfd51bd410e687
2022-06-22T14:05:55.721000
 REPORT RequestId: 2ba3fb1b-7717-4a6c-b22d-296d70f577a6        Duration:
569.42 ms       Billed Duration: 570 ms        Memory Size: 128 MB
Max Memory Used: 86 MB
```

The function executed, but was the DynamoDB insertion successful? We can do two things to verify this; we can either go to the Web Console and explore the items in the table, or we can issue an `aws-cli` call. Notice that we printed the table name to the terminal so that we can use it in a `scan` command, but it's probably best to output the table name in the `Outputs` section of our template. Let's scan the `images` table:

```
$ aws dynamodb scan -table-name imagecatalog-ImagesTable-1VE6QDFPON4MO
```

which produces the following output:

```
{
    "Items": [
        {
            "id": {
                "S": "images/test_dynamo2.png"
            },
            "ts": {
                "S": "Wed, 22 Jun 2022 14:05:55 GMT"
            }
        }
    ],
    "Count": 1,
    "ScannedCount": 1,
    "ConsumedCapacity": null
}
```

This too was successful. You have just created your first DynamoDB-powered search index for S3-stored images. The architecture of this application looks like Figure 5.2.

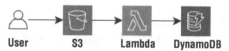

User   S3   Lambda   DynamoDB

Figure 5.2: Application architecture

Cleaning Up

You're all done with this simple pipeline, so remember to clean up your resources by running this:

```
$ aws cloudformation delete-stack --stack-name imagecatalog
```

Now that you are familiar with setting up and tearing down a data engineering pipeline with AWS SAM, let's explore more complex cases.

The code for this entire AWS SAM application is available at https://github .com/techfort/aws-sam-basic-s3-lambda-dynamodb-pipeline.

Serverless Ingestion

There are many ways to perform data ingestion in AWS through serverless technologies, but by far the most popular are Lambda and Fargate. These two technologies have a lot in common, although they are intended for entirely different use cases.

AWS Fargate

Fargate is a serverless tool that allows you to deploy containers without worrying about provisioning the underlying infrastructure. Fargate's concepts of tasks and services are parallel to the ideas of pods and deployments in Kubernetes. If you are familiar with Kubernetes, then you will clearly understand how containers are put to work. You can think of Fargate as a deployment mode, rather than a service in its own right.

An elastic load balancer can be mapped to Fargate services to allow web traffic to reach your containers so that they can perform work in response to web requests. Developing for Fargate has the same workflow as any other container-based development you are used to. In this respect, it's entirely possible to deploy an API with Fargate consisting of a single container handling all the endpoints, interacting with resources whose address and details are going to be injected as environment variables. Unlike Lambda, Fargate has no time execution limits and is in fact aimed at long-running tasks.

In addition to "permanent" tasks, you can configure Fargate tasks to be triggered by CloudWatch events or schedules, so your container will be invoked, much like a Lambda, perform its work without fear of breaking a time limit, and shut down. And you will only pay for whatever time your container was running.

Since AWS SAM is capable of instantiating any CloudFormation resource, you could even use SAM to create pipelines that contain Fargate tasks and configure trigger events.

Fargate operates on top of Amazon Elastic Container Service (ECS) and Amazon Elastic Kubernetes Service (EKS), AWS's tools to run container-based applications. To create and run a Fargate application, first you need to create an ECS/EKS environment and then deploy the container image you developed, which can then be kept permanently running or configured to run on demand or invoked by events.

AWS Lambda

We have already talked about AWS Lambda extensively, so we will only focus on how Lambda functions can be used as a means to data ingestion within an import pipeline in AWS. The one thing to remember about Lambdas is that they are an ideal workhorse for tasks that are predictable in terms of frequency and workload.

A daily API call that should be computed in a short amount of time (less than 15 minutes) and should not require more than 10 GB of memory is a classic case. In fact, the constraints I just mentioned are extremes; in my experience, 512 MB of memory for API calls that can be executed and processed in less than a minute is more representative of the typical use case. Think, for example, of incremental changes retrieved from a third-party API, or a query that generates some aggregates/statistics to be stored in S3.

Example Architecture: Fargate-Based Periodic Batch Import

Let's assume you are monitoring a social media site, where posts are coming in at a steady rate, and a near-real-time batch ingestion is perfectly acceptable. In this case, we could set up a Fargate task that periodically interrogates some API (the social media website we are monitoring) and processes the result. We are going to skip the processing of the result since it is not very important at this point. We want to focus on creating a basic app, containerizing it, then deploying it on Fargate.

The very basic architecture is shown in Figure 5.3 (where *datalake* is an S3 bucket).

Figure 5.3: Fargate-based periodic batch import

The Basic Importer

Let's create a basic node.js app that retrieves a list of posts from social media every five seconds. We are going to use a very handy website called {JSON} Placeholder (https://jsonplaceholder.typicode.com), which fakes an API response—in our case, a list of posts. (I highly recommend this product, as it allows you to rapidly prototype applications).

So, our application looks like this:

```
import axios from 'axios';

const endpoint = 'https://jsonplaceholder.typicode.com/posts';

const saveToS3 = (data) => {
```

```
        // here is where you would process your data
        console.log(data);
        return data;
    }

const batchImport = async () => {
    const { data } = await axios.get(endpoint);
    return saveToS3(data);
}

const run = () => {
    setInterval(batchImport, 5000);
};

run();
```

As I pointed out, the `saveToS3` operation is a dummy; it's not important.
If we run this in our terminal by using Node.js we get the following output:

```
$ node index.js
[
  {
    userId: 1,
    id: 1,
    title: 'sunt aut facere repellat provident occaecati excepturi optio
reprehenderit',
    body: 'quia et suscipit\n' +
      'suscipit recusandae consequuntur expedita et cum\n' +
      'reprehenderit molestiae ut ut quas totam\n' +
      'nostrum rerum est autem sunt rem eveniet architecto'
  },
  {
    userId: 1,
    id: 2,
    title: 'qui est esse',
    body: 'est rerum tempore vitae\n' +
      'sequi sint nihil reprehenderit dolor beatae ea dolores neque\n' +
      'fugiat blanditiis voluptate porro vel nihil molestiae ut
reiciendis\n' +
      'qui aperiam non debitis possimus qui neque nisi nulla'
  },
  ...
]
```

By default, this fake API returns 100 records.

Now that we verified that the application works, let's create a Dockerfile to package it into a container and then build the image for deployment. Our Dockerfile follows the simple pattern of using the node:16 base image (Node.js version 16), then copies the application code and the `package.json` file (necessary to retrieve dependencies), installs the dependencies, copies them across to the container, and then runs the application:

```
FROM node:16

WORKDIR /usr/src/app

COPY package*.json ./

RUN npm install

COPY . .

CMD ["node", "index.js"]
```

At this point, we can run the `docker build` command to produce an image:

```
$ docker build . -t fargate-ingestion:v0.1
Sending build context to Docker daemon  900.1kB
Step 1/6 : FROM node:16
 ---> b9f398d30e45
Step 2/6 : WORKDIR /usr/src/app
 ---> Using cache
 ---> a30a90223c7d
Step 3/6 : COPY package*.json ./
 ---> Using cache
 ---> 58c8ae4d4200
Step 4/6 : RUN npm install
 ---> Using cache
 ---> 12193f7c799a
Step 5/6 : COPY . .
 ---> Using cache
 ---> cc81df16aac6
Step 6/6 : CMD ["node", "index.js"]
 ---> Using cache
 ---> e1f66ae60a5b
Successfully built e1f66ae60a5b
Successfully tagged fargate-ingestion:v0.1
```

If you don't have the base image already on your machine, then this operation might take a few minutes while node:16 downloads. Subsequent build operations, however, will be near instantaneous.

Now that we have an image for our application, we want to deploy it on Fargate. We'll use AWS Copilot CLI for this, but I feel ECS CLI deserves a mention, as it is the equivalent of AWS CLI for ECS-based work. AWS Copilot CLI is fully supported, so its installation and usage are documented on AWS in the same section as ECS CLI (at this address: https://docs.aws.amazon.com/AmazonECS/latest/developerguide/AWS_Copilot.html).

ECS CLI

The first step is to install ECS CLI. ECS CLI is a tool that allows you to manage ECS clusters from the command line, much like `kubectl` for Kubernetes. The installation instructions are available at `https://docs.aws.amazon.com/AmazonECS/latest/developerguide/ECS_CLI_installation.html`, but here's a quick summary of the process:

1. Download the executable for your platform and move into your `$PATH`.
2. Download the public ECS key.
3. Download the signatures for the executable.
4. Import the public key with GPG.
5. Verify the signature.
6. Verify the version of ECS CLI.

At the end of my installation process, I have the following version:

```
$ ecs-cli --version
ecs-cli version 1.21.0 (bb0b8f0)
```

ECS CLI is a very complete tool that allows you to create and configure clusters and tasks on AWS ECS.

AWS Copilot CLI

There is a neat tool maintained by AWS that makes life on ECS incredibly easier, and I strongly encourage you to try it. It's called AWS Copilot CLI. With this tool, you can initialize and deploy a project containing a Dockerfile with a couple of commands. Installation documentation is available at the following URL: `https://docs.aws.amazon.com/AmazonECS/latest/developerguide/AWS_Copilot.html`), but let's go through it in detail.

First, let's install the tool:

```
$ sudo curl -Lo /usr/local/bin/copilot https://github.com/aws/copilot-
cli/releases/latest/download/copilot-linux \
    && sudo chmod +x /usr/local/bin/copilot \
    && copilot --help
```

The output of the installation is a very friendly help message:

```
🏗️🚀  Launch and manage containerized applications on AWS.
Commands
  Getting Started 🌱
    init       Create a new ECS or App Runner application.
    docs       Open the copilot docs.
```

Develop 🎇

```
    app           Commands for applications.
                  Applications are a collection of services and
environments.
    env           Commands for environments.
                  Environments are deployment stages shared between
services.
    svc           Commands for services.
                  Services are long-running ECS or App Runner services.
    job           Commands for jobs.
                  Jobs are tasks that are triggered by events.
    task          Commands for tasks.
                  One-off Amazon ECS tasks that terminate once their work
is done.

  Release 🚀
    pipeline      Commands for pipelines.
                  Continuous delivery pipelines to release services.
    deploy        Deploy a Copilot job or service.

  Extend 🧸
    storage       Commands for working with storage and databases.
    secret        Commands for secrets.
                  Secrets are sensitive information that you need in your
application.

  Settings ⚙️
    version       Print the version number.
    completion    Output shell completion code.

Flags
  -h, --help      help for copilot
  -v, --version   version for copilot

Examples
  Displays the help menu for the "init" command.
  `$ copilot init --help`
```

Next, we want to initialize our project, so let's move to the directory where we created the Dockerfile for the `fargate-ingestion` project and run the following:

```
$ copilot init
```

Of the many options prompted by the command, we want to choose Backend Service; as you will notice it specifies ECS On Fargate.

NOTE If you are curious about the underlying architectures for each of the deployment options, visit `https://aws.github.io/copilot-cli/docs/concepts/services`.

Our Backend Service has the architecture shown in Figure 5.4.

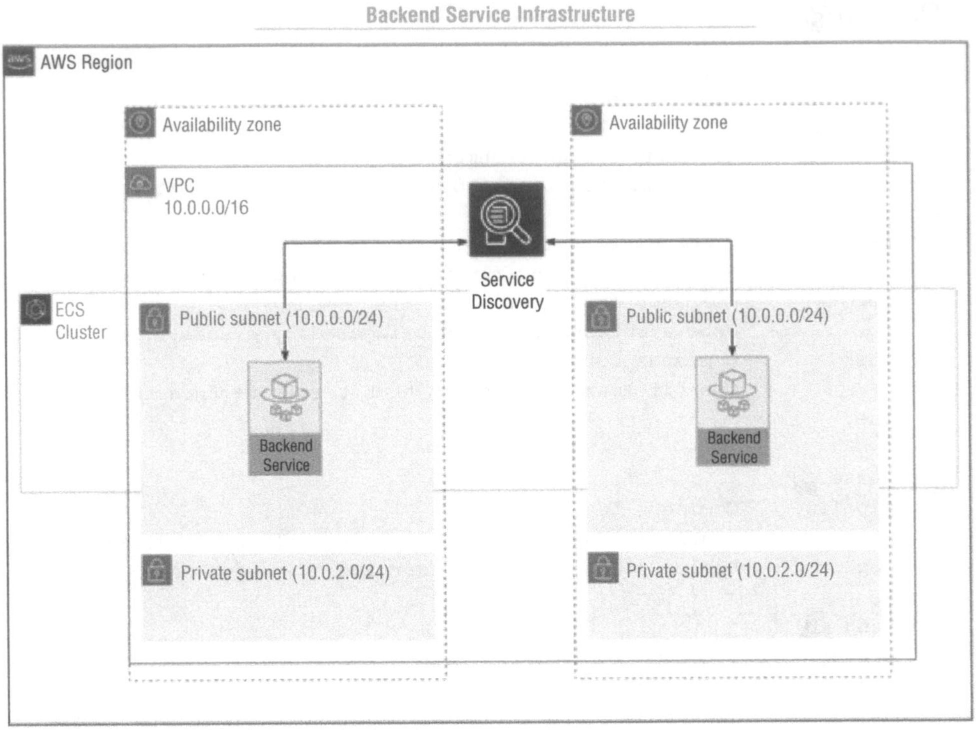

Backend Service Infrastructure

Figure 5.4: Backend Service infrastructure

> **NOTE** For the sake of simplicity in the example (and because we are mainly focused not on security, but on the construction of an import pipeline), we have placed back-end services in a public subnet. In the real world these would be in private subnets, accessible through VPC endpoints or NAT gateways, but it would greatly complicate the diagram in Figure 5.4.

Once you've specified all the options (they are few and trivial, mainly naming the application and service), you will get the following output:

```
$ copilot init
Note: It's best to run this command in the root of your Git repository.
Welcome to the Copilot CLI! We're going to walk you through some
questions
to help you get set up with a containerized application on AWS. An
application is a collection of
containerized services that operate together.

Application name: fargate-ingestion
Workload type: Backend Service
Service name: socialmedia-ingestion
Dockerfile: ./Dockerfile
```

```
parse EXPOSE: no EXPOSE statements in Dockerfile ./Dockerfile
Ok great, we'll set up a Backend Service named socialmedia-ingestion in
application fargate-ingestion.

✓ Created the infrastructure to manage services and jobs under
application fargate-ingestion.
✓ The directory copilot will hold service manifests for application
fargate-ingestion.
✓ Wrote the manifest for service socialmedia-ingestion at copilot/
socialmedia-ingestion/manifest.yml.

Your manifest contains configurations like your container size and port.

✓ Created ECR repositories for service socialmedia-ingestion.

All right, you're all set for local development.
Deploy: No

No problem, you can deploy your service later:
- Run `copilot env init --name test --profile default --app fargate-
ingestion` to create your staging environment.
- Run `copilot deploy` to deploy your service.
```

- Be a part of the Copilot ✥ community ✥!

```
   Ask or answer a question, submit a feature request...
   Visit 🔗 https://aws.github.io/copilot-cli/community/get-involved/ to
see how!
```

It is tempting to answer "yes" to deployment (and indeed, it works just fine), but let's not rush ahead too quickly. Instead, let's create a staging environment and then deploy our app in it. So run the following:

```
$ copilot env init --name test --profile default --app fargate-ingestion
```

where --*name* indicates the environment name and --*app* refers to the application you named during the init phase.

At the end of the whole operation, which may take a few minutes, you should get an output like the following:

```
Default environment configuration? Yes, use default.
✓ Linked account 972520707061 and region eu-west-1 to application
fargate-ingestion.

✓ Proposing infrastructure changes for the fargate-ingestion-test
environment.
- Creating the infrastructure for the fargate-ingestion-test
environment.
[create complete]  [72.5s]
   - An IAM Role for AWS CloudFormation to manage resources
[create complete]  [18.4s]
```

```
     - An ECS cluster to group your services
[create complete]   [10.2s]
     - An IAM Role to describe resources in your environment
[create complete]   [18.2s]
     - A security group to allow your containers to talk to each other
[create complete]   [5.5s]
     - An Internet Gateway to connect to the public internet
[create complete]   [19.6s]
     - Private subnet 1 for resources with no internet access
[create complete]   [5.5s]
     - Private subnet 2 for resources with no internet access
[create complete]   [5.5s]
     - A custom route table that directs network traffic for the public
subnets  [create complete]   [14.8s]
     - Public subnet 1 for resources that can access the internet
[create complete]   [5.5s]
     - Public subnet 2 for resources that can access the internet
[create complete]   [5.5s]
     - A private DNS namespace for discovering services within the
environment   [create complete]   [45.8s]
     - A Virtual Private Cloud to control networking of your AWS resources
[create complete]   [13.4s]

✓ Created environment test in region eu-west-1 under application
fargate-ingestion.
```

Incredibly helpful if you ask me. Creating and configuring networking correctly can be at times complicated and painful.

Now, we can deploy our app with `copilot deploy`, so let's examine the (quite lengthy) output:

```
$ copilot deploy
Only found one workload, defaulting to: socialmedia-ingestion
Only found one environment, defaulting to: test
Environment test is already on the latest version v1.10.1, skip upgrade.
Sending build context to Docker daemon  904.7kB
Step 1/6 : FROM node:16
 ---> b9f398d30e45
Step 2/6 : WORKDIR /usr/src/app
 ---> Using cache
 ---> a30a90223c7d
Step 3/6 : COPY package*.json ./
 ---> Using cache
 ---> 58c8ae4d4200
Step 4/6 : RUN npm install
 ---> Using cache
 ---> 12193f7c799a
Step 5/6 : COPY . .
 ---> Using cache
 ---> 254b65bdca54
Step 6/6 : CMD ["node", "index.js"]
```

```
---> Using cache
---> 53278fac8d0b
Successfully built 53278fac8d0b
Successfully tagged
XXXXXXXXXXXX.dkr.ecr.eu-west-1.amazonaws.com/fargate-ingestion/
socialmedia-ingestion:latest
```

The first thing Copilot will do is retrieve a list of environments; we only have one (test), so it will proceed with that. Next, it will build our container image and warn us about the storage of credentials on our local machine:

```
WARNING! Your password will be stored unencrypted in /home/joe/.docker/
config.json.
Configure a credential helper to remove this warning. See
https://docs.docker.com/engine/reference/commandline/
login/#credentials-store
```

After that, it will push the container image it just built into a newly created ECR repository:

```
Login Succeeded
Using default tag: latest
The push refers to repository [XXXXXXXXXXXX.dkr.ecr.eu-west-1.amazonaws.
com/fargate-ingestion/socialmedia-ingestion]
3dd464bf310a: Layer already exists
f8c094b1cefd: Layer already exists
7f5c666daeb7: Layer already exists
60d123ff4c7b: Layer already exists
27c708b9165c: Layer already exists
ff8e37fde8f2: Layer already exists
a09864edc19a: Layer already exists
607ee9ffddc: Layer already exists
e6fd4ebbaaab: Pushed
261e5d6450d3: Layer already exists
65d22717bade: Layer already exists
3abde9518332: Layer already exists
0c8724a82628: Layer already exists
latest: digest:
sha256:f8c5f55c0d60d4bb03f29bdc6b25305bde89c3d3df6294fcd64e1b2b6b70b886
size: 3049
```

At this point, Copilot describes the infrastructure changes it will apply to accommodate the deployment of your application, and finally deploy it:

```
✓ Proposing infrastructure changes for stack
fargate-ingestion-test-socialmedia-ingestion
- Creating the infrastructure for stack fargate-ingestion-test-
socialmedia-ingestion  [create complete]  [87.1s]
  - Service discovery for your services to communicate within the VPC
[create complete]  [2.4s]
```

```
    - Update your environment's shared resources
[create complete]   [0.0s]
    - An IAM role to update your environment stack
[create complete]   [20.8s]
    - An IAM Role for the Fargate agent to make AWS API calls on your
behalf          [create complete]   [17.4s]
    - A CloudWatch log group to hold your service logs
[create complete]   [2.4s]
    - An ECS service to run and maintain your tasks in the environment
cluster         [create complete]   [42.4s]
    Deployments
                Revision  Rollout      Desired  Running  Failed  Pending
       PRIMARY  1              [completed]  1        1        0       0
    - An ECS task definition to group your containers and run them on ECS
[create complete]   [0.0s]
    - An IAM role to control permissions for the containers in your tasks
[create complete]   [20.8s]

✓ Deployed service socialmedia-ingestion.
```

According to Copilot, it worked! But we don't just trust that—we want to see it in action, maybe by observing some logs. So, let's explore what other Copilot commands are available for this purpose:

```
$ copilot svc help
Commands for services.
Services are long-running ECS or App Runner services.

Usage
  copilot svc [command]

Available Commands
  init       Creates a new service in an application.
  ls         Lists all the services in an application.
  package    Prints the AWS CloudFormation template of a service.
  deploy     Deploys a service to an environment.
  delete     Deletes a service from an application.
  show       Shows info about a deployed service per environment.
  status     Shows status of a deployed service.
  logs       Displays logs of a deployed service.
  exec       Execute a command in a running container part of a service.
  pause      Pause running App Runner service.
  resume     Resumes a paused service.

Flags
  -h, --help   help for svc
```

Since we want to explore the logs, let's call the help for the `logs` subcommand:

```
$ copilot svc logs help
Displays logs of a deployed service.

Usage
  copilot svc logs [flags]
```

```
Flags
  -a, --app string          Name of the application. (default "fargate-
ingestion")
      --end-time string     Optional. Only return logs before a specific
date (RFC3339).
                            Defaults to all logs. Only one of end-time /
follow may be used.
  -e, --env string          Name of the environment.
      --follow              Optional. Specifies if the logs should be
streamed.
  -h, --help                help for logs
      --json                Optional. Outputs in JSON format.
      --limit int           Optional. The maximum number of log events
returned. Default is 10
                            unless any time filtering flags are set.
      --log-group string    Optional. Only return logs from specific
log group.
  -n, --name string         Name of the service.
      --since duration      Optional. Only return logs newer than a
relative duration like 5s, 2m, or 3h.
                            Defaults to all logs. Only one of start-time
/ since may be used.
      --start-time string   Optional. Only return logs after a specific
date (RFC3339).
                            Defaults to all logs. Only one of start-time
/ since may be used.
      --tasks strings       Optional. Only return logs from specific
task IDs.

Examples
  Displays logs of the service "my-svc" in environment "test".
  `$ copilot svc logs -n my-svc -e test`
  Displays logs in the last hour.
  `$ copilot svc logs --since 1h`
  Displays logs from 2006-01-02T15:04:05 to 2006-01-02T15:05:05.
  `$ copilot svc logs --start-time 2006-01-02T15:04:05+00:00 --end-time
2006-01-02T15:05:05+00:00`
  Displays logs from specific task IDs.
  `$ copilot svc logs --tasks
709c7eae05f947f6861b150372ddc443,1de57fd63c6a4920ac416d02add891b9`
  Displays logs in real time.
  `$ copilot svc logs --follow`
  Display logs from specific log group.
  `$ copilot svc logs --log-group system`
```

If you remember, the code of our application was performing an API call every five seconds, so if we issue a `copilot svc logs --follow` command we should be able to see the JSON output of the JSON Placeholder API, which is the case:

```
$ copilot svc logs --follow
Found only one deployed service socialmedia-ingestion in
environment test
```

```
copilot/socialmedia-inges [
copilot/socialmedia-inges    {
copilot/socialmedia-inges       userId: 1,
copilot/socialmedia-inges       id: 1,
copilot/socialmedia-inges       title: 'sunt aut facere repellat provident
occaecati excepturi optio reprehenderit',
copilot/socialmedia-inges        body: 'quia et suscipit\n' +
copilot/socialmedia-inges         'suscipit recusandae consequuntur
expedita et cum\n' +
copilot/socialmedia-inges          'reprehenderit molestiae ut ut quas
totam\n' +
copilot/socialmedia-inges          'nostrum rerum est autem sunt rem
eveniet architecto'
copilot/socialmedia-inges    },
```

Perfect. Our application is up and running and performing its job.

If you wanted, you could extend this exercise by saving the output of an API call as a file in S3, using the timestamp in the object key so you don't overwrite old objects.

Clean Up

Running `copilot svc delete` will delete everything:

```
$ copilot svc delete
Only found one service, defaulting to: socialmedia-ingestion
Sure? Yes
✓ Deleted service socialmedia-ingestion from environment test.
✓ Deleted resources of service socialmedia-ingestion from application
fargate-ingestion.

✓ Deleted service socialmedia-ingestion from application
fargate-ingestion.
Recommended follow-up action:
  - Run `copilot pipeline deploy` to update the corresponding pipeline
if it exists.
```

And you're done! Congratulations; you now know how to build and deploy containerized applications with AWS Copilot CLI on AWS Fargate.

AWS Kinesis Ingestion

I've already introduced Kinesis as a serverless streaming tool. Kinesis as an ingestion mechanism is widely used, especially in serverless architectures. Data can be published onto Kinesis with the AWS SDK in a plethora of programming languages, and whatever program publishes records on a Kinesis stream is defined as a *producer*, whereas any programming using the SDK to receive and consume the data published on streams is called a *consumer*. Of the three types of streams Kinesis provides (Data, Delivery, and Analytics), the first two are suited to ingestion.

AWS Lambda functions can be used as both producers and consumers in general, but they make great Kinesis consumers since AWS EventBridge takes care of the triggering of the Lambda itself.

Example Architecture: Two-Pronged Delivery

To illustrate how Kinesis can be used to both carry information into the data lake architecture and deliver it to a target store, we'll use a forked architecture where data is sucked into the lake with Kinesis data, and one prong delivers it to S3 and the other to DynamoDB using a Lambda consumer. Figure 5.5 is a graphical representation of the architecture.

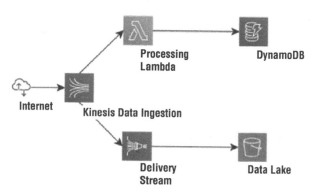

Figure 5.5: Two-pronged delivery

So, once records are published onto the source data stream, we should see two final effects: objects stored in S3 and records appearing in DynamoDB.

We are going to use the same kind of records we used for the Fargate inges-tion example (social media posts). This time, though, at the Lambda level we will augment the record with a computed attribute (specifically, the length in characters of the body of a post) and store that in DynamoDB. We'll do this simply so we can illustrate the purpose of having an intermediate Lambda performing some computing operation as opposed to using another Firehose stream to deliver directly to DynamoDB (which is perfectly feasible).

Just looking at Figure 5.5 we can identify five resources:

- A Kinesis data stream that ingests data into the architecture
- A processing Lambda function
- A Firehose delivery stream
- An S3 bucket
- A DynamoDB table

The entire architecture is serverless, so SAM seems an easy way to approach this. Here's the template file, which we'll explore in detail:

```yaml
AWSTemplateFormatVersion: '2010-09-09'
Transform: AWS::Serverless-2016-10-31
Description: >
  kinesis-ingestion

  Sample SAM Template for kinesis-ingestion

# More info about Globals: https://github.com/awslabs/
serverless-application-
model/blob/master/docs/globals.rst
Globals:
  Function:
    Timeout: 30


Parameters:
  DatalakeRawAreaBucketName:
    Type: String
    Default: daitawsc-datalake-raw


Resources:
  Datalakes3RawAreaBucket:
    Type: AWS::S3::Bucket
    Properties:
      BucketName: !Ref DatalakeRawAreaBucketName

  KinesisIngestionStream:
    Type: AWS::Kinesis::Stream
    Properties:
      Name: "kinesis-ingestion"
      RetentionPeriodHours: 24
      ShardCount: 2

  KinesisS3DeliveryStream:
    Type: AWS::KinesisFirehose::DeliveryStream
    Properties:
      DeliveryStreamName: "kinesis-s3-delivery"
      DeliveryStreamType: KinesisStreamAsSource
      KinesisStreamSourceConfiguration:
        KinesisStreamARN: !GetAtt KinesisIngestionStream.Arn
        RoleARN: arn:aws:iam::972520707061:role/FIrehoseToS3Role
      S3DestinationConfiguration:
        BucketARN: !Sub 'arn:aws:s3:::${Datalakes3RawAreaBucket}'
        CompressionFormat: UNCOMPRESSED
        ErrorOutputPrefix: "error/"
        Prefix: "data/"
        RoleARN: arn:aws:iam::972520707061:role/FIrehoseToS3Role

  ProcessedItemsTable:
    Type: AWS::Serverless::SimpleTable
    Properties:
```

```
        PrimaryKey:
          Name: id
          Type: Number
        ProvisionedThroughput:
          ReadCapacityUnits: 2
          WriteCapacityUnits: 2


  KinesisConsumerFunction:
    Type: AWS::Serverless::Function
    Properties:
      PackageType: Image
      Architectures:
        - x86_64
      Policies:
        # Give Create/Read/Update/Delete Permissions to the SampleTable
        - DynamoDBCrudPolicy:
            TableName: !Ref ProcessedItemsTable
      Environment:
        Variables:
          # Make table name accessible as environment variable from
function code during execution
          ITEMS_TABLE: !Ref ProcessedItemsTable
      Events:
        Kinesis:
          Type: Kinesis
          Properties:
            BatchSize: 50
            Stream: !GetAtt KinesisIngestionStream.Arn
            StartingPosition: TRIM_HORIZON

    Metadata:
      DockerTag: nodejs14.x-v1
      DockerContext: ./kinesisingestion
      Dockerfile: Dockerfile

Outputs:
  KinesisStreamArn:
    Description: "ARN of KinesisDataSource"
    Value: !GetAtt KinesisIngestionStream.Arn
  KinesisDeliveryStreamArn:
    Description: "ARN of KinesisDeliveryStream"
    Value: !GetAtt KinesisS3DeliveryStream.Arn
  KinesisConsumerLambdaArn:
    Description: "ARN of KinesisConsumerLambdaArn"
    Value: !GetAtt KinesisConsumerFunction.Arn
```

I created this project using the Hello World template. Some of the templates are very useful and will come with my preconfigured resources, but I find starting from Hello World a good way to learn about SAM and CloudFormation.

Let's go in order and identify resources with dependencies, since we want to declare them last. I find that a bottom-up approach works well for this purpose, so just looking at Figure 5.5 we can tell that the DynamoDB table and the S3 bucket do not have any dependencies. The Kinesis data stream also does not have any dependencies, so we can declare these three resources first. In order to give some reusability to the template (in particular to reconstruct the S3 bucket ARN in dependent resources), we will declare the bucket name as a parameter of type `String`.

So those resources are fairly straightforward:

```
Resources:
  DataLakeS3RawAreaBucket:
    Type: AWS::S3::Bucket
    Properties:
      BucketName: !Ref DatalakeRawAreaBucketName

  KinesisIngestionStream:
    Type: AWS::Kinesis::Stream
    Properties:
      Name: "kinesis-ingestion"
      RetentionPeriodHours: 24
      ShardCount: 2

  ProcessedItemsTable:
    Type: AWS::Serverless::SimpleTable
    Properties:
      PrimaryKey:
        Name: id
        Type: Number
      ProvisionedThroughput:
        ReadCapacityUnits: 2
        WriteCapacityUnits: 2
```

By now you should be familiar with resource declaration. If not, be sure to review the examples earlier in this and the previous chapter.

Now for the two resources with dependencies: the Kinesis Firehose delivery stream and the processing Lambda that works as a Kinesis consumer.

```
  KinesisS3DeliveryStream:
    Type: AWS::KinesisFirehose::DeliveryStream
    Properties:
      DeliveryStreamName: "kinesis-s3-delivery"
      DeliveryStreamType: KinesisStreamAsSource
      KinesisStreamSourceConfiguration:
        KinesisStreamARN: !GetAtt KinesisIngestionStream.Arn
        RoleARN: arn:aws:iam::972520707061:role/FIrehoseToS3Role
      S3DestinationConfiguration:
        BucketARN: !Sub 'arn:aws:s3:::${DataLakeS3RawAreaBucket}'
        CompressionFormat: UNCOMPRESSED
        ErrorOutputPrefix: "error/"
        Prefix: "data/"
        RoleARN: arn:aws:iam::972520707061:role/FIrehoseToS3Role
```

```
    KinesisConsumerFunction:
      Type: AWS::Serverless::Function
      Properties:
        PackageType: Image
        Architectures:
          - x86_64
        Policies:
          # Give Create/Read/Update/Delete Permissions to the SampleTable
          - DynamoDBCrudPolicy:
              TableName: !Ref ProcessedItemsTable
        Environment:
          Variables:
            # Make table name accessible as environment variable from
function code during execution
            ITEMS_TABLE: !Ref ProcessedItemsTable
        Events:
          Kinesis:
            Type: Kinesis
            Properties:
              BatchSize: 50
              Stream: !GetAtt KinesisIngestionStream.Arn
              StartingPosition: TRIM_HORIZON
```

These two resources are a little more complex. A Kinesis Firehose can be used directly (you can publish records directly on it for delivery to a target store) or it can use a Kinesis data stream as source so that the data in the data stream can also be used by other consumers, as our forked pipeline illustrates.

For this reason, `KinesisS3DeliveryStream` specifies `KinesisStreamAsSource` as the stream type. If you wanted to publish data straight onto the delivery stream, then you would use `DirectPut`.

Now for the source and destination configurations. For the source stream, we only need the ARNs of the data stream and the execution role to access it. (In this case, I created a role in IAM separately to this SAM application because I will have a lot of similar use cases; this way, I can just reference it through the ARN. But nothing stops you from creating an IAM role specifically for the purpose, and even in the template as part of the stack.)

We obtain the ARN of the stream using the `!GetAtt` function of CloudFormation and appending `.Arn` to the end of the resource ID, just like most programming languages would do to access a property of a struct or object.

As for the S3 destination configuration:

- I specify the ARN of the bucket (here I reconstruct it to demonstrate the use of `!Sub` but you could also use the `!GetAtt` approach shown earlier).

- I specify UNCOMPRESSED for the compression type (you can use GZIP, Snappy, ZIP, among others).

- I specify the prefix for errors and for successfully delivered data (error output will be delivered under the `errors/` subfolder and normally delivered data under the `data/` subfolder).

■ I specify the role used to access S3, which is the same we specified earlier for accessing Kinesis, since I created a role and attached the policies granting Full Access to S3 and Kinesis.

You probably want to be more restrictive than that in real-life scenarios.

Finally, I print some output to get the ARN of the newly created streams and Lambda function.

Before building and deploying the application, let's take a quick look at the code inside the Lambda performing the data augmentation:

```javascript
// Create clients and set shared const values outside of the handler.
import { DynamoDBClient } from '@aws-sdk/client-dynamodb';
import { DynamoDBDocument } from '@aws-sdk/lib-dynamodb';

// Create a DocumentClient that represents the query to add an item
const client = new DynamoDBClient();
const docClient = DynamoDBDocument.from(client);
const tableName = process.env.ITEMS_TABLE;

console.log('Loading function');

export const handler = async (event) => {
    console.log(`Will write to ${tableName}`);
    let successes = 0;
    let failures = 0;
    await Promise.all(event.Records.map(async (record) => {
        // Kinesis data is base64 encoded so decode here
        try {
            var payload = JSON.parse(Buffer.from(record.kinesis.data,
'base64').toString('ascii'));
            payload.bodyLength = payload.body.length;
            console.log('Decoded payload:', payload);
            await docClient.put({
                TableName: tableName,
                Item: payload,
            });
            successes++;
        } catch (err) {
            failures++;
            console.log('ERROR', err);
        }
    }));
    return {
        message: "success",
        statusCode: 200,
        successes,
        failures,
    };
};
```

These are operations performed by this code:

1. Receive a batch of events from Kinesis.

2. Map the array of received events to an array of `Promises`, each delivering the records to DynamoDB (we could do a batch insert but this illustrates the idea a little better).

3. Augment the record with a `bodyLength` field containing the number of characters in the body of the record.

4. Store to DynamoDB.

5. Keep track of successes and failures.

6. Exit the Lambda.

Now we're ready to build and deploy using the usual approach:

```
$ sam build -use-container && sam deploy -guided
```

If all goes well, your application should be up and running. Now we want to test, so let's reuse the approach of launching a logs terminal and triggering events in another terminal window. So in terminal 1 we issue

```
$ sam logs -tail -stack-name <your-stack-name>
```

In my case, I used `kinesis-ingestion` for the stack name when running the guided deploy.

In the second terminal window, we put a record onto the Kinesis data stream. The record itself can be passed as base64-encoded data, so in this case the post

```
{
    "userId": 1,
    "id": 2,
    "title": "qui est esse",
    "body": "est rerum tempore vitae\nsequi sint nihil reprehenderit
dolor beatae ea dolores neque\nfugiat blanditiis voluptate porro vel
nihil molestiae ut reiciendis\nqui aperiam non debitis possimus qui
neque nisi nulla"
}
```

is base64-encoded into this string:

ewogICAgInVzZXJJZCI6IDEsCiAgICAiaWQiOiAyLAogICAgInRpdGxlIjogInF1aSBlc3Qg
ZXNzZSIsCiAgICAiYm9keSI6ICJlc3QgcmVydW0gdGVtcG9yZSB2aXRhZVxuc2VxdWkgc21
udCBuaWhpbCByZXByZWhlbmRlcml0IGRvbG9yIGJlYXRhZSBlYSBkb2xvcmVzIG5lcXVlXG5
mdWdpYXQgYmxhbmRpdGlpcyB2b2x1cHRhdGUgcG9ycm8gdmVsIG5paGlsIG1vbGVzdGlhZSB
1dCByZWljaWVuZGlzXG5xdWkgYXBlcmlhbSBub24gZGViaXRpcyBwb3NzaW11cyBxdWkgbm
VxdWUgbmlzaSBudWxsYSIKICB9

So the command to publish the record on Kinesis looks like this:

```
$ aws kinesis put-record --stream-name kinesis-ingestion --data
"ewogICAgInVzZXJJJZCI6IDEsCiAgICAiaWQiOiAyLAogICAgInRpdGxlIjogInFlaSB1c3Q
gZXNzZSIsCiAgICAiYm9keSI6ICJlc3QgcmVydW0gdGVtcG9yZSB2aXRhZVxuc2VxdWkgc2l
udCBuaWhpbCByZXByZWhlbmRlcml0IGRvbG9yIGJlYXRhZSBlYSBkb2xvcmVzIG5lcXVlXG5
mdWdpYXQgYmxhbmRpdGlpcyB2b2x1cHRhdGUgcG9ycm8gdmVsIG5paGlsIG1vbGVzdGlhZSB
1dCByZWljaWVuZGlzXG5xdWkgYXBlcmlhbSBub24gZGViaXRpcyBwb3NzaW1lcyBxdWkgbm
VxdWUgbmlzaSBudWxsYSIKICB9"
--partition-key id
{
    "ShardId": "shardId-000000000001",
    "SequenceNumber": "49630888878509674900451029917175578267617965789096
706066"
}
```

The output of the command represents the shard that handled the operation and the sequence number of the operation.

Since obtaining shard and sequence number indicates a successful put operation, we can move to the logs window, where we should observe a Lambda execution:

```
$ sam logs --tail --stack-name kinesis-ingestion

2022/06/28/[$LATEST]cec34f61a1074617aef7ded7f2e8f679
2022-06-28T18:03:27.994000 START
 RequestId: 6d03772f-9bc5-4b1c-9aca-769fb2c74afe Version: $LATEST
2022/06/28/[$LATEST]cec34f61a1074617aef7ded7f2e8f679
2022-06-28T18:03:27.994000 2022-06-
28T18:03:27.994Z        undefined        INFO        Loading function
2022/06/28/[$LATEST]cec34f61a1074617aef7ded7f2e8f679
2022-06-28T18:03:28.050000 2022-06-
28T18:03:28.050Z        6d03772f-9bc5-4b1c-9aca-769fb2c74afe        INFO
Will write to
 kinesis-ingestion-ProcessedItemsTable-R0R926TCY0C1
} bodyLength: 206non debitis possimus qui neque nisi nulla',t
reiciendis\n' +00 2022-06-
28T18:03:28.091Z        6d03772f-9bc5-4b1c-9aca-769fb2c74afe        INFO
Decoded payload: {
2022/06/28/[$LATEST]cec34f61a1074617aef7ded7f2e8f679
2022-06-28T18:03:28.610000 END RequestId:
 6d03772f-9bc5-4b1c-9aca-769fb2c74afe
2022/06/28/[$LATEST]cec34f61a1074617aef7ded7f2e8f679
2022-06-28T18:03:28.610000 REPORT
RequestId: 6d03772f-9bc5-4b1c-9aca-769fb2c74afe        Duration: 599.09
ms        Billed
Duration: 1551 ms        Memory Size: 128 MBMax Memory Used: 83 MB
Init Duration:
951.31 ms
```

Great! The Lambda seems to have executed correctly, and to verify this, we only need to check the content of the DynamoDB table and the S3 bucket, so let's do that. To check the bucket, we issue a `ls` command to the bucket name we specified in the template:

```
$ aws s3 ls --recursive s3://daitawsc-datalake-raw/
2022-06-28 14:01:13        302 data/2022/06/28/13/
kinesis-s3-delivery-1-2022-06-
28-13-56-11-2a040a04-7b31-4ecb-a84f-e9995ad4c13a
2022-06-28 14:13:50        302 data/2022/06/28/14/
kinesis-s3-delivery-1-2022-06-
28-14-08-48-2538d85c-76e9-49a3-9398-7b2b5a85d0d8
2022-06-28 14:27:29        302 data/2022/06/28/14/
kinesis-s3-delivery-1-2022-06-
28-14-22-26-bb11c928-00b5-4680-993f-e3bbd955f90e
2022-06-28 14:34:13        604 data/2022/06/28/14/
kinesis-s3-delivery-1-2022-06-
28-14-29-11-dca24bbb-a9b1-4a77-9094-3d2ec00acdf6
2022-06-28 14:42:01        604 data/2022/06/28/14/
kinesis-s3-delivery-1-2022-06-
28-14-36-58-83f7f45e-f3bf-4e49-bb18-398652762ebd
2022-06-28 14:51:45        302 data/2022/06/28/14/
kinesis-s3-delivery-1-2022-06-
28-14-46-43-3a424276-6dd1-44a2-9603-e6b6a1c266d7
2022-06-28 15:09:31        576 data/2022/06/28/15/
kinesis-s3-delivery-1-2022-06-
28-15-04-29-1b2b3e97-928b-4b0d-89f7-fb08d059c7e4
2022-06-28 18:10:16        288 data/2022/06/28/18/
kinesis-s3-delivery-1-2022-06-
28-18-03-25-1677d2cd-664d-4411-a87c-527acb1f9dc0
```

Note the automatic partitioning applied by Firehose: each object delivered to S3 is automatically partitioned by YEAR/MONTH/DAY/HOUR in the format YYYY/MM/DD/HH. This will come in very handy when we start analyzing data with Athena.

The Firehose branch of our architecture worked well. Now let's scan the content of the DynamoDB table. Since we didn't actually specify a table name in the template, SAM created one automatically. However, we need that name to be able to explore the items contained in the table itself.

Not to worry—a handy command will reveal all tables in DynamoDB:

```
$ aws dynamodb list-tables
```

and the output:

```
{
    "TableNames": [
        "kinesis-ingestion-ProcessedItemsTable-R0R926TCY0C1"
    ]
}
```

So now that we have the name of the table, we can scan it with the `scan` subcommand of the `aws dynamodb` command:

```
$ aws dynamodb scan --table-name
kinesis-ingestion-ProcessedItemsTable-R0R926TCY0C1
{
    "Items": [
        {
            "bodyLength": {
                "N": "206"
            },
            "id": {
                "N": "2"
            },
            "userId": {
                "N": "1"
            },
            "title": {
                "S": "qui est esse"
            },
            "body": {
                "S": "est rerum tempore vitae\nsequi sint nihil
reprehenderit
 dolor beatae ea dolores neque\nfugiat blanditiis voluptate porro
vel nihil
molestiae ut reiciendis\nqui aperiam non debitis possimus qui neque
nisi nulla"
            }
        },
    ],
    "Count": 1,
    "ScannedCount": 1,
    "ConsumedCapacity": null
}
```

Excellent! Both branches of the pipeline performed their jobs successfully. You now know the basics of using Kinesis data streams and Firehose for serverless ingestion.

Fully Managed Ingestion with AppFlow

If you are creating a data lake for the purpose of analytics, chances are that you will be trying to join data coming from third-party services that your company uses, such as CRM solutions like Salesforce, ticketing/helpdesk software, payment/invoicing products like Stripe, and other products dealing with important domains such as Marketing, Sales, and Finance.

AppFlow is a solution released by AWS in 2020 that allows you to create a direct pipeline of data transfer from an external product into your AWS account, normally into S3 (but other storage solutions are available, too). AppFlow resolves many headaches in terms of periodic data import from third parties, since it eliminates the need to create and maintain services whose only purpose is to interrogate these third parties' APIs to retrieve data incrementally and store it into your AWS account. Failures, retries, and quotas are all managed by AWS—you only have to supply credentials for the source service and a destination for the data.

Let's explore a common use case, which is also referenced in the AWS documentation: the daily import of Salesforce data into S3.

The basic pipeline in AppFlow is referred to as a flow. This represents the definition of a data transfer job from the designated source to the designated target. In our example the source is Salesforce, and the target is S3. We will accomplish this through CloudFormation templates and the AWS CLI tool. This way, should you ever want to create a SAM application that includes a flow, you can reuse the code.

We will need two resources: a credentials definition and a flow definition. Credentials define the connection details to a source. Normally, third-party services provide credentials in the form of username/password pairs, or API keys, or some other combination of secret and public details.

Let's take a look at a credentials definition for Salesforce:

```
AWSTemplateFormatVersion: '2010-09-09'
Resources:
  MySalesforceConnection:
    Type: AWS::AppFlow::ConnectorProfile
    Properties:
      ConnectorProfileName: MySalesforceConnection
      ConnectorType: Salesforce
      ConnectionMode: Public
      ConnectorProfileConfig:
        ConnectorProfileProperties:
          Salesforce:
            InstanceUrl: https://<instance-name>.my.salesforce.com
            IsSandboxEnvironment: false
        ConnectorProfileCredentials:
          Salesforce:
            AccessToken: <access-token-value>
            RefreshToken: <refresh-token-value>
            ConnectorOAuthRequest:
              AuthCode: <auth-code-0075e>
              RedirectUri: https://login.salesforce.com/
            ClientCredentialsArn: <secret-arn-value>
```

As usual, our template's main section is the `Resources` one, which contains a resource with logical ID `MySalesforceConnection` of type `AppFlow::ConnectorProfile`, which defines a connection.

Under `Properties`, we find a few interesting fields:

- `ConnectorProfileName`: Identifies the connector
- `ConnectorType`: One of a list of supported types (`Amplitude` | `CustomConnector` | `CustomerProfiles` | `Datadog` | `Dynatrace` | `EventBridge` | `Googleanalytics` | `Honeycode` | `Infornexus` | `LookoutMetrics` | `Marketo` | `Redshift` | `S3` | `Salesforce` | `SAPOData` | `Servicenow` | `Singular` | `Slack` | `Snowflake` | `Trendmicro` | `Upsolver` | `Veeva` | `Zendesk`)
- `ConnectionMode`: Can be either `Private` or `Public`

The `ConnectorProfileConfig` field is a bit more complicated in that it consists of two embedded properties: `ConnectorProfileProperties` and `ConnectorProfileCredentials`. Each of the services listed has its own set of parameters filled, since they all connect in their own ways. Salesforce, for example, uses OAuth, much like Google, and therefore you need to specify `AccessToken`, `RefreshToken`, and `RedirectUri` for successful login operations. Because of this, you can use one of the provided connectors, or you can create your own if you know the authentication mechanism for the third party.

For example, if you want to connect to a hypothetical third-party service called ACME that allows connection through API keys, you could use the `ApiKeyCredentials` `ConnectorType` and provide API key credentials details in its properties.

A full list of `ConnectorTypes` is available here: `https://docs.aws.amazon.com/AWSCloudFormation/latest/UserGuide/aws-resource-appflow-connectorprofile.html`.

Finally, in our example, if you are using a Secrets Manager for storing credentials you need to provide its ARN.

Now for the flow itself. The template for the flow looks like this:

```
AWSTemplateFormatVersion: '2010-09-09'
Resources:
  MySalesforceToS3Flow:
    Type: AWS::AppFlow::Flow
    Properties:
      FlowName: MySalesforceToS3Flow
      TriggerConfig:
        TriggerType: OnDemand
      SourceFlowConfig:
        ConnectorType: Salesforce
        ConnectorProfileName: MySalesforceConnection
        SourceConnectorProperties:
```

```
        Salesforce:
            Object: Account
    DestinationFlowConfigList:
      - ConnectorType: S3
        DestinationConnectorProperties:
          S3:
              BucketName: <s3-bucket-name>
              S3OutputFormatConfig:
                  FileType: CSV
    Tasks:
      - TaskType: Map_all
        SourceFields: []
        ConnectorOperator:
          Salesforce: NO_OP
```

Let's go through it in detail. Under `Resources` we find the flow definition with logical ID `MySalesforceToS3Flow`, which is of type `AppFlow::Flow`. Under `Properties` we find:

- `FlowName`: A human-readable identifier for the flow, which you supply.

- `TriggerConfig`: A configuration parameter that specifies whether the flow is triggered on demand or on a schedule. The value of `TriggerType` can be `Event` | `OnDemand` | `Scheduled`.

- `SourceFlowConfig`: Where we specify the details of the connector we created.

- `DestinationFlowConfigList`: Where we specify the target of our flow. In this case, since `DestinationConnectorProperties` specifies an S3 target, we need to specify the bucket name and the output format of the data (in our case, CSV).

- `Tasks`: A list of YAML configuration objects that specify different import tasks. Of particular note are

  - `Type`: One of `Arithmetic` | `Filter` | `Map` | `Map_all` | `Mask` | `Merge` | `Truncate` | `Validate`.

  - `SourceFields`: Here we include the fields we want to apply a particular task to.

  - `ConnectorOperator`: Here we specify the filter operation to apply to field values. In Salesforce's case, the list is `ADDITION` | `BETWEEN` | `CONTAINS` | `DIVISION` | `EQUAL_TO` | `GREATER_THAN` | `GREATER_THAN_OR_EQUAL_TO` | `LESS_THAN` | `LESS_THAN_OR_EQUAL_TO` | `MASK_ALL` | `MASK_FIRST_N` | `MASK_LAST_N` | `MULTIPLICATION` | `NO_OP` | `NOT_EQUAL_TO` | `PROJECTION` | `SUBTRACTION` | `VALIDATE_NON_NEGATIVE` | `VALIDATE_NON_NULL` | `VALIDATE_NON_ZERO` | `VALIDATE_NUMERIC`, where `NO_OP` means no filter is applied.

If you merge the two templates as shown next, you obtain a CloudFormation template that you can run with AWS CLI:

```
AWSTemplateFormatVersion: '2010-09-09'
Resources:

  MySalesforceConnection:
    Type: AWS::AppFlow::ConnectorProfile
    Properties:
      ConnectorProfileName: MySalesforceConnection
      ConnectorType: Salesforce
      ConnectionMode: Public
      ConnectorProfileConfig:
        ConnectorProfileProperties:
          Salesforce:
            InstanceUrl: https://<instance-name>.my.salesforce.com
            IsSandboxEnvironment: false
        ConnectorProfileCredentials:
          Salesforce:
            AccessToken: <access-token-value>
            RefreshToken: <refresh-token-value>
            ConnectorOAuthRequest:
              AuthCode: <auth-code-0078e>
              RedirectUri: https://login.salesforce.com/
            ClientCredentialsArn: <secret-arn-value>

  MySalesforceToS3Flow:
    Type: AWS::AppFlow::Flow
    Properties:
      FlowName: MySalesforceToS3Flow
      TriggerConfig:
        TriggerType: OnDemand
      SourceFlowConfig:
        ConnectorType: Salesforce
        ConnectorProfileName: MySalesforceConnection
        SourceConnectorProperties:
          Salesforce:
            Object: Account
      DestinationFlowConfigList:
        - ConnectorType: S3
          DestinationConnectorProperties:
            S3:
              BucketName: <s3-bucket-name>
              S3OutputFormatConfig:
                FileType: CSV
      Tasks:
        - TaskType: Map_all
          SourceFields: []
          TaskProperties:
          - Key: EXCLUDE_SOURCE_FIELDS_LIST
            Value: '[]'
          ConnectorOperator:
            Salesforce: NO_OP
```

You may remember from previous chapters that we can deploy the template with

```
$ aws cloudformation deploy
```

Specifically, if we save the YAML as `salesforce_appflow.yaml`, we can run it with

```
$ aws cloudformation deploy -template-file salesforce_appflow.yaml
-stack-name
 salesforce_appflow_ingestion
```

At the end of this operation, you will have an operational flow that will funnel data into the data lake (or whatever other store you targeted).

Remember to clean up (if you are only testing this) by issuing the usual

```
$ aws cloudformation delete-stack -stack-name <your_stack_name>
```

to avoid incurring unwanted costs.

Operational Data Ingestion with Database Migration Service

The last ingestion method we are going to explore is Database Migration Service (DMS), which is a widely used tool to siphon data from operational databases (typically transactional databases that are backing live products) into an isolated processing facility, like a data lake.

Copying data into a data lake is ideal for processing and analyzing data without applying pressure to operational databases that are not quite built for reporting (and it isn't their intended purpose, anyway).

DMS Concepts

There are four basic concepts to DMS: instance, task, source endpoints, and target endpoints. Tasks can operate one or both of two operations: Full Load and Capture Data Change (CDC). Let's take a closer look.

DMS Instance

A DMS instance is a dedicated EC2 instance upon which tasks run. Like any other EC2, you can configure its size, which clearly has to be proportional to the amount of work it's going to perform, and it can be deployed as a single instance or in a highly available configuration.

In practical terms, an instance is the worker machine.

DMS Endpoints

DMS supports a number of sources and targets. Both sources and targets are endpoints and have to be independently declared. If you want to use DMS to transfer data from database A to database B, you need to create the endpoints first.

Configuring endpoints is not complicated, especially in the case of RDS database sources—it's really just a matter of specifying host and credentials (be it username/password combinations or IAM authentication). Configuring a target store like S3, however, can get a little more complex, so we'll explore that scenario in more detail.

To recap: Endpoints are connection configurations that can be either the source or the target of a migration operation.

DMS Tasks

Tasks define the work performed by DMS. Typically, in a data platform context, you want to simply copy the data from operational databases into the raw area of a data lake, maybe even in a suboptimal format like CSV, which has the advantage of being human readable.

DMS can be used for a variety of migrations, both into and out of the cloud as well as between clouds (for example, different engines, or operations such as migrating from Oracle to PostgreSQL). But in our case we will focus on the most common usage: ingesting data into the data lake architecture. A common task definition is that of copying data from all tables in all databases on a server into an S3-based data lake.

Tasks are highly configurable, so you can specify filters, transformations, and which columns/tables to include or leave out. As mentioned, tasks can be Full Loads, Capture Data Change (CDC), or both:

- A Full Load task simply takes the selected content of a configured data source and loads it into the target, then it stops.
- A CDC task only captures the changes applied to the source and copies them over to the target.
- A Full Load + CDC task does both: it operates an initial load and then keeps track of the changes.

Typically, for data analytics purposes, you'll want to create a Full Load + CDC task.

Summary of the Workflow

To summarize, putting a DMS ingestion pipeline in place involves the following steps:

1. Create a DMS instance that will perform the work.
2. Create a source endpoint and a target endpoint.
3. Create a task that connects to a source and migrates the data to a target.

One instance can run multiple tasks, so the number of instances and tasks running on each instance should be correctly configured in order to avoid instances being excessively strained (and incurring errors) or being too idle (which will represent a cost higher than it needs to be). But this is something that you can only find out through trial and error—no magic bullet exists to define the perfect configuration.

Common Use of DMS

The most common use case (in data analytics) is to transfer operational data into the raw area of the data lake. To do this, we need to follow the previous steps; therefore, putting a DMS instance in place is the first step. Then, we are going to create the source and target endpoints. The source is going to be a MySQL database and the target S3. Finally, we'll start a task that performs a full load and then keeps track of changes.

DMS does not perform record-level updates, since it does not have a concept of awareness of the data that is contained in the target store. Instead, it works in an "append-only" fashion, where new records are simply stored as additional entries into S3.

So, when going to perform analytics on this data, we have an important trade-off between the benefit of point-in-time analysis (we possess all historical versions of a record in a database since the moment a DMS task was started) and the complexity of finding the current state of a record, and also building queries that only take into account one version (possibly the latest) of a record.

If you imagine a very simple users table with attributes ID, NAME, and AGE, you may operate a full load from DMS into S3 and have two records looking like this:

ID	NAME	AGE
1	joe	47
2	jack	22

But if you update record number 1 (for example, if you changed the age from 47 to 51), the total number of records in your data lake would be three, like so:

ID	NAME	AGE
1	joe	47
2	jack	22
1	joe	51

So whereas in a normal relational database a query returning the count of users will give the number 2 as a result, running the same query in the data lake will return 3, which clearly is not what you want.

In Chapter 6, "Processing Data," we explore in more detail what you can do to avoid this issue and end up with a cleaned version of the dataset that only mirrors what is currently stored in the original database. For now, we will only worry about producing an output that will help us with the multiple versions of a record issue.

Example Architecture: DMS to S3

The most common use of DMS in the context of an analytics data platform is transferring data from operational databases into the raw area of a data lake. For this we need:

- An existing transactional database with some data
- A DMS instance
- An S3 bucket (the data lake)
- A DMS endpoint for the database source
- A DMS endpoint for the S3 target
- A DMS task transferring data from the database to S3 in Parquet format

I set up a minimal RDS MySQL database and uploaded some sample data I found on the Internet. The content of the data is actually quite unimportant at this point, since I just want to demonstrate how ingestion works.

NOTE If you are worried about costs, create a free-tier database. The instance itself will be of `micro` type, which will be more than sufficient for you to familiarize yourself with the infrastructure. You can then turn off and delete the database once you are done using it.

Also remember to create a security group that allows traffic on the relevant network ports. If you are working with MySQL or MariaDB, this port is 3306. Also, make a note of the database credentials such as the username/password combination and the database endpoint—you will need them to create a source endpoint in DMS.

NOTE Every database engine/vendor is different. You need to check the requirement at the configuration level for replication to work correctly. For example, in MySQL/MariaDB, `binlog` (binary log) has to be turned on, and its format needs to be set to `ROW` in order for replication tasks to work. Without it, DMS cannot react to changes.

DMS Instance

Let's now move to DMS in the Web Console. Type **DMS** in the search bar and select the result (which will be displayed as *Database Migration Service*). Click Replication Instances and then click the Create Instance button. You will be required to fill in some details, like those shown in Figure 5.6.

Create replication instance

Replication instance configuration

Name
The name must be unique among all of your replication instances in the current AWS region.

```
daitawsc-dms
```

Replication instance name must not start with a numeric value

Descriptive Amazon Resource Name (ARN) - *optional*
A friendly name to override the default DMS ARN. You cannot modify it after creation.

```
Friendly-ARN-name
```

Description

```
daitawsc dms instance
```

The description must only have unicode letters, digits, whitespace, or one of these symbols: _.:/=+-@. 1000 maximum character.

Instance class Info
Choose an appropriate instance class for your replication needs. Each instance class provides differing levels of compute, network and memory capacity. DMS pricing ☑

```
dms.t3.small
2 vCPUs    2 GiB Memory                    ▼
```

🔘 Include previous-generation instance classes

Engine version
Choose an AWS DMS version to run on your replication instance. DMS versions ☑

```
3.4.7                                      ▼
```

🔘 Include Beta DMS versions

> ⓘ **Upgrades to versions 3.4.7 and higher**   [View endpoints]
> Upgrades to AWS DMS versions 3.4.7 and higher require that you configure AWS
> DMS to use VPC endpoints or use public routes. This requirement applies to
> source and target endpoints for S3, Kinesis, Secrets Manager, DynamoDB,
> Amazon Redshift, and OpenSearch Service. Learn more ☑

Allocated storage (GiB) Info
Choose the amount of storage space you want for your replication instance. AWS DMS uses this storage for log files and cached transactions while replication tasks are in progress.

```
50
```

VPC
Choose an Amazon Virtual Private Cloud (VPC) where your replication instance should run.

```
vpc-d84496a1                               ▼
```

Multi AZ
The Multi-AZ option deploys a primary replication instance in one Availability Zone (AZ) and a standby in another AZ. The Single-AZ option deploys a single replication instance in one AZ. Billing is based on DMS pricing.

Figure 5.6: Create Replication Instance

Be sure to include the security group that allows traffic in the relevant connectivity option, as shown in Figure 5.7.

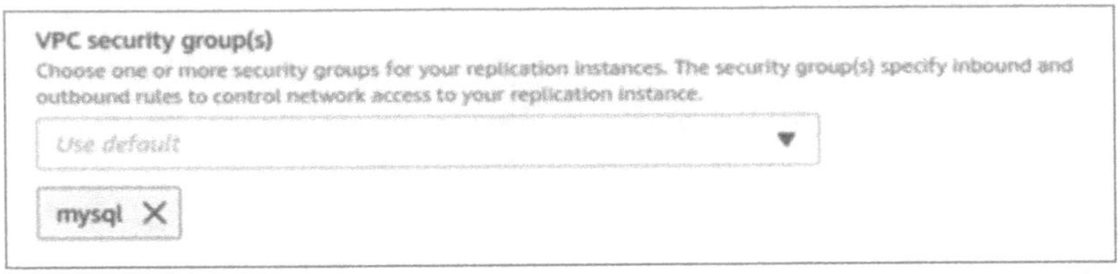

VPC security group(s)
Choose one or more security groups for your replication instances. The security group(s) specify inbound and outbound rules to control network access to your replication instance.

Use default   ▼

mysql ✕

Figure 5.7: Specifying the security group

In this example I called this security group `mysql` to ensure I chose the correct one.

Now go ahead and create the replication instance. In a few minutes, you will see the instance up and running and marked as available, if all goes as it's supposed to.

DMS Endpoints

Now for the source endpoint. In DMS, click Endpoints on the right side, and click Create Endpoint. You will be prompted with a form similar to the one shown in Figure 5.8.

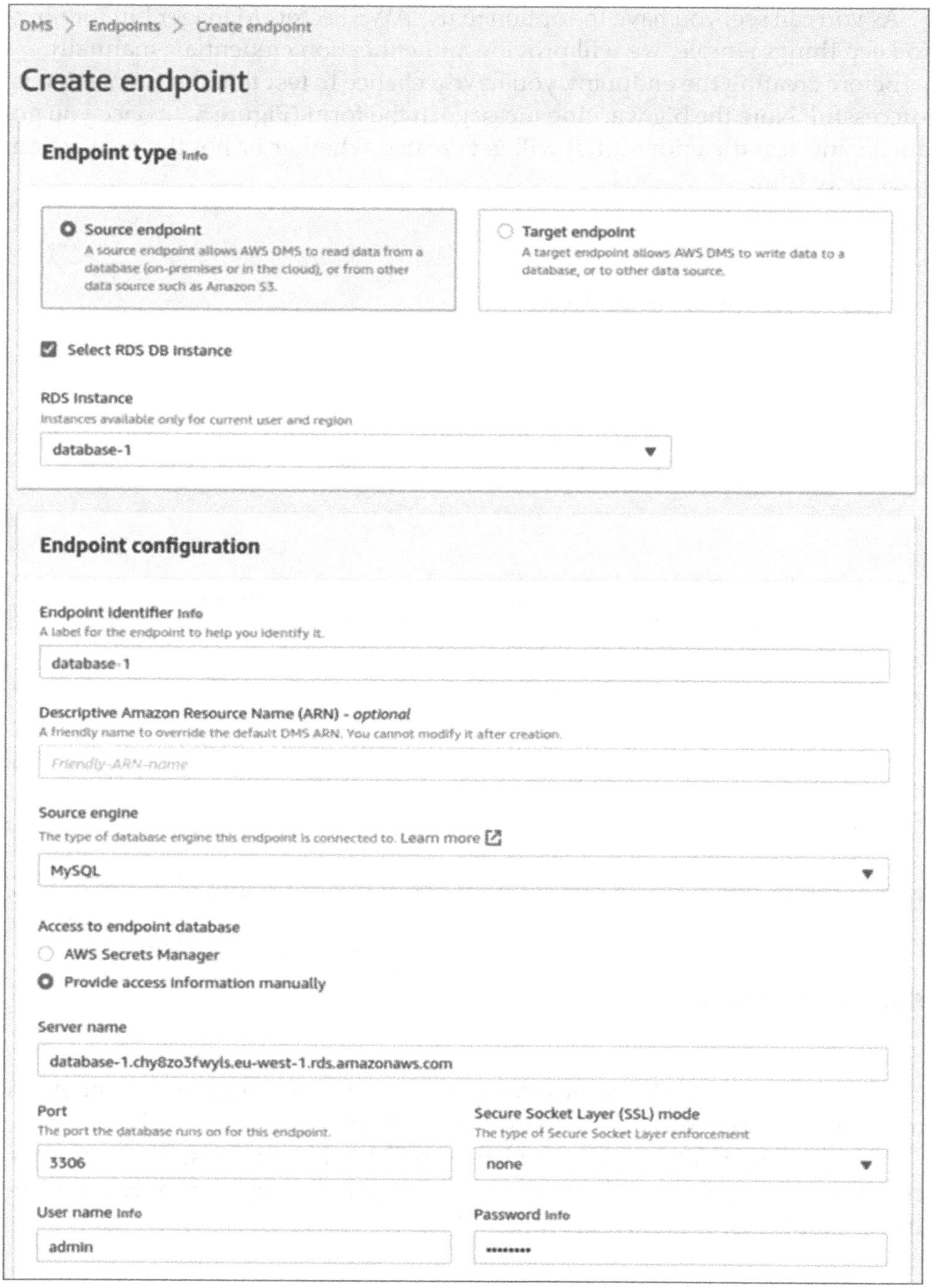

DMS ⟩ Endpoints ⟩ Create endpoint

Create endpoint

Endpoint type Info

○ **Source endpoint**
A source endpoint allows AWS DMS to read data from a database (on-premises or in the cloud), or from other data source such as Amazon S3.

○ **Target endpoint**
A target endpoint allows AWS DMS to write data to a database, or to other data source.

☑ **Select RDS DB instance**

RDS Instance
Instances available only for current user and region

| database-1 | ▼ |

Endpoint configuration

Endpoint identifier Info
A label for the endpoint to help you identify it.

| database-1 |

Descriptive Amazon Resource Name (ARN) - optional
A friendly name to override the default DMS ARN. You cannot modify it after creation.

| Friendly-ARN-name |

Source engine
The type of database engine this endpoint is connected to. Learn more ☑

| MySQL | ▼ |

Access to endpoint database
○ AWS Secrets Manager
● Provide access information manually

Server name

| database-1.chy8zo3fwyls.eu-west-1.rds.amazonaws.com |

Port
The port the database runs on for this endpoint.

| 3306 |

Secure Socket Layer (SSL) mode
The type of Secure Socket Layer enforcement

| none | ▼ |

User name Info

| admin |

Password Info

| •••••••• |

Figure 5.8: Create Endpoint

As you can see, you have the option to use AWS Secrets Manager but for now, to keep things simple, we will provide authentication credentials manually.

Before creating the endpoint, you have a chance to test that the connection is successful. Note the big warning message in the form (Figure 5.9); once you go ahead and test the endpoint, it will get created whether or not the connection was successful.

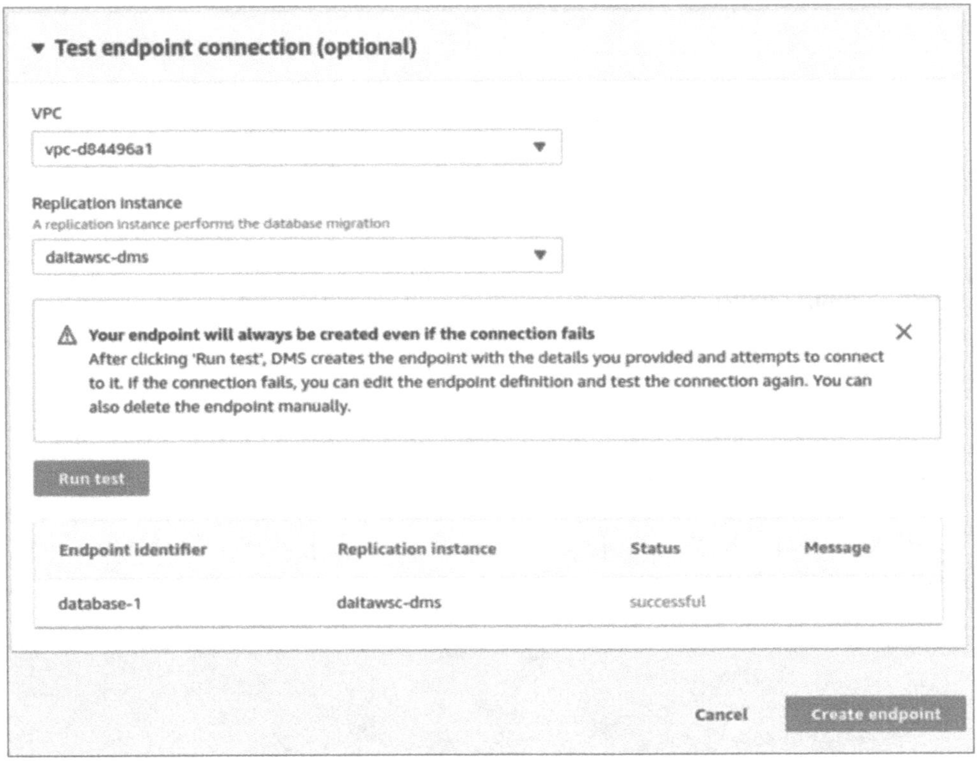

Figure 5.9: Test Endpoint Connection

As you can see, my test was successful, so next click Create Endpoint. All is ready for this source endpoint to migrate data from an operational database.

Now for the target endpoint, which is an S3 bucket. The first thing we do is click Create Endpoint and this time specify Target as the type. Then we complete the usual details, as shown in Figure 5.10.

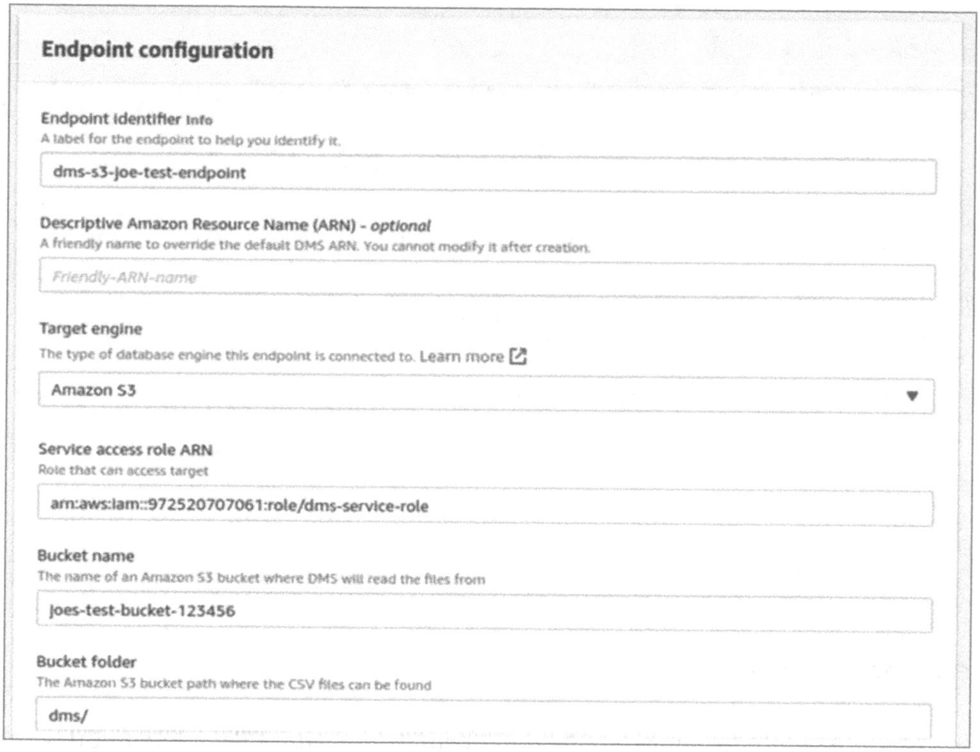

Figure 5.10: Endpoint Configuration

Note the Service Role ARN. This is a role I specifically created for this endpoint because when you go to create the role in IAM, you need to specify the service for the role's use case, in our case DMS. By doing so, DMS is added to the trusted entities of the role. If you did not do so, and simply attached a Write or Full Access S3 policy to the role, AWS would impede the writing operations because DMS is not an allowed source entity to write to S3.

Before testing the endpoint, we need to configure it. There are many ways to write data coming from a database into S3. Ultimately this is up to you and your data needs. The full list of options available to configure an S3 target is available here:

```
https://docs.aws.amazon.com/dms/latest/userguide/CHAP_Target.
S3.html#CHAP_Target.S3.Configuring
```

For our example, I specified the options shown in Figure 5.11, which we will talk about in detail.

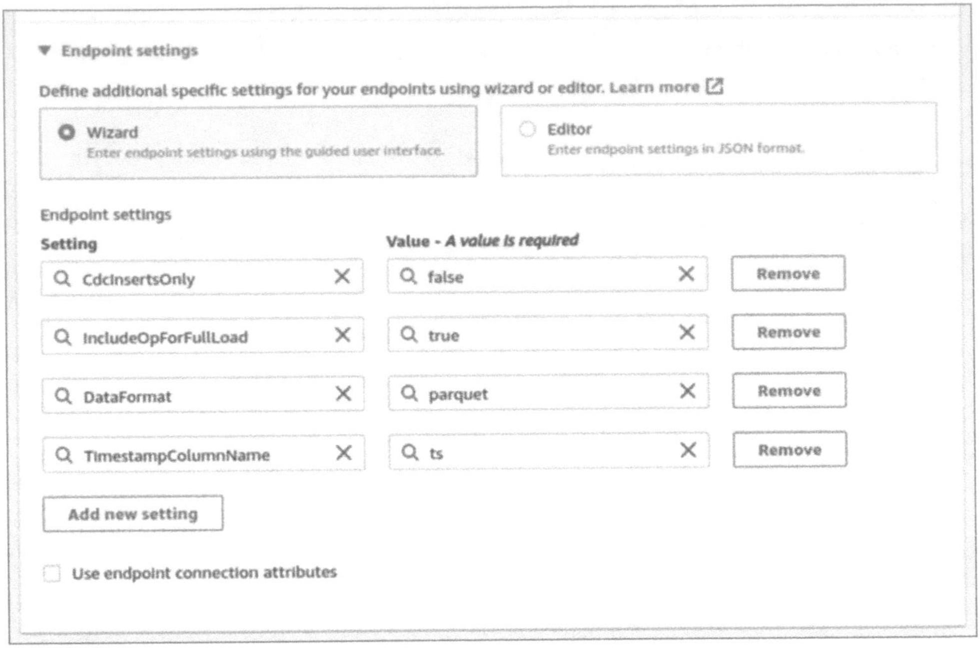

Figure 5.11: Endpoint Settings

Let's start with the simplest: the data format. I specified Parquet; if you want human-readability you can specify CSV. However, be aware of CSV's suboptimal performance for queries. Since CSV uses a comma character (,) to separate fields, if fields contain commas it is probably best to specify some other uncommon character as a separator. Escaping is handled by DMS, but in my experience, some problem always arises, so there is little value to exporting to CSV unless you have a specific case (such as a machine learning training dataset).

Next, we'll talk about two related parameters: `includeOpForFullLoad` and `CdcInsertsOnly`, which are set to `true` and `false`, respectively. When migrating data from a database into S3, if we are just doing a full load, then S3 will simply contain a snapshot of the data. But this is rarely how DMS is used. Instead, we want to capture changes and store those in S3, too.

Not only that, but we possibly want to know what kind of an operation was performed on a record: was it an Insert (I), an Update (U), or a Delete (D)? To capture this, we set the `IncludeOpForFullLoad` flag to `true`. By setting this flag to `true`, we ensure that each record imported at Full Load time will have an additional column called `Op`, which will specify the type of operation. All records migrated at Full Load are considered inserts, so the `Op` value for all those records will be `I`. By setting `CdcInsertsOnly` to `false`, we are also capturing the operation flag for all subsequent records, so new inserts will be marked with `I`, updates to existing records will have a new record in S3 but will be marked with `U`, and deletion will be marked with `D`.

The two tables shown in Figure 5.12 and Figure 5.13 are taken from the documentation and are a good summary. The first table (Figure 5.12) is for Parquet and CSV, and the second table (Figure 5.13) is for CSV only.

With these parameter settings		DMS sets target records as follows for .csv and .parquet output	
includeOpForFullLoad	cdcInsertsOnly	For full load	For CDC load
true	true	Added first field value set to I	Added first field value set to I
false	false	No added field	Added first field value set to I, U, or D
false	true	No added field	No added field
true	false	Added first field value set to I	Added first field value set to I, U, or D

Figure 5.12: For Parquet and CSV

With these parameter settings		DMS sets target records as follows for .csv output	
includeOpForFullLoad	cdcInsertsAndUpdates	For full load	For CDC load
true	true	Added first field value set to I	Added first field value set to I or U
false	false	No added field	Added first field value set to I, U, or D
false	true	No added field	Added first field value set to I or U
true	false	Added first field value set to I	Added first field value set to I, U, or D

Figure 5.13: For CSV only

The last parameter is `TimestampColumnName`. If specified, this parameter creates an additional column (with the value of the parameter as the column name) that contains the timestamp of when the record was migrated by DMS. This is handy for retrieving the latest version of a record in S3, which should also correspond to what is currently contained in our operational database.

Now we can test this endpoint, and if it is successful, create it (Figure 5.14).

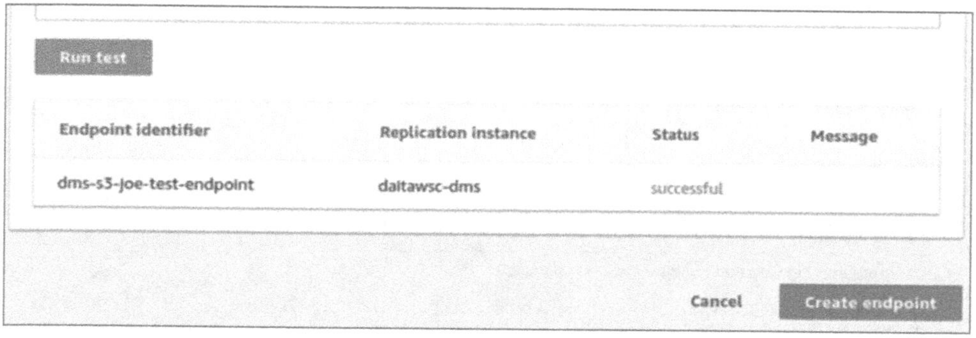

Figure 5.14: Test run

Great! Now we have two endpoints configured: one to retrieve data from our operational database and one to store the data into an S3 bucket.

DMS Task

Now for the last part, where it all comes together: the DMS task.

In DMS we choose Database Migration Tasks from the sidebar menu and select Create Replication Tasks. The first part of the configuration is pretty straightforward: we name the task and specify the source and target endpoints we created. Then we need to establish if this task will simply operate a full load, only operate CDC, or do both, as shown in Figure 5.15.

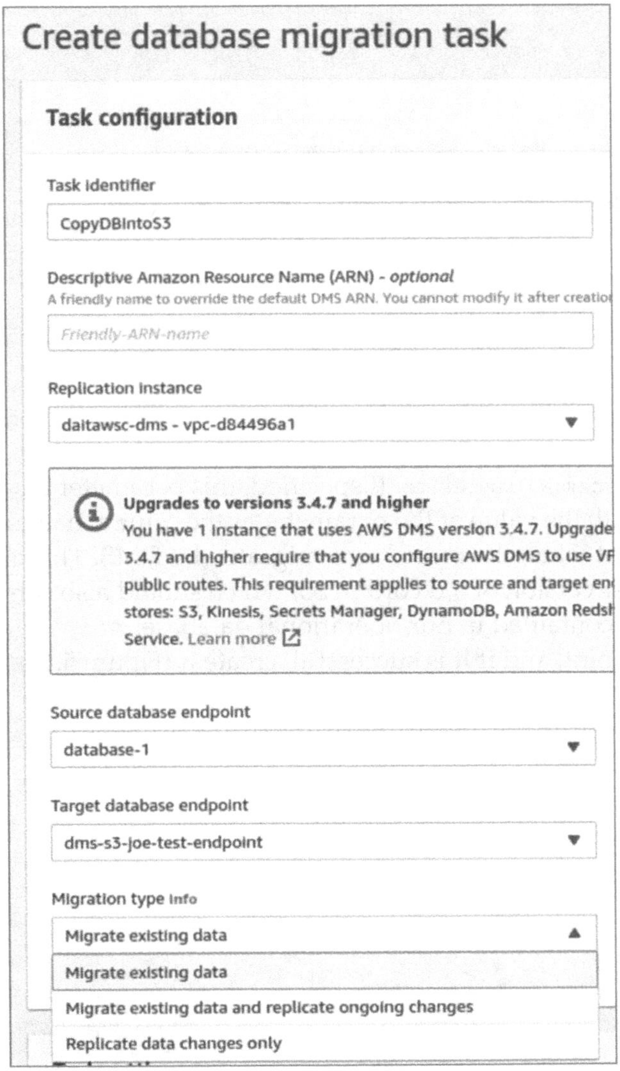

Create database migration task

Task configuration

Task identifier

CopyDBintoS3

Descriptive Amazon Resource Name (ARN) - *optional*
A friendly name to override the default DMS ARN. You cannot modify it after creation

Friendly-ARN-name

Replication instance

daitawsc-dms - vpc-d84496a1   ▼

ⓘ **Upgrades to versions 3.4.7 and higher**
You have 1 instance that uses AWS DMS version 3.4.7. Upgrade
3.4.7 and higher require that you configure AWS DMS to use VP
public routes. This requirement applies to source and target en
stores: S3, Kinesis, Secrets Manager, DynamoDB, Amazon Redsh
Service. Learn more ↗

Source database endpoint

database-1   ▼

Target database endpoint

dms-s3-joe-test-endpoint   ▼

Migration type Info

Migrate existing data   ▲

Migrate existing data

Migrate existing data and replicate ongoing changes

Replicate data changes only

Figure 5.15: Create Database Migration Task

We will choose the second option: Migrate Existing Data And Replicate Ongoing Changes. This will allow us to test the creation of new entries for all updates we issue in our operational database.

Next, we need to create table mappings. In practice, this is where we define what the task will be doing. Configuring table mappings is very straightforward. You can make use of wildcards (%) for matching patterns, so if you want to match everything, you just specify %. If you want to match all tables in a single database (such as `daitawsc-db`) you specify the value `daitawsc-db.%`, and so on for columns and the like. In this particular example (and to be honest, in most cases in real-life scenarios) we will take everything in. The configuration looks like Figure 5.16.

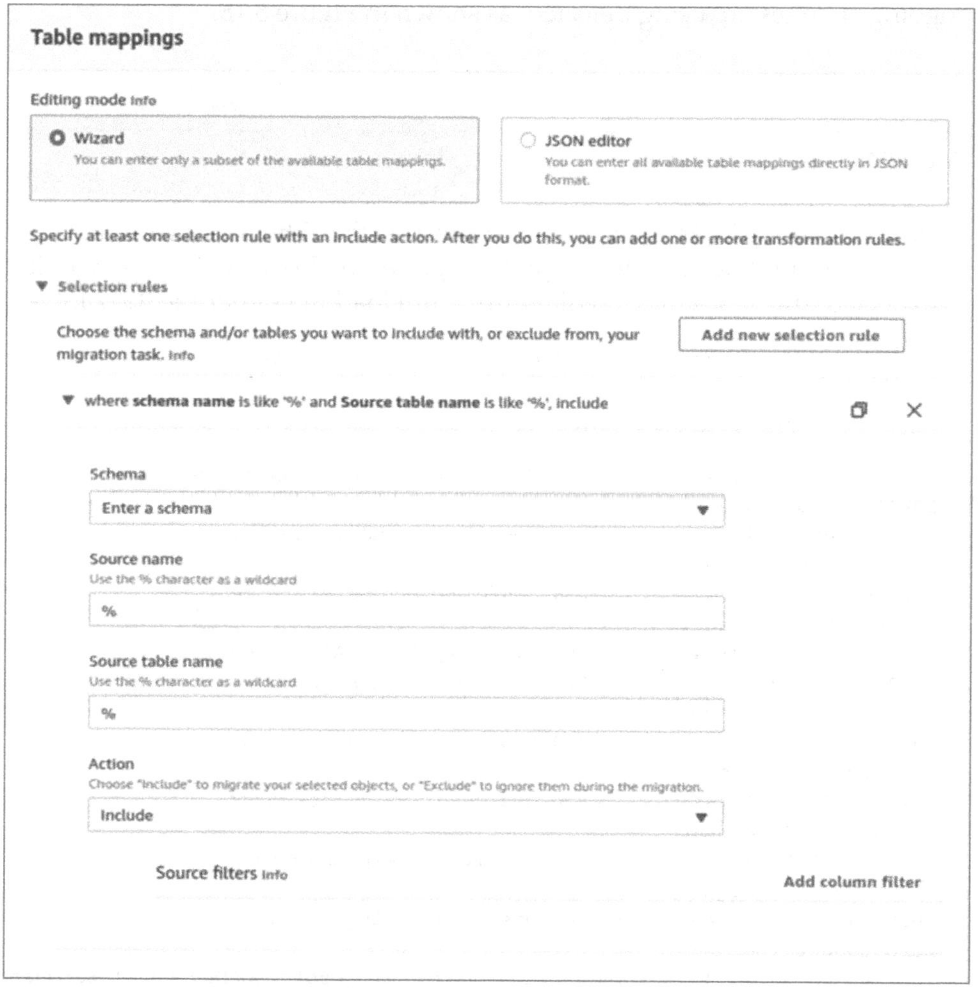

Figure 5.16: Table Mappings

Once you click Create Task, you will be asked if you want the task to start immediately after creation. Then it will appear in the dashboard and you can inspect its status, as shown in Figure 5.17.

Figure 5.17: Inspecting the migration task status

After a while (a length of time proportional to the amount of data you have in your database), you should see that the full load was successful and that ongoing changes are being detected, as shown in Figure 5.18.

Figure 5.18: Full load successful

Since everything looks good, we can now inspect the S3 bucket. If you remember, we specified a folder dms/ for the data migrated by DMS, so if all is working as expected, this aws-cli call will return a full load file under the dms/ folder:

```
$ aws s3 ls --recursive  s3://joes-test-bucket-123456/dms/
```

And the result is as expected:

```
2022-07-05 17:40:43       23543 dms/classicmodels/customers/
LOAD00000001.parquet
2022-07-05 17:40:43        4871 dms/classicmodels/employees/
LOAD00000001.parquet
2022-07-05 17:40:44        3066 dms/classicmodels/offices/
LOAD00000001.parquet
2022-07-05 17:40:44        4405 dms/mysql/db/LOAD00000001.parquet
2022-07-05 17:40:44        1964 dms/mysql/engine_cost/
LOAD00000001.parquet
2022-07-05 17:40:44        5369 dms/mysql/global_grants/
LOAD00000001.parquet
2022-07-05 17:40:44        4820 dms/mysql/help_category/
LOAD00000001.parquet
2022-07-05 17:40:45       56492 dms/mysql/help_keyword/
LOAD00000001.parquet
2022-07-05 17:40:45      104949 dms/mysql/help_relation/
LOAD00000001.parquet
2022-07-05 17:40:45     1142058 dms/mysql/help_topic/LOAD00000001.parquet
```

```
2022-07-05 17:40:45          9202 dms/mysql/innodb_index_stats/
LOAD00000001.parquet
2022-07-05 17:40:45          2927 dms/mysql/innodb_table_stats/
LOAD00000001.parquet
2022-07-05 17:40:45          1720 dms/mysql/proxies_priv/
LOAD00000001.parquet
2022-07-05 17:40:45          2071 dms/mysql/rds_configuration/
LOAD00000001.parquet
2022-07-05 17:40:45           877 dms/mysql/rds_heartbeat2/
LOAD00000001.parquet
2022-07-05 17:40:46          2699 dms/mysql/rds_history/
LOAD00000001.parquet
2022-07-05 17:40:46          2243 dms/mysql/rds_replication_status/
LOAD00000001.parquet
2022-07-05 17:40:46          1033 dms/mysql/replication_group_
configuration_version/LOAD00000001.parquet
2022-07-05 17:40:46          2087 dms/mysql/replication_group_member_
actions/LOAD00000001.parquet
2022-07-05 17:40:46          1864 dms/mysql/server_cost/
LOAD00000001.parquet
2022-07-05 17:40:47          2136 dms/mysql/tables_priv/
LOAD00000001.parquet
2022-07-05 17:40:47         86515 dms/mysql/time_zone/LOAD00000001.parquet
2022-07-05 17:40:47        117244 dms/mysql/time_zone_name/
LOAD00000001.parquet
2022-07-05 17:40:47       7024967 dms/mysql/time_zone_transition/
LOAD00000001.parquet
2022-07-05 17:40:47        579600 dms/mysql/time_zone_transition_type/
LOAD00000001.parquet
2022-07-05 17:40:47         11527 dms/mysql/user/LOAD00000001.parquet
2022-07-05 17:40:48          3978 dms/performance_schema/binary_log_
transaction_compression_stats/LOAD00000001.parquet
2022-07-05 17:40:51         18301 dms/performance_schema/global_status/
LOAD00000001.parquet
2022-07-05 17:40:51         43846 dms/performance_schema/global_variables/
LOAD00000001.parquet
2022-07-05 17:40:51          8264 dms/performance_schema/host_cache/
LOAD00000001.parquet
2022-07-05 17:40:53         18569 dms/performance_schema/session_status/
LOAD00000001.parquet
2022-07-05 17:40:53         45298 dms/performance_schema/session_variables/
LOAD00000001.parquet
2022-07-05 17:40:54         59813 dms/performance_schema/variables_info/
LOAD00000001.parquet
2022-07-05 17:40:55          1741 dms/sys/sys_config/LOAD00000001.parquet
```

The data structure is very intuitive. Each separate database is stored under a prefix, so the sample database I am using to work on this sample architecture will be stored under the prefix `classicmodels`. You can go ahead and download one of the files and inspect its content:

```
$ aws s3 cp s3://joes-test-bucket-123456/dms/classicmodels/employees/
LOAD00000001.parquet employees.parquet
download: s3://joes-test-bucket-123456/dms/classicmodels/employees/
LOAD00000001.parquet to ./employees.parquet
```

We can use `parquet-tools` to explore the content of a Parquet file, shown in Figure 5.19.

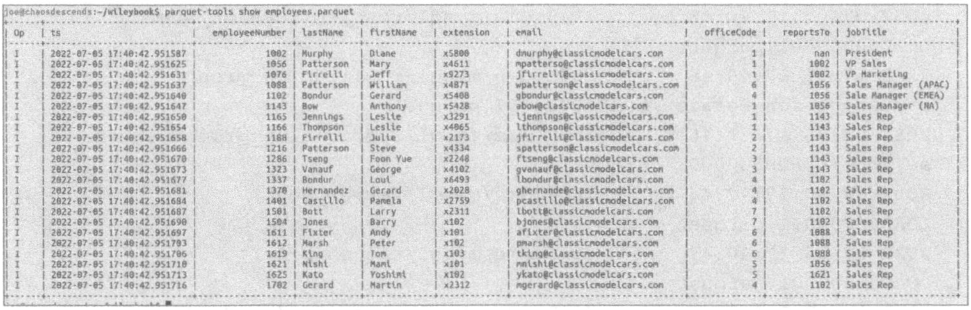
joe@chaosdescends:~/wileybook$ parquet-tools show employees.parquet

Op	ts	employeeNumber	lastName	firstName	extension	email	officeCode	reportsTo	jobTitle
I	2022-07-05 17:40:42.951587	1002	Murphy	Diane	x5800	dmurphy@classicmodelcars.com	1	nan	President
I	2022-07-05 17:40:42.951625	1056	Patterson	Mary	x4611	mpatterso@classicmodelcars.com	1	1002	VP Sales
I	2022-07-05 17:40:42.951631	1076	Firrelli	Jeff	x9273	jfirrelli@classicmodelcars.com	1	1002	VP Marketing
I	2022-07-05 17:40:42.951637	1088	Patterson	William	x4871	wpatterson@classicmodelcars.com	6	1056	Sales Manager (APAC)
I	2022-07-05 17:40:42.951640	1102	Bondur	Gerard	x5408	gbondur@classicmodelcars.com	4	1056	Sale Manager (EMEA)
I	2022-07-05 17:40:42.951647	1143	Bow	Anthony	x5428	abow@classicmodelcars.com	1	1056	Sales Manager (NA)
I	2022-07-05 17:40:42.951650	1165	Jennings	Leslie	x3291	ljennings@classicmodelcars.com	1	1143	Sales Rep
I	2022-07-05 17:40:42.951654	1166	Thompson	Leslie	x4065	lthompson@classicmodelcars.com	1	1143	Sales Rep
I	2022-07-05 17:40:42.951658	1188	Firrelli	Julie	x2173	jfirrelli@classicmodelcars.com	2	1143	Sales Rep
I	2022-07-05 17:40:42.951666	1216	Patterson	Steve	x4334	spatterson@classicmodelcars.com	2	1143	Sales Rep
I	2022-07-05 17:40:42.951670	1286	Tseng	Foon Yue	x2248	ftseng@classicmodelcars.com	3	1143	Sales Rep
I	2022-07-05 17:40:42.951673	1323	Vanauf	George	x4102	gvanauf@classicmodelcars.com	3	1143	Sales Rep
I	2022-07-05 17:40:42.951677	1337	Bondur	Loui	x6493	lbondur@classicmodelcars.com	4	1102	Sales Rep
I	2022-07-05 17:40:42.951681	1370	Hernandez	Gerard	x2028	ghernande@classicmodelcars.com	4	1102	Sales Rep
I	2022-07-05 17:40:42.951684	1401	Castillo	Pamela	x2759	pcastillo@classicmodelcars.com	4	1102	Sales Rep
I	2022-07-05 17:40:42.951687	1501	Bott	Larry	x2311	lbott@classicmodelcars.com	7	1102	Sales Rep
I	2022-07-05 17:40:42.951690	1504	Jones	Barry	x102	bjones@classicmodelcars.com	7	1102	Sales Rep
I	2022-07-05 17:40:42.951697	1611	Fixter	Andy	x101	afixter@classicmodelcars.com	6	1088	Sales Rep
I	2022-07-05 17:40:42.951703	1612	Marsh	Peter	x102	pmarsh@classicmodelcars.com	6	1088	Sales Rep
I	2022-07-05 17:40:42.951706	1619	King	Tom	x103	tking@classicmodelcars.com	6	1088	Sales Rep
I	2022-07-05 17:40:42.951710	1621	Nishi	Mami	x101	mnishi@classicmodelcars.com	5	1056	Sales Rep
I	2022-07-05 17:40:42.951713	1625	Kato	Yoshimi	x102	ykato@classicmodelcars.com	5	1621	Sales Rep
I	2022-07-05 17:40:42.951716	1702	Gerard	Martin	x2312	mgerard@classicmodelcars.com	4	1102	Sales Rep

Figure 5.19: Exploring the content of the Parquet file

Notice the first two columns: `Op` and `ts`. As promised, data was augmented by DMS to include the operation applied to the record and the timestamp of its creation.

So far, we have tested that the full load works. Now we want to update one of the records and repeat the download of the file to see if the change was captured and reflected. We'll change the first record in the table and change the `President` name from `Murphy, Diane` to `Minichino, Joe` (I'm writing the book, I might as well be president). If all works as it should, we should get an additional record, marked with a `U` for update, with a different name for the president. This additional record, however, will not be put in the `LOAD0000001.parquet` file. It will be stored in an additional file.

Let's first check the content of the `employees` subfolder of `dms/classicmodels`:

```
$ aws s3 ls s3://joes-test-bucket-123456/dms/classicmodels/employees/
2022-07-05 18:03:55        2067 20220705-180354959.parquet
2022-07-05 17:40:43        4871 LOAD00000001.parquet
```

Let's download that file and inspect it (Figure 5.20):

```
$ aws s3 cp s3://joes-test-bucket-123456/dms/classicmodels/
employees/20220705-180354959.parquet update.parquet
download: s3://joes-test-bucket-123456/dms/classicmodels/
employees/20220705-180354959.parquet to ./update.parquet
```

```
+----+----------------------------+----------------+----------+-----------+-----------+------------------------------+------------+----------+-----------+
| Op | ts                         | employeeNumber | lastName | firstName | extension | email                        | officeCode | reportsTo | jobTitle |
+----+----------------------------+----------------+----------+-----------+-----------+------------------------------+------------+----------+-----------+
| U  | 2022-07-05 18:02:51.000000 |           1002 | Minichino | Joe      | x5800     | dmurphy@classicmodelcars.com |            |        1 | nan | President |
+----+----------------------------+----------------+----------+-----------+-----------+------------------------------+------------+----------+-----------+
```

Figure 5.20: Inspecting the downloaded file

Perfect! DMS did its job, and I am now president!

We now have an operation identifier U that indicates it's an update, and a timestamp of that event capture.

This concludes the DMS section, and hopefully you have realized how this is going to play a vital part in any architecture that includes migration of operational data into a data lake.

Summary

This chapter explored the various data ingestion mechanisms for serverless and traditional architectures. You learned how to ingest data with Kinesis, Fargate, Lambda, and DMS. This provides you with a range of solutions you can adopt for all your ingestion use cases. Now that we possess the means to ingest data, let's explore how this data is processed in preparation for analysis.

Summary

Processing Data

In this chapter we are going to dig deep into how we ingest, process, and enrich data, preparing it for analysis.

Specifically, we will be looking at serverless and traditional data engineering technologies and practices to perform extract, transform, and load (ETL) to turn raw data that is unusable into clean data stored in optimized formats for whatever analytics purpose you have in mind.

By and large, the main tool for performing all sorts of data processing tasks is AWS Glue, since Glue is more of a family of tools than a single one. AWS Glue enables you to connect to source master systems, using them for extraction or querying. It enables you to build a data catalog, allowing you to describe what data you have, where it is, what form it is in, as well as other metadata. AWS Glue also enables you to perform simple and complex jobs on this data, such as joining it with other datasets, cleaning it, and storing it in new locations, ready for consumption.

Phases of Data Preparation

Clearly every business has its own peculiar use cases and nuances to deal with, but if we were to describe the typical phases of data preparation, we could identify at least two very common ones:

- Raw data that gets validated, then wrangled and stored in optimized formats, which we will call the "cleanup" phase.

- Cleaned data that is often manipulated, enriched, or filtered to form datasets for specific analysis use cases. This we will call the "curation" phase.

Obviously, you may find yourself with more intermediary steps needed in which you perform more specific cleanup or curation tasks, but these should work well as a reference.

The technologies you adopt to perform these steps depend on a number of factors:

1. Skill sets available in your team

2. Nature of the data being manipulated:

   a. **Volume:** How big is the dataset we need to process? Simple jobs can be manipulated using something as simple as Microsoft Excel, but as soon as the dataset becomes larger, you have to think about distributed processing of your data.

   b. **Veracity:** How fast is your dataset updating? Is it once per day, once per hour, or thousands of times a second? This shift in speed means a very different approach to how you architect your data processing pipelines.

   c. **Variety:** Is the data you are processing changing its schema? Or does it remain well defined and structured? A changing schema needs to be accommodated within your data catalog and downstream consumers, whereas more static schemas enable you to simplify your processing pipeline.

   (Some of you might recognize these as the *3 V's of Big Data*.)

We will explore all the technologies available in AWS to perform these steps, including AWS's own technologies, AWS's own offerings/versions of third-party technologies, and serverless and traditional technology.

What Is ETL? Why Should I Care?

Extract, transform, and load (ETL) is a data processing step that takes data from a source (extract), transforms the data (both in terms of structure and format), and loads it into another data store. Why do you need this? Because in the context of analytics it is not really an option to have data analyzed in place, especially when the current store is an operational database. Attempting to create enterprise-level analytics on data residing in an operational/transactional database will result—among other negative consequences—in the following:

- Limited Insights capability since many operational databases are not capable of enriching/joining data across database instances and/or different engines
- Degradation of live database performance due to heavy OLAP-type queries on OLTP systems

Let me expand a little on the second aspect. In a large number of cases, companies start trying to analyze their data in the only stores they have available, which are their operational stores, databases used by the product to set and retrieve application state. These kind of databases, mostly relational databases, are designed to handle a large number of concurrent small transactions. But the nature of analytics is as far away from this as you could imagine, since analytical processing is a single query analyzing enormous amounts of data, often using aggregation computations. OLTP databases were never designed to do this, which puts the store under undue pressure, because it is also simultaneously busy sustaining all those transactions coming from product users. So have mercy on your transactional store and let it do what it does best—small transactions— and let other stores and engines run your analytical queries.

I have seen attempts at running analytics on operational databases, mainly due to resistance to set up an isolated analytics facility and a fear of the costs and learning curve involved in the construction and maintenance of a data lake. These attempts have always resulted in failure and a horrendous false economy move, since the costs of degrading the performance of your operational stores (which may include product downtime) far exceed the cost of setting up and maintaining an analytics pipeline.

Therefore, the industry standard is to extract data from its original source (be it an operational database, a third-party service, a data stream, or whatever else the world may throw at you), transform the data structure and format so that it is suitable for analysis, and load it into a centralized store like a data lake. ETL is thus a vital step in data engineering.

ETL Job vs. Streaming Job

One very important distinction we have to keep in mind is the difference between standard ETL and streaming. Normal ETL jobs take data from a source, load it in memory, process it, and store it into a target destination. Streaming jobs, however, don't use sources such as databases or S3 buckets, but rather streaming resources such as a Kinesis data stream or a Kafka topic.

Stream processing is obtained through the processing of batches of records. For pure stream processing (meaning where records are individually processed as they are published on the stream), I recommend that you look at products such as Apache Flink, which is included in Amazon EMR (formerly Elastic MapReduce).

Overview of ETL in AWS

There are many ways of performing ETL in AWS, but by far the most common are using AWS Glue, using AWS Lambda (and AWS Step Functions), and using Apache Airflow. AWS is making Apache Airflow available to its customers through a managed offering called AWS Managed Airflow.

Some of you, especially the more experienced data engineers, might be wondering why Spark is not getting a mention. After all, it is the industry standard and possibly best-in-class in matters ETL. We are indeed going to be using Spark as part of AWS Glue ETL jobs, but with the advantage that we do not have to set up and provision the cluster (and ancillary services such as Apache ZooKeeper).

Let's start from the beginning, though—we will go through all the options in good time.

ETL with AWS Glue

Glue is an orchestrator, and it's also able to perform lightweight transformations. It allows you to create jobs that perform ETL. You can do this through code, notebooks, or even visual tools.

Normally I'm not one to suggest visual tools over manually written code (I like visibility on code, and I find automatically generated code is rarely optimized for the task), but ETL is a special case in which I suggest you give visual tools a go before dismissing them.

When you create a Glue job, you are given the choice of the underlying infrastructure, which can consist of technology such as Spark, Hadoop, Hive, Presto, Pig, and, generally speaking, all those tools that make up the Hadoop ecosystem.

ETL with Lambda Functions

Lambdas are very suited to perform ETL operations, with some advantages and disadvantages compared to other systems. The number one disadvantage is the limits in terms of memory and execution time. Recall that Lambda functions are particularly suited to computing with predictable workloads, and by that I mean that Lambdas have an execution time limit, so you have to take that into consideration. That said, Lambda handles bursts and unpredictable workloads, too, if you apply clever batching and chunking of work across invocations.

In this respect, using Lambda functions to process a precise amount of stream records (such as records coming from Kinesis, Kafka, or AWS MSK [Managed Kafka]) that have a similar structure and size gives you the ability to predict with a certain level of precision what memory will be required by the Lambda and what timeout to configure on it, as well as the number of invocations based on the traffic you are receiving. Therefore, in these conditions it is quite easy to estimate the cost of a Lambda-based infrastructure.

One "gotcha" to be kept in mind when attempting to perform ETL with Lambdas is the complexity of the processing pipeline. The pipeline might prove too complicated for a single Lambda or a simple linear chain of Lambdas. For this purpose, you can use AWS Step Functions, which allow you to conditionally invoke Lambdas (depending on the success or failure of a function execution), and even iterate through a cycle.

Another trade-off to be aware of is that Lambdas need to be coded; there is no "no-code" alternative to it. You may think this is trivial, but many people in the industry actually believe you should not write ETL jobs unless absolutely necessary. To an extent I can get behind the idea that using visual tools that automate the transformation of data in one format to another format should be done by tools and not by code written by humans.

However, sometimes the transformation isn't straightforward and/or involves complex conditions, so code is necessary.

ETL with Hadoop/EMR

Another major alternative is to run ETL jobs in EMR, Amazon's managed Hadoop offering, which makes it trivial to set up a cluster and create your ETL jobs. Amazon also offers Serverless EMR, which has the usual on-demand pricing model, very convenient for those who desire to work with Hadoop but are concerned about the costs of an online cluster that is mostly idle.

Other Ways to Perform ETL

Naturally there are other ways to perform ETLs in AWS, such as Managed Airflow or custom containers running on Fargate. There is no magic-bullet way of doing this, but Glue should cover the vast majority of standard scenarios.

ETL Job Design Concepts

If ETL jobs were simply used to move data around, we would not have ETL programmers. Whether you are using a visual tool or manually authoring code, it is vital to understand that an ETL job requires design. To design it properly, you need to know what you are trying to accomplish. Let's start from the very beginning, the moment a data analytics team is asked to deliver some analytical insight.

Source Identification

The first step is to identify the data sources. The data may reside in an existing reliable source like an operational database, or it may reside in some third-party service only accessible through APIs. For more complex cases, you may have several sources that need to be blended into a single dataset. Fortunately, I've seen how to build and deploy ingestion pipelines for most scenarios. You should be armed with the necessary tools to move the data to a place where an ETL job can easily access it. If following a traditional data lake architecture, your data will probably be in an S3 data lake or similarly accessible intermediary/landing store.

Destination Identification

Based on your requirements, you will have to store the data in a particular fashion (in the majority of cases parquet or AVRO, which are optimized formats for analytics), or maybe use a particular tool. For example, many business intelligence (BI) tools on the market are easily connected with Amazon Redshift since it is a favorite of many data analysts and BI developers.

Typically, a business analyst or a data analyst produces a specification that illustrates how the raw dataset for their analysis is shaped, what data is needed and in what format, and where the data is going to be stored. An ETL job might even have multiple destinations.

Mappings

Data might come with fields and attributes named in a way that does not comply with the company's policies or best practices and conventions. Some attributes may need to have their data type changed to be interpreted correctly. You can perform this transformation with *mappings*.

Validation

Some records may be corrupted or simply unsuitable for inclusion because they're missing a required attribute. Corrupted or invalid records are difficult to deal with if they are allowed to trickle into data for analysis. They can break a query and impede the production of results, or in the worst-case scenario, they may falsify Insights or skew a machine learning model in a silent and deadly fashion, where no error was recorded but the output is simply incorrect.

Filter

Not all of the data is going to be needed. You can probably filter out a good considerable amount of records that simply do not have a place in the Insight you want to deliver.

Join, Denormalization, Relationalization

One of the most important functions of an ETL job is relationalizing and denormalizing data. It is important to understand that when it comes to BI and analytics, we produce datasets based on their "read pattern"—that is, each record needs to be represented in a particular way in order to be useful for analysis, so you may end up with several different versions of related datasets, each specifically designed and optimized to suit a particular piece of analytics. Don't try to reach for one dataset to suit several analyses—there's very little benefit in that.

Building a single record that is the joined representation of different tables or data sources is done with a join operation and produces a denormalized view of the data itself. For example, if you have a table of employees with these fields:

```
EMPLOYEE_ID | NAME | JOB_TITLE | OFFICE_ID
```

and a table of offices (which are referenced in the `employees` table with an `officeID` attribute) with the fields

```
OFFICE_ID | OFFICE_NAME | ADDRESS | COUNTRY | ZIP
```

then a denormalized representation of an employee-office record looks like this:

```
EMPLOYEE_ID | NAME | JOB_TITLE | OFFICE_ID | OFFICE_NAME | ADDRESS |
COUNTRY | ZIP
```

The flattening of deep/nested data like JSON is where denormalization is often used. For example, you may have a JSON representation of an employee that has the following schema:

```
{
        "employeeId": 1,
        "name": "Joe Minichino",
        "job_title": "engineer",
        "office": {
        "id": 1,
        "name": "Cork Office",
        "address": "Cork City",
        "zip": 12345
        }
}
```

and you want to obtain a denormalized representation as illustrated earlier.

Relationalization is a fancy term that obtains just the opposite result of a denormalization. Using the previous JSON as an example, *relationalizing* it would mean creating two tables suitable for either relational databases or data warehouse solutions like Redshift.

AWS Glue for ETL

Let's take a quick look at Glue Studio's interface, shown in Figure 6.1, which will give us an idea of what we can do with AWS Glue.

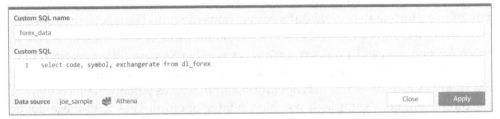

Figure 6.1: AWS Glue interface in the Web Console

First, AWS Glue is in fact a very extensive tool that also allows you to manage data cataloging and indexing, something we will explore in detail in Chapter 7, "Cataloging, Governance, and Search." For now, we'll concentrate on ETL and general data processing features of Glue.

In the left-hand sidebar navigation, the top block of options is related to ETL and processing. The options under Glue Console are specifically for cataloging.

If you click Jobs, you will be prompted with the above interface, which gives you multiple choices to create a new Glue job.

Here's an overview of our options before we go into detail for every one of them.

Really, It's Just Spark

The reality is that as of 2023, Spark has been the de facto standard in matters ETL. AWS Glue jobs are Spark jobs.

Visual

AWS Glue gives you a handy visual tool that allows you to manually drag and drop sources and targets of an ETL job into a diagram, as well as the intermediary manipulation steps such as the application of mappings and other kinds of transformations.

I have successfully witnessed many jobs being created this way and have to admit that most run-of-the-mill ETL tasks are better solved this way rather than reinventing the wheel over and over. There are two variants of visual job: blank canvas and "with source and target." The latter has two convenient drop-downs that specify where the data is coming from and where it's going to be stored.

Spark Script Editor

If you have more complex needs, or if you simply prefer to write Spark code by hand, the Spark Script Editor is the option for you. A nice inline editor will let you write your code for Spark jobs that the ETL job will then execute either on demand, on schedule, or when triggered by an event.

Python Shell Script Editor

Similar to the Spark Editor, the Python Shell Editor lets you write Python shell scripts.

Jupyter Notebook

This is an extremely interesting option for the development of Spark jobs and a relatively recent one. Jupyter Notebooks were normally the bread and butter of data scientists who wanted to avoid repeating lengthy and tedious data manipulations and discovery work ahead of training and testing machine learning models.

But the fact that Notebooks originated in data science does not actually preclude them from being used in data engineering, and in fact it greatly enhances the developer experience of developing ETL jobs. Where you previously had to run a job to test it and endure very lengthy start times before witnessing your code failing, now you can limit yourself to rewriting problematic code blocks and only rerun that code, which has a tremendous impact on productivity. And your sanity for that matter.

Connectors

A prerequisite to any ETL job is to connect to data sources. You could, potentially, create connections in the scripts, but that's an antipattern, since you should create connectors that can be shared across jobs and inject credentials through Secrets Manager as opposed to specifying them in either code or environment variables.

Connectors represent the mechanism through which you connect to a data source or a target data store. This concept is very similar to the idea of endpoints in AWS Data Migration Service (DMS), as you'll recall from Chapter 5, "Data Ingestion."

Creating Connections

A connector encapsulates a connection, which stores credentials for connecting to a particular data source (or target store). So, in order to create a connector, you must create a connection first.

Creating Connections with the Web Console

You can create a connection using the Web Console or through the command line. In the Web Console, you can reach the interface to create connections by choosing Glue Studio ➢ Connectors, as shown in Figure 6.2.

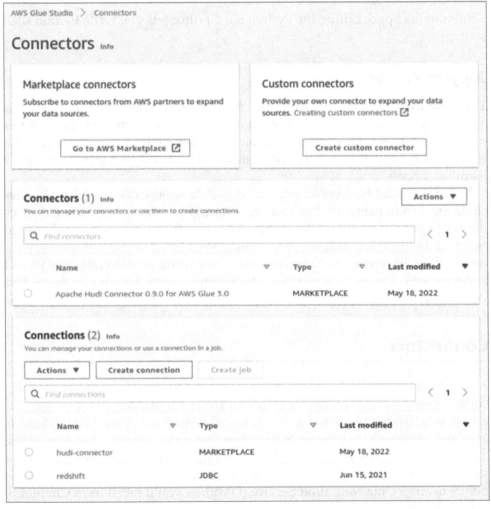

Figure 6.2: Connectors screen

Click Create Connection to open a screen that allows you to specify credentials. You could specify them there, but this is not the most secure way of doing so. Instead, credentials of all kinds should be stored in AWS Secrets Manager, so on the Connection Access screen click Secret, as shown in Figure 6.3.

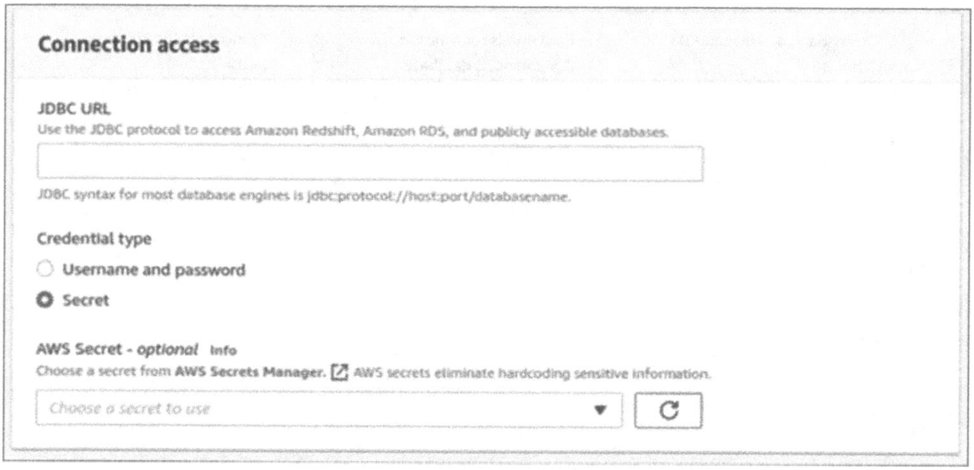

Figure 6.3: Connector Access

The link to Secrets Manager will bring you to a form that provides you with handy templates for the kind of connection you want to create (such as an RDS database), as shown in Figure 6.4.

Note that upon choosing the option to create credentials for RDS, the UI even picks up the existing databases. That means you don't have to specify the value for the host as it will be automatically populated by AWS.

Creating Connections with the AWS CLI

If instead you want to create secrets from the command line, you'll find the documentation for creating a database secret here:

```
https://docs.aws.amazon.com/secretsmanager/latest/userguide/cre-
ate_database_secret.htm
```

Let's try it out. From the documentation we can see that the creation of a secret is actually a one-line operation, provided we have the secret's information saved in a JSON file that follows this structure:

```
{
  "engine": "mysql",
  "host": "<instance host name/resolvable DNS name>",
  "username": "<username>",
  "password": "<password>",
  "dbname": "<database name. If not specified, defaults to None>",
  "port": "<TCP port number. If not specified, defaults to 3306>"
}
```

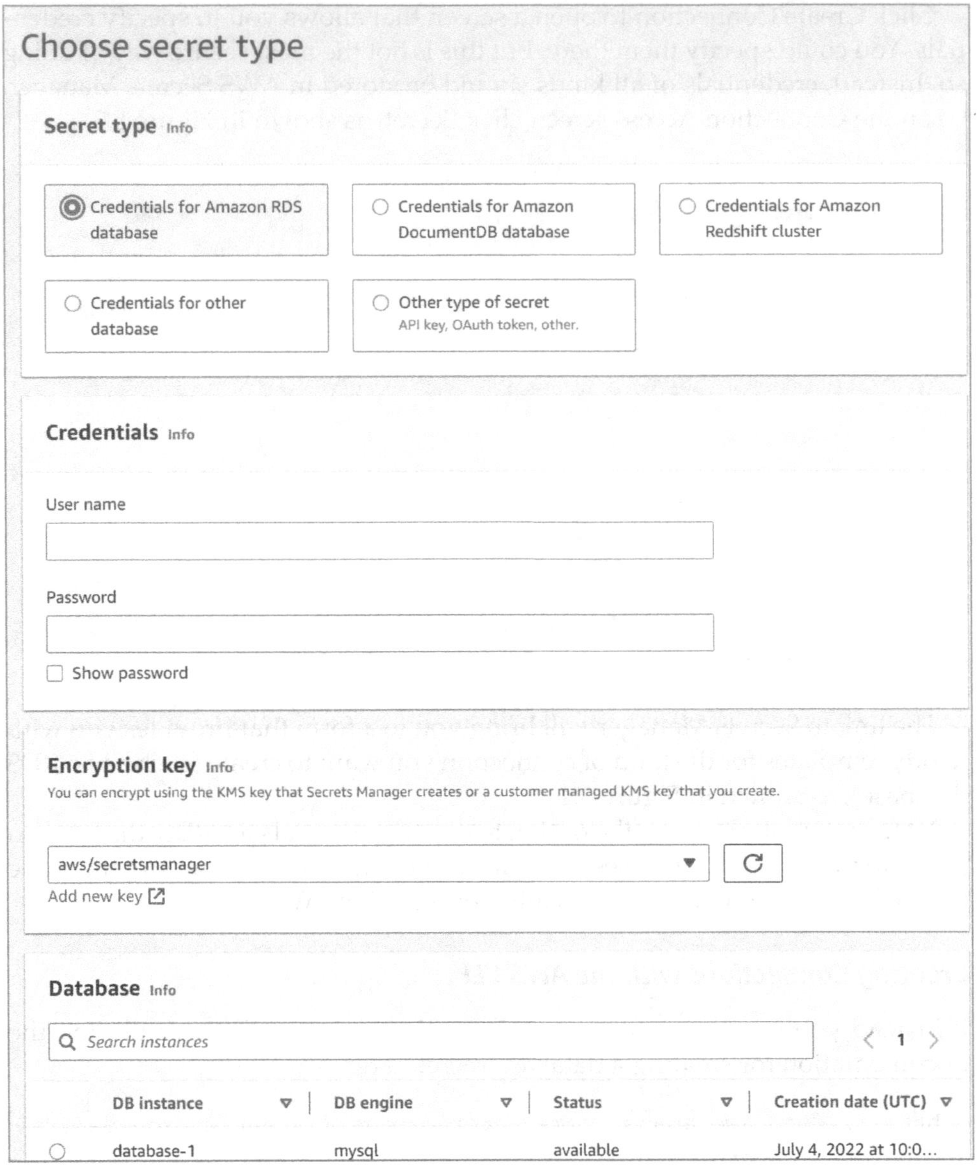

Choose secret type

Secret type Info

(●) Credentials for Amazon RDS database

(○) Credentials for Amazon DocumentDB database

(○) Credentials for Amazon Redshift cluster

(○) Credentials for other database

(○) Other type of secret
API key, OAuth token, other.

Credentials Info

User name

Password

☐ Show password

Encryption key Info

You can encrypt using the KMS key that Secrets Manager creates or a customer managed KMS key that you create.

aws/secretsmanager ▼ | ⟳

Add new key ☑

Database Info

Q Search instances   ‹ 1 ›

DB instance	DB engine	Status	Creation date (UTC)
○ database-1	mysql	available	July 4, 2022 at 10:0…

Figure 6.4: Secrets Manager

This seems fairly easy; all we need is the host, username, and password of the database we are connecting to. So save the above JSON as `creds.json`, then edit the username and password to match the values you set for your data source. In our case we will connect to the sample RDS instance I created for the DMS ingestion pipeline, so I can retrieve the necessary information by describing the db instance in the command line with

```
$ aws rds describe-db-instances
```

whose output is a JSON object starting with these details:

```
{
    "DBInstances": [
        {
            "DBInstanceIdentifier": "database-1",
            "DBInstanceClass": "db.t3.micro",
            "Engine": "mysql",
            "DBInstanceStatus": "available",
            "MasterUsername": "admin",
            "Endpoint": {
                "Address": "database-1.chy8zo3fwyls.eu-west-1.rds.
amazonaws.com",
                "Port": 3306,
                "HostedZoneId": "Z29XKXDKYMONMX"
            },
            "AllocatedStorage": 100,
            "InstanceCreateTime": "2022-07-04T10:04:48.914000+00:00",
            "PreferredBackupWindow": "23:14-23:44",
            "BackupRetentionPeriod": 7,
            "DBSecurityGroups": [],
            "DBParameterGroups": [
                {
                    "DBParameterGroupName": "daitawsc",
                    "ParameterApplyStatus": "in-sync"
                }
            ],
// continues ...
```

Note the `Endpoint.Address` value, which is our host. We copy that into the `host` property of the `creds.json` file, and we are ready to create the secret:

```
$ aws secretsmanager create-secret—name joe/sample-rds-db—secret-string
file://creds.json
{
    "ARN": "arn:aws:secretsmanager:eu-west-1:XXXXXXXXXXX:secret:joe/
sample-rds-db-OLiiNG",
    "Name": "joe/sample-rds-db",
    "VersionId": "3c40cbc9-4242-4810-845d-70db4e37bc8e"
}
```

Perfect! Now we should be able to see our newly created secret, both in the Web Console and in the command line.

```
$ aws secretsmanager list-secrets
{
  "SecretList": [
        {
            "ARN": "arn:aws:secretsmanager:eu-west-1:XXXXXXXXX:
secret:joe/sample-rds-db-OLiiNG",
            "Name": "joe/sample-rds-db",
            "LastChangedDate": "2022-07-14T14:38:16.234000+00:00",
```

```
            "SecretVersionsToStages": {
                "3c40cbc9-4242-4810-845d-70db4e37bc8e": [
                    "AWSCURRENT"
                ]
            },
            "CreatedDate": "2022-07-14T14:38:16.193000+00:00"
        }
    ]
}
```

It has been created correctly, so we can now use it in an AWS Glue Connector. You can do so in the command line with

```
$ aws glue create-connection
```

which requires you to specify the `--connection-input` option in either short-hand syntax:

```
Name=string,Description=string,ConnectionType=string,MatchCriteria=strin
g,string,ConnectionProperties={KeyName1=string,KeyName2=string},Physical
ConnectionRequirements={SubnetId=string,SecurityGroupIdList=[string,
string],AvailabilityZone=string
}
```

or JSON:

```
{
            "Name": "string",
            "Description": "string",
            "ConnectionType":
"JDBC"|"SFTP"|"MONGODB"|"KAFKA"|"NETWORK"|"MARKETPLACE"|"CUSTOM",
            "MatchCriteria": ["string", ...],
            "ConnectionProperties":
{"HOST"|"PORT"|"USERNAME"|"PASSWORD"|"ENCRYPTED_PASSWORD"|"JDBC_
DRIVER_JAR_URI"|"JDBC_DRIVER_CLASS_NAME"|"JDBC_ENGINE"|"JDBC_
ENGINE_VERSION"|"CONFIG_FILES"|"INSTANCE_ID"|"JDBC_CONNECTION_
URL"|"JDBC_ENFORCE_SSL"|"CUSTOM_JDBC_CERT"|"SKIP_CUSTOM_JDBC_CERT_
VALIDATION"|"CUSTOM_JDBC_CERT_STRING"|"CONNECTION_URL"|"KAFKA_BOOTSTRAP_
SERVERS"|"KAFKA_SSL_ENABLED"|"KAFKA_CUSTOM_CERT"|"KAFKA_SKIP_CUSTOM_
CERT_VALIDATION"|"KAFKA_CLIENT_KEYSTORE"|"KAFKA_CLIENT_KEYSTORE_
PASSWORD"|"KAFKA_CLIENT_KEY_PASSWORD"|"ENCRYPTED_KAFKA_CLIENT_KEYSTORE_
PASSWORD"|"ENCRYPTED_KAFKA_CLIENT_KEY_PASSWORD"|"SECRET_ID"|"CONNECTOR_
URL"|"CONNECTOR_TYPE"|"CONNECTOR_CLASS_NAME": "string"
                ...},
            "PhysicalConnectionRequirements": {
              "SubnetId": "string",
              "SecurityGroupIdList": ["string", ...],
              "AvailabilityZone": "string"
            }
        }
```

Or you can use the Web Console form, which at this point will pick up the newly created secret, shown in Figure 6.5.

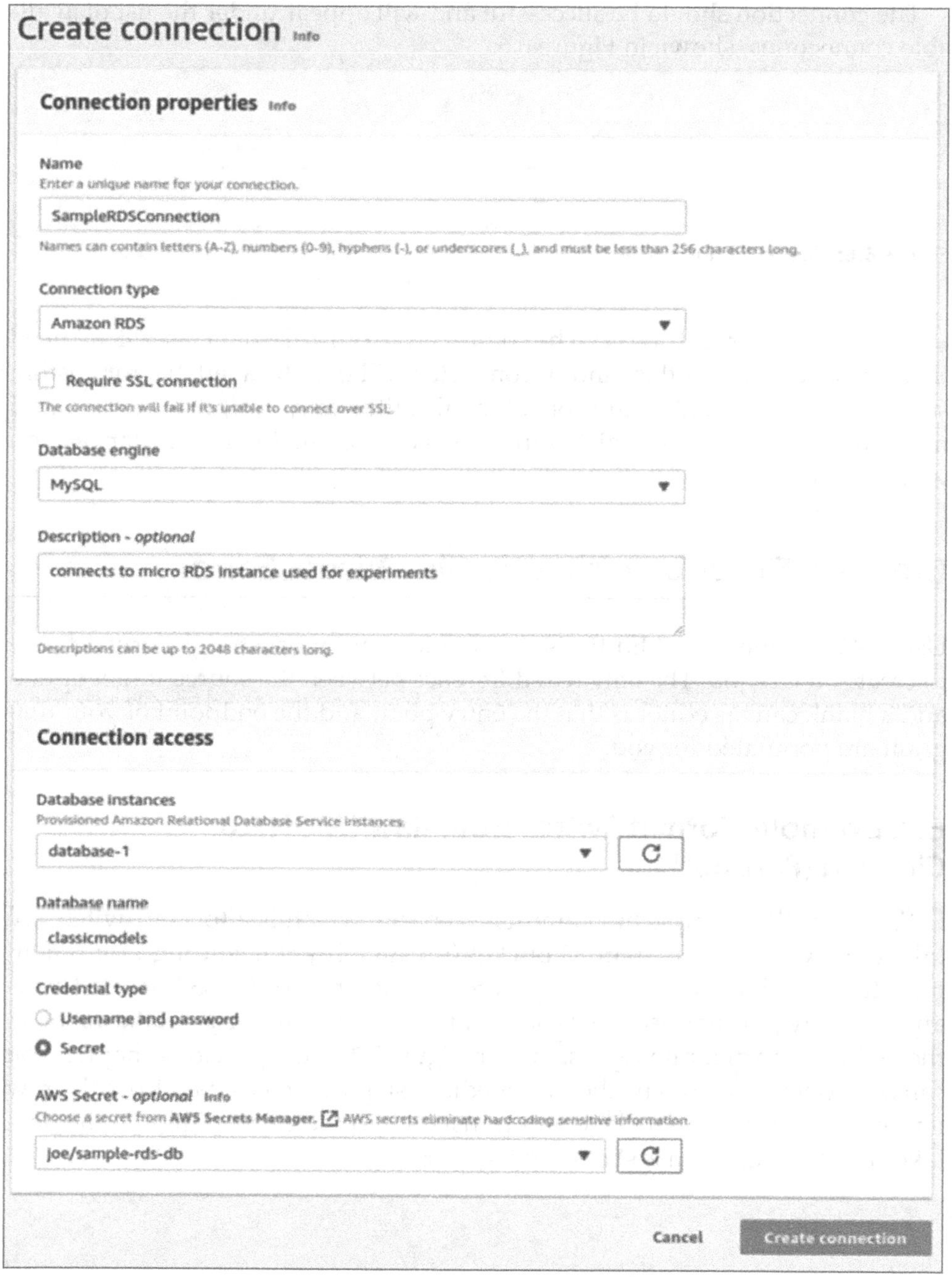

Figure 6.5: Connection Properties section

The connection should be successful and will appear under the list of available connections, shown in Figure 6.6.

Name	▽	Type	▽	Last modified	▼
○ SampleRDSConnection		JDBC		Jul 14, 2022	

Figure 6.6: Custom connectors list

Great! Now our ETL jobs can be connected to our RDS databases if we need them to, but note that this kind of connector will only be available for custom script jobs, not Visual Editor jobs. Visual Editor only supports custom and marketplace connectors, which you can specify on the Job Details tab, as you will see later.

Creating ETL Jobs with AWS Glue Visual Editor

Using AWS Glue Visual Editor is the simplest and most straightforward way to create an ETL job. The only real difference between the source-target option and a blank canvas editor is that the entry point and the endpoint of your diagram are populated for you.

ETL Example: Format Switch from Raw (JSON) to Cleaned (Parquet)

Let's start with a simple but common scenario, which is a format switch: we take the JSON content of an S3 bucket (presumably the landing point of an ingestion pipeline) and we convert it to parquet in another S3 bucket. This is an extremely popular use of ETL jobs in the industry, and if you take a look at the architecture diagram represented in Figure 5.1 in the previous chapter, you can see how this would be the intermediary step that takes data from the raw landing area of your data lake and transfers it to the cleaned area of the data lake. The ETL diagram is shown in Figure 6.7.

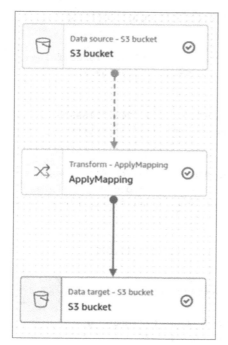

Figure 6.7: ETL diagram in the Editor

In the properties of the source bucket, we specify that it's a JSON format, and obviously the location (which in my case is a bucket called `joes-test-jsonbucket`). As for the destination, we specify its location (another bucket called `joes-test-parquetbucket`) and the format (`parquet`). As for the content of the source bucket, I copied an export of the posts resource of the fake API we mentioned in Chapter 5 (available at this address: `https://jsonplaceholder.typicode.com/posts`). So at the end of the exercise, we should see a parquet version of the JSON file in the original JSON bucket deposited into the parquet destination bucket. Once you tab over to the Job Details and specify a name and an IAM role for the job, you can save it and run it. Once you do, open a terminal window to follow the progress of the job by running the `aws logs` command like so:

```
$ aws logs tail—follow  /aws-glue/jobs/logs-v2
```

which will produce an output similar to

```
2022-07-14T19:09:43.980000+00:00
jr_9f18561c2f7fdb945891821f34a9b87a7704aba97d764352db4748461159806e-
driver 22/07/14 19:09:43 INFO Utils: Successfully started service
'sparkDriver' on port 46687.
2022-07-14T19:09:47.088000+00:00
jr_9f18561c2f7fdb945891821f34a9b87a7704aba97d764352db4748461159806e-
driver 22/07/14 19:09:47 INFO GlueContext: GlueMetrics configured
and enabled
```

These lines indicate that the job has been started correctly. Then

```
[some omitted verbose output]
22/07/14 19:10:07 INFO MultipartUploadOutputStream: close closed:false
s3://aws-glue-assets-972520707061-eu-west-1/sparkHistoryLogs/spark-
application-1657825784357.inprogress
2022-07-14T19:10:08.385000+00:00
jr_9f18561c2f7fdb945891821f34a9b87a7704aba97d764352db4748461159806e-6
22/07/14 19:10:08 INFO NewHadoopRDD: Input split: s3://joes-test-
jsonbucket/posts.json:0+27520
2022-07-14T19:10:10.151000+00:00
jr_9f18561c2f7fdb945891821f34a9b87a7704aba97d764352db4748461159806e-6
22/07/14 19:10:10 INFO MultipartUploadOutputStream: close closed:false
s3://joes-test-parquetbucket/export/run-S3bucket_node3-5-part-block-0-
r-00000-gzip.parquet
```

These lines indicate that the file has been written correctly, too.

```
2022-07-14T19:10:10.371000+00:00
jr_9f18561c2f7fdb945891821f34a9b87a7704aba97d764352db4748461159806e-
driver
 22/07/14 19:10:10 INFO DAGScheduler: ResultStage 0 (runJob at
GlueParquetHadoopWriter.scala:176) finished in 19.036 s
```

And finally, we get confirmation of the successful run.

If you want to see the files appearing in real time you can always run the sync subcommand of the aws s3 command, which makes a directory on your machine mirror the contents of an S3 bucket (and vice versa for that matter, depending on the order of the arguments).

```
$ aws s3 sync s3://joes-test-parquetbucket .--dryrun
(dryrun) download: s3://joes-test-parquetbucket/export/run-S3bucket_
node3-5-part-block-0-r-00000-gzip.parquet
to export/run-S3bucket_node3-5-part-block-0-r-00000-gzip.parquet
```

The --dryrun flag is very handy because it shows what operations would be performed if you went ahead with the sync. Since I want to explore and confirm that the parquet file generated by Glue actually contains the records that were in the original JSON file, I will go ahead and run the command without the --dryrun (and therefore download the bucket's contents), and then use parquet-tools (as shown in previous chapters) to check if the records are there and they look correct.

All looks good, as shown in Figure 6.8.

```
joe@choosdescends:~/wileybook/synced-dir$ parquet-tools show export/run-S3bucket_node3-5-part-block-0-r-00000-gzip.parquet
  userid |  id | title                                                     | body
---------------------------------------------------------------------------------
     1  |   2 | qui est esse                                              | est rerum tempore vitae
        |     |                                                           | sequi sint nihil reprehenderit dolor beatae ea dolores neque
        |     |                                                           | fugiat blanditiis voluptate porro vel nihil molestiae ut reiciendis
     1  |   3 | ea molestias quasi exercitationem repellat qui ipsa sit aut| qui aperiam non debitis possimus qui neque nisi nulla
        |     |                                                           | et iusto sed quo iure
        |     |                                                           | voluptatem occaecati omnis eligendi aut ad
        |     |                                                           | voluptatem doloribus vel accusantium quis pariatur
     1  |   4 | eum et est occaecati                                       | molestiae porro eius odio et labore et velit aut
        |     |                                                           | ullam et saepe reiciendis voluptatem adipisci
        |     |                                                           | sit amet autem assumenda provident rerum culpa
        |     |                                                           | quis hic commodi nesciunt rem tenetur doloremque ipsam iure
        |     |                                                           | quis sunt voluptatem rerum illo velit
```

Figure 6.8: Inspecting parquet

> **TIP** If you want a near–real-time view (or even synchronization) of what's happening in an S3 bucket, you can run a simple infinite loop in your command line that runs a sync (either `--dryrun` or actual) like so:
>
> ```
> $ while true; do aws s3 sync –delete s3://<my bucket id here> <my
> local dir here> && sleep 2; done
> ```
>
> This will keep attempting to sync every two seconds and can be interrupted by the usual Ctrl+C (or however the `SIGTERM` is issued in your terminal).

Job Bookmarks

If you try to rerun the job, you will notice that nothing will happen. This is confusing, but also entirely justified. AWS Glue ETL jobs have—by default—a feature called Job Bookmark enabled, which keeps track of the objects and the data that has been processed so you don't erroneously process it a second time (which could lead to duplicate records in the target store). The idea of Job Bookmark is extremely important; do consider it with attention. It is the difference between processing only new data and erroneously reprocessing all the data, which could be in the terabytes or even petabytes. Since our first file was processed, rerunning the job will look only for new data, and upon not finding it, it will simply terminate.

There are situations, especially during the development phase, where you would want to reprocess data, in which case you have two options:

- Click Actions in the Job Details screen and choose Reset Bookmark. This will erase the current bookmark and the next run will consider all of the data as new.

- Disable or pause the Job Bookmark on the Job Details screen, as illustrated in Figure 6.9.

Job bookmark Info

Specifies how AWS Glue processes job bookmark when the job runs. It can remember previously processed data (Enable), update state information (Pause), or ignore state information (Disable).

Enable ▲
🔍
Enable
Pause
Disable

Figure 6.9: Bookmark Enable/Disable option

Transformations

During an ETL job, a lot of transformations can be applied to a dataset. You can change field names, filter data, and so forth. Let's see what the Visual Editor makes available for us.

Adding transforms to our diagram is very simple: click the background canvas of the diagram to make sure no step is selected. Then, click the Transform option in the option bar at the top of the diagram and select any of the options given, as shown in Figure 6.10.

Figure 6.10: Available transformations

A new node will appear in the diagram. Select the node, select the Node Properties tab, and from the Node Parent drop-down, choose any of the existing nodes. The transform will be applied immediately after the step you specified as parent of the node.

Apply Mapping

You must have noticed that there is a mapping step in the diagram. In our case it didn't do anything, in a sort of passthrough fashion. However, you could specify all sorts of mappings at that point of the ETL job. For example, you may want to rename a column or change its data type. To do so, click the mapping step in the diagram, which will bring up its properties on the right-hand pane. The Transform tab will contain the form shown in Figure 6.11.

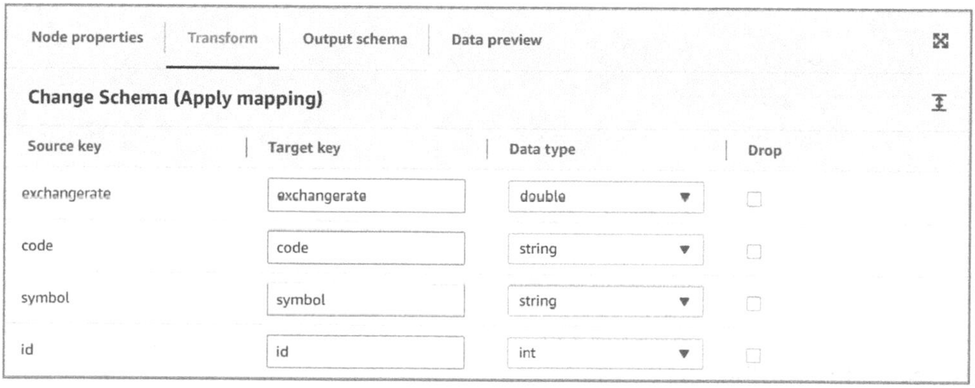

Node properties	Transform	Output schema	Data preview		⋈
Change Schema (Apply mapping)					⊥
Source key	Target key	Data type		Drop	
exchangerate	exchangerate	double ▼		☐	
code	code	string ▼		☐	
symbol	symbol	string ▼		☐	
id	id	int ▼		☐	

Figure 6.11: Mapping transformation

This process is very intuitive and allows you to apply basic transformations, including dropping a field if you don't feel it is needed.

Filter

The Filter transform allows you to keep records that comply with a set of rules. Let's add a Filter Transform to our ETL job by following the previous steps and then selecting the top ApplyMapping as the parent node for the Filter transform. At that point, the ApplyMapping node will have two "child" nodes, the original destination bucket and the filter. But we want the filter to be executed after the mapping. All we need to do is remove the ApplyMapping as parent of the bucket node and specify the filter as the new parent. Nodes can have multiple parent or child nodes, so selecting one node as parent does not automatically remove another one. You have to take care of doing that explicitly. Once you are finished with this, the diagram should look something like Figure 6.12.

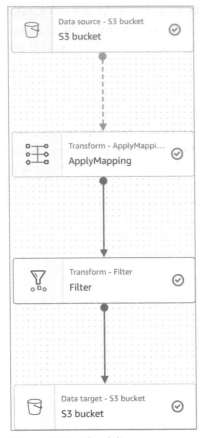

Figure 6.12: Edited diagram

At this point, however, our Filter transform does not do anything, so let's fix that. Let's assume you have a business rule whereby entries with userID 1 are considered bogus (maybe they're identified as spam, or banned users, or are test accounts), and therefore you don't want their posts processed and included in your analytics. Selecting the properties of the Filter node, you can create a rule that keeps all entries except for userIDs 1s, as shown in Figure 6.13.

Bear in mind that depending on how you construct the rules you will allow the records to be kept, rather than allowing them to be excluded, so when you filter your records with userIDs 1s, you need to specify that "if a userID does *not* have value 1, then it can be kept."

Other Available Transforms

There are plenty more transforms, all very intuitive, such as field renaming, dropping null values, filling null values with default values, unions, and aggregates. By and large all these ready-made transforms aim at resolving common

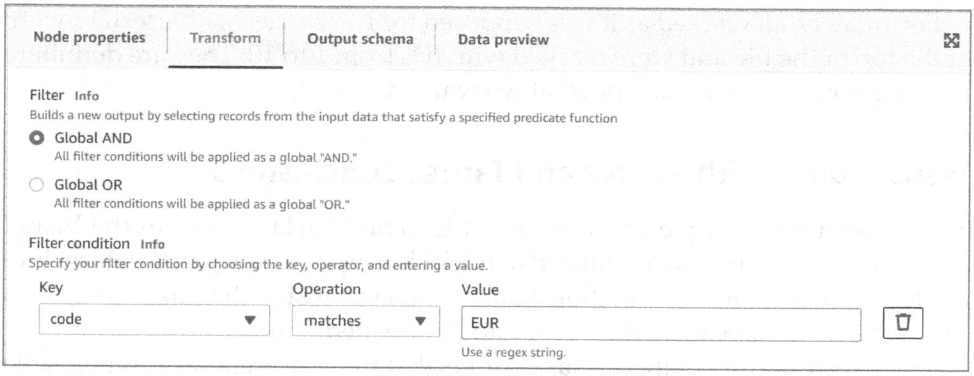

Figure 6.13: Node Properties

manipulation use cases. If you need something more complex, you will have to write it by hand. However, before you end up scrapping the Visual Editor, check out the Custom Transform option. You can create a transform in code and inject it into your diagram, which is a great last resort before having to dump the Visual Editor altogether and start writing code from scratch.

Run the Edited Job

Now that we've applied some changes, we can run the job again, taking care to reset the bookmark. Optionally you can run the looped `aws s3 sync` command I showed you earlier for real-time monitoring, and in another terminal you can follow the logs of the Glue job. If all goes well, you will see the file in your local directory, as shown in Figure 6.14.

```
joe@chaosdescends:~/wileybook/synced-dir$ while true; do aws s3 sync --delete s3://joes-test-parquetbucket .  && sleep 2; done
download: s3://joes-test-parquetbucket/export/run-S3bucket_node3-16-part-block-0-r-00000-snappy.parquet to export/run-S3bucket_node3-16-part-block-0-r-00000-snappy.parquet
```

Figure 6.14: Viewing local files

Note that the default compression is snappy, which is great because the smaller the objects on S3, the less money you pay for storage. Let's now take a look with parquet tools to verify that we have no entries with userID equal to 1 (shown in Figure 6.15).

```
joe@chaosdescends:~/wileybook/synced-dir$ parquet-tools show export/run-S3bucket_node3-16-part-block-0-r-00000-snappy.parquet
+--------------------------------------------------------------------+------------------------------------------------------+--------+----+
| body                                                               | title                                                | userid | id |
|--------------------------------------------------------------------+------------------------------------------------------+--------+----|
| delectus reiciendis molestiae occaecati non minima eveniet qui voluptatibus | et ea vero quia laudantium autem               |      2 | 11 |
| accusamus in eum beatae sit                                        |                                                      |        |    |
| vel qui neque voluptates ut commodi qui incidunt                   |                                                      |        |    |
| ut animi commodi                                                   |                                                      |        |    |
| itaque id aut magnam                                               | in quibusdam tempore odit est dolorem                |      2 | 12 |
| praesentium quia et ea odit et ea voluptas et                      |                                                      |        |    |
| sapiente quia nihil amet occaecati quia id voluptatem              |                                                      |        |    |
| incidunt ea est distinctio odio                                    |                                                      |        |    |
| aut dicta possimus sint mollitia voluptas commodi quo doloremque   | dolorum ut in voluptas mollitia et saepe quo animi   |      2 | 13 |
| iste corrupti reiciendis voluptatem eius rerum                     |                                                      |        |    |
| sit cumque quod eligendi laborum minima                            |                                                      |        |    |
| perferendis recusandae assumenda consectetur porro architecto ipsum ipsam |                                               |        |    |
| fuga et accusamus dolorum perferendis illo voluptas                | voluptatem eligendi optio                            |      2 | 14 |
| non doloremque neque facere                                        |                                                      |        |    |
```

Figure 6.15: Inspecting parquet

Fortunately, all worked as it was supposed to. The entries with userID 1 were at the top of the file and were marked with IDs from 1 to 10. They are definitely missing now, which is exactly what we wanted.

Visual Editor with Source and Target Conclusions

You've seen how simple and effective it is to build ETL jobs with the Visual Editor. In the example we simulated a quick cleanup of a raw JSON dataset into a filtered parquet one, completing a data engineering step that takes data from the raw/landing area of a data lake into the cleaned one.

One handy feature of the Visual Editor is that the code generated is available on the Script tab, so you can copy it and store it in your version control system of choice, such as GIT.

Creating ETL Jobs with AWS Glue Visual Editor (without Source and Target)

Frankly there is not much more to say about this option, other than the fact that you may want to specify a source that is not included in the drop-down options (it may require a connection to an API, for example). But even if that is your case, all of the knowledge you acquired here stands: a source of an ETL job will have child nodes but no parent ones, a target will have parent node(s) but no child ones, and the transforms in between can be added the same way you've seen in the previous section.

Creating ETL Jobs with the Spark Script Editor

When choosing to create ETL jobs with the Spark Script Editor, you can create Spark jobs with manually authored code. Glue gives you two options: start with some pregenerated boilerplate code or upload a local file. We will focus on the boilerplate option because if you are familiar with Spark and have developed an application locally that you can upload to AWS Glue, then it is safe to say you possess the necessary expertise and familiarity that this book aims to provide you with.

That said, the configuration options we have seen in the previous section are going to be the same, so you can retain and use that knowledge.

When you choose to create a script using the editor, the following code will be pregenerated and included in the editor:

```
import sys
from awsglue.transforms import *
from awsglue.utils import getResolvedOptions
```

```
from pyspark.context import SparkContext
from awsglue.context import GlueContext
from awsglue.job import Job

## @params: [JOB_NAME]
args = getResolvedOptions(sys.argv, ['JOB_NAME'])

sc = SparkContext()
glueContext = GlueContext(sc)
spark = glueContext.spark_session
job = Job(glueContext)
job.init(args['JOB_NAME'], args)
job.commit()
```

Your code will have to be placed between these two lines:

```
job.init(args['JOB_NAME'], args)
job.commit()
```

Once you have written your code, you can save the job and run it just like you did with the Visual Editor.

Although a handy option for those who are familiar with Spark and who may have developed scripts locally and intend to deploy them in AWS Glue, the Script Editor is not my first choice when it comes to Spark code development. Developing with the Script Editor means that—to test the correctness of your code—you need to run your job. Nowadays, startup times and execution times have been greatly reduced, even compared with just a few years back, but it is still a very slow development workflow when you take into account the time it takes to actually execute the job (which can be lengthy).

If you want to familiarize yourself with the AWS Glue Jobs API, to see the differences between it and Spark and to have a more trial-and-error approach, then notebooks are far more suited. I suggest developing with notebooks, and you may optionally deploy the code you developed in notebooks in a Script Editor job, using the local file upload facility.

Developing ETL Jobs with AWS Glue Notebooks

If you choose the option to create a job with a notebook, you will be presented with a code editor that should look very familiar if you're used to working with Jupyter Notebooks.

> **NOTE**   A notebook is a great idea for prototyping and experimental work, but it should never be considered a production job artifact. The aforementioned option of version-controlling the generated script is the way to go.

What Is a Notebook?

A notebook is a relatively recent evolution in code development that allows you to run code chunks as opposed to running an entire program. Why is this important? Because as you write code that works, you never have to rerun those parts of the code for your program to work. Take our simple ETL job that we created with the Visual Editor; it executes the following steps:

1. Load data from S3 in JSON format.
2. Map it.
3. Filter it.
4. Save it to S3 in parquet format.

Traditionally we'd write a program, probably make some mistake at some point, we'd have to hunt down that bug or mistake, and rerun the program to verify that it works as expected.

But with a notebook, we could split the job into four *cells* (that's the notebook terminology for chunks of code), run step 1, verify it works, move to step 2, stumble upon some problem, fix it, rerun, and move on to the next step. If at some point you find you have committed some kind of mistake at an earlier point in the code (e.g., you successfully loaded data, but maybe it was the wrong data to load), then you only need to rerun the code as far back as the changes you applied.

This approach is particularly useful in data science and engineering because some steps are cumbersome, resource intensive, lengthy, and generally better executed once. In our case it prevents us from having to wait for a long time for a Spark job to be executed, only to fail with some obscure message.

So let's take a look at the notebook's interface, which should clarify a lot.

Notebook Structure

When loading a notebook, you will be presented with what you see in Figure 6.16.

```
[*]:  import sys
      from awsglue.transforms import *
      from awsglue.utils import getResolvedOptions
      from pyspark.context import SparkContext
      from awsglue.context import GlueContext
      from awsglue.job import Job

      sc = SparkContext.getOrCreate()
      glueContext = GlueContext(sc)
      spark = glueContext.spark_session
      job = Job(glueContext)
```

Figure 6.16: What you see when you load a notebook

If you place the cursor in the text field containing the code (the cell) and either press Shift+Enter or click the Play button at the top of the interface, it will execute the code, which in Jupyter Notebook jargon is called *running the cell*. You will get an output similar to this:

```
Welcome to the Glue Interactive Sessions Kernel
For more information on available magic commands, please type %help in
any new cell.


Please view our Getting Started page to access the most up-to-date
information on the Interactive Sessions kernel:
https://docs.aws.amazon.com/glue/latest/dg/interactive-sessions.html
It looks like there is a newer version of the kernel available. The
latest version is 0.31 and you have 0.30 installed.
Please run `pip install—upgrade aws-glue-sessions` to upgrade
your kernel
Authenticating with environment variables and user-defined glue_role_
arn: arn:aws:iam::XXXXXXXXXXXXXX:role/joes-glue-notebook-role
Attempting to use existing AssumeRole session credentials.
Trying to create a Glue session for the kernel.
Worker Type: G.1X
Number of Workers: 5
Session ID: 9af39864-c7d2-4bf8-91dd-b5d8420b3e78
Applying the following default arguments:
—glue_kernel_version 0.30
—enable-glue-datacatalog true
Waiting for session 9af39864-c7d2-4bf8-91dd-b5d8420b3e78 to get into
ready status...
Session 9af39864-c7d2-4bf8-91dd-b5d8420b3e78 has been created
```

If you get this output, we're in business. If not, and you get an error message, then chances are you have not applied the correct permissions to the IAM role with which you are executing the notebook. For notebooks to run correctly, you need AWS Glue as a trusted entity, and `glue:CreateSession` and `iam:PassRole` permissions. As usual my advice is that you start with a very loose `glue:*` policy and restrict as you go—just don't forget to apply those restrictions!

Now we want to replicate our ETL job that we created with the Visual Editor, but this time we are going to use manually authored code.

> **NOTE**   I really like Spark, and I believe modern data engineering heavily depends on it and for good reason: it's a fast, scalable, user-friendly technology that simplifies the lives of those professionals involved in moving and transforming data, and ETL in general. We will go through some rather simple examples of ETL jobs written with PySpark, but Spark itself is a subject worth many books in its own right. So keep in mind our focus is on how Spark jobs fit into the data platform for analytics, not Spark code itself.

Step 1: Load Code into a *DynamicFrame*

`DataFrame` is a very familiar term for anyone who has worked with Spark or Pandas (the data manipulation library for Python). `DynamicFrame` is an AWS wrapper class of the underlying Spark `DataFrame` class aimed at resolving schema inconsistencies that are otherwise handled by defining fields with a type of `string` (in Spark), whereas `DynamicFrame` uses a `union` field that allows all types found in the data already loaded in memory. So aside from niche uses, `DynamicFrame` will be our class of reference.

The first step is to load data into a `DynamicFrame`, which is done by creating a `DynamicFrame` from the AWS Glue context of the ETL job. So create a cell and include the following code:

```
connection_type = "s3"
connection_options = {"paths": ["s3://joes-test-jsonbucket/"],
"recurse": True}
postsDF = glueContext.create_dynamic_frame_from_options(connection_type =
connection_type, connection_options = connection_options, format = "json")
postsDF.printSchema()
```

The magic here is performed by the `create_dynamic_frame_from_options` method of the Glue context, which needs to know the connection type (`s3`), the options (the S3 bucket and recursive read), and the format of the input (JSON). After this, we print the schema that was inferred:

```
root
|—userId: int
|—id: int
|—title: string
|—body: string
```

All looks good. Now let's say we want to apply basic mapping by capitalizing the fields and maybe changing that `id` into a more meaningful `PostID` and `body` to `Content`. We can do this by creating a mappings array, with each element of the array a four-element Python tuple with the following values (in order):

- The current name of the field
- Its current type
- The new name of the field
- Its new type

So our mappings will look something like this:

```
mappings = [("userId", "int", "UserID", "int"), ("id", "int", "PostID",
"int"), ("title", "string", "Title", "string"), ("body", "string",
"Content", "string")]
```

Step 2: Apply Field Mapping

Now, if you remember our Visual Editor job, we apply the mapping. For this we need a class from the `awsglue.transforms` module called `ApplyMappings`, which gets applied to a `DynamicFrame` with the `apply` method, like so:

```
mappedPostsDF = ApplyMapping.apply(frame = postsDF, mappings = mappings)
mappedPostsDF.printSchema()
```

which produces the following output:

```
root
|—UserID: int
|—PostID: int
|—Title: string
|—Content: string
```

If you want, you can use `show` to print a few records and verify everything is okay:

```
mappedPostsDF.show()
```

Here is the example output:

```
{"UserID": 1, "PostID": 2, "Title": "qui est esse", "Content": "est
rerum tempore vitae
sequi sint nihil reprehenderit dolor beatae ea dolores neque
fugiat blanditiis voluptate porro vel nihil molestiae ut reiciendis
qui aperiam non debitis possimus qui neque nisi nulla"}
```

So, the mapping was applied successfully. Now for the filtering.

Step 3: Apply the Filter

The idea of applying a filter is the same as with the mapping, so import the `Filter` class from `awsglue.transforms`, then apply it with the `apply` method.

To verify that our filtering works, let's take stock of how many posts we have in memory before we apply the filter:

```
mappedPostsDF.count()
99
```

Now let's import the filter:

```
from awsglue.transforms import Filter
```

Then create the `filter` function:

```
filter_func = lambda r: r["UserID"] not in [1, 3, 7]
```

Compared to the Visual Editor job, we pushed it up a notch and decided to exclude all posts by UserIDs 1, 3, and 7.

Now let's apply the filter:

```
filteredPostsDF = Filter.apply(frame = mappedPostsDF, f = filter_func,
transformation_ctx = "filteredPostsDF")
filteredPostsDF.count()
```

which returns the output

```
70
```

This makes sense because UserID 1 had posts with IDs 1–9, so in total we have lost 29 posts in the filtering.

Step 4: Write to S3 in Parquet Format

Now for the final step: we want to take the filter/mapped JSON input and save it as parquet in our destination bucket. This is not so different from the initial load that we performed in the script: instead of creating a `DynamicFrame`, we will be writing the `DynamicFrame` with the `write_dynamic_frame` method of the Glue context (which returns a `DynamicFrameWriter` class). We'll then call the `from_options` method on it, which specifies very similar details to the read (connection type, connection options, format, format options).

Let's see it in practice:

```
write_connection_type = "s3"
write_connection_options = {"path": "s3://joes-test-parquetbucket/
etlexport"}
write_format = "parquet"
write_format_options = {"compression": "snappy"}

write_operation = glueContext.write_dynamic_frame.from_options(
    frame = filteredPostsDF,
    connection_type = write_connection_type,
    connection_options = write_connection_options,
    format = write_format,
    format_options = write_format_options
)
```

Now, to verify that everything worked as expected, let's first check that a parquet file is there in the new subfolder `etlexport` of our parquet bucket. Then we download it, expecting to see that the first entries in the file belong to UserID 2, as we filtered UserID 1 out (see Figure 6.17).

And there you have it.

```
joe@chaosdescends:~$ aws s3 ls --recursive  s3://joes-test-parquetbucket/
2022-07-17 15:20:04     9664 etlexport/part-00000-415bc8df-7828-4b11-bf9c-f27501462685-c000.snappy.parquet
2022-07-17 15:19:58        8 etlexport_$folder$
2022-07-15 13:39:35    11489 export/run-53bucket_node3-16-part-block-0-r-00000-snappy.parquet
joe@chaosdescends:~$ aws s3 cp s3://joes-test-parquetbucket/etlexport/part-00000-415bc8df-7828-4b11-bf9c-f27501462685-c000.snappy.parquet test-write.snappy.parquet
download: s3://joes-test-parquetbucket/etlexport/part-00000-415bc8df-7828-4b11-bf9c-f27501462685-c000.snappy.parquet to ./test-write.snappy.parquet
joe@chaosdescends:~$ parquet-tools show test-write.snappy.parquet
```

Title	Content	UserID	PostID
et ea vero quia laudantium autem	delectus reiciendis molestiae occaecati non minima eveniet qui voluptatibus accusamus in eum beatae sit vel qui neque voluptates ut commodi qui incidunt ut animi commodi	2	11
in quibusdam tempore odit est dolorem	itaque id aut magnam praesentium quia et ea odit et ea voluptas et sapiente quia nihil amet occaecati quia id voluptatem incidunt ea est distinctio odio	2	12
dolorum ut in voluptas mollitia et saepe quo animi	aut dicta possimus sint mollitia voluptas commodi quo doloremque iste corrupti reiciendis voluptatem eius rerum	2	13

Figure 6.17: Verifying the first entries in the file

Example: Joining and Denormalizing Data from Two S3 Locations

Let's see an example in which we take nested data in JSON format from two different sources, join it, then flatten it to produce a denormalized representation of each record.

Let's assume we upload a file containing users' information, with one example record looking like this:

```
{
    "id": 10,
    "name": "Clementina DuBuque",
    "username": "Moriah.Stanton",
    "email": "Rey.Padberg@karina.biz",
    "address": {
      "street": "Kattie Turnpike",
      "suite": "Suite 198",
      "city": "Lebsackbury",
      "zipcode": "31428-2261",
      "geo": {
        "lat": "-38.2386",
        "lng": "57.2232"
      }
    },
    "phone": "024-648-3804",
    "website": "ambrose.net",
    "company": {
      "name": "Hoeger LLC",
      "catchPhrase": "Centralized empowering task-force",
      "bs": "target end-to-end models"
    }
}
```

And let's assume we want to join this dataset to the previous blog post dataset, using the id in the users JSON as the key to join to the userID in the posts JSON.

We will do this manually, so launch a Script Editor job, and after the initial boilerplate code, we are going to retrieve posts, retrieve users, join them, and flatten them.

Retrieving posts should look familiar:

```
postsDF = glueContext.create_dynamic_frame.from_options(
    connection_type = "s3",
    connection_options = {"paths": ["s3://joes-test-jsonbucket/"],
"recurse": True},
    format = "json"
)
postsDF.printSchema()
```

We print the schema, as it is relevant to our scenario:

```
root
|—userId: int
|—id: int
|—title: string
|—body: string
```

Then we retrieve the users' data:

```
employeesDF = glueContext.create_dynamic_frame.from_options(
    connection_type="s3",
    connection_options={"paths":["s3://joes-test-bucket-123456/
sampleusers/"], "recurse": "false"},
    format="json"
)
employeesDF.printSchema()
```

We also check the schema:

```
root
|—id: int
|—name: string
|—username: string
|—email: string
|—address: struct
|      |—street: string
|      |—suite: string
|      |—city: string
|      |—zipcode: string
|      |—geo: struct
|      |      |—lat: string
|      |      |—lng: string
|—phone: string
|—website: string
|      |—name: string
|      |—catchPhrase: string
|—company: struct
|      |—bs: string
```

Now we join them:

```
joinedDF = Join.apply(postsDF,employeesDF,"userId","id")
joinedDF.printSchema()
```

The arguments in order are `frame1`, `frame2`, `keys1`, and `keys2`. Keys can be an array of keys if you are joining on multiple fields.

The resulting schema looks as expected:

```
root
|—username: string
|—company: struct
|      |—name: string
|      |—catchPhrase: string
|      |—bs: string
|—address: struct
|      |—street: string
|      |—suite: string
|      |—city: string
|      |—zipcode: string
|      |—geo: struct
|      |      |—lat: string
|      |      |—lng: string
|—.id: int
|—body: string
|—name: string
|—userId: int
|—title: string
|—website: string
|—email: string
|—phone: string
|—id: int
```

A call to `joinedDF.show()` produces output with a sample record looking like this:

```
{
  "username": "Moriah.Stanton",
  "company": {
    "name": "Hoeger LLC",
    "catchPhrase": "Centralized empowering task-force",
    "bs": "target end-to-end models"
  },
  "address": {
    "street": "Kattie Turnpike",
    "suite": "Suite 198",
    "city": "Lebsackbury",
    "zipcode": "31428-2261",
    "geo": {
      "lat": "-38.2386",
      "lng": "57.2232"
    }
```

```
    },
    ".id": 91,
    "body": "libero voluptate eveniet aperiam sedsunt placeat suscipit
molestias similique fugit nam natusexpedita consequatur consequatur
dolores quia eos et placeat",
    "name": "Clementina DuBuque",
    "title": "aut amet sed",
    "userId": 10,
    "email": "Rey.Padberg@karina.biz",
    "website": "ambrose.net",
    "id": 10,
    "phone": "024-648-3804"
}
```

So far so good! All the details from both datasets are included in every record. However, this is not very parquet, CSV, or Redshift friendly. Let's flatten it using this:

```
unnestDF = UnnestFrame.apply(joinedDF)
unnestDF.printSchema()
```

which produces the following schema:

```
root
|—username: string
|—company.name: string
|—company.catchPhrase: string
|—company.bs: string
|—address.street: string
|—address.suite: string
|—address.city: string
|—address.zipcode: string
|—address.geo.lat: string
|—address.geo.lng: string
|—.id: int
|—body: string
|—name: string
|—userId: int
|—title: string
|—website: string
|—email: string
|—phone: string
|—id: int
```

As you can see, the `UnnestFrame` transform has taken every nested field and flattened it using a dot notation.

From here, you can store the data where it suits your use case, be it S3, Redshift, or a relational database.

Conclusions for Manually Authored Jobs with Notebooks

Notebooks are a very handy tool that allows you to focus on problematic code areas, something that is of particular value in data engineering when startup and execution times of lengthy and heavy operations can turn development into a tedious and frustratingly slow experience.

But no more. Look at the image in Figure 6.18 of the notebook we just developed. Each of those blocks is an independently executable piece of code that can be edited to resolve problems and continue with development.

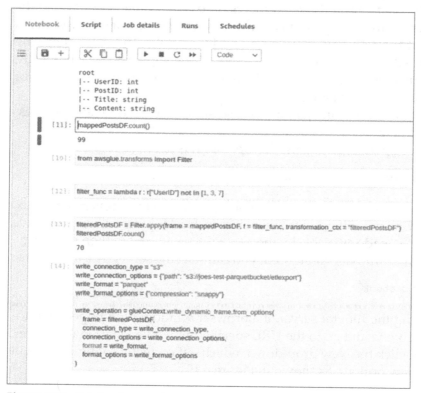

Figure 6.18: Notebook example

Once you are finished developing a notebook, you can then download the code and use it for deployment in a standard ETL job.

The basic syntax highlighting also makes the job a bit easier, and later you will see how Jupyter Notebooks in Amazon SageMaker even support autocompletion.

While Visual Editor jobs are extremely easy to develop and deploy, the UI to create a filter (for example) is actually a more complex experience than writing that one-liner Lambda shown in Figure 6.18. So in real life, if the job goes beyond simple and straightforward processing, I tend to write the code myself as opposed to using the Visual Editor.

That said, the Visual Editor is incredibly useful as a boilerplate generator, so I often find myself creating a job with the Visual Editor and then editing the code.

> **NOTE** When you manually edit the code of a Visual Editor job, you permanently turn that job into a Script Editor job.

Creating ETL Jobs with AWS Glue Interactive Sessions

Another incredibly useful tool that AWS Glue has made available to its users is *interactive sessions*. Even those engineers used to a remote workflow in the end always crave the ability to run code locally, with instantaneous results, in the comfort of their favorite tools, such as editors, IDEs, and even operating systems. Interactive sessions retain the benefit of developing Spark jobs locally, but make your notebook code on AWS Glue's resources, which is a superior benefit in terms of performance.

The prerequisites for running interactive sessions and the installation process are illustrated here:

For all major operating systems, this operation is needed:

```
pip3 install—upgrade jupyter boto3 aws-glue-sessions
```

From this point on, instructions for the setup of interactive sessions on Linux, macOS, and Windows differ, but the point is to instruct Jupyter on how to include the new kernels made available by the `aws-glue-sessions` Python package.

When you have Jupyter configured, you can start the server by running this:

```
$ jupyter notebook
```

After starting the Jupyter server, if a browser window hasn't opened automatically, open one and go to the URL specified when you started the server. Then you can click the New drop-down, which—if correctly configured—will include two new options, as shown in Figure 6.19.

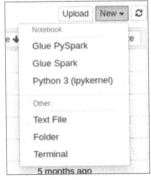

Figure 6.19: Available kernels

Choosing PySpark will start a new interactive session.

It's Magic

Well, more specifically, *magics*. *Magics* are a series of directives that you can include in your notebook that will perform special operations, shown in Table 6.1. One such operation is the `%iam_role` magic, which will specify the IAM role used during the interactive session. This is very important to specify, and when you do, make sure that Glue is a trusted entity of that role and that you have an identity-based policy that specifies `glue:CreateSession` on it.

Table 6.1: The magics available in AWS Glue

MAGIC	TYPE	DESCRIPTION
`%%configure`	Dictionary	A JSON-formatted dictionary consisting of all configuration parameters for a session. Each parameter can be specified here or through individual magics.
`%profile`	String	Specify a profile in your AWS configuration to use as the credentials provider.
`%iam_role`	String	Specify an IAM role to execute your session with.
`%region`	String	Specify the AWS region in which to initialize a session.
`%session_id`	String	Returns the session ID for the running session.
`%connections`	List	Specify a comma-separated list of connections to use in the session.
`%additional_python_modules`	List	Comma-separated list of PIP packages, S3 paths, or private PIP arguments.
`%extra_py_files`	List	Comma-separated list of additional Python files from S3.
`%extra_jars`	List	Comma-separated list of additional JARs to include in the cluster.
`%number_of_workers`	Integer	The number of workers of a defined `worker_type` that are allocated when a job runs. `worker_type` must be set, too.
`%worker_type`	String	Standard, G.1X, *or* G.2X. `number_of_workers` must be set, too. Default is G.1X.

Continues

Table 6.1 (*continued*)

MAGIC	TYPE	DESCRIPTION
`%glue_version`	String	The version of Glue to be used by this session. Currently, the only valid options are 2.0 and 3.0.
`%security_configuration`	String	Define a security configuration to be used with this session.
`%sql`	String	Run SQL code. All lines after the initial `%%sql magic` will be passed as part of the SQL code.
`%streaming`	String	Changes the session type to Glue Streaming.
`%etl`	String	Changes the session type to Glue ETL.
`%status`		Returns the status of the current Glue session, including its duration, configuration, and executing user/role.
`%stop_session`		Stops the current session.
`%list_sessions`		Lists all currently running sessions by name and ID.

As you can see, you have plenty of configuration options, such as what profile to use, or what kind of worker type and how many of them. The IAM role and region magics can be configured through local AWS credentials the same way you would configure your AWS CLI or SAM CLI tools.

Development Workflow

At this point, you are free to create ETL jobs the same way you did with notebooks, with the added benefit that local Jupyter Notebooks also support autocomplete and you are not limited to the Jupyter interface (which is absolutely fine) but you can use tools such as Visual Studio Code, Vim, or your favorite code editor and development environment. For reference, the interactive session will look more or less like Figure 6.20.

```
import sys
from awsglue.transforms import *
from awsglue.utils import getResolvedOptions
from pyspark.context import SparkContext
from awsglue.context import GlueContext
from awsglue.job import Job

sc = SparkContext.getOrCreate()
glueContext = GlueContext(sc)
spark = glueContext.spark_session
job = Job(glueContext)

Welcome to the Glue Interactive Sessions Kernel
For more information on available magic commands, please type %help in any new cell.

Please view our Getting Started page to access the most up-to-date information on the Interactive Sessions kernel: https://docs.aws.amazon.co
m/glue/latest/dg/interactive-sessions.html
It looks like there is a newer version of the kernel available. The latest version is 0.31 and you have 0.30 installed.
Please run `pip install --upgrade aws-glue-sessions` to upgrade your kernel
Authenticating with environment variables and user-defined glue_role_arn: arn:aws:iam::972520707061:role/joes-glue-notebook-role
Attempting to use existing AssumeRole session credentials.
Trying to create a Glue session for the kernel.
Worker Type: G.1X
Number of Workers: 5
Session ID: 003688dd-b3b0-4098-86a2-b5083c797a04
Applying the following default arguments:
--glue kernel version 0.30
--enable-glue-datacatalog true
Waiting for session 003688dd-b3b0-4098-86a2-b5083c797a04 to get into ready status...
Session 003688dd-b3b0-4098-86a2-b5083c797a04 has been created
```

Figure 6.20: Interactive sessions in a notebook

Note the necessary IAM magic statement at the top (if you haven't configured a role in the credentials) and the session being created remotely from your local Jupyter Notebook.

Streaming Jobs

ETL jobs are a vital part of your data engineering pipelines. However, up until this point we have taken cold data and processed it, and this may not always be the optimal approach. Data may be coming in from a streaming source, such as a Kinesis data stream or a Kafka topic. This incoming data may need the same kind of processing you applied in classic ETL jobs, but its ingestion and manipulation are different. With AWS Glue you receive records in batches, define a processing function, and apply that to all the batches that are received.

As you may know, Spark is somewhat simulating stream processing by working on micro batches, as opposed to true stream-processing tools such as Apache Flink that process each record received individually in real time. For this reason, you need to be aware that working in small batches means introducing a bit of latency between when the original data was published on a streaming channel and when it gets processed. This may work well in the majority of scenarios, but if you are in need of real-time processing (such as video data or chat messages), you will have to opt for true stream processing.

But in the context of building a data platform for analytics in a business, real time is almost never a requirement, as daily, weekly, or even monthly frequency of data refresh for Insights is common practice. Therefore, a few minutes between data being published and being processed is normally acceptable.

Differences with a Standard ETL Job

At a high level, a standard ETL job follows this algorithm:

LOAD data FROM source

PROCESS data

STORE data INTO target

A streaming job is essentially the same thing, except the PROCESS step only applies to the current batch of records being processed as opposed to the entire set of data loaded at the start of an ETL job. At the AWS Glue level, the difference is that in the job details you can switch from ETL to Streaming.

Other than these two major differences, nothing else changes.

Streaming Sources

AWS Glue streaming jobs support a number of sources. Kafka, MSK (AWS's own fully managed Kafka offering), and Kinesis are a few. Data published on one of these streaming channels (Kinesis streams or Kafka topics) can be processed by a streaming job.

Example: Process Kinesis Streams with a Streaming Job

Let's take a look at a standard scenario, fully based on AWS technology. We will publish data on a Kinesis stream and process it with an AWS Glue job. Let's first create a Kinesis data stream, then a streaming job that processes data in small batches. The Web Console form to create a basic data stream is extremely simple (see Figure 6.21).

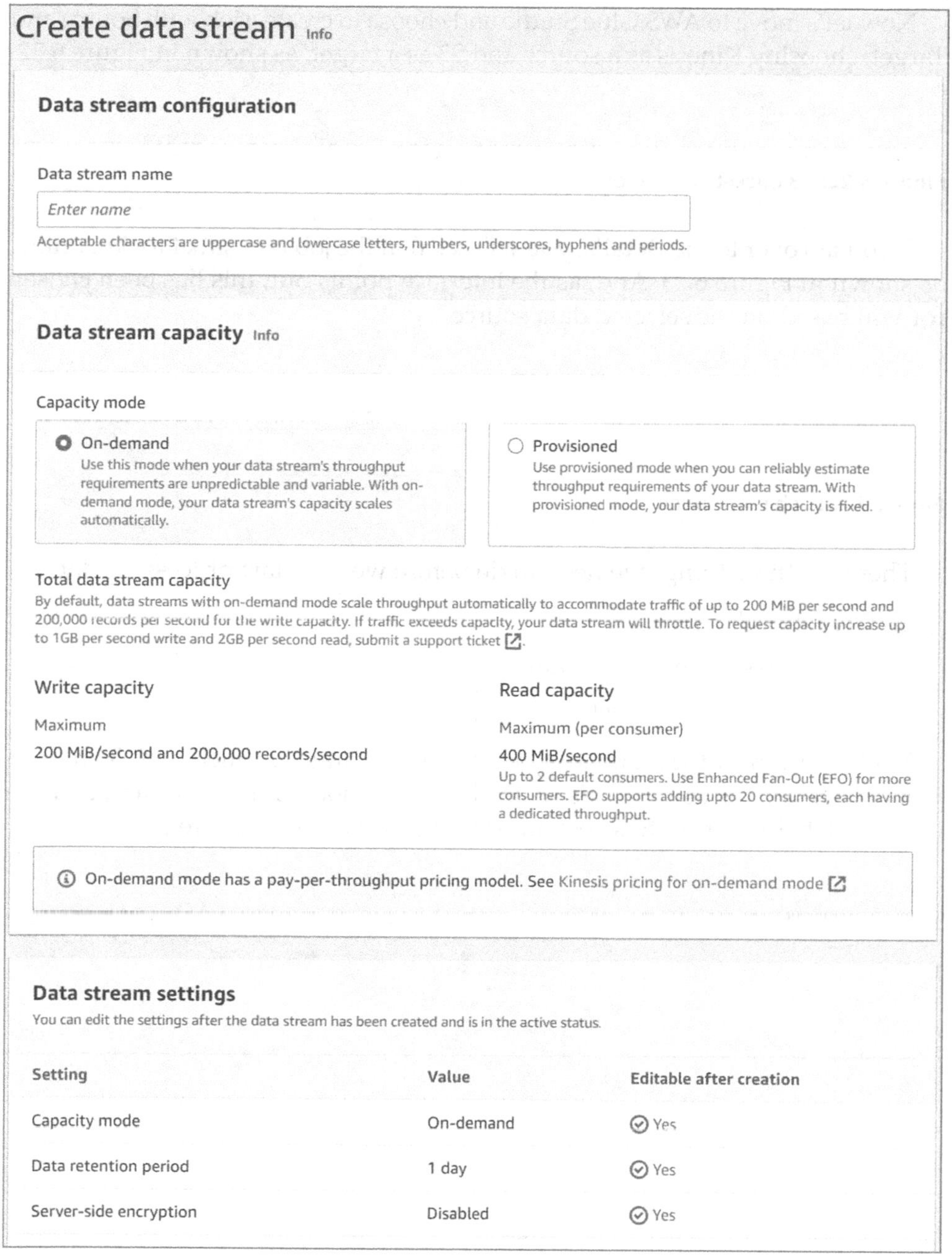

Create data stream Info

Data stream configuration

Data stream name

```
Enter name
```

Acceptable characters are uppercase and lowercase letters, numbers, underscores, hyphens and periods.

Data stream capacity Info

Capacity mode

⦿ **On-demand**
Use this mode when your data stream's throughput requirements are unpredictable and variable. With on-demand mode, your data stream's capacity scales automatically.

◯ **Provisioned**
Use provisioned mode when you can reliably estimate throughput requirements of your data stream. With provisioned mode, your data stream's capacity is fixed.

Total data stream capacity

By default, data streams with on-demand mode scale throughput automatically to accommodate traffic of up to 200 MiB per second and 200,000 records per second for the write capacity. If traffic exceeds capacity, your data stream will throttle. To request capacity increase up to 1GB per second write and 2GB per second read, submit a support ticket 🔗.

Write capacity

Maximum

200 MiB/second and 200,000 records/second

Read capacity

Maximum (per consumer)

400 MiB/second
Up to 2 default consumers. Use Enhanced Fan-Out (EFO) for more consumers. EFO supports adding upto 20 consumers, each having a dedicated throughput.

ⓘ On-demand mode has a pay-per-throughput pricing model. See Kinesis pricing for on-demand mode 🔗

Data stream settings

You can edit the settings after the data stream has been created and is in the active status.

Setting	Value	Editable after creation
Capacity mode	On-demand	✓ Yes
Data retention period	1 day	✓ Yes
Server-side encryption	Disabled	✓ Yes

Figure 6.21: Kinesis Create Data Stream

If you want to keep all the defaults (which is okay for testing out a Kinesis stream), you are only required to give the stream a unique name. The stream creation takes a few seconds.

Now let's move to AWS Glue Studio and choose to create a job with Source and Target, choosing Kinesis as a source and S3 as a target, as shown in Figure 6.22.

Figure 6.22: S3 bucket exploration

If you tab over to Job Details, you will see that the job type is set to Streaming, as shown in Figure 6.23. And, as the interface points out, this has been chosen for you based on the selected data source.

Figure 6.23: Job type option

There are three things we need to do before we can start processing data:

1. Give the job a name.
2. Select the source data stream.
3. Select the target S3 bucket.

You've seen how to rename the job from the default "Untitled Job" (in the Job Details). As for the source, let's select the source node in the diagram, and tab over to Data Properties to select our stream, as shown in Figure 6.24.

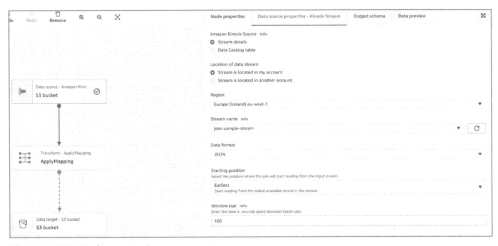

Figure 6.24: Node properties

And we do the same for the target bucket. Notice that I left the format as uncompressed JSON (Figure 6.25).

Figure 6.25: Target node properties

Before saving, remove the `ApplyMapping` node since it's not supported for Kinesis (it is if you write the code for it—you'll see this later). Now save the job.

If we now click Run, we can test that the processing works by publishing some data on Kinesis and seeing it being stored in S3 (as shown in Figure 6.26).

Figure 6.26: Seeing data stored in S3

I find the easiest way to publish records is using AWS CLI:

```
$ aws kinesis put-record –stream-name joes-sample-stream –partition-
key userId
–data <base64-encoded data>
```

Notice that I used `userId` as a partition key because I'm using the JSON placeholder data we used in previous examples, and `userId` is a good field for partitioning.

Now if we check in S3, we should be able to see entries coming from the streaming job:

```
$ aws s3 ls–recursive s3://joes-test-bucket-123456/stream-processing/
2022-07-27 11:10:08          0 stream-
processing/ingest_year=2022/ingest_month=07/ingest_day=27/
ingest_hour=11/run-1658920205704-part-r-00000
2022-07-27 11:10:08          0 stream-
processing/ingest_year=2022/ingest_month=07/ingest_day=27/
ingest_hour=11/run-1658920205704-part-r-00001
2022-07-27 11:10:08       6930 stream-
processing/ingest_year=2022/ingest_month=07/ingest_day=27/
ingest_hour=11/run-1658920205704-part-r-00002
2022-07-27 11:10:08          0 stream-
processing/ingest_year=2022/ingest_month=07/ingest_day=27/
ingest_hour=11/run-1658920205704-part-r-00003
```

Great! Not only did the job store the data, but it also used the hive partitioning pattern, which is going to be very handy for analytics later on.

You will notice that there are numbers before the names of the objects being listed, and as you may recall from earlier chapters, this is the size of the object itself. Some of them are 0s, meaning the objects are empty, but one of them has size 6930. If you want to check the content of an object, always make sure you are not trying to download and open something empty—it is not dangerous; it's just a waste of time.

Sure enough, when you go to download the object, it has the exact content of the data we posted.

Let's now make this a little more complex, by adding a processing step to it, and doing it in an interactive session. We will keep the Kinesis stream we have created to publish data.

The next step is to create a table in the AWS Glue Data Catalog and set Kinesis as a source. This step is necessary so that we can define the schema of the incoming data in Kinesis.

> **NOTE** The AWS Glue Data Catalog is a very important concept that is going to be extensively explored in the next chapter. Simply follow the instructions for now—you will better understand the role of it soon enough.

So in the AWS Glue console, go to Database and add a new database (this is trivial—just give it a name), so we don't add tables to production databases. Then click Tables and select Add Tables ➤ Manually. You will be prompted with a wizard consisting of several steps. The first one asks you to assign the table's name and the database it will be stored in (Figure 6.27).

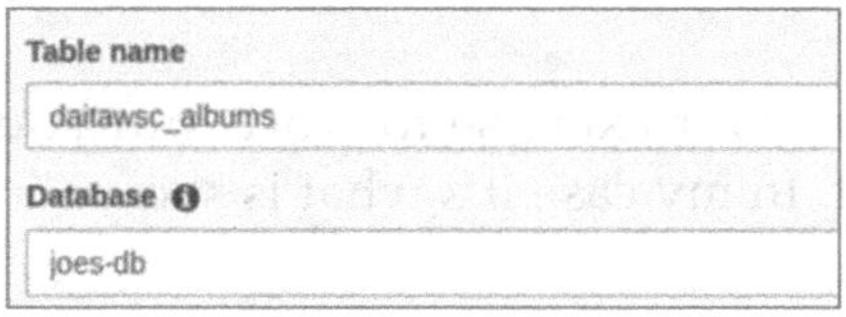

Table name

daitawsc_albums

Database ❶

joes-db

Figure 6.27: Table and database selection

The second step is to add the data store, which is where we set Kinesis as the source and specify the Kinesis stream (Figure 6.28).

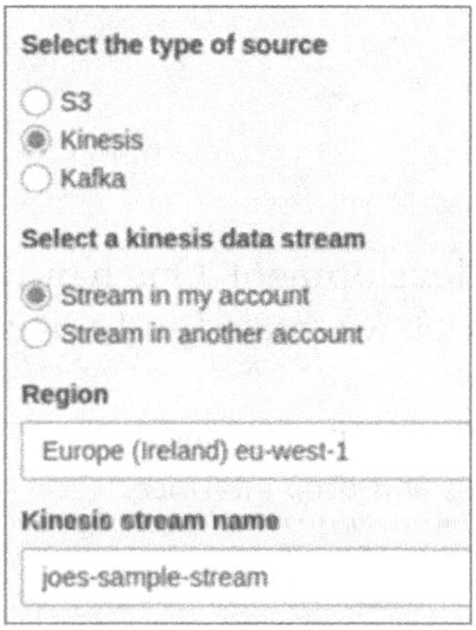

Select the type of source

○ S3
◉ Kinesis
○ Kafka

Select a kinesis data stream

◉ Stream in my account
○ Stream in another account

Region

Europe (Ireland) eu-west-1

Kinesis stream name

joes-sample-stream

Figure 6.28: Setting Kinesis as the source

Then we have to specify the format of the data, in our case JSON (Figure 6.29).

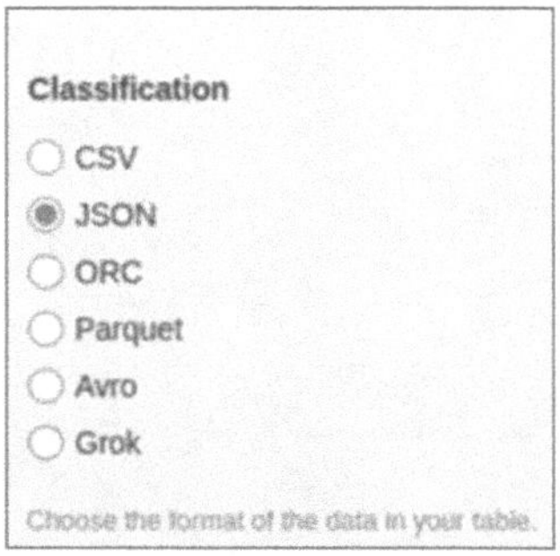

Classification

○ CSV
◉ JSON
○ ORC
○ Parquet
○ Avro
○ Grok

Choose the format of the data in your table.

Figure 6.29: File format selection

After that, we have to specify the schema. In our case, a single JSON item looks like this:

```
{
"userId": 1,
"id": 1,
"title": "quidem molestiae enim"
}
```

You can use whatever data you want for your exercise to work, but you will have to specify a schema that reflects it. In my case it's what is shown in Figure 6.30.

	Column name	Data type
1	userId	int
2	id	int
3	title	string

Figure 6.30: Sample schema

And that's it! You can complete the table creation.

Now we want to proceed with the streaming job development. One handy option we can adopt is to go into the script of the visual job we created and edit it.

> **NOTE** As previously mentioned, once you edit a script the job is permanently changed into a Script Editor job; you cannot go back to a drag-and-drop interface. Fortunately, the Web Console warns you of this fact.

In real life, you will always be working with development, staging, and production resources, so you need not worry. While you are developing a script, use a test S3 bucket (or target resource) to verify that your work is correctly behaving, and you can switch resources through job parameters.

Let's now take a look at the job's code:

```
import sys
from awsglue.transforms import *
from awsglue.utils import getResolvedOptions
from pyspark.context import SparkContext
from awsglue.context import GlueContext
from awsglue.job import Job

from pyspark.sql import DataFrame, Row
import datetime
from awsglue import DynamicFrame
```

```
args = getResolvedOptions(sys.argv, ["JOB_NAME"])
sc = SparkContext()
glueContext = GlueContext(sc)
spark = glueContext.spark_session
job = Job(glueContext)
job.init(args["JOB_NAME"], args)

dataframe_KinesisStream_node1 = glueContext.create_data_frame.
from_catalog(
    database="joes-db",
    table_name="daitawsc_albums",
    transformation_ctx="dataframe_KinesisStream_node1",
    additional_options={"startingPosition":"TRIM_HORIZON",
"inferSchema":"true"}
)

def processBatch(data_frame, batchId):
    if data_frame.count() > 0:
        KinesisStream_dyf = DynamicFrame.fromDF(
            data_frame, glueContext, "from_data_frame"
        )
        now = datetime.datetime.now()
        year = now.year
        month = now.month
        day = now.day
        hour = now.hour

        KinesisStream_dyf.printSchema()

        # Script generated for node S3 bucket
        S3bucket_node3_path = (
            "s3://joes-test-bucket-123456/stream-processing"
            + "/ingest_year="
            + "{:0>4}".format(str(year))
            + "/ingest_month="
            + "{:0>2}".format(str(month))
            + "/ingest_day="
            + "{:0>2}".format(str(day))
            + "/ingest_hour="
            + "{:0>2}".format(str(hour))
            + "/"
        )

        S3bucket_node3 = glueContext.write_dynamic_frame.from_options(
            frame=KinesisStream_dyf,
            connection_type="s3",
            format="json",
            connection_options={"path": S3bucket_node3_path,
"partitionKeys": []},
            transformation_ctx="S3bucket_node3",
        )
```

```
glueContext.forEachBatch(
    frame=dataframe_KinesisStream_node1,
    batch_function=processBatch,
    options={
        "windowSize": "100 seconds",
        "checkpointLocation": args["TempDir"] + "/" + args["JOB_NAME"] +
"/checkpoint/",
    },
)
job.commit()
```

As you may have already guessed, the biggest difference between an ETL and a streaming job is in the `forEachBatch` invocation at the end of the script, which applies the batch processing function (`processBatch`) to each batch.

As for the way we ingest data, you can see how the dynamic frame for ingestion is created through the `from_catalog` method, in which we specify the database and the table we created in the Glue Catalog at the beginning of this exercise.

Now—to ensure our job works correctly—we publish some data on our Kinesis stream and it should appear in the destination bucket we indicated in the job, correctly partitioned with the Hive pattern `ingest_*="` we see in the `glueContext.write_dynamic_frame.from_options` call.

If all goes well, you will be able to see objects appearing in the S3 bucket, which I monitor with a simple inline Bash script illustrated earlier:

```
$ while true; do aws s3 ls –recursive s3://<my-s3-bucket>/<my-prefix> &&
sleep 5;
done
```

For me, the operation produced the following output:

```
2022-07-28 13:46:15          0 stream-
processing/ingest_year=2022/ingest_month=07/ingest_day=28/
ingest_hour=13/run-1659015974104-part-r-00003
2022-07-28 13:46:22          0 stream-
processing/ingest_year=2022/ingest_month=07/ingest_day=28/
ingest_hour=13/run-1659015981582-part-r-00000
2022-07-28 13:46:22          0 stream-
processing/ingest_year=2022/ingest_month=07/ingest_day=28/
ingest_hour=13/run-1659015981582-part-r-00001
2022-07-28 13:46:22       6930 stream-
processing/ingest_year=2022/ingest_month=07/ingest_day=28/
ingest_hour=13/run-1659015981582-part-r-00002
2022-07-28 13:46:22          0 stream-
processing/ingest_year=2022/ingest_month=07/ingest_day=28/
ingest_hour=13/run-1659015981582-part-r-00003
```

which goes to indicate that one of the objects has content that, when downloaded, reveals exactly what we expected.

Streaming ETL Jobs Conclusions

All in all, there is not much of a difference between an ETL job running on a schedule and a streaming job, especially when you consider the fact that Spark streaming is not "true" streaming, but more simulated streaming through processing of micro batches.

All of the transforms and manipulations we saw in the standard ETL jobs are applicable. They just have to be included in the `processBatch` function.

Summary

In this chapter we have explored a number of ways in which you can perform data processing for the purpose of cleaning up raw data and then curating it to create a dataset specifically aimed at producing some specific piece of analytics or insight. At the core of processing is the idea of ETL (extract, transform, load), which consists of taking data from a source, validating it, filtering it, manipulating it, and then storing it into a separate location. In AWS-land, the tool of choice for ETL is AWS Glue, which is responsible not only for creating and monitoring ETL jobs but also for creating and maintaining connections, notebooks, and other useful tools like crawlers, which help automate the population of the AWS Glue Data Catalog. In the next chapter we will explore the Data Catalog in detail and learn to analyze the data we have so far ingested and curated.

CHAPTER

7

Cataloging, Governance, and Search

In this chapter, you'll learn how to discover data, regulate access, and query it. You'll learn about the vital role a data catalog plays in the construction of a data platform and how to catalog your datasets for the purpose of specifying schemas. We'll discuss tagging and granting access to data as well as performing queries that allow you to build datasets for your data consumers and clients, including business intelligence (BI) tools. We'll be working with AWS Glue and Amazon Athena in this chapter.

Cataloging with AWS Glue

Cataloging data is a vital process for the automated data platform. Without it, ingestion, processing, and analytics are entirely useless, as your data is not made available to query engines to perform analytics. Let's explore tools and techniques to catalog data in AWS.

AWS Glue and the AWS Glue Data Catalog

We have explored some of the features of AWS Glue, but in this chapter, we will clarify in detail the role that AWS Glue has in an AWS-based data lake architecture. AWS Glue is called that because it glues together several parts of the architecture, enabling them to work together seamlessly.

At a high level, AWS Glue:

- Allows you to process data
- Allows you to catalog data
- Enables cross-tool communication and integration via schema definition

The AWS Data Catalog is a pivotal point of the data lake architecture, and it performs vital functions such as the following:

- Storing databases and tables
- Storing crawlers and classifiers
- Storing connections
- Working as a schema registry

Let's explore these in detail.

Glue Databases and Tables

Databases in AWS Glue are a concept similar to what you are probably used to in standard relational databases, where you store groups of tables that belong together in the same database.

This is not just semantics; different databases can be associated to different locations in your data lake and their access can be limited to specific users. A governance tool called Lake Formation allows you to specify these permissions and govern your data in compliance with your business's policies.

Databases

So how do you create a database and the tables within it? In the previous chapter we have seen how this can be done with the Web Console, by navigating to AWS Glue, clicking Databases, and creating a database.

You can also use the AWS CLI. For example:

```
$ aws glue create-database --database-input "{\Name\":
\"joes-glue-sample-db\",
 \"Description\": \"joes sample glue db created with the aws cli\"}"
```

As of this writing, this is the full set of options you can pass into the command; however, bear in mind these can change:

```
{
        "Name": "string",
        "Description": "string",
        "LocationUri": "string",
        "Parameters": {"string": "string"
```

```
          ...},
        "CreateTableDefaultPermissions": [
          {
            "Principal": {
              "DataLakePrincipalIdentifier": "string"
            },
            "Permissions":
["ALL"|"SELECT"|"ALTER"|"DROP"|"DELETE"|"INSERT"|"CREATE_DATABASE"|
"CREATE_TABLE"|"DATA_LOCATION_ACCESS", ...]
          }
          ...
        ],
        "TargetDatabase": {
          "CatalogId": "string",
          "DatabaseName": "string"
        }
      }
```

All the parameters are actually optional except for the name (you have to name the database).

In the previous chapter I created the `joes-db` database, so I will continue working on that.

The Idea of Schema-on-Read

Tables in AWS Glue are schema definitions. This sounds like a simple definition, but it is in fact a significant departure from the implementation of tables in standard relational databases; in RDBS systems, tables define the schema and also apply constraints to the data that is being stored. If you have a `users` table with the fields

```
ID (int) | NAME (varchar) | AGE (int)
```

you will not be able to store a record with an additional field ADDRESS in it or try to store `forty two years old` as the value for the AGE field. Tables are strict definitions that cannot be broken, not at store time and not at read time.

But when it comes to big data and analytics, the quantity and diversity of the data stored makes this approach far too restrictive and unmaintainable. Imagine storing petabytes of data and having to apply a field change—it sounds like the data engineer's idea of a night terror.

Instead, in recent times, the idea of *schema-on-read* was developed, which is simply the decoupling of the data and the schema. The schema definition is never applied to the data being stored (in most cases, from a practical perspective, this would not make sense, as you are simply storing objects in S3 and there is no schema to adhere to) and is only applied to the data being read at query time. This approach not only makes data lake maintenance much easier but also makes analytics far more agile and flexible. It also allows a different interpretation of the same raw data.

Let's look at an example. Let's say you stored a CSV file in S3 that has the following data in it:

```
ID,NAME,AGE,EMAIL,COUNTRY,USERNAME
1,"joe",47,"joe@example.com","Ireland","joe"
2,"jill",52,"jill@example.com","USA","jill"
```

Because we apply schema-on-read operations, we can have a lot of schema permutations applicable to this raw dataset. Here are some examples:

```
ID int, NAME string, AGE int
NAME string, COUNTRY string, USERNAME string
ID int, EMAIL string, AGE int
```

The hawk-eyed reader might be wondering how it is possible for a query engine to correctly discern fields (some of the example schemas are "skipping" fields compared to the original dataset), and the last example even switches the order of fields in the schema as they are found in the raw file.

And you would be right in thinking this is more work for the query engine, but this is analytics and we are not interested in millisecond performance differences, although performance does have a role, which we will explain soon. To answer the question, query engines have to perform a lot of preliminary scans before they can apply schemas, so some formats are more suited than others for this kind of analytical work.

The format in which you store data impacts performance greatly, which is why columnar formats such as Apache Parquet perform better, especially considering that each page of data in parquet is described in detail by its metadata. Also, the compression algorithm you choose is very important as it has cost and performance implications, as illustrated here: `https://docs.aws.amazon.com/athena/latest/ug/compression-formats.html`. "Skipping" columns in Parquet is not an issue, as the entire block storing a certain field can be skipped.

CSV has the great advantage of being human readable, but it is not ideal for querying, which is why we tend to find it a lot in raw/landing areas of data lakes but rarely beyond that (unless it's used as machine learning training data).

Bearing in mind that schema-on-read is the approach taken by AWS's main analytical engine (Amazon Athena), we can move on to defining tables for our data.

Tables

Tables in AWS Glue are a resource like everything else, so we can create them with the Web Console, AWS CLI, or CloudFormation.

There are three ways of adding tables in the console: manually defining the schema, with a crawler, or from an existing schema.

Create Table Manually

When creating a table in the Glue Console, you will always have to specify what database it belongs to. After that, you need to establish a source, which can be S3, Kafka, or Kinesis. This is to indicate that we are applying schema-on-read to data that is already stored in our data lake (in S3) or is incoming through a streaming platform, either Kinesis or Kafka.

In this example I'm going to add a table that uses an example bucket already used in previous scenarios, as shown in Figure 7.1.

Next is the data format. This is important because it determines the parsers that are going to try to decipher the data contained in your source. Needless to say, if you specify the wrong format you will incur errors when trying to query the data. The choices are Avro, JSON, XML, Parquet, CSV, and ORC. Another derivative aspect to this initial choice is that it immediately makes you aware of the fact that you have to commit to similar formats in data lake locations. A data lake by nature can contain any kind of information in any format, but mixing plain text, JSON, CSV, and Parquet is not good practice, and inevitably you will experience problems.

The only file I have in this bucket is the output of a JSON Placeholder REST call for the Posts resource, which has this structure:

```
id int, userId int, title string, body string
```

So I will replicate that in Glue, as shown in Figure 7.2.

Next up is partitioning. I don't have partitions in this case, but you could create them by using key prefixes as we have seen on numerous occasions already in Chapter 5, "Data Ingestion."

For example, you could have posts stored by data and have partitions such as year, month, day, and hour (which is the default partitioning schema applied by Kinesis Firehose when delivering to target stores).

There are two "syntaxes" to do so: the AWS/Kinesis way is to prefix the S3 objects with the values separated by slashes, so for our date partitioning we would structure the S3 key like so:

```
2022/08/01/13/posts.json
```

When defining partitions, you can specify year, month, day, and hour.
The Hive syntax for partitioning is more explicit; it looks like the following:

```
year=2022/month=08/day=01/hour=13
```

When performing automatic detection of partitions, this results in the partitions being called the terms you supplied as opposed to the automatic Partition 0, Partition 1, etc., which would be the output of automatic partition detection for the first type of syntax. In our case we don't have partitions, so we skip that part.

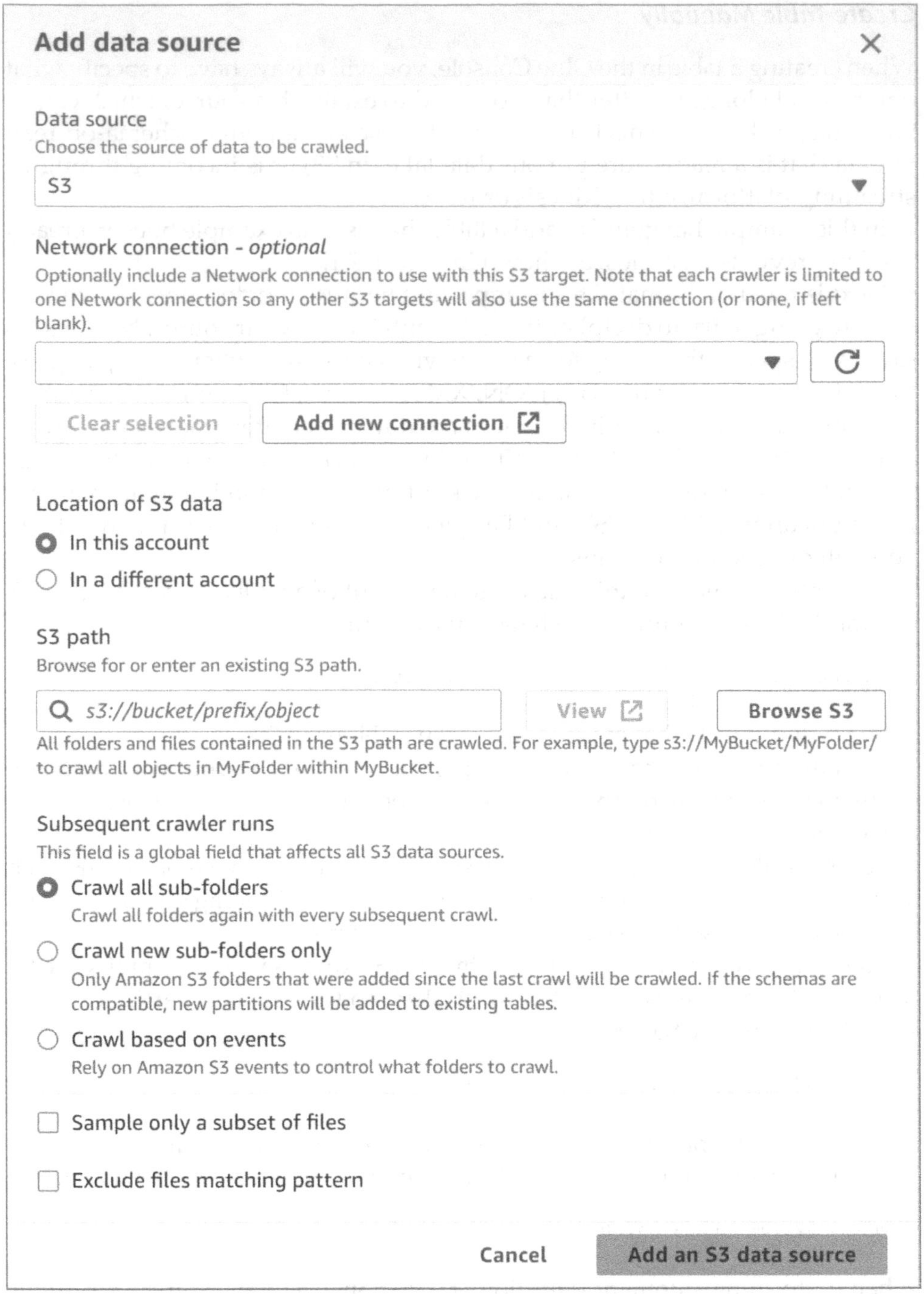

Add data source ✕

Data source
Choose the source of data to be crawled.

S3	▼

Network connection - *optional*
Optionally include a Network connection to use with this S3 target. Note that each crawler is limited to one Network connection so any other S3 targets will also use the same connection (or none, if left blank).

	▼	⟳

Clear selection	Add new connection ⬀

Location of S3 data
⦿ In this account
◯ In a different account

S3 path
Browse for or enter an existing S3 path.

🔍 s3://bucket/prefix/object	View ⬀	Browse S3

All folders and files contained in the S3 path are crawled. For example, type s3://MyBucket/MyFolder/ to crawl all objects in MyFolder within MyBucket.

Subsequent crawler runs
This field is a global field that affects all S3 data sources.

⦿ Crawl all sub-folders
   Crawl all folders again with every subsequent crawl.

◯ Crawl new sub-folders only
   Only Amazon S3 folders that were added since the last crawl will be crawled. If the schemas are compatible, new partitions will be added to existing tables.

◯ Crawl based on events
   Rely on Amazon S3 events to control what folders to crawl.

☐ Sample only a subset of files

☐ Exclude files matching pattern

Cancel	Add an S3 data source

Figure 7.1: Adding a table

Schema (4)
View and manage the table schema.

Q *Filter schemas*

#	Column name	Data type
1	id	int
2	userid	int
3	title	string
4	body	string

Figure 7.2: Table schema

A nice overview of the table in Figure 7.3 offers a summary of the object we are about to create.

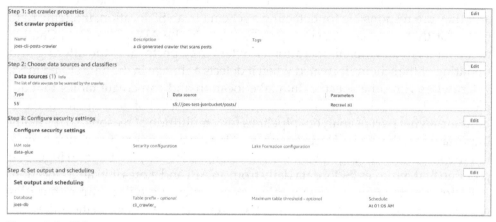

Figure 7.3: Object summary

All is going well. Our table will appear in the list of tables in the Glue Console.

Creating a Table from an Existing Schema

Creating a table from an existing schema is very similar to creating it manually, with the exception that you don't have to specify the schema. You will have to choose a database and a table to "clone" (so to speak), but you will still have to specify a source type, a location, and partitions.

I find this to be useful when constructing development, staging, or production environments to ensure identical schemas.

Creating a Table with a Crawler

Crawlers are a topic deserving of their own section, so we will explore them in detail, together with classifiers, later in the chapter, in their own dedicated section, "Crawlers." In short, crawlers perform data scans that infer schemas and create tables accordingly.

Summary on Databases and Tables

AWS Glue offers a Data Catalog that works as a metastore for schemas that can either be created manually, copied from existing ones, or created automatically through crawlers.

These schemas are applied on-read to incoming data (from Kinesis and Kafka) or to cold data (S3) by analytical engines so the underlying data can be queried. As part of the Data Catalog, these schemas can then be referenced in AWS Glue ETL jobs for both reading and storing purposes.

Crawlers

Crawlers are a major feature of AWS Glue and a vital part of an automated architecture. Crawlers are "scanning" jobs that can run on a schedule or on demand, and they are responsible for detecting a schema in an S3 location, inferring data types for that schema, and storing the schema in the AWS Glue Data Catalog metastore. An additional operation crawlers may perform is the altering and updating of the schema it created when it detects a change in the data stored in S3.

Crawlers run off a specific data lake location and can create tables that are partitioned, enabling optimization of queries and a level of data isolation. Partitions are a vital part of analytics pipelines for a multitude of reasons, so it's really important that these are detected correctly. However, identifying a partition key is not the same as detecting a partition. For example, let's say we have an ingestion pipeline that retrieves JSON data daily from an API and stores it in an S3 location.

Following the conventions you've seen earlier, we will assume that files retrieved on two consecutive days will have keys looking similar to the following:

```
2022/08/01/posts.json
2022/08/02/posts.json
```

The partitioning pattern is year/month/day and the data is stored in files called `posts.json` (it's actually a good idea to give unique names to files by using something like UUIDs, but let's keep it simple for now).

If a crawler ran on the first day, it would detect the year/month/day partitions and would add partitions with the following values:

```
Year = 2022
Month = 08
Day = 01
```

The following day, if the crawler didn't run, the partition `Day = 02` would never get added to the table. If you tried to query the data for that partition, the query would fail.

So for every partition you create, you need to do one of two things:

- Add the partition manually.
- Run a crawler to detect the new partitions.

Let's try to create a crawler from the Web Console and then see how we could create the equivalent from the AWS CLI.

First of all, we go to AWS Glue ➤ Crawlers ➤ Add Crawler. The wizard prompts us to provide a name (see Figure 7.4).

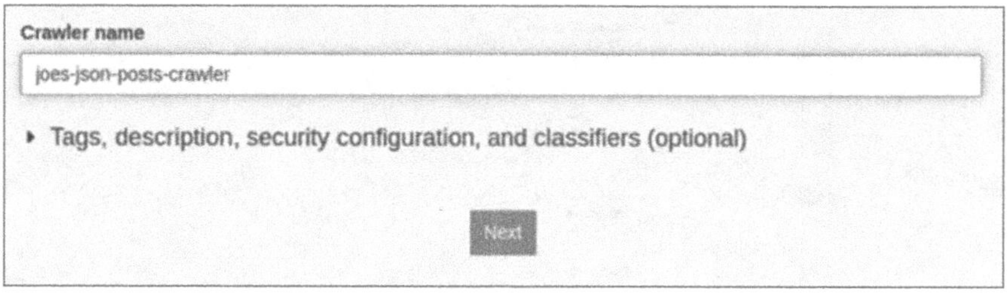

Crawler name

joes-json-posts-crawler

▶ Tags, description, security configuration, and classifiers (optional)

Next

Figure 7.4: Crawler Name field

Then we have to specify the kind of data store we are going to crawl. The vast majority of times you will find yourself creating crawlers for data that has landed in S3, but that's not the only store that can be targeted. DynamoDB, a JDBC connection, a MongoDB database, and Data Catalog tables are all plausible targets.

Let's stick to our most common scenario, S3, as shown in Figure 7.5.

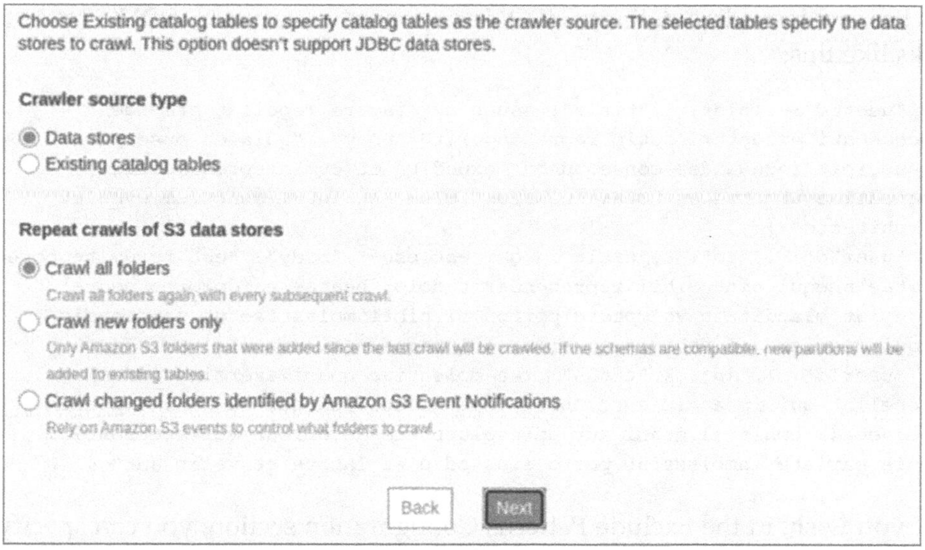

Choose Existing catalog tables to specify catalog tables as the crawler source. The selected tables specify the data stores to crawl. This option doesn't support JDBC data stores.

Crawler source type

⦿ Data stores
◯ Existing catalog tables

Repeat crawls of S3 data stores

⦿ Crawl all folders
  Crawl all folders again with every subsequent crawl.
◯ Crawl new folders only
  Only Amazon S3 folders that were added since the last crawl will be crawled. If the schemas are compatible, new partitions will be added to existing tables.
◯ Crawl changed folders identified by Amazon S3 Event Notifications
  Rely on Amazon S3 events to control what folders to crawl.

Back Next

Figure 7.5: Crawler creation, source, and stores options

The ingestion pipeline architecture for your use case will help you decide if you want to crawl all folders or only new folders. If you place new data in existing prefixes, then you have to scan all folders. If you create new prefixes (e.g., through partitioning by date), you can limit the scans to new folders. This is the better approach when it is feasible.

Now we have to provide a location for the crawler. Note that it can be a bucket, but it can also be a prefix within that bucket so that you can have multiple crawlers running for the same bucket in different prefixes (Figure 7.6).

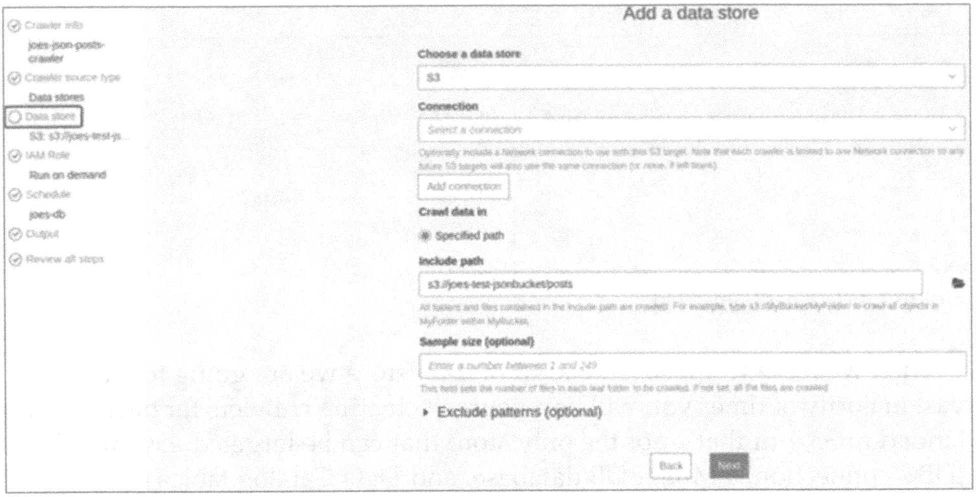

Figure 7.6: Crawler creation, folder, and path field

We will scan the JSON bucket with the posts data from JSON Placeholder, this time with newline-delimited JSON as opposed to standard JSON. The data looks like this:

```
{ "userId": 1,"id": 1,"title": "sunt aut facere repellat provident
occaecati excepturi optio reprehenderit","body": "quia et suscipit\
nsuscipit recusandae consequuntur expedita et cum\nreprehenderit
molestiae ut ut quas totam\nnostrum rerum est autem sunt rem eveniet
architecto" }
{ "userId": 1,"id": 2,"title": "qui est esse","body": "est rerum tempore
vitae\nsequi sint nihil reprehenderit dolor beatae ea dolores neque\
nfugiat blanditiis voluptate porro vel nihil molestiae ut reiciendis\
nqui aperiam non debitis possimus qui neque nisi nulla" }
{ "userId": 1,"id": 3,"title": "ea molestias quasi exercitationem
repellat qui ipsa sit aut","body": "et iusto sed quo iure\nvoluptatem
occaecati omnis eligendi aut ad\nvoluptatem doloribus vel accusantium
quis pariatur\nmolestiae porro eius odio et labore et velit aut" }
```

If you wish, in the Exclude Patterns Configuration section, you can specify Glob-style patterns to exclude sub-prefixes from the scanning.

After this section, you have to provide an IAM role. At this point you should have some roles that are configured as AWS Glue Service Roles with S3 permissions, but if you don't, go to IAM, create a role, choose AWS Glue as your use case (remember, this is so that Glue is a trusted entity on the role), then add the appropriate S3 policy (a read-only permission for a crawler is actually enough) and specify that as the role for the crawler.

Now we have to specify a schedule, and these are the options available:

- On Demand
- Hourly
- Daily
- Choose Days
- Weekly
- Monthly
- Custom

The Choose Days option will let you run the crawler only on certain days of the week and the Custom option on a custom schedule. Either way, the maximum frequency of the crawler runs is hourly (although a cron-style schedule is not the only option to trigger a rescan; you can also hook a crawler run to EventBridge, as in the case of S3 events, or use API calls).

The last screen of the wizard is where you specify which database you want to store the new table in and what prefix to give to the tables created by the crawler (see Figure 7.7). Next, though, is a slightly tricky bit that you will want to pay attention to if you don't want to spend hours trying to figure out why your queries are breaking for no apparent reason.

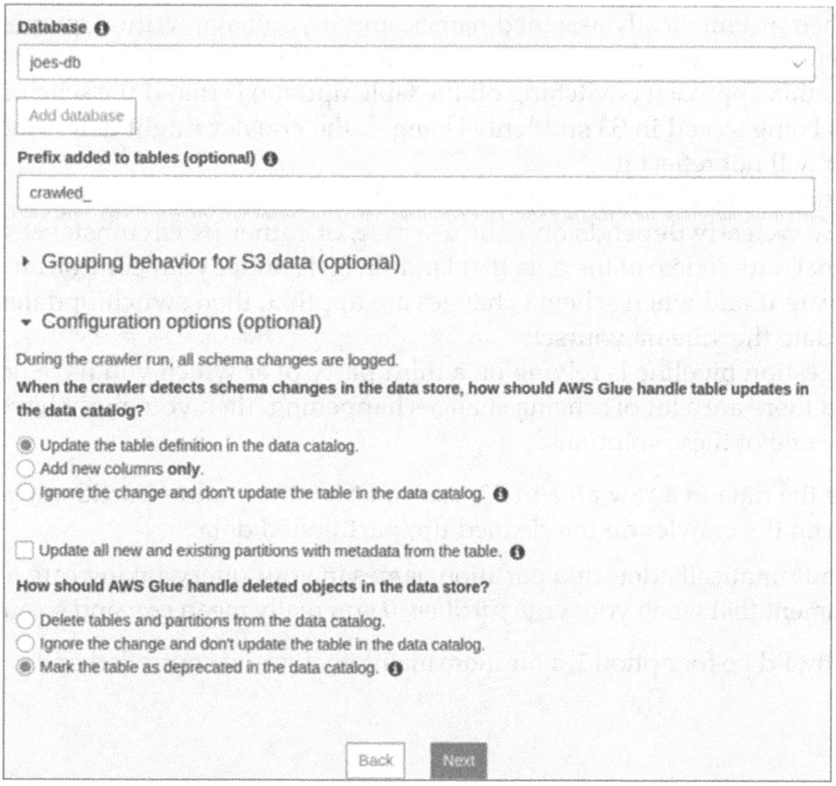

Database ❶

joes-db

Add database

Prefix added to tables (optional) ❶

crawled_

▸ Grouping behavior for S3 data (optional)

▾ Configuration options (optional)

During the crawler run, all schema changes are logged.

When the crawler detects schema changes in the data store, how should AWS Glue handle table updates in the data catalog?

◉ Update the table definition in the data catalog.
◯ Add new columns **only**.
◯ Ignore the change and don't update the table in the data catalog. ❶

☐ Update all new and existing partitions with metadata from the table. ❶

How should AWS Glue handle deleted objects in the data store?

◯ Delete tables and partitions from the data catalog.
◯ Ignore the change and don't update the table in the data catalog.
◉ Mark the table as deprecated in the data catalog. ❶

Back   Next

Figure 7.7: Crawler creation, prefix field

Also note the Sample Size parameter. As the documentation explains it, "Sets the number of files in each leaf folder to be crawled when crawling sample files in a dataset." In other words, you can set a number of files that will be sampled to detect schema changes. If you set this parameter to a really low number, it will speed up crawler execution but at the risk of missing a schema detection. So this aspect depends on what you are working on and how data is deposited into S3. If you don't set it, all files are crawled; it will be slower but it's safer. In my experience, crawlers with a daily schedule are mostly run overnight so that analytics datasets are refreshed by the morning, the time when analysts traditionally start working on producing Insights. Therefore, the time it takes to scan folders is not that important, as long as it's completed by morning.

Updating or Not Updating?

Note the Configuration options. The first option is Update The Table Definition In The Data Catalog. Clearly this is what we want *at first*. But after the first run, if you adopted the AWS-style partition prefixes in S3, you would have to manually edit the Schema to change partition names from the automatic *partition_0*, *partition_1*, and so on to the more meaningful *year, month, day*, and so on.

If you don't change the configuration option from table update to Ignore The Change And Don't Update The Table In The Data Catalog, your partitions will revert to their automatically assigned names, and if you have written queries (between crawler runs) that are using year/month/day, they will break. The trade-off of this approach (switching off the table update) is that if the schema of the data being stored in S3 suddenly changes, the crawler might detect the change but will not reflect it.

So the question is, should you update or not?

The answer clearly depends on your use case, or rather its circumstances. If the original data source of the data that lands in S3 is under your control, and you are aware if and when schema changes are applied, then switch updates off and update the schema yourself.

If the ingestion pipeline is relying on a third party over which you have no control and there are a lot of schema changes happening, then you might have to settle for one of these solutions:

- Store the data in a raw area in S3, use an ETL to normalize partitioning, and run the crawler on the cleaned up/partitioned data.

- Use automatically detected partition names in your query, taking care to document that when you write *partition_0* you really mean *year* and so on.

Personally, I'd go for option 1, a far more maintainable and controlled option.

Running the Crawler

As for our crawler, let's take care to check the box that updates the partitions, and leave the rest of the options at their defaults. Now we are ready to create and run the crawler.

First, you will see the crawler appearing in the list of crawlers (Figure 7.8).

Then, roughly after a few minutes (depending on how much data you are scanning), the crawler will update with information on the job duration and the number of tables added (Figure 7.9).

| ☐ | joes-json-posts-crawler | ⊘ Ready | ⊘ Succeeded |

Figure 7.8: Crawler list

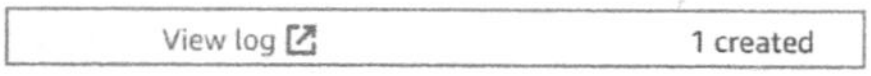

| View log ☐ | 1 created |

Figure 7.9: Crawler list, run information

In our case, one table was added, or so the summary says. To verify it, we go to AWS Glue ➤ Databases ➤ Tables, and check if the newly created table is there. According to the options we provided, the table should have the prefix `crawled_`, which helps us identify it.

It's good practice to prefix tables in such a way that you can identify which crawler generated them (see Figure 7.10).

Figure 7.10: Generated tables

Now for the last test, where we verify the correctness of the schema. Before showing the results, note that since I don't like to have to edit the schema to rename partitions, I use the Hive pattern:

```
$ aws s3 ls --recursive  s3://joes-test-jsonbucket/posts/
2022-08-01 19:08:36      2500 posts/year=2022/month=08/day=01/posts.json
```

As mentioned, partitions are explicitly named in the prefix, so the crawler should detect them—and it does (see Figure 7.11).

The schema is the familiar one we used in previous examples, plus the year/month/day partitions.

Our pipeline can now be augmented with scheduled scanning of the data to automatically create partitioned tables in our Data Catalog.

Creating a Crawler from the AWS CLI

As well as showing you how to create a crawler from the CLI, this section will clarify a little more about the options available because the generated YAML

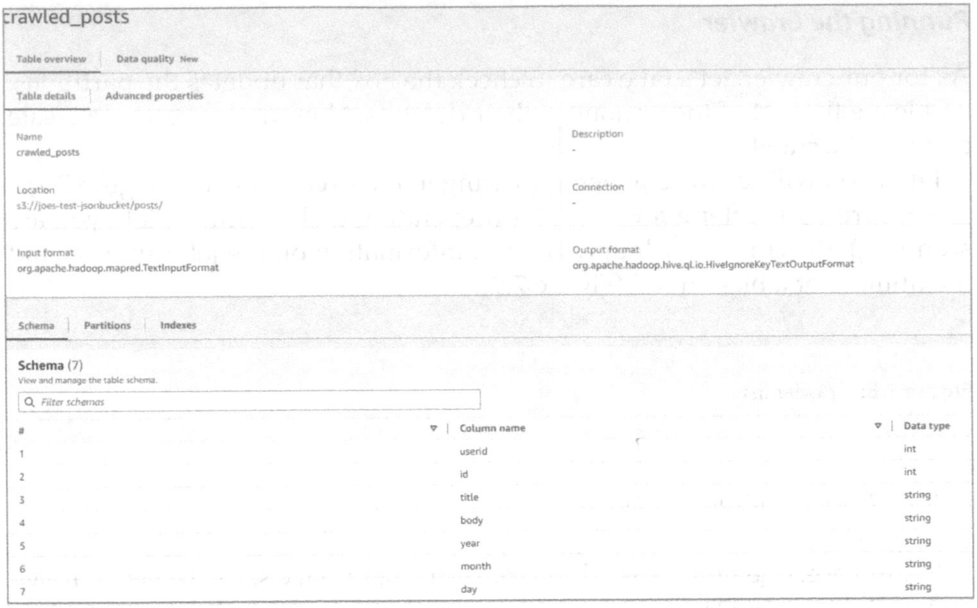

Figure 7.11: Generated schema

input is very well documented and shows which options are required and what aspect of the crawler they configure.

Let's start with generating the skeleton YAML:

```
$ aws glue create-crawler --generate-cli-skeleton yaml-input >
crawler.yaml
```

This produces a file with all sorts of target options, so we will trim it down a bit to focus on the S3 target:

```
Name: 'joes-cli-posts-crawler'  # [REQUIRED] Name of the new crawler.
Role: 'arn:aws:iam::<account id>:role/<your role>' # [REQUIRED] The
IAM role or Amazon Resource Name (ARN) of an IAM role used by the new
crawler to access customer resources.

DatabaseName: 'joes-db' # The Glue database where results are written
Description: 'a cli generated crawler that scans posts' # A description
of the new crawler.

Targets: # [REQUIRED] A list of collection of targets to crawl.
  S3Targets:  # Specifies Amazon Simple Storage Service (Amazon S3)
targets.
    - Path: 's3://joes-test-jsonbucket/posts/'  # The path to the Amazon
S3 target.


Schedule: 'cron(5 1 * * ? *)' # A cron expression used to specify the
schedule (see Time-Based Schedules for Jobs and Crawlers.
```

```
TablePrefix: 'cli_crawler_' # The table prefix used for catalog tables
that are created.
SchemaChangePolicy:
  UpdateBehavior: LOG

  DeleteBehavior: DEPRECATE_IN_DATABASE
RecrawlPolicy:
  RecrawlBehavior: CRAWL_EVERYTHING

LineageConfiguration:
  CrawlerLineageSettings: DISABLE
```

I used default settings and a cron expression to make the Crawler execute every night at 1:05 am. Make sure to save the code to a file, which I called create_crawler.yaml.

Now let's create it with the usual `cli-input` option:

```
$ aws glue create-crawler --cli-input-yaml file://create_crawler.yaml
```

And sure enough, here it is in the list of crawlers (Figure 7.12).

| ☐ | joes-json-posts-crawler | ⊘ Ready | ⊘ Succeeded |

Figure 7.12: Crawler created with the CLI

And since we are using the CLI, you can also list the crawlers with this:

```
$ aws glue list-crawlers
```

And we can start it with:

```
$ aws glue start-crawler --name joes-cli-posts-crawler
```

Retrieving Table Information from the CLI

Let's make sure the crawler did its job and retrieved table information. If you remember we gave the crawler the instruction to create a table prefixed by `cli_crawler_`. Since the prefix detected by the crawler is `posts`, we can assume the table created is called `cli_crawler_posts` (but you can verify that by checking the list of tables in the Glue Console or from the CLI). We can retrieve table information by using this:

```
$ aws glue get-table -database-name joes-db --name cli_crawler_posts
```

Which outputs the following:

```
{
    "Table": {
        "Name": "cli_crawler_posts",
        "DatabaseName": "joes-db",
        "Owner": "owner",
```

```
        "CreateTime": "2022-08-02T08:52:47+00:00",
        "UpdateTime": "2022-08-02T08:52:47+00:00",
        "LastAccessTime": "2022-08-02T08:52:47+00:00",
        "Retention": 0,
        "StorageDescriptor": {
            "Columns": [
                {
                    "Name": "userid",
                    "Type": "int"
                },
                {
                    "Name": "id",
                    "Type": "int"
                },
                {
                    "Name": "title",
                    "Type": "string"
                },
                {
                    "Name": "body",
                    "Type": "string"
                }
            ],
            "Location": "s3://joes-test-jsonbucket/posts/",
            "InputFormat": "org.apache.hadoop.mapred.TextInputFormat",
            "OutputFormat":
"org.apache.hadoop.hive.ql.io.HiveIgnoreKeyTextOutputFormat",
            "Compressed": false,
            "NumberOfBuckets": -1,
            "SerdeInfo": {
                "SerializationLibrary": "org.openx.data.jsonserde.
JsonSerDe",
                "Parameters": {
                    "paths": "body,id,title,userId"
                }
            },
            "BucketColumns": [],
            "SortColumns": [],
            "Parameters": {
                "CrawlerSchemaDeserializerVersion": "1.0",
                "CrawlerSchemaSerializerVersion": "1.0",
                "UPDATED_BY_CRAWLER": "joes-cli-posts-crawler",
                "averageRecordSize": "250",
                "classification": "json",
                "compressionType": "none",
                "objectCount": "1",
                "recordCount": "10",
                "sizeKey": "2500",
                "typeOfData": "file"
            },
            "StoredAsSubDirectories": false
        },
```

```
    "PartitionKeys": [
        {
            "Name": "year",
            "Type": "string"
        },
        {
            "Name": "month",
            "Type": "string"
        },
        {
            "Name": "day",
            "Type": "string"
        }
    ],
    "TableType": "EXTERNAL_TABLE",
    "Parameters": {
        "CrawlerSchemaDeserializerVersion": "1.0",
        "CrawlerSchemaSerializerVersion": "1.0",
        "UPDATED_BY_CRAWLER": "joes-cli-posts-crawler",
        "averageRecordSize": "250",
        "classification": "json",
        "compressionType": "none",
        "objectCount": "1",
        "recordCount": "10",
        "sizeKey": "2500",
        "typeOfData": "file"
    },
    "CreatedBy": "arn:aws:sts::123456789012:assumed-role/data-glue/
AWS-Crawler",
    "IsRegisteredWithLakeFormation": false,
    "CatalogId": "123456789012"
    }
}
```

This is a nice and complete summary of the table your crawler has created. Note that the JSON summary specifies that your table was indeed created by a crawler, not manually.

Classifiers

While I never had to resort to classifiers in a production scenario, a word on them is definitely warranted. For the vast majority of cases, the data you deal with will be stored in common formats that can be correctly identified and deciphered by AWS Glue, and a correct schema will be generated as a result of the crawler scan operation.

However, sometimes you may want to generate a different set of columns from the default interpretation of the file, or the crawler may not be able to correctly detect the schema of a file. In that case you may resort to classifiers, which will help the crawler make sense of the file.

Classifier Example

In previous chapters we have used data returned by the JSON Placeholder API, which is standard JSON, and therefore the response to our request is a JSON Array containing objects, something like this:

```
[
{ "userId": 1,"id": 1,"title": "sunt aut facere repellat provident
occaecati excepturi optio reprehenderit","body": "quia et suscipit\
nsuscipit recusandae consequuntur expedita et cum\nreprehenderit molestiae
ut quas totam\nnostrum rerum est autem sunt rem eveniet architecto"
},
{
"userId": 1,"id": 2,"title": "qui est esse","body": "est rerum tempore
vitae\nsequi sint nihil reprehenderit dolor beatae ea dolores neque\
nfugiat blanditiis voluptate porro vel nihil molestiae ut reiciendis\
nqui aperiam non debitis possimus qui neque nisi nulla"
}
]
```

If you were to crawl this data, the detected schema would look like Figure 7.13. You could still use that in Athena (you can extract JSON in queries), but that is suboptimal and not what we want. What we want is the usual schema we have detected in the previous example, which worked well because it was newline-delimited JSON.

#	▽ Column name	▽ Data type
1	array	array

Figure 7.13: Crawler-generated schema, single array field

Here is a classic case where we can build a classifier to obviate this problem. In the Glue Console, go to Classifier, click Add Classifier, enter a name for it, and type the JSON path `$[*]`, which represents the path where the Classifier will look for the data, as shown in Figure 7.14.

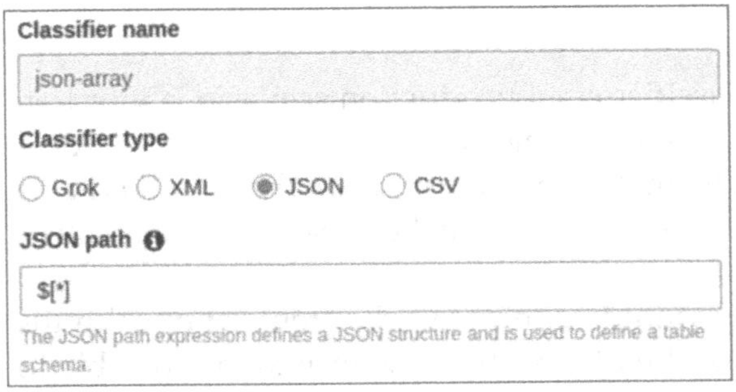

Classifier name

> json-array

Classifier type

◯ Grok   ◯ XML   ⦿ JSON   ◯ CSV

JSON path ❶

> $[*]

The JSON path expression defines a JSON structure and is used to define a table schema.

Figure 7.14: Adding a classifier

Now, let's go back to the crawler and add this newly created classifier into it (Figure 7.15).

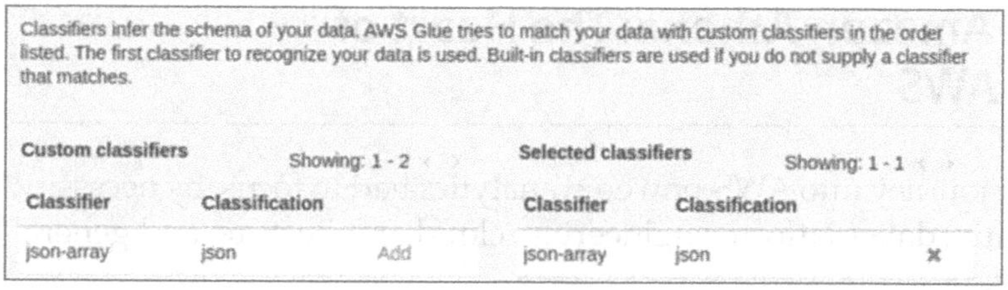

Classifiers infer the schema of your data. AWS Glue tries to match your data with custom classifiers in the order listed. The first classifier to recognize your data is used. Built-in classifiers are used if you do not supply a classifier that matches.

Custom classifiers		Showing: 1 - 2	Selected classifiers		Showing: 1 - 1
Classifier	Classification		Classifier	Classification	
json-array	json	Add	json-array	json	✖

Figure 7.15: Add the classifier to the crawler

Now let's rerun the crawler and you will see that the schema has correctly been detected, as in Figure 7.16.

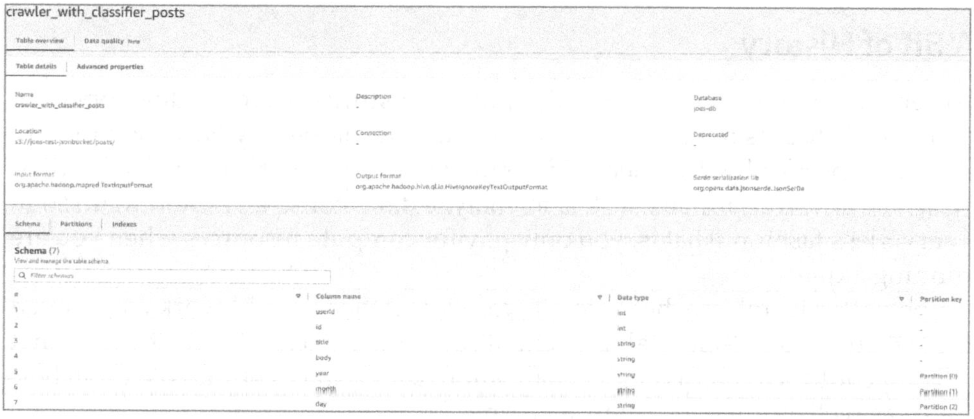

Figure 7.16: Newly generated schema with classifier

The classifier allowed us to leave the pipeline unchanged and still make sense of the schema contained in the files.

Crawlers and Classifiers Summary

Crawlers are a vital part in automating schema creation and maintenance in an AWS Data Lake architecture. With crawlers, you can scan data deposited in S3 buckets (and many more data stores) and automate the creation of tables in the AWS Glue Data Catalog representing the data schema for the content of those files.

Classifiers let you resolve more complex deciphering challenges so that you can leave the rest of the ingestion and processing pipeline untouched.

Search with Amazon Athena: The Heart of Analytics in AWS

Up until now, our journey into AWS-powered analytics had to focus, by necessity, on data engineering, data platform engineering, cloud architecture, and general SysOps/DevOps.

Before we could dream of analyzing data, we had to acquire it, validate it, filter it, clean it, and curate it by enriching and augmenting data from cleaned sources.

If you forgive me a food expression (I am Italian, after all), we have been boiling the water for a long time—it's time to throw the pasta in!

A Bit of History

Athena is a wondrous and frankly quite monstrous machine developed by Amazon. It has its roots in Presto, a database developed by Facebook in 2012 that was specifically designed and optimized to analyze terabytes of flat files. Athena's first and primary task is to analyze data stored in S3, and to do so in a serverless fashion. That is, you only pay for compute resources when you are running a query.

Soon after its release, however, it was clear Athena could work as so much more than just a flat-file analyzer capable of immense scale. It became clear that Athena could work as a data virtualization layer and cover the role of orchestrator as well as query/analytical engine.

So that's what Amazon Athena really is nowadays: a serverless analytical engine capable of analyzing large-scale quantities of data stored in S3 and other federated data sources and producing Insights and datasets suited for analytics.

Interface Overview

First of all, data in Athena is searched and retrieved with SQL—specifically, the Presto dialect of SQL, which is very similar to the ANSI standard, plus the addition of utility functions that are ideal for analyzing data that has originated in the web. Functions like URL parsing, extracting hosts/domains, and so on are trivial operations. The full documentation for the query language used in Athena is available here:

```
https://docs.aws.amazon.com/athena/latest/ug/ddl-sql-reference.html
```

You can access Athena's interactive service on the Web Console by typing **Athena** in the search bar.

You will be presented with a query editor; on the left side a drop-down list of catalogs, databases, and tables; and on the right side a query editor at the top and a results pane at the bottom. Let's take a quick look at these components (Figure 7.17).

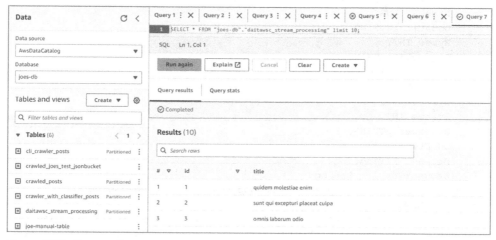

Figure 7.17: Query editor

As you can see, Data Source is the first drop-down list. This is a list of catalogs you have created in your AWS account. The first and default data source is the AWS Glue Data Catalog, with which we have worked a lot in Chapter 6, "Processing Data." In fact, all of the tables I have created either manually or with crawlers are now appearing in the list of tables.

It should become apparent at this point that all the work we have put into creating ingestion and processing pipelines, followed by automated cataloging, was a preliminary phase to our ability to query the data we have manipulated up to this point.

Creating Tables Manually

Before we can run any queries, we need tables. If you have completed any of the crawler exercises, your catalog will contain some tables ready to query. If you don't want to use crawlers to create tables, or you can't, you can create tables manually, although this is not something I advise you do. However, there may be circumstances where this your only choice, so let's see how you do that. The full documentation on creating tables is available here: https://docs.aws.amazon.com/athena/latest/ug/creating-tables .html#creating-tables-how-to.

Athena's DDL looks very familiar to anyone accustomed to SQL, with a few additions. First, tables are *external*, so you have to use the keyword EXTERNAL in the table definition. What does *external* mean? It means that when you drop the table only the metadata will be dropped; the data will remain there. Fortunately, I might add!

Let's take a look at the example listed in the documentation:

```
CREATE EXTERNAL TABLE IF NOT EXISTS cloudfront_logs (
    `Date` Date,
    Time STRING,
    Location STRING,
    Bytes INT,
    RequestIP STRING,
    Method STRING,
    Host STRING,
    Uri STRING,
    Status INT,
    Referrer STRING,
    OS String,
    Browser String,
    BrowserVersion String
) ROW FORMAT SERDE 'org.apache.hadoop.hive.serde2.RegexSerDe'
WITH SERDEPROPERTIES (
"input.regex" = "^(?!#)([^ ]+)\\s+([^ ]+)\\s+([^ ]+)\\s+([^ ]+)\\s+([^
]+)\\s+([^ ]+)\\s+([^ ]+)\\s+([^ ]+)\\s+([^ ]+)\\s+([^ ]+)\\s+[^\(]+[\(]
([^\;]+).*\%20([^\/]+)[\/](.*)$"
) LOCATION 's3://athena-examples-MyRegion/cloudfront/plaintext/';
```

Things to note:

- A field can be encapsulated in backticks if the field name is a keyword.
- Field types can be capitalized or mixed cases; it does not matter. It all gets reduced to lowercase by Athena.
- Since data is in S3, you need to specify the library responsible for deciphering data. In the previous example it's regex parsing of server logs, but it can be Parquet, CSV, JSON, AVRO, and so on.
- You need to specify the location of the data in S3.

Athena Data Types

Athena supports a number of familiar data types, plus a few interesting additions. You can read the full documentation on data types here: https://docs .aws.amazon.com/athena/latest/ug/data-types.html. Let's take a look at them:

- Boolean: true or false
- Integer types: tinyint, smallint, int, bigint

- Precision types: `float`, `double`, `decimal`
- Text: `char`, `varchar` and `string` (which are all Hive data types)
- `Binary`: for Parquet formats
- Time: `date` and `timestamp`

Complex Types

Athena supports complex types—that is, fields that store complex data structures as opposed to single primitive values. These are arrays, maps, and structs.

Array < data_type >

The `array` type allows you to specify a type, and you can store multiple values of a single type in one field. The retrieved type will be an array. For example, you can use this:

```
CREATE EXTERNAL TABLE example (myarray array<integer>) LOCATION ' . . . '
INSERT INTO example(myarray) values (array[1,2,3])
```

Retrieving the value will return

```
[1, 2, 3]
```

Map < primitive_type, data_type >

`Map` allows you to specify a pair of values. For example:

```
CREATE EXTERNAL TABLE example (mymap array<integer, string>)
LOCATION ' . . . '
INSERT INTO example(mymap) values (map(1, 'foo'))
```

Note that the first of the two types declared in a `map` has to be a primitive.

Struct < col_name: data_type >

With a struct you create complex structures holding data. This is ideal for nested data such as is commonly found in JSON. A common example is

```
CREATE EXTERNAL TABLE users (id int, address struct <street: string,
zip: int, city: string>)
```

Note that you can also create nested structs:

```
address struct<street: string, zip: int, city: string, geo: struct<lat:
float, lon: float>>
```

Running a Query

Let's try to run a query. You could start typing SQL right away in the editor, but if you click one of those ellipses (three dots) next to the table names, you will be presented with a few interesting options, shown in Figure 7.18.

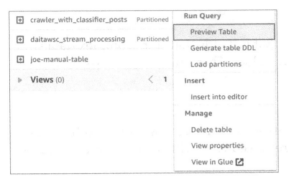

Figure 7.18: Table options in Athena

The first option, Preview Table, immediately injects a standard query that retrieves only 10 records from the table and displays them in the results pane. Let's do that. This is the query generated by Athena:

```
SELECT * FROM "joes-db"."crawler_with_classifier_posts" limit 10;
```

The query returns the data we uploaded in the posts.json file, with the schema detected by the crawler. Athena's interface also has two very handy options at the top right of the results pane (shown in Figure 7.19).

Figure 7.19: Copy and Download Results buttons

You can either copy the data or download the results in a CSV format.

I am copying the first row of results here to show the format in which Athena copies the result set into the clipboard:

```
#  userid  id  title  body  year  month  day
1  1  1  sunt aut facere repellat provident occaecati excepturi optio
reprehenderit        quia et suscipit
```

```
suscipit recusandae consequuntur expedita et cum
reprehenderit molestiae ut ut quas totam
nostrum rerum est autem sunt rem eveniet architecto  2022  08  01
```

So far, so good, and nothing exotic if you are used to working with SQL.

Connecting with JDBC and ODBC

The Web Console interface for Athena is not the only editor you can use to construct your queries. You can also connect with JDBC and ODBC drivers. This
allows you to use your favorite query editor. The full documentation on how
to connect to Athena using JDBC and ODBC is available here: `https://docs`
`.aws.amazon.com/athena/latest/ug/connect-with-jdbc.html`.

Query Stats

Another interesting feature of Athena is Query Stats. Every time you run a query,
you get a detailed overview of the amount of space scanned, the execution time
(all details relevant to calculate the cost of the query), and a breakdown of the
various phases of the execution (Figure 7.20).

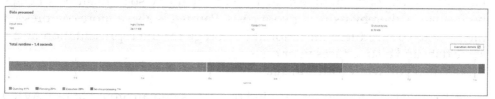

Figure 7.20: Query Stats graph

We are going to talk about Athena's pricing model soon, so this information
is very relevant.

Recent Queries and Saved Queries

Another very helpful feature of Athena is the ability to save queries with a name
and a history of recent queries. Even more relevant, when browsing the history
of queries, the result sets are available for download since—as you learned—
they are permanently stored in S3 (Figure 7.21).

Clicking the Execution ID opens the corresponding query where you can
click Download Results if you wish.

☐	ID		Name
☐	d063775f-f63c-43f1-8fd0-282ef3bc2c9a		PQL Checks Specific Accounts
☐	30468c1c-34af-48ef-bc75-dd34ede668f2		ops_report: new_biz
☐	42f94585-6533-4662-a0e0-6120c26129b3		mql_validation

Figure 7.21: Saved queries

The Power of Partitions

Let's change the previous query to use the power of partitions. At a practical level, partitions can be used as query fields in `where` clauses of your SQL queries so that you can limit the amount of data scanned by Athena. Why does this matter?

Athena Pricing Model

Athena's serverless pricing model is a function of the amount of space scanned in S3 and the time it took to execute your queries. So, if you scan the whole table location for results, the query will cost you more, because it will scan more space than it should and because that will take longer to execute.

This is also where storing data in the right format is extremely relevant. Parquet is orders of magnitude faster than CSV to query, so it enhances Athena's performance, thereby reducing your costs. Parquet is also a more compressed file format, so it reduces the amount of storage for the representation of the same data and also reduces your costs.

So, when you work with Athena:

- Use the right format for the kind of queries you are going to use: AVRO for record retrieval, Parquet for large datasets.
- Utilize partitions to limit the amount of space scanned.
- Curate your datasets so they only contain data that is relevant to the queries you are going to build and no unnecessary space is scanned.

Returning to our query, let's see how we can use partitions in our WHERE clauses. If you remember, in the JSON bucket previously used, we specified some Hive-style partitions—specifically, these two objects are under different partitions:

```
$ aws s3 ls --recursive s3://joes-test-jsonbucket/posts
2022-07-14 17:16:02      27520 posts.json
2022-08-01 19:08:36       2500 posts/year=2022/month=08/day=01/posts.json
2022-08-02 15:02:12       2500 posts/year=2022/month=08/day=02/posts.json
```

So before going to retrieve actual data, let's count the records for each partition, which should be identical, given that I performed a copy.

Here's a query that does that:

```
select distinct day, count(id) from "cli_crawler_posts" group by 1;
```

Note that you can use the position of the field to perform aggregations, and unlike most things in programming, fields are 1-indexed, not 0-indexed.

The results, as expected, are identical:

```
#   day   _col1
1   02    10
2   01    10
```

Automatic Naming

Unnamed aggregations will follow the convention _covX, where X is a number representing the position of the field relative to all unnamed fields. Now that we know we have two identical partitions, let's perform a query that only returns data from one partition:

```
select userId, id as postId from "cli_crawler_posts" p where p.day = '02';
```

This very simple query actually shows off all the power of Athena and partitions, believe it or not. By specifying that where p.day = '02' in the WHERE clause, Athena knew to scan files where the day partition is '02'. If you refer to the bucket contents a few lines above, that means Athena did not scan the first of the two items for relevant results, as its day partition had the value '01'. In a real-life scenario, you could use a query with that kind of condition to only retrieve data for the first day of the month, which is quite a common request.

It's important to understand that there is no concept of hierarchy in partitions. You don't need to specify year and month before you can query for day. That too is an advantage. How can Athena do this? The secret is in the object prefixes; if you recall, in Chapter 3, we explained that S3 does not have a concept of folder. What you see represented as a folder is a sort of "rendering" that the S3 UI applies to the underlying data by grouping objects with common key prefixes. But in reality, each object is an independent entity, with its own key.

So, when Athena scans our files in S3, there's no such thing as recursing through folders. There are only two separate S3 objects with the following keys:

```
posts/year=2022/month=08/day=01/posts.json
posts/year=2022/month=08/day=02/posts.json
```

Through the AWS Data Catalog, Athena is now aware of the existence of a partition called day, and therefore it does not scan the data in the first file, since the value corresponding to the day= part of the prefix is not '02'.

Any kind of SQL operation performed on fields is also available on partitions. For example, although the partition values are strings, you could cast them to integer values. In this example, we want to retrieve all partitions from a year greater than 2021:

```
select userId, id as postId from "cli_crawler_posts" p where cast(p.year
as int) > 2021;
```

which works just fine.

Athena Query Output

A very important aspect of Athena is that each query produces a CSV output that's written to S3. You can configure this output location in the settings, or you can specify it in the query.

This is actually a very useful feature because some Athena queries may take a very long time to execute, so keeping a program lingering, waiting for a result set, is not feasible or convenient. But thanks to AWS EventBridge, as soon as the result is written to S3, you can trigger the execution or processing of the result set through the s3:* events.

Recently, for example, I produced a report through Athena and configured an output location. When Athena is finished producing the result, a Lambda is triggered that picks up the location of the report, generates a presigned URL, and sends the link in an email to relevant parties.

Athena Peculiarities (SQL and Not)

There are a few aspects to be careful of when working with Athena; let's explore the main ones.

Computed Fields Gotcha and WITH Statement Workaround

Let's take the following query:

```
select id as postId, length(body) as bodyLength from "cli_crawler_posts"
where bodyLength > 10;
```

This query would work on most RDBS systems; unfortunately, it does not in Athena. Athena can only retrieve fields from a catalog or from a temporary view or table that you create within the query itself.

WITH statements are a perfect workaround, and although they lengthen the query a bit, they also make it easier to read and modify.

So we can refactor the previous query with this:

```
with results as (
select id as postId, length(body) as bodyLength
from "cli_crawler_posts")
select r.postId, r.bodyLength from results r where r.bodyLength > 180
order by 2 desc;
```

which produces expected results, shown in Figure 7.22.

Results (6)

# ▽	postId	▽	bodyLengt
1	2		206
2	2		206
3	6		194
4	6		194

Figure 7.22: Result of query

Also note that you can reference one WITH statement from another:

```
with raw as (
select id as postId, userId, length(body) as bodyLength
from "cli_crawler_posts"),
results as (
select r.postId, r.userId, r.bodyLength
from raw r
where r.bodyLength > 180
)
select r.postId, r.bodyLength from results r order by 2 desc;
```

Lowercase!

Athena does not support capital letters or capitalization in table names and columns, and in fact it automatically switches all table names and columns to lowercase. Why is this a big deal, then, if Athena is taking care of it? Because as you will see later, Athena supports federated queries that can connect to external data stores, and there you may have capital letters littered in your queries.

Even worse, Athena's errors are sometimes quite obscure and misleading. So how do you work around this? There are two major approaches:

- In the original database, which contains capitalized tables and columns, create views that only have lowercase fields.
- Put a system such as a ProxySQL (https://proxysql.com) in place to create rules. You will find many benefits of a system like ProxySQL since it can better manage database credentials, replicas, shards, etc.

Query Explain

You can click a button that explains the queries you execute. This feature produces a nice diagram, or you can even export to JSON. The previous query, for example, produces the following EXPLAIN output:

```
{
  "0" : {
    "plan" : {
  "id" : "18",
  "name" : "Output",
  "identifier" : "[postId, bodyLength]",
  "details" : "postId := id\nbodyLength := length\n",
  "children" : [ {
    "id" : "289",
    "name" : "RemoteMerge",
    "identifier" : "[1]",
    "details" : "",
    "children" : [ ],
    "remoteSources" : [ "1" ]
  } ],
  "remoteSources" : [ ]
}
  },
  "1" : {
    "plan" : {
  "id" : "322",
  "name" : "LocalMerge",
  "identifier" : "[length DESC_NULLS_LAST]",
  "details" : "",
  "children" : [ {
    "id" : "290",
    "name" : "PartialSort",
    "identifier" : "[length DESC_NULLS_LAST]",
    "details" : "",
    "children" : [ {
      "id" : "288",
      "name" : "RemoteSource",
      "identifier" : "[2]",
      "details" : "",
```

```
      "children" : [ ],
      "remoteSources" : [ "2" ]
    } ],
    "remoteSources" : [ ]
  } ],
  "remoteSources" : [ ]
}
  },
  "2" : {
    "plan" : {
  "id" : "1",
  "name" : "ScanFilterProject",
  "identifier" : "[table = awsdatacatalog:HiveTableHandle{schemaName=
joes-db, tableName=cli_crawler_posts, analyzePartitionValues=Optional.
empty}, filterPredicate = (\"length\"(\"body\") > BIGINT '180')]",
  "details" : "length := \"length\"(\"body\")\nLAYOUT: joes-db.cli_
crawler_posts\nid := id:int:1:REGULAR\nbody := body:string:3:REGULAR\
nmonth:string:-1:PARTITION_KEY\n    :: [[08]]\nyear:string:-1:PARTITION_
KEY\n    :: [[2022]]\nday:string:-1:PARTITION_KEY\n    :: [[01],
[02]]\n",
  "children" : [ ],
  "remoteSources" : [ ]
}
  }
}
```

Moreover, you can export the Distributed Plan and the Logical Plan, each showing the steps performed and the time it took to execute them (and why). With the output of EXPLAIN you can inspect a query and understand what kind of merge, repartition, join, and replication operations were performed to complete the query you issued. The full documentation of Athena EXPLAIN is available here:

```
https://docs.aws.amazon.com/athena/latest/ug/athena-explain-
statement-understanding.html
```

This feature is particularly useful when connecting a third-party tool to Athena, as it may clarify the reasons why a certain query is taking too long to run, something that is most likely very difficult to inspect in the third-party tool itself.

Deduplicating Records

When working with S3 and ingestion pipelines, you may find yourself creating daily snapshots of data, which means that at least part of the data may be identical to the previous snapshot you created. When you go to create reports, you may find yourself with numerous copies of the same record, with no guarantee of the number of such copies. For example, imagine you are monitoring customers' revenue that they generate for your business. Your leadership team has asked you to start tracking the customers' subscription value on a daily basis so that you can ultimately create a timeline of revenues by segment, indicating which customers went up or down in value in what cohort or group.

Customer Acme Inc. has a recurring revenue that changes rarely, but you are storing a copy of their record every day, so when asked to create a report of the latest record you are going to have to do a lot of ordering and limiting.

It is useful to bear the following information in mind:

- Always timestamp the ingestion of a record.

- If asked for the latest version, only query the latest partition.

- If your dataset isn't partitioned, you can use the functions RANK() and ROW_NUMBER().

RANK works well when you want to score records according to a particular set of criteria. For example, if your customer records have a ts column that represents the timestamp of ingestion, you could create a WITH statement that ranks all records, and then you can select only the most recent, like so:

```
WITH records AS (
SELECT c.customerId, c.revenue,
  RANK() OVER (PARTITION BY c.customerId ORDER BY c.ts DESC) as rnk
  FROM customers c
)
SELECT * FROM records r WHERE r.rnk = 1;
```

Remember that the WITH statement is necessary since computed fields cannot be used in a WHERE clause.

ROW_NUMBER() works in the same way. It's ideal when some records are entirely identical, but inevitably the engine will return one record before the other, and you can use that value to only retrieve one copy, for example.

Working with JSON, Flattening, and Unnesting

Perhaps one of the aspects that deserves a little more attention when it comes to querying data with Athena is working with JSON, flattening, and unnesting data. If you are used to standard SQL and working with relational databases, you may find some of these concepts a bit exotic at first. But there is no reason to panic—Athena makes it quite easy.

Working with JSON can be done in two ways: by using extraction functions (from the SQL reference documentation) or by using dot notation. If you used a crawler to create a schema and your raw data is contained deep within or nested in JSON, you may find yourself with a complex schema like the struct example we listed earlier:

```
address struct<street: string, zip: int, city: string, geo: struct<lat:
float, lon: float>>
```

If you wanted to query this field, you would use the dot notation, which should be familiar if you are used to JSON or even the majority of programming languages when it comes to field access:

```
SELECT u.id, u.address.geo.lat, u.address.geo.lon FROM users u;
```

Sometimes, however, you may deal with JSON data that contains arrays of data in a field. The Athena documentation has a whole section dedicated to working with arrays because they clearly pose a challenge when trying to unravel the data into a format that's suitable for reporting. The documentation is available here:

```
https://docs.aws.amazon.com/athena/latest/ug/querying-arrays.html
```

We are going to take a quick look at the most challenging aspect, which is creating a single object containing an array and creating a single row per element of the array.

Imagine you have a raw dataset in JSON with the following data in it:

```
{   "department": "engineering",
"users": ['Sharon', 'John', 'Bob', 'Sally']
}
```

After we create a crawler and scan the data, we obtain a table named `dataset`. Now we want to create a report indicating each user and the department they work in. The query to accomplish this task is as follows:

```
SELECT d.department, names FROM dataset d
CROSS JOIN UNNEST(d.users) as t(names)
```

The more unusual elements in the query are the CROSS JOIN and UNNEST keywords. The meaning of the query can be defined as follows: create a relation *names* by flattening the *users* field of the *dataset* table, and CROSS JOIN it with the *department* field.

This special type of JOIN that Athena uses to flatten data is the perfect intermediary step between a nested dataset and a flat format like CSV or Parquet.

Athena Views

Athena views are very similar to views that you may be accustomed to while working with relational databases. The principle of a view is simple: you have a query, most likely a complex one, and you want simplified access to the filter that the query provides, something of a shortcut to the original query. Or maybe you want to query a subset of the data, especially if you are limiting your query to certain partitions.

A view is a perfect way to do so. As you will see, this property of views fits perfectly well in the wider analytics pipeline and workflow.

Where views find their perfect application is in hiding the complexity of queries that join numerous tables. For example:

```
SELECT x.a, x.b, y.c, z.d, z.e, SUM(z.f), AVG(y.a)
FROM x
JOIN y on x.a = y.a
JOIN z on z.a = y.a
WHERE . . .
GROUP BY 1, 2, 3, 4, 5
ORDER BY 6 DESC
```

You could save this query and run it when you need it. But—especially if there is automated work involved—a better approach is to create a view:

```
CREATE VIEW myView AS <query>
```

The immediate benefit is that *this view is added to the catalog* and your view is now accessible like any other table. ETL jobs can interrogate it, and you can use it to retrieve data, to run analytics, or even use it in other views, greatly simplifying your analytics life.

It's important to understand that views are not materialized. The underlying query will always be run to obtain the data you need in the view.

Since Athena Views have a fundamental role in enabling, optimizing, and governing access to data, Athena's UI makes it very easy to create a view from a query by just clicking the Create button at the bottom of the SQL editor.

CREATE TABLE AS SELECT (CTAS)

If Views are a metadata description of a query, but the underlying query is always run and the data is untouched, CTAS creates a materialized version of a SELECT query. So when you issue CREATE TABLE AS SELECT a new table will be added to the catalog, with a LOCATION property for this new table located at the S3 bucket and prefix of the output of the Athena query.

Why would you use CTAS? A common example is that you have a huge dataset, stored in a format that is not ideal for the work you want to conduct, so you create a table as a SELECT of the original table. The result set is then stored in a different S3 location, set as the LOCATION property of the new table, and you can specify a different storage format for your original query so that not only is your new table smaller but its format is optimized.

Please refer to the documentation on considerations and limitations of working with CTAS here:

```
https://docs.aws.amazon.com/athena/latest/ug/considerations-
ctas.html
```

NOTE Unlike with normal tables, backticks to wrap field names are not allowed, and the format conversions are more limited than plain Athena tables.

Saving Queries and Reusing Saved Queries

It is possible in Athena to save queries with a name. To do so, click the Save drop-down menu at the bottom of the query editor text field, as shown in Figure 7.23.

This allows you to associate a name to the query and reopen it at a later time. You will be prompted with a modal dialog box, where you can enter a name and an optional description (Figure 7.24).

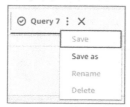

Figure 7.23: Save button drop-down options

Save query   ✕

Query name
The name used to reference this saved query in the query editor.

Use 1-128 characters

Query description - *optional*

Use up to 1024 characters. 1024 characters remaining.

Preview SQL query

SELECT * FROM "joes-db"."daitawsc_stream_processing" where userid = 1;

Cancel   **Save query**

Figure 7.24: Save Query dialog box

If you click the Saved Queries tab above the query editor, you will be shown a list of saved queries. If you click the ID, the query opens in the editor (Figure 7.25).

	ID	Name
☐		
☐	78ea2813-4d3a-4ab2-8e39-18f04fa1ac59	joe-retrieve-post

Figure 7.25: Query editor

Running Parameterized Queries

You may have noticed that the query in our example contains a ? (question mark). This is how you create parameterized queries in Athena. To enter the desired parameter, click Run. The Athena editor will recognize that you need to supply a value for the parameter, and it will bring up a parameter form (Figure 7.26).

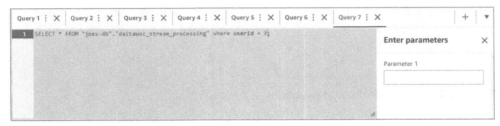

Figure 7.26: Parameterized query

Supply a value and click Run to execute the query as normal. As you can see from the previous example, it is entirely possible to save a parameterized query.

Athena Federated Queries

Athena has occupied a revolutionary role in producing analytics. One feature that has represented a groundbreaking innovation or evolution in AWS-land is federated queries.

Federated engines for databases have been around for some time, but in AWS, the ability to combine data lake analysis with federation has boosted the potential of analytics and search.

So what does it mean to perform a federated query in Athena? In short, you can perform queries that join data coming from your data lake with external sources, which can be any of the following:

- Relational and NoSQL databases in your account
- Relational and NoSQL databases in other AWS accounts
- External data stores
- Caches, logs
- Data warehouses

And pretty much any reachable data store that you can think of.

So in a single SQL query you could join data from your data lake, a Redis instance, an Elasticsearch index, a relational database, and even log files on a server. This blows your ability to create meaningful Insights wide open, and the potential for data enrichment and augmentation is vastly increased.

Let's see how we can connect data sources to Athena first and then perform federated queries.

Athena Lambda Connectors

To connect to a data source, go to the Athena interface, select Data Sources, and then click Create Data Source. You will be presented with a list of possible data connectors. Pick whatever data source suits your use case; in my example, I will be connecting to an RDS instance that I used in Chapter 5, "Data Ingestion," a sample database. Since the RDS is MySQL, I will choose MySQL from the list.

After selecting your desired engine, you will be brought to an interface where you can name the data connector and specify the Lambda function that handles the connection and data retrieval. We don't have any Lambda for the purpose, so we will have to create it.

In the Connection Details pane of the interface, click the Create Lambda Function button, as shown in Figure 7.27.

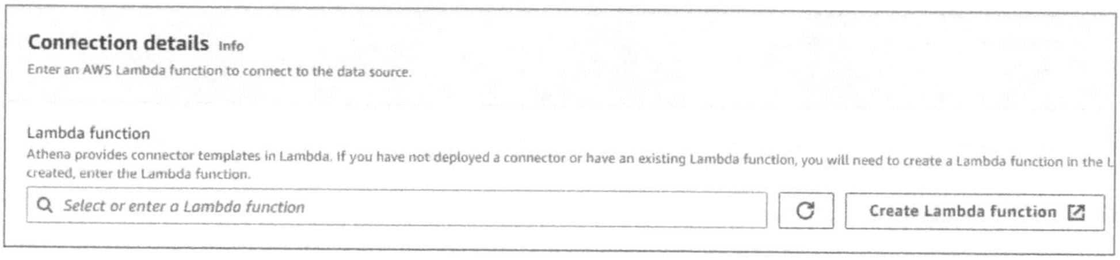

Figure 7.27: Connection Details pane

This will bring you to an interface that will allow you to create a Lambda for the purpose of connecting a data source. All you need to do is fill the details in the form:

- An application name.
- A secret in the Secrets Manager. This is for the purpose of creating necessary IAM permissions and to inject credentials in the JDBC connection string, which you should not type in clear text in the function configuration.

- A spill bucket, which is the S3 bucket where the connection will store the data for Athena to perform merges with result sets coming from other data sources.
- A function name.
- The Lambda memory.
- The Lambda timeout.
- Security groups.
- SpillPrefix, the prefix applied to keys used for spill result sets.
- Subnets.

Subnets and security groups all depend on the data source you are using. In AWS, these are easily found in the resource itself.

Note on Connection Errors

Sometimes when trying out the new connector you may be presented with a connection string error, similar to the error shown in Figure 7.28.

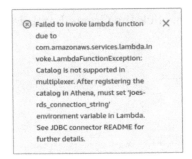

ⓒ Failed to invoke lambda function   ✕
due to
com.amazonaws.services.lambda.in
voke.LambdaFunctionException:
Catalog is not supported in
multiplexer. After registering the
catalog in Athena, must set 'joes-
rds_connection_string'
environment variable in Lambda.
See JDBC connector README for
further details.

Figure 7.28: Connection error

Simply go into the Lambda configuration and duplicate the connection string environment variable to the name indicated in the error. In my case the environment variable `default` had to be duplicated to `joes-rds_connection_string` (an environment variable name that actually will not work; see the following note). All should work well after that.

> **NOTE** If you are going to use CloudFormation to create this connector, the name of the environment variable storing the connection string is a concatenation of the application name plus `_connection_string`. Also very important, do not name your application with dashes (-); doing so will break the constraints of the characters considered to be valid. The only non-alphanumeric character that can be used is the underscore.

Performing Federated Queries

In previous query examples, we have interrogated tables using simply their name, which is perfectly fine. But this only works because we had `AWSDataCatalog` and `joes-db` selected as our data source and database. When performing federated queries, every time we specify a table, we need to indicate the data source and the database within that data source. So while in standard SQL queries to a relational database you would use the `database.tablename` format, in Athena federated queries you need an additional data source identifier, so the format is `datasource.database.tablename`. Anything under the default AWS Glue Data Catalog is identified with `AwsDataCatalog`. So a query retrieving all data from `cli_crawler_posts` would be formulated like this:

```
SELECT * FROM "AwsDataCatalog"."joes-db"."cli_crawler_posts"
```

Clearly this query has little "federated" to it. Let's see a real example.

After the creation of the data source, I am now presented with the ability to choose it from the drop-down menu on the left, and I can see the tables in it, more or less like those shown in Figure 7.29.

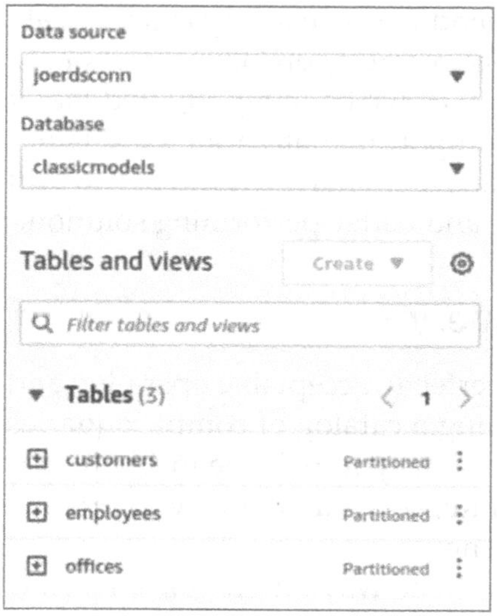

Figure 7.29: Databases and tables in Athena

Now let's say we want to join a table from the data lake (so S3-based) with one stored in a MySQL RDS database. Following the pattern illustrated earlier, all we need to do is to prefix each table with its data source and database. In my example I'll go to enrich the posts data from the data lake with employees data in the RDS instance to create a result set where each post record also contains information about its author (in the hypothetical scenario that userId in posts refers to an ID in the employees table).

So the resulting query looks like the following:

```
SELECT
p.userId,
e.name,
p.id,
p.title,
p.body
FROM "AwsDataCatalog"."joes-db"."cli_crawler_posts" p
JOIN "joerdsconn"."classicmodels"."employees" e on p.userId = e.employeeId
LIMIT 10;
```

Running this query effectively performs an operation of some complexity, since Athena substantially applied schema-on-read to S3-based JSON data and used MySQL's engine to query RDS data, performed separate dataset retrievals, and then did a merge.

In my experience, joining data coming from S3 (in multiple formats such as compressed JSON, CSV, and Parquet), RDS, or other relational databases, Redshift, and other stores such as DocumentDB or Elasticsearch, all in one query, is quite common. That said, I highly recommend that you always import data into S3 for analysis or enrichment, as the pressure you apply on transactional/operational stores to run analytical queries is, as we have highlighted many times before, entirely unnecessary. Consider importing data from those tables residing in OLTP databases into your data lake and analyze it there. You will find this to be a more resilient, cost-effective, and better-performing solution.

Creating a View from a Federated Query

Creating a view from a federated query is a perfectly acceptable operation and one you will find yourself doing a lot. Creating a catalog of complex queries through views is in fact standard practice, and as you will see in Chapter 8, "Data Consumption, BI, Visualizations, and Reports," a vital way to provide curated datasets for visualization and reporting.

The view generated by a federated query is in no way different from a view created from a standard query.

Governing: Athena Workgroups, Lake Formation, and More

Governing a data lake in AWS can be complicated, but it does not have to be. Bearing in mind that IAM alone is capable of enforcing any kind of restrictions through identity-based policies, AWS offers a number of tools to govern the access to the data in your data lake.

Athena Workgroup is one such feature of Athena, but for a wider, more generic management of data access, Lake Formation is a better solution.

Athena Workgroups

Athena Workgroup is a feature of Athena that stands somewhere in between governance and search; therefore I am including it under the Governing heading.

An Athena Workgroup is a type of resource that allows you to isolate query execution and query history between users, teams, or applications. From a technical perspective, this means you have a completely separate resource with which to perform the queries against your data lake. From a governance perspective, you can limit access to data and set query limits on a particular workgroup, which naturally affects the ability of users to access data or the frequency with which they query it. Assigning users or teams to a particular workgroup means enabling (or disabling) access to querying data, but also enforcing cost control. Let's see how you can create a workgroup.

In the Web Console, this is as easy as going to Athena, selecting Workgroups on the left side, and clicking Create Workgroup. This will bring you to a form where you can fill in all the necessary details, such as the top-level information (name and description), shown in Figure 7.30, but also various settings, shown in Figure 7.31.

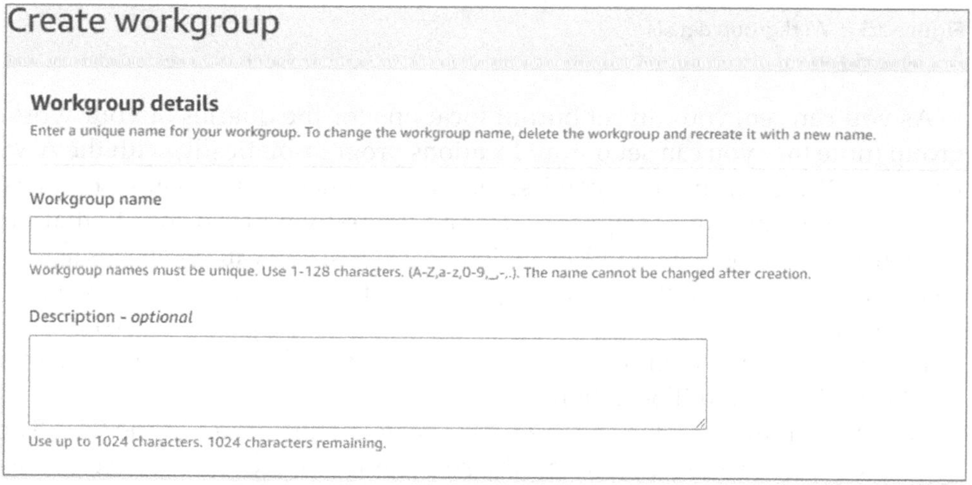

Figure 7.30: Create Workgroup

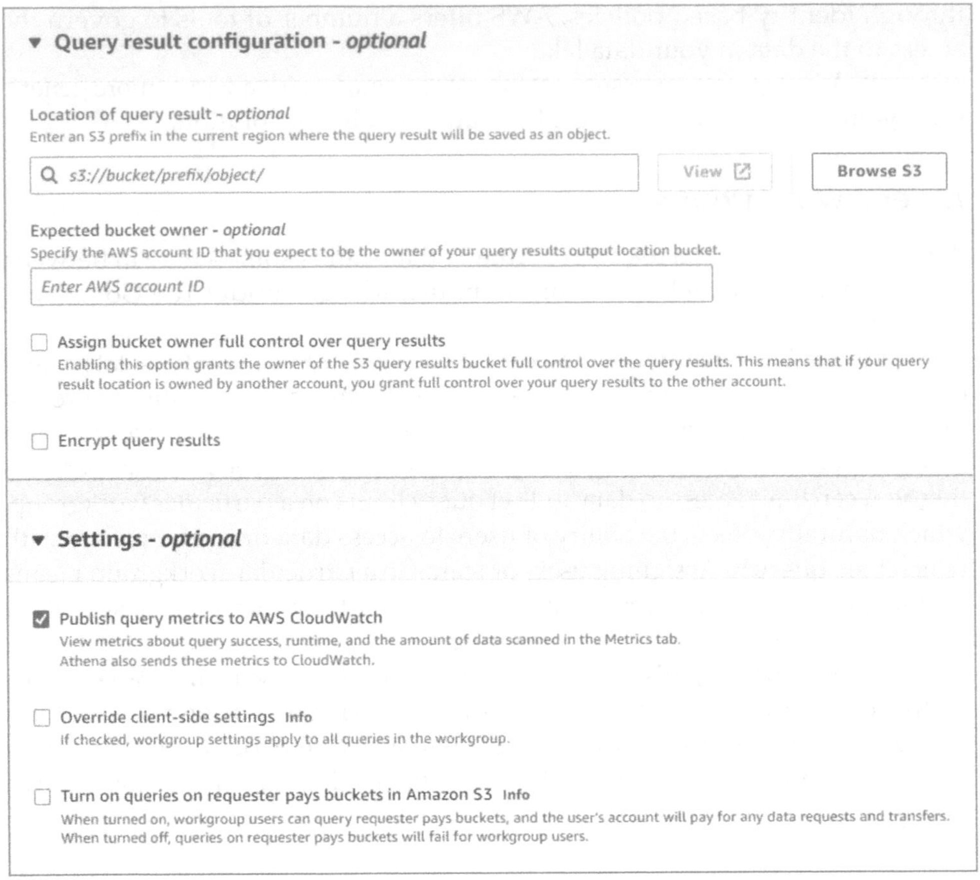

Figure 7.31: Workgroup details

As you can see, you can set output locations for the queries of your workgroup (note that you can set output locations programmatically, with the AWS Athena SDK, for each query you issue). As mentioned, you can also set query limits for the workgroup (Figure 7.32). And naturally you can specify that the workgroup have no data limits at all. On top of this, you can set alarms associated with your data limits so you can get notified in case the limits are reached.

While creating workgroups with the Web Console is easy, in the wider context of maintaining a data platform, the preferred way to do this is through either the AWS CLI or CloudFormation.

Let's take a quick look at how we can create a workgroup in the CLI. The service of reference is `athena` and the subcommand is `create-work-group`. Let's run the command to generate the input skeleton in YAML and see what the resulting output is:

```
$ aws athena create-work-group --generate-cli-skeleton yaml-input >
athena_workgroup.yaml
```

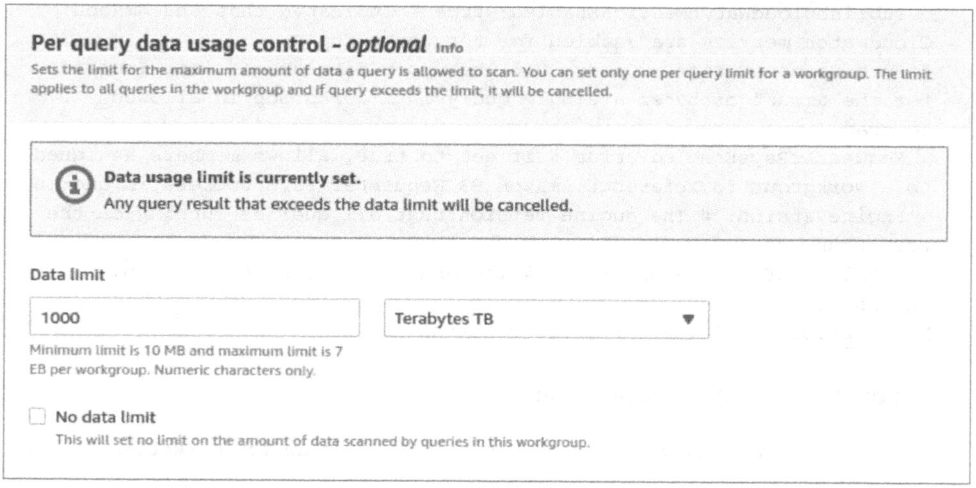

Figure 7.32: Setting query limits for the workgroup

The YAML:

```
Name: ''  # [REQUIRED] The workgroup name.
Configuration: # The configuration for the workgroup, which includes
the location in Amazon S3 where query results are stored, the
encryption configuration, if any, used for encrypting query results,
whether the Amazon CloudWatch Metrics are enabled for the workgroup,
the limit for the amount of bytes scanned (cutoff) per query, if
it is specified, and whether workgroup's settings (specified with
EnforceWorkGroupConfiguration) in the WorkGroupConfiguration override
client-side settings.
  ResultConfiguration:  # The configuration for the workgroup, which
includes the location in Amazon S3 where query results are stored and
the encryption option, if any, used for query results.
    OutputLocation: ''  # The location in Amazon S3 where your query
results are stored, such as s3.
    EncryptionConfiguration: # If query results are encrypted in Amazon
S3, indicates the encryption option used (for example, SSE-KMS or CSE-
KMS) and key information.
      EncryptionOption: SSE_S3  # [REQUIRED] Indicates whether Amazon S3
server-side encryption with Amazon S3-managed keys (SSE-S3), server-side
encryption with KMS-managed keys (SSE-KMS), or client-side encryption
with KMS-managed keys (CSE-KMS) is used. Valid values are: SSE_S3, SSE_
KMS, CSE_KMS.
      KmsKey: '' # For SSE-KMS and CSE-KMS, this is the KMS key
ARN or ID.
    ExpectedBucketOwner: '' # The Amazon Web Services account ID that
you expect to be the owner of the Amazon S3 bucket specified by
ResultConfiguration$OutputLocation.
  EnforceWorkGroupConfiguration: true # If set to "true", the settings
for the workgroup override client-side settings.
```

```
    PublishCloudWatchMetricsEnabled: true # Indicates that the Amazon
CloudWatch metrics are enabled for the workgroup.
    BytesScannedCutoffPerQuery: 0 # The upper data usage limit (cutoff)
for the amount of bytes a single query in a workgroup is allowed
to scan.
    RequesterPaysEnabled: true # If set to true, allows members assigned
to a workgroup to reference Amazon S3 Requester Pays buckets in queries.
    EngineVersion: # The engine version that all queries running on the
workgroup use.
        SelectedEngineVersion: ''  # The engine version requested by
the user.
Description: '' # The workgroup description.
```

An example template would be:

```
Name: 'MarketingWorkgroup'  # a fictitious workgroup for marketing analysts
Configuration:
  ResultConfiguration:
    OutputLocation: 's3://mycompany-marketing-analytics/athena-output/'
    EncryptionConfiguration:
      EncryptionOption: SSE_KMS  # server-side encryption with KMS-
managed keys (SSE-KMS)
      KmsKey: 'my-kms-key' # ID of the KMS
    ExpectedBucketOwner: '123456789012' # The Amazon Web Services
account ID
  BytesScannedCutoffPerQuery: 0
  RequesterPaysEnabled: true
Description: 'Workgroup allocated to Marketing Data Analytics department'
```

Now you can potentially create the workgroup by issuing this:

```
$ aws athena create-work-group –cli-input-yaml file://my_template.yaml
```

Note that this will require the `athena:CreateWorkGroup` permission on the role currently associated to your AWS CLI profile.

By configuring the workgroup to send metrics to CloudWatch, you will be able to inspect all sorts of details about query performance and workgroup data utilization.

Fine-Grained Athena Access with IAM

Since you can create databases in the AWS Glue Data Catalog, it is possible to control what data is accessible to what user through IAM policies. In particular, you can use a resource-based policy to control the users that have access to a workgroup, and you can use identity-based policies to control the actions that are allowed to an identity.

The full documentation with examples is available here: `https://docs.aws.amazon.com/athena/latest/ug/fine-grained-access-to-glue-resources.html`. But let's take a peek at example policies that work as fine-grained control.

In this policy, we allow the user to list databases, get database information, and create databases:

```
{
    "Effect": "Allow",
    "Action": [
        "glue:GetDatabase",
        "glue:GetDatabases",
        "glue:CreateDatabase"
    ],
    "Resource": [
      "arn:aws:glue:us-east-1:123456789012:catalog",
      "arn:aws:glue:us-east-1:123456789012:database/default",
      "arn:aws:glue:us-east-1:123456789012:database/example_db"
    ]
}
```

You will notice that the first resource allowed by the policy is `catalog`. There are four entities in the AWS Glue Data Catalog that follow a precise hierarchy: CATALOG, DATABASE, TABLE, and FUNCTION.

> **NOTE**   To obtain access to databases, you need to grant access to the catalog.

Table 7.1 is a handy reference of policy actions you need to allow to grant privileges to a user to perform database actions.

Table 7.1: Permissions needed

DATABASE OPERATION	PERMISSIONS NEEDED
ALTER DATABASE	glue:GetDatabase
	glue:UpdateDatabase
CREATE DATABASE	glue:CreateDatabase
	glue:GetDatabase
CREATE TABLE	glue:GetDatabase
	glue:GetTable
	glue:CreateTable
DROP DATABASE	glue:GetDatabase
	glue:DeleteDatabase
	glue:GetTables
	glue:GetTable
	glue:DeleteTable

Table 7.1: Permissions needed *(continued)*

DATABASE OPERATION	PERMISSIONS NEEDED
DROP TABLE	glue:GetDatabase
	glue:GetTable
	glue:DeleteTable
	glue:GetPartitions
	glue:GetPartition
	glue:DeletePartition
MSCK REPAIR TABLE	glue:GetDatabase
	glue:GetTable
	glue:GetPartitions
	glue:GetPartition
	glue:BatchCreatePartition
SHOW DATABASES	glue:GetDatabases
SHOW TABLES	glue:GetDatabase
	glue:GetTables

If you are wondering why many write/update operations require `Get*` permissions, that is because you need to be able to obtain information about databases before you can update them.

The trend of adoption of attribute-based access control is growing, so you may want to consult the following site to explore the option to integrate Athena with Corporate Directory: `https://aws.amazon.com/blogs/security/how-to-scale-authorization-needs-using-attribute-based-access-control-with-s3`.

Recap of Athena-Based Governance

Athena workgroups are a good way to govern access to data by associating certain identities to certain workgroups that may or may not have access to data. Identity-based and resource-based IAM policies are a good way to enforce fine-grained control over access to data and the ability to perform certain actions. Combined, IAM and Athena Workgroup give you a solid way of monitoring costs and governing data access and security over your data lake.

For a more generic approach to governance, however, you can use Lake Formation, as you will see next.

AWS Lake Formation

Lake Formation is a fully managed service for managing your data lakes. Note the plural here, since the level of granularity Lake Formation provides is such that you can build and maintain several data lakes, achieving total isolation and ease of management.

The underlying security and permission system in AWS is entirely based on IAM, so it is important to understand that Lake Formation only represents a central facility where you can easily manage access and permissions but that it is entirely possible to replicate the same exact security policies simply through the creation of IAM policies attached to IAM roles. It is therefore no wonder that when you attempt to grant some database permissions to a user, you will be asked to supply the ARN of the IAM user or role.

First take a look at the interface on the Web Console, to familiarize yourself with the options offered by Lake Formation. The left sidebar menu looks like Figure 7.33.

Figure 7.33: Lake Formation menu

By default, navigating to Lake Formation from the search bar will land you on the dashboard page, where you can set up a data lake. There are three stages to a data lake setup:

1. Registering a S3 location
2. Creating a database
3. Assigning permissions

In substance, a data lake in AWS is an S3 bucket registered with Lake Formation. The process of registering the location allows Lake Formation to manage permissions on that location, but this is all just for your convenience; again, you could simply create an S3 bucket and define bucket policies to obtain an equivalent result, but with more manual work.

Registering a Location in Lake Formation

If you click Register An S3 Location, you will be prompted with the form shown in Figure 7.34.

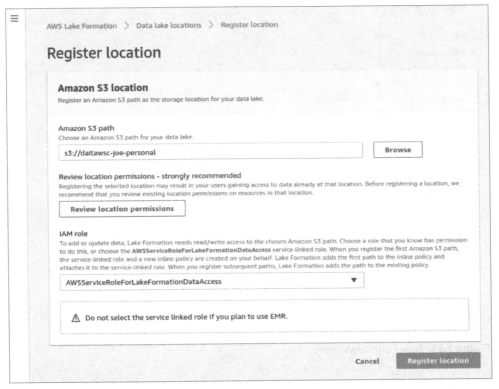

Figure 7.34: Registering location in Lake Formation

I filled in the form with a bucket created for the purpose. When you supply the S3 location, the Location Permission Review button is enabled. You can click it to review the permissions, but since this is a brand-new bucket there will be nothing of worth there.

At this point you can either create an IAM role that has Lake Formation as a linked service or you can simply leave the default role offered by AWS. I suggest the latter unless, as the warning message shows, you intend to use EMR.

This location registration is the equivalent of the AWS CLI tool command:

```
$ aws lakeformation register-resource --resource-arn
arn:aws:s3:::daitawsc-joe-personal --use-service-linked-role
```

if the role you use from the AWS CLI has Lake Formation as a linked service; otherwise, provide an ARN with the `--role-arn` option.

Once the registration is performed, as well as the new location appearing in the Web Console, you will be able to retrieve a list of registered resources with this:

```
$ aws lakeformation list-resources
{
    "ResourceInfoList": [
        {
            "ResourceArn": "arn:aws:s3:::daitawsc-joe-personal",
            "RoleArn": "arn:aws:iam::XXXXXXXXXXXX:role/aws-service-
role/lakeformation.amazonaws.com/AWSServiceRoleForLakeFormationDataAccess",
            "LastModified": "2022-09-01T12:00:19.053000+00:00"
        }
    ]
}
```

If you want to de-register the location, you can use this:

```
$ aws lakeformation deregister-resource --resource-arn
arn:aws:s3:::daitawsc-joe-personal
```

This operation may result in the following error:

```
An error occurred (InvalidInputException) when calling the
DeregisterResource
operation: Must manually delete service-linked role to deregister last
S3 location.
```

This does not mean that the deregistration operation failed, but rather that deregistering a resource does not silently imply the deletion of the IAM role you associated with the location, and that, if you want to delete the role, you have to do it manually. This can be done in the Web Console but also with the CLI tool with the following command:

```
$ aws iam delete-role -role-name <role name>
```

In any case, once you have registered a location, it should appear in the list, as shown in Figure 7.35.

Figure 7.35: List of registered locations

Creating a Database in Lake Formation

At this point, we can create a database, using the registered location as the location for the database itself. If you click the Stage 2 button to create a database in the Web Console, you will be shown the form in Figure 7.36.

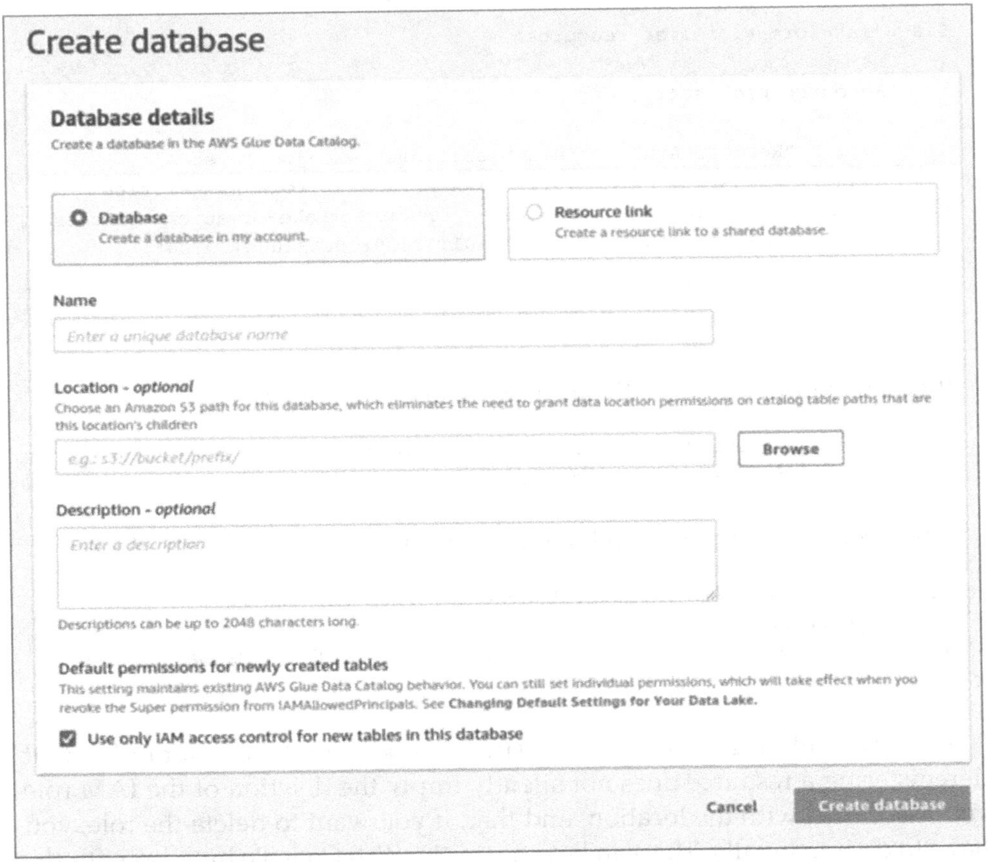

Figure 7.36: Create Database form

A name and the S3 location are the only details you need to complete to create the database. It will now appear in the Lake Formation databases screen (Figure 7.37).

Figure 7.37: List of databases

Assigning Permissions in Lake Formation

Once you have databases and tables, you can assign permissions to access these resources. Permissions are in DBMS-style with GRANT/REVOKE statements such as

```
GRANT SELECT ON table TO username
```

Note that the IAM role you use to perform the grant/revoke action needs to be allowed the following actions in a IAM policy:

```
lakeformation:ListPermissions
lakeformation:GrantPermissions
lakeformation:BatchGrantPermissions
lakeformation:RevokePermissions
lakeformation:BatchRevokePermissions
```

When assigning permissions, these are the details you will need to specify: a principal (who the permission applies to), the action (such as SELECT permissions), and the resource (a database, or a table in a database).

In the AWS CLI tool, the generated skeleton for granting permissions has the following structure.

```
$ aws lakeformation grant-permissions --generate-cli-skeleton yaml-input
CatalogId: ''  # The identifier for the Data Catalog.
Principal: # [REQUIRED] The principal to be granted the permissions on
the resource.
  DataLakePrincipalIdentifier: ''  # An identifier for the Lake
Formation principal.
Resource: # [REQUIRED] The resource to which permissions are to be granted.
  Catalog: {}  # The identifier for the Data Catalog.
  Database: # The database for the resource.
    CatalogId: ''  # The identifier for the Data Catalog.
    Name: '' # [REQUIRED] The name of the database resource.
  Table: # The table for the resource.
    CatalogId: ''  # The identifier for the Data Catalog.
    DatabaseName: '' # [REQUIRED] The name of the database for the table.
    Name: '' # The name of the table.
    TableWildcard: {} # A wildcard object representing every table under
a database.
```

```
TableWithColumns: # The table with columns for the resource.
   CatalogId: ''  # The identifier for the Data Catalog.
   DatabaseName: '' # [REQUIRED] The name of the database for the table
with columns resource.
     Name: '' # [REQUIRED] The name of the table resource.
     ColumnNames: # The list of column names for the table.
     - ''
     ColumnWildcard: # A wildcard specified by a ColumnWildcard object.
       ExcludedColumnNames:  # Excludes column names.
       - ''
   DataLocation: # The location of an Amazon S3 path where permissions
are granted or revoked.
      CatalogId: ''  # The identifier for the Data Catalog where the
location is registered with Lake Formation.
      ResourceArn: '' # [REQUIRED] The Amazon Resource Name (ARN) that
uniquely identifies the data location resource.
   DataCellsFilter: # A data cell filter.
      TableCatalogId: ''  # The ID of the catalog to which the table belongs.
      DatabaseName: '' # A database in the Glue Data Catalog.
      TableName: '' # The name of the table.
      Name: '' # The name of the data cells filter.
   LFTag: # The LF-tag key and values attached to a resource.
      CatalogId: ''  # The identifier for the Data Catalog.
      TagKey: '' # [REQUIRED] The key-name for the LF-tag.
      TagValues: # [REQUIRED] A list of possible values an attribute
can take.
      - ''
   LFTagPolicy: # A list of LF-tag conditions that define a resource's
LF-tag policy.
      CatalogId: ''  # The identifier for the Data Catalog.
      ResourceType: DATABASE # [REQUIRED] The resource type for which the
LF-tag policy applies. Valid values are: DATABASE, TABLE.
      Expression: # [REQUIRED] A list of LF-tag conditions that apply to
the resource's LF-tag policy.
      - TagKey: ''  # [REQUIRED] The key-name for the LF-tag.
        TagValues: # [REQUIRED] A list of possible values an attribute
can take.
        - ''
Permissions: # [REQUIRED] The permissions granted to the principal on
the resource.
- ALL
PermissionsWithGrantOption: # Indicates a list of the granted
permissions that the principal may pass to other users.
- CREATE_DATABASE
```

As you can see, the permissions themselves are listed under the `Permissions` property. This is the simplest way of granting permissions in Lake Formation. However, you will notice the presence of LF-Tag-related properties and `DataCell` security. This is the preferred way of managing permissions in Lake Formation, and the subject of the next section.

LF-Tags and Permissions in Lake Formation

Now that you have registered a location and created a database, you can assign permissions. Before you do this, you need to understand the idea of LF-Tags (Lake Formation tags) and their role in permission management.

Managing permissions with tags is not the only way. You could use named resources, but this approach is a less scalable and maintainable way to manage a large number of resources, so we do not recommend it. LF-Tags is best practice, even according to AWS's own documentation, which contains the following statement:

> *Lake Formation tag-based access control (LF-TBAC) is the recommended method to use to grant Lake Formation permissions when there is a large number of Data Catalog resources. LF-TBAC is more scalable than the named resource method and requires less permission management overhead.*

With that in mind, let's proceed on with our exploration of tags.

The concept of tags is very popular with social media, for example, and LF-Tags are similar. LF-Tags are key-value pairs, like normal resource tags used in AWS. The only difference is that these tags are registered within Lake Formation and are used for access control and permission management. Policy management is a complex discipline, and especially in rapidly growing businesses and environments, it can be very difficult to exercise. LF-Tags are simple, effective, scalable, and easy to manage as the business grows and as governance complexity grows as well.

A common use of tags is to define the domain or use case of a certain resource. For example, a database table representing marketing data could have a `domain=marketing` tag associated with it.

Before moving to a practical example, let's illustrate some rules and features of tag assignment:

- You need to create tags before you can assign them.

- You can assign multiple tags to a resource, but not two tags of the same type. For example, you can have `region=EU`, `department=Marketing`, but you cannot have `department=Marketing, Sales`.

- You can only tag existing resources; you cannot tag resources at creation time.

- You can grant permissions based on simple tags or tag expressions; for example, `region=EU AND department=(Marketing or Sales)`.

- You can tag a database, a table, or even a column.

- At first only data lake administrators can create tags, but they can then grant permissions to other principals (IAM users or roles), specifically `DESCRIBE` and `ASSOCIATE`, which allow you to inspect and associate tags on a resource.

Let's create our first LF-Tag. We can do this in the Web Console or the CLI. In the Web Console, from Lake Formation, expand Administrative Roles And Tasks in the left side navigation bar and click LF-Tags. If you don't have any tags created, you will see the screen in Figure 7.38.

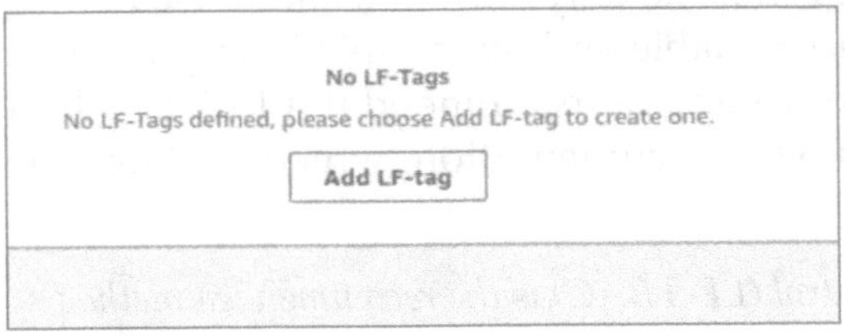

No LF-Tags

No LF-Tags defined, please choose Add LF-tag to create one.

Add LF-tag

Figure 7.38: Add LF-Tag button

Clicking Add LF-Tag will bring you to the Tag creation form (Figure 7.39).

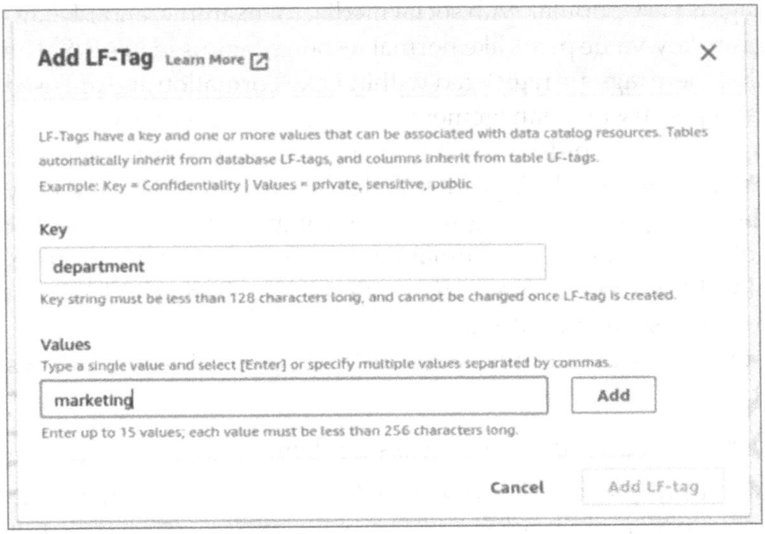

Add LF-Tag   Learn More ☐   ✕

LF-Tags have a key and one or more values that can be associated with data catalog resources. Tables automatically inherit from database LF-tags, and columns inherit from table LF-tags.
Example: Key = Confidentiality | Values = private, sensitive, public

Key

department

Key string must be less than 128 characters long, and cannot be changed once LF-tag is created.

Values
Type a single value and select [Enter] or specify multiple values separated by commas.

marketing   Add

Enter up to 15 values; each value must be less than 256 characters long.

                                   Cancel   Add LF-tag

Figure 7.39: LF-Tag creation form

In my example, I created a tag with key `department` and values `marketing`. Upon clicking Add, you will create a key-value pair, and if you want to create multiple values in one go, just separate them with a comma, like my example in Figure 7.40. This will create two more key-value pairs with one Add operation.

Now we can click Create LF-Tag, and our tag will appear on the list of tags.

From the AWS CLI, the operation is even simpler. In Teamwork we have multiple products, so for example if I wanted to create tags for the product that the data in question relates to, I could use the following command:

```
$ aws lakeformation create-lf-tag --tag-key product --tag-value Teamwork
Desk Chat
```

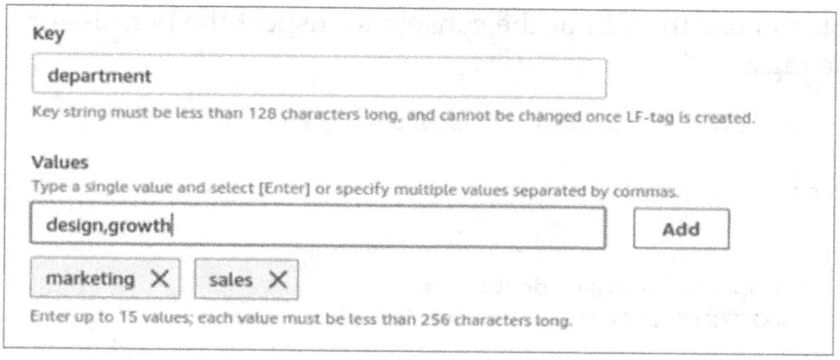

Figure 7.40: Adding key and values

NOTE If the profile you are using with the AWS CLI does not have `lakeformation` actions in an identity-based policy and it's not in the Data Lake administrators list, then it won't be allowed to create tags.

Let's retrieve the tags list from the CLI:

```
$ aws lakeformation list-lf-tags
{
"LFTags": [
    {
        "CatalogId": "972520707061",
        "TagKey": "department",
        "TagValues": [
            "marketing",
            "design",
            "growth",
            "sales"
        ]
    },
    {
        "CatalogId": "972520707061",
        "TagKey": "product",
        "TagValues": [
            "Chat",
            "Desk",
            "Teamwork"
        ]
    }
]
}
```

As expected, the tags created from the web console and the CLI are both appearing.

At this point you can use the CLI or the console to inspect the permissions associated with the tags:

```
$ aws lakeformation list-permissions --resource-type LF_TAG
{
    "PrincipalResourcePermissions": [
        {
            "Principal": {
                "DataLakePrincipalIdentifier":
"arn:aws:iam::XXXXXXXXXXXX:role/tw-data-and-analytics-team"
            },
            "Resource": {
                "LFTag": {
                    "CatalogId": "972520707061",
                    "TagKey": "department",
                    "TagValues": [
                        "*"
                    ]
                }
            },
            "Permissions": [
                "DESCRIBE"
            ],
            "PermissionsWithGrantOption": [
                "DESCRIBE"
            ]
        },
```

The list continues on for all tags and all permissions (ASSOCIATE, DESCRIBE) for each principal that has been granted permissions.

Now that you know how to create LF-Tags, let's try to assign them to resources. By selecting a database from Lake Formation, you will be brought to a screen where you can edit the LF-Tags. If no tags are associated with the resource, you will have a button like the one shown in Figure 7.41 in place of the tags list.

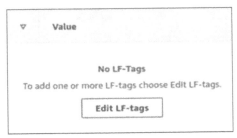

Figure 7.41: Empty tag list

Clicking Edit will bring up a modal window in which you can associate tags. The UI will only give you the option to choose from existing tags, which is very handy (Figure 7.42).

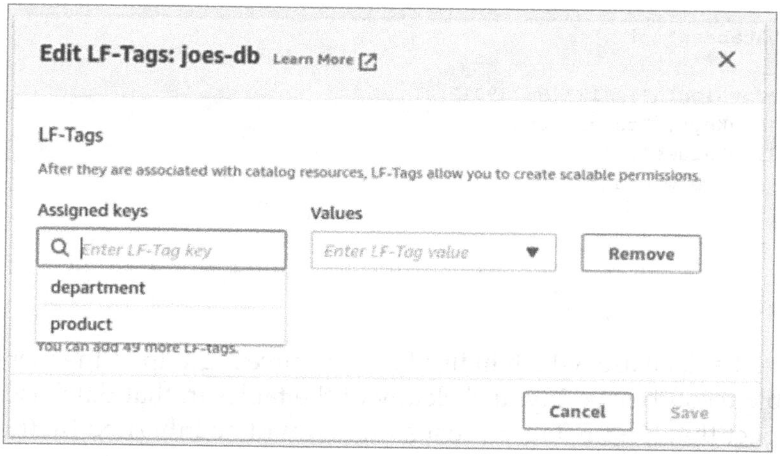

Edit LF-Tags: joes-db Learn More ☐   ✕

LF-Tags

After they are associated with catalog resources, LF-Tags allow you to create scalable permissions.

Assigned keys   **Values**

🔍 Enter LF-Tag key   Enter LF-Tag value   ▼   Remove

  department

  product

You can add 49 more LF-tags.

                                                        Cancel   Save

Figure 7.42: Edit LF-Tag form

At this point we need to choose the desired key and the value and click Save. As mentioned earlier, you can only tag the resource with one key-value pair per key. So if you tried to associate two `department` tag keys, the interface would prevent you from associating the tags, as shown in Figure 7.43.

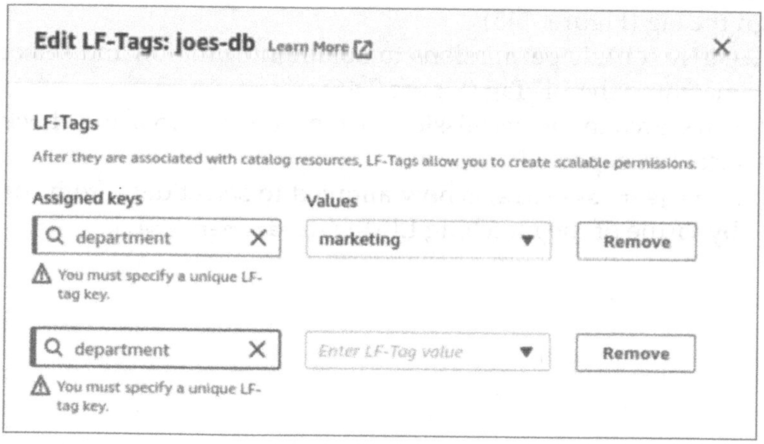

Edit LF-Tags: joes-db Learn More ☐   ✕

LF-Tags

After they are associated with catalog resources, LF-Tags allow you to create scalable permissions.

Assigned keys   **Values**

🔍 department   ✕   marketing   ▼   Remove

⚠ You must specify a unique LF-
   tag key.

🔍 department   ✕   Enter LF-Tag value   ▼   Remove

⚠ You must specify a unique LF-
   tag key.

Figure 7.43: LF-Tag validation

The tags will be listed in the Web Console, but you can also check with the AWS CLI:

```
$ aws lakeformation get-resource-lf-tags --resource {\"Database\":{\"Nam
e\":\"joes-db\"}}
{
    "LFTagOnDatabase": [
        {
            "CatalogId": "123456789012",
            "TagKey": "department",
            "TagValues": [
                "marketing"
            ]
        }
    ]
}
```

We have tagged a database, which in itself is a resource high up in the hierarchy of taggable resources. So if you click any of the tables in that database, you should expect that the LF-Tag we just assigned will be inherited by the tables contained in the database.

The last step we need to perform is to create an IAM role with an associated LF-Tag that will enable it to use the tagged database. I created `lf-tag-test-role` for the purpose, which is a Glue service role with the S3FullAccess policy attached to it.

In the Lake Formation console, let's go to Data Lake Permissions and click Grant. Here we can assign the permission to the newly created role. First, we select the role (Figure 7.44).

Then, we assign the tag (Figure 7.45).

At this point, we give it basic permissions to obtain information and select data on resources matching the LF-Tag (Figure 7.46).

And finally, we can search in the permissions list for the principal and check that everything worked as expected.

This new role, `lf-tags-test-role`, is now allowed to select data from the `joes-db` database by virtue of the matching LF-Tag `department=marketing`.

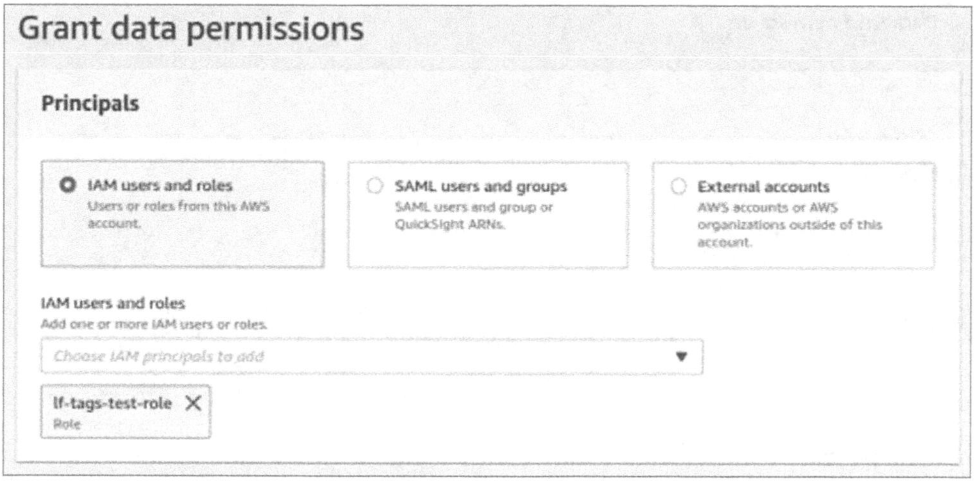

Figure 7.44: Grant data permissions form

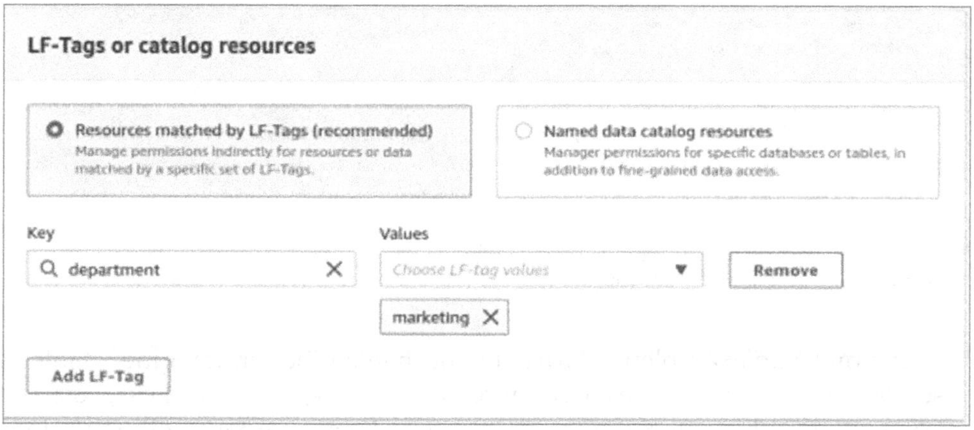

Figure 7.45: LF-Tag-based permission

Data Filters

Another, more granular option to manage security and governance in AWS is through the use of data filters. Data filters substantially grant discretionary access to databases, tables, but also columns and rows (through the use of filter conditions), consequently achieving cell-level security.

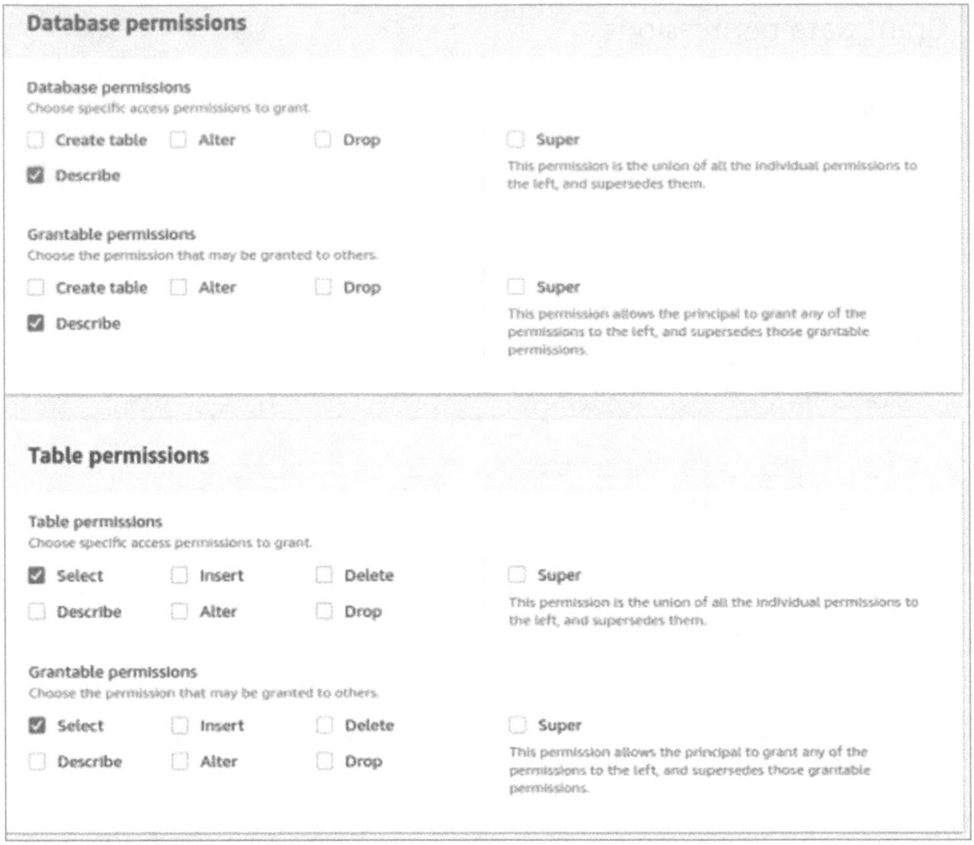

Figure 7.46: Database Permissions

Let's make an example to clarify the mechanism better. Imagine a table of user data in which you have the columns ID, NAME, AGE, EMAIL, ADDRESS, COUNTRY, and PRODUCT, which stores users' details for a SaaS company selling various products and would look similar to the following:

ID	NAME	AGE	ADDRESS	COUNTRY	PRODUCT
1	Joe	47	<address>	IE	1
2	Jill	32	<address>	US	2
3	Anna	26	<address>	DE	3

In our hypothetical use case, we want to grant use of the data to an external consultant conducting some demographic analysis, but we do not want to allow them to access private details such as geolocation/address data. Also, we are not interested in analyzing data related to the product with ID 3.

So the idea would be to create a filter that excludes the ADDRESS and COUNTRY columns, but also rows where the value for the PRODUCT column is 3. Effectively, the data we want to allow is the content of the italicized cells here:

ID	NAME	AGE	ADDRESS	COUNTRY	PRODUCT
1	*Joe*	*47*	<address>	*IE*	*1*
2	*Jill*	*32*	<address>	*US*	*2*
3	Anna	26	<address>	DE	3

This is where data filters come into the picture. Let's go ahead and create a data filter on one of our sample tables.

From Lake Formation, select Data Filters and click Create Data Filter. This will bring up a modal window for the creation of the filter. In my example, I will create a filter on the crawled posts S3 data we used in Chapter 6, excluding the Body column and discarding any row where the userId is 2, as shown in Figure 7.47.

Now, to enforce the filter, we need to grant permissions to an IAM role using the data filter restriction. We follow the same procedure we adopted for adding LF-Tag–based permissions, but this time we select Named Resources (as opposed to LF-Tags), select the correct database and table, and add the data filter, which will become available in the Filters drop-down list (Figure 7.48).

And there you go. The IAM role lf-tags-test-role is now only allowed to SELECT data from the cli_crawler_posts table according to the conditions listed in the data filter we created.

Governance Conclusions

Clearly, you can push a combination of LF-Tags and data filters to the extreme for the most granular security and governance policy. The possibilities are endless, and the flexibility granted by these two systems is clearly adaptable to any use case or business.

Whether you are an agile startup with an offensive data strategy that does not turn the screws on data access, or a government institution that needs thorough review of access policies for each individual data point that is used, Lake Formation covers all your needs.

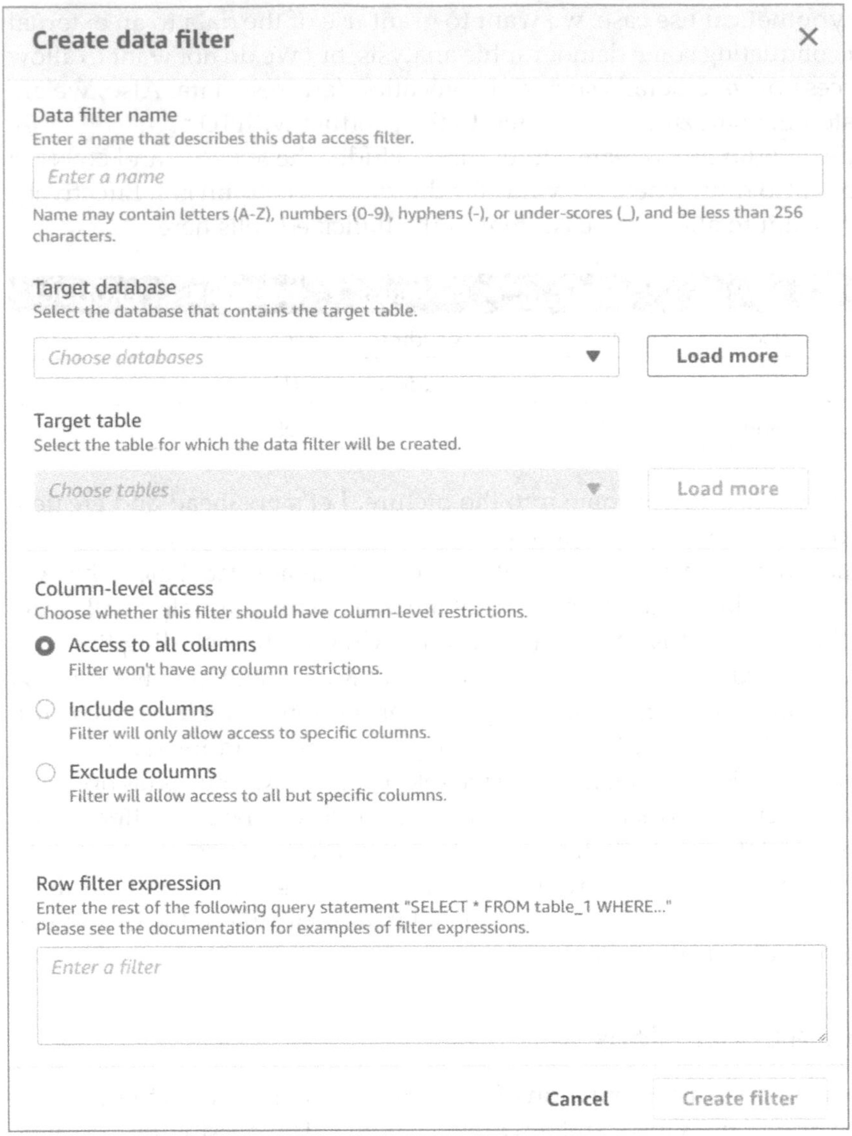

Create data filter   ✕

Data filter name
Enter a name that describes this data access filter.

> Enter a name

Name may contain letters (A-Z), numbers (0-9), hyphens (-), or under-scores (_), and be less than 256 characters.

Target database
Select the database that contains the target table.

| Choose databases ▼ | | Load more |

Target table
Select the table for which the data filter will be created.

| Choose tables ▼ | | Load more |

Column-level access
Choose whether this filter should have column-level restrictions.

🔘 **Access to all columns**
   Filter won't have any column restrictions.

◯ **Include columns**
   Filter will only allow access to specific columns.

◯ **Exclude columns**
   Filter will allow access to all but specific columns.

Row filter expression
Enter the rest of the following query statement "SELECT * FROM table_1 WHERE..."
Please see the documentation for examples of filter expressions.

> Enter a filter

Cancel   Create filter

Figure 7.47: Data filter creation form

Summary

In this chapter we explored the tools provided by AWS to catalog, search, and govern your data platform. The main actors are Glue, Athena, and Lake Formation. These three tools provide you with everything you need to discover your data, catalog it, and make it available to your analytical engines, and then allow (or restrict) access to the data through tags and filters.

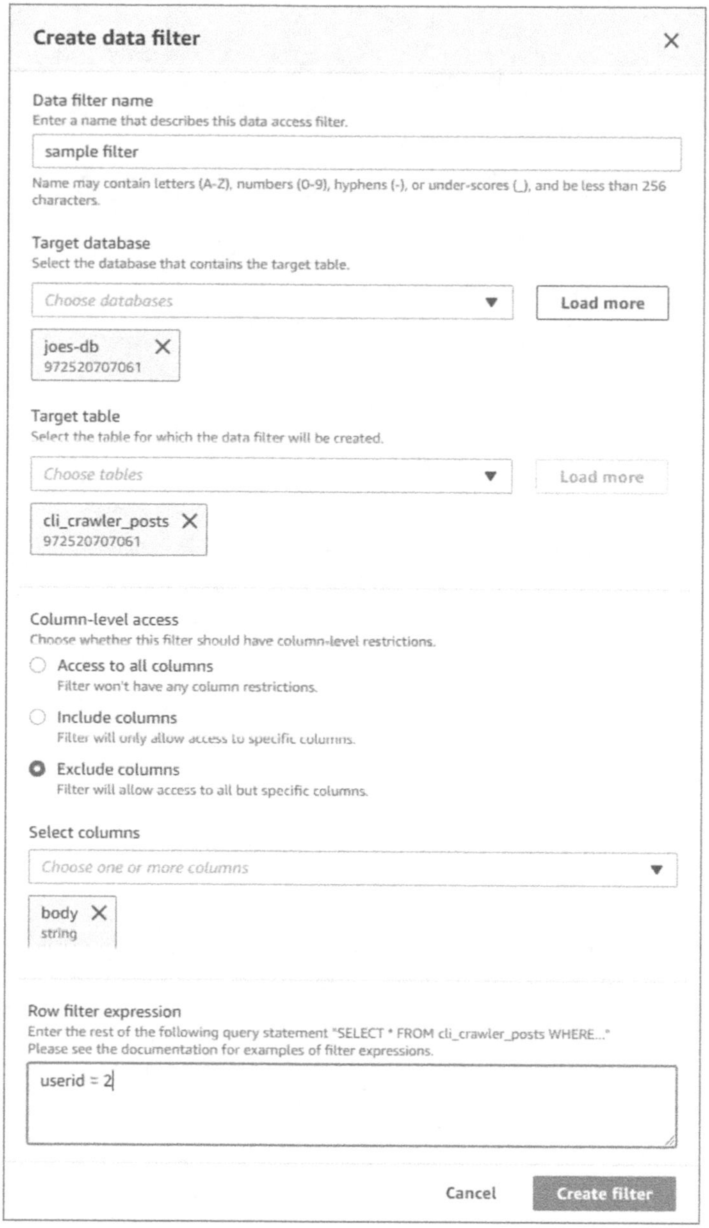

Create data filter   ✕

Data filter name
Enter a name that describes this data access filter.

    sample filter

Name may contain letters (A-Z), numbers (0-9), hyphens (-), or under-scores (_), and be less than 256 characters.

Target database
Select the database that contains the target table.

    Choose databases   ▼   Load more

    joes-db   ✕
    972520707061

Target table
Select the table for which the data filter will be created.

    Choose tables   ▼   Load more

    cli_crawler_posts ✕
    972520707061

Column-level access
Choose whether this filter should have column-level restrictions.
○ Access to all columns
   Filter won't have any column restrictions.
○ Include columns
   Filter will only allow access to specific columns.
◉ Exclude columns
   Filter will allow access to all but specific columns.

Select columns

    Choose one or more columns   ▼

    body ✕
    string

Row filter expression
Enter the rest of the following query statement "SELECT * FROM cli_crawler_posts WHERE..."
Please see the documentation for examples of filter expressions.

    userid = 2

                                        Cancel   Create filter

Figure 7.48: LF-Tag available in form

We are nearing the end of our journey: our data has been imported, processed, cataloged, and analyzed. All we need to do now is visualize it!

Data Consumption: BI, Visualization, and Reporting

All the work you have done up to now to prepare and implement a data lake architecture would make no sense unless the data was used for its purpose: to create actionable Insights. These can be business intelligence (BI) dashboards, reports, or any other kind of Insight, such as forecasts.

There are several ways to produce reports, but the AWS way is with Amazon QuickSight.

QuickSight

QuickSight is a BI and visualization tool that does not differ tremendously from other similar tools, such as Tableau or Power BI, offering similar features and developer experience.

However, where QuickSight really shines in your AWS-based architecture is in the following aspects:

- It's serverless, and therefore you do not need to manage servers to run it.
- It seamlessly integrates with AWS data sources, especially with your AWS Data Catalog/Glue, Athena, and Redshift, but also with relational databases, including Amazon Relational Database Service (RDS).

- It seamlessly integrates with Amazon SageMaker, for real-time (and offline) augmentation of data through machine learning (ML) model predictions and forecasts.

- It's very fast due to its computing in-memory engine, SPICE, which leverages an underlying highly provisioned storage unit.

- It's very easy to use; creating a highly informative visual is only a matter of dragging and dropping fields into field wells.

The main concepts in QuickSight are User & Group, Data Source, Dataset, Analysis, Visual, Insight, and Dashboard. Let's explore these ideas and see what they represent, but first let's get QuickSight set up.

Signing Up for QuickSight

QuickSight is somewhat of an outlier in that it requires you to specify the pricing model you are going to adopt. There are two: Standard and Enterprise. You need to have an AWS account and when you sign up for QuickSight you must specify the pricing model—but you do get an initial trial period (free) of 30 days. You can upgrade or downgrade at any time after signing up.

QuickSight is in the same landscape as tools such as Tableau, Power BI, and Google Data Studio, so it has a subscription model like all the other actors in this field. Monthly charges are determined by the roles of your users (Admin, Author, Reader).

Standard Plan

As of this writing, a price of $9/month (for annual subscriptions) and $12/month (for monthly payments) is applicable for Authors in QuickSight.

Enterprise Plan

The Enterprise pricing model is more complex and includes features such as QuickSight Q, an AI/ML capability that allows users to ask questions of your data in natural language. The model has been pretrained on domains such as sales, marketing, financial services, healthcare, and sports analytics. The Enterprise tier also enables sessions that are used to permit external users to consume QuickSight data, especially by embedding it in websites. The full details for pricing are available at `https://aws.amazon.com/quicksight/pricing`.

Users and User Groups

QuickSight has users. Anyone with a valid email address can be invited to be a user in QuickSight. This feature enables organizations to invite external users to produce visuals and dashboards, since not all companies and businesses will have a dedicated BI department. On the Enterprise plan, QuickSight also supports external federation, which is useful if your company has an external identity store, such as Active Directory.

When you issue an invitation to an email address, you can specify the role this new user will have within QuickSight, whether they are ADMIN, AUTHOR, or READER. That said, when you create a user, you can specify whether or not they are also an IAM user with an associated email address within the AWS account.

Clearly, if you are only creating users who are in your organization, associating the account with an IAM user is a better choice since you can govern their account with IAM policies.

Here is an overview of user-related concepts in QuickSight:

Administrators   Admins in QuickSight can manage the platform and therefore can create and delete top-level resources such as users, groups, data sources, and datasets. They can invite new users, change the user role, and add to or remove users from groups.

Author   Authors are BI developers who can use the tool for creating Insights and can therefore create new data sources and datasets and visualize them in an analysis.

Reader   Readers are users with read-only access to QuickSight. They can consume analytics, but they cannot modify anything within the platform.

Groups   User groups are not dissimilar to what you are probably familiar with in other contexts, or even AWS itself. Grouping users gives administrators the possibility to assign policies that are common to all the users in the group. That way, you can manage groups of users and ensure consistency of policy across departments.

Managing Users and Groups

QuickSight has a generic Manage QuickSight option available in the drop-down menu displayed by clicking the User icon on the top-right corner of the screen. After you click Users, you will see a User list page with an Invite User button used to create a user in QuickSight. Clicking that button brings up a window where you can type the email address of the user. Once you do, you will have to specify the rest of the details, such as the user's role and whether or not this user is an IAM user as well, as shown in Figure 8.1.

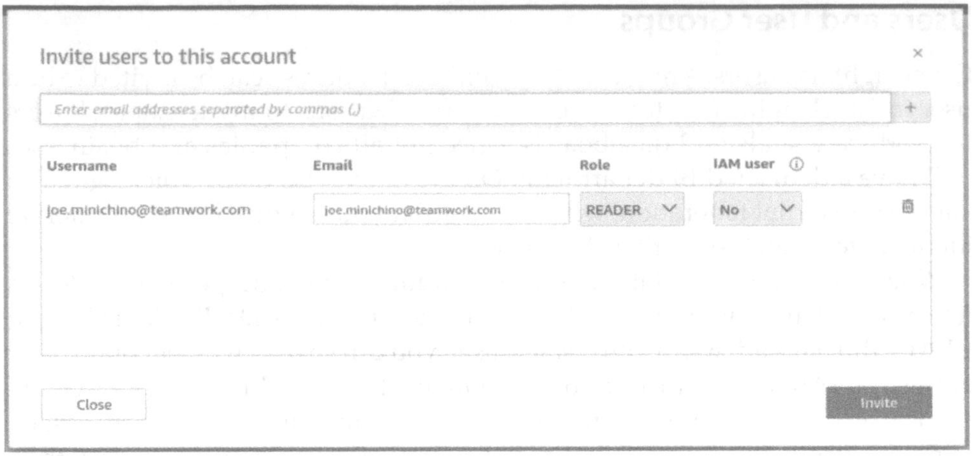

Figure 8.1: User invitation

Once the invitation has been issued, the user will be marked as pending until such time as they accept the invitation. Then they will appear as normal, with their role associated with them.

Managing groups is also available on the Manage QuickSight page, and creating a group is as easy as clicking New Group (see Figure 8.2).

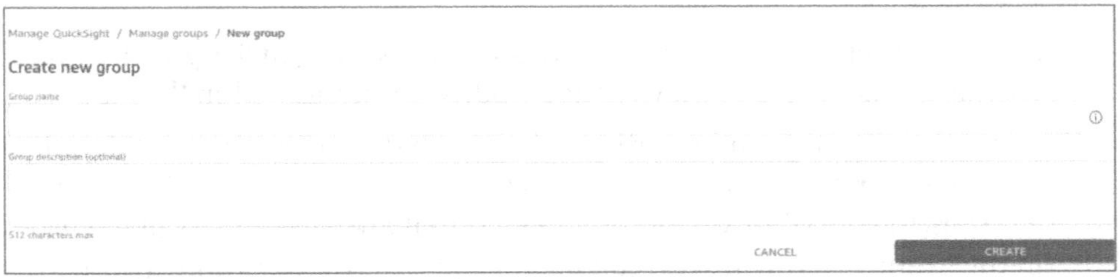

Figure 8.2: Create New Group

Managing QuickSight

There are several aspects of QuickSight that require your attention in order to ensure that data can be accessed correctly, both by QuickSight and by QuickSight users, as well as AWS Services.

Click the User icon at the top-right corner of the screen and then select Manage QuickSight to access the management console. Let's explore it.

Users and Groups

In this section, you can invite or delete users, change their permissions, include them or exclude them from a group, as well as create and delete groups.

Your Subscriptions

In this section, you can check the status of your subscription, including the estimated cost per month. Depending on your pricing plan, you will be shown data about sessions or reader costs, as shown in Figure 8.3.

Figure 8.3: Cost analysis in QuickSight

SPICE Capacity

Here you can check your SPICE usage, purchase more space, or release unused SPICE space, as shown in Figure 8.4.

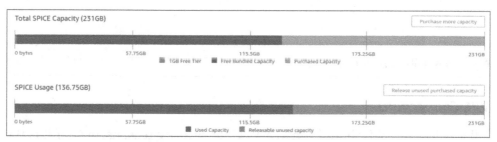

Figure 8.4: SPICE usage graph

Account Settings

In this section, you can set the email for administrators and even delete your QuickSight account.

Security and Permissions

In this section, you can manage QuickSight's security. Of particular note is the access to other AWS services, as shown in Figure 8.5.

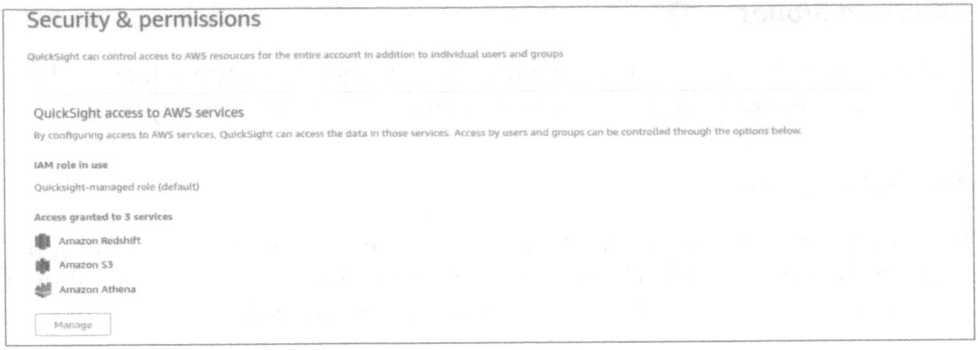

Security & permissions

QuickSight can control access to AWS resources for the entire account in addition to individual users and groups

QuickSight access to AWS services

By configuring access to AWS services, QuickSight can access the data in those services. Access by users and groups can be controlled through the options below.

IAM role in use

Quicksight-managed role (default)

Access granted to 3 services

🔲 Amazon Redshift

🔲 Amazon S3

📊 Amazon Athena

Manage

Figure 8.5: QuickSight access to AWS services

By clicking Manage, you can select what services QuickSight can gain access to. Note that retrieving data from Redshift or Athena will not work unless you explicitly grant access to those services from QuickSight. Even if you have granted access to Athena, you will need to also grant access to the underlying S3 bucket where the actual data is stored.

Other settings are IP restrictions to whitelist IPs that are contacting QuickSight (this is especially relevant for embedding analytics) and the public access to dashboards, which is a single toggle for all dashboards (Figure 8.6).

Manage public access to dashboards

⬤▬▬ Anyone on the internet
This will allow dashboards to be shared with public. Data on dashboards will be available to the public.

Figure 8.6: Public access to dashboards

VPC Connections

All services in AWS should run in a VPC for security reasons, even if it is the default one that gets created when you create your AWS account. However, QuickSight is a fully managed service running on its own servers (managed and scaled automatically by AWS), so you need to configure access to VPCs in your account.

All you need is the VPC ID you want to connect to and a relevant security group for the resources you are trying to access. For example, if you are trying to access a Redshift cluster running in a VPC, you will need the VPC ID where the cluster runs, and you will need a security group configured to allow traffic on port 5439 (the default for Redshift) or whatever port you have configured Redshift to allow traffic on.

Mobile Settings

Mobile access to QuickSight can be configured to require biometrics authentication, have a maximum session length, and force the requirement of the latest operating system version available on the device attempting access.

Domains and Embedding

Here you can configure the domains that are allowed to contain embedded visuals from QuickSight.

Single Sign-On

Single sign-on (SSO) is a common method of authentication these days that relies on identity providers. In other words, rather than storing a user's credentials, you leverage the identity this user possesses already with other identity providers such as Amazon, Google, or Facebook. If the user is logged in with one of these providers, then authentication can be authorized through those providers.

To configure SSO, you need to activate it and provide the URL used by the identity provider for the authentication, as well as the URL the user will be redirected to once authentication is successful.

SSO as a topic is outside the scope of this chapter. You can see the full documentation on how to use federation and SSO here: `https://docs.aws.amazon.com/quicksight/latest/user/external-identity-providers.html`.

Data Sources and Datasets

There are several ways to import data into QuickSight so that you can analyze it, including uploading files such as CSV files. In the context of the construction of a data platform, however, you will likely rely on a data lake and cataloged resources, and then connect QuickSight to those resources to create analyses and dashboards.

These are the data sources supported by QuickSight:

- Amazon Athena
- Amazon Aurora
- Amazon OpenSearch Service
- Amazon Redshift
- Amazon Redshift Spectrum
- Amazon S3
- Amazon S3 Analytics

- Apache Spark 2.0 or later
- AWS IoT Analytics
- Exasol 7.1.2 or later
- MariaDB 10.0 or later
- Microsoft SQL Server 2012 or later
- MySQL 5.1 or later
- Oracle 12c or later
- PostgreSQL 9.3.1 or later
- Presto 0.167 or later
- Snowflake
- Teradata 14.0 or later
- Timestream

Since this list is always growing, consult the following site for an up-to-date version:

```
https://docs.aws.amazon.com/quicksight/latest/user/supported-data-
sources.html
```

Note that Redshift, Athena, and RDS must be within an AWS environment to be available.

If you take a look at QuickSight's navigation menu (see Figure 8.7), it does not list "Data Sources." This is because QuickSight allows you to create a data source only when you initiate the creation of a dataset from the web interface. You can, however, create a data source on its own from the AWS CLI, as you will see later in the "Creating a Data Source from the AWS CLI" section.

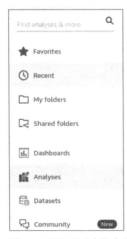

Figure 8.7: QuickSight's navigation menu

Once you create the data source, you can reuse it across datasets. Given this premise, let's go ahead and create a data source by clicking Datasets and then clicking the New Dataset button at the top right.

Creating an Athena Data Source

At this point, you will be asked to pick your data source, which is one of the options just listed as well as a few social media–related sources such as Twitter and Adobe Analytics, as shown in Figure 8.8.

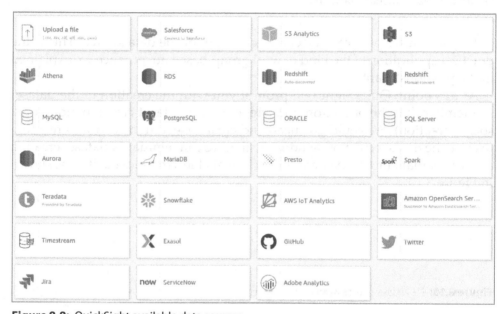

Figure 8.8: QuickSight available data sources

In our case, most of our data should reside in S3, Athena, or Redshift. Choosing Athena has the advantage that it will allow you to use underlying federated queries that you may have wrapped in a view cataloged under AwsDataCatalog, which is available by default. Selecting Athena brings up the data source creation window shown in Figure 8.9.

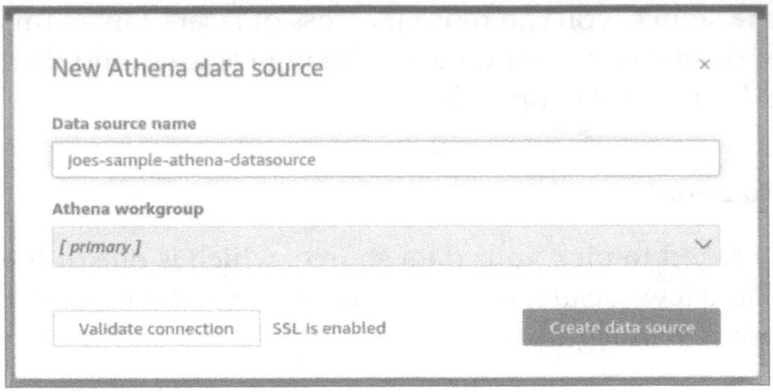

New Athena data source   ✕

Data source name

joes-sample-athena-datasource

Athena workgroup

[primary]   ⌄

Validate connection   SSL is enabled   Create data source

Figure 8.9: New Athena Data Source

As you can see, you can select a workgroup for the data source. This is the practical application of the kind of workgroup-based governance we explained in the previous chapter.

At this point, QuickSight will prompt you with the creation of the dataset (remember that the operation you triggered is a dataset creation, not a data source creation). We could go ahead and create one, but instead we are going to close the dataset creation window so that we can reinitiate a dataset creation and verify that our Athena data source is available. And indeed, it is, as shown in Figure 8.10.

FROM EXISTING DATA SOURCES

joes-sample-athena-dat...
Updated 2 minutes ago

Figure 8.10: New data source available

Creating Other Data Sources

You always initiate the creation of a data source through the creation of a dataset. Athena data sources and S3 data sources are very straightforward because they require no credentials or configuration. However, any other kind of data source will possibly require configuration details such as the host of the data source, maybe a username/password credential pair, port number, and database name. Needless to say, you should possess this information before you can create an RDS data source, for example.

Creating a Data Source from the AWS CLI

The CLI tool, unlike the web interface, allows you to create a data source without creating a dataset. Use this command to create a data source:

```
$ aws quicksight create-data-source
```

There are a few details you have to supply, as illustrated by the help message:

```
SYNOPSIS
        create-data-source
    --aws-account-id <value>
    --data-source-id <value>
    --name <value>
    --type <value>
    [--data-source-parameters <value>]
    [--credentials <value>]
    [--permissions <value>]
    [--vpc-connection-properties <value>]
    [--ssl-properties <value>]
    [--tags <value>]
    [--cli-input-json | --cli-input-yaml]
    [--generate-cli-skeleton <value>]
```

For an Athena data source, most options are not applicable, and the creation is straightforward. All you need to do is supply the required flag values and specify **ATHENA** as the data source type. Let's give it a try, using the usual `generate-cli-skeleton` approach. If you try the option, it will generate a YAML file that serves as a template for your command. I saved mine and edited it by eliminating all options that do not relate to an Athena data source. It looks like this:

```
AwsAccountId: '123456789012'
DataSourceId: 'joes-cli-qs-datasource'
Name: 'joes-cli-qs-datasource'
Type: ATHENA
DataSourceParameters:
  AthenaParameters:
    WorkGroup: 'primary'

Tags:
- Key: 'use'
  Value: 'joes-stuff'
```

If you try to run it with this:

```
$ aws quicksight create-data-source cli-input-yaml file://athena_
datasource.yaml
```

and if it all goes well, you will receive an output similar to this:

```
$ aws quicksight create-data-source --cli-input-yaml file://athena_
quicksight_datasource.yaml
{
    "Status": 202,
    "Arn": "arn:aws:quicksight:eu-west-1:123456789012:datasource/
joes-cli-qs-datasource",
```

```
        "DataSourceId": "joes-cli-qs-datasource",
        "CreationStatus": "CREATION_IN_PROGRESS",
        "RequestId": "74076498-b794-4157-9dea-7d2b580c6569"
}
```

And if you then use the command $ **aws quicksight list-data-sources**
--aws-account-id 123456789012, you will obtain output similar to the following:

```
{
            "Arn": "arn:aws:quicksight:eu-west-1:972520707061:datasource/
da86e0ed-127b-4b37-8420-e422d4344b09",
            "DataSourceId": "da86e0ed-127b-4b37-8420-e422d4344b09",
            "Name": "joes-sample-athena-datasource",
            "Type": "ATHENA",
            "Status": "CREATION_SUCCESSFUL",
            "CreatedTime": "2022-09-07T14:34:46.148000+00:00",
            "LastUpdatedTime": "2022-09-07T14:34:46.148000+00:00",
            "DataSourceParameters": {
                "AthenaParameters": {
                    "WorkGroup": "primary"
                }
            },
            "SslProperties": {
                "DisableSsl": false
            }
        }
}
```

indicating that your data source was created successfully.

Creating a Dataset from a Table

Now that we have our data source in place, we can create a dataset. Let's go
ahead and select the original Athena data source, then choose the database and
table we want to import into QuickSight, as shown in Figure 8.11.

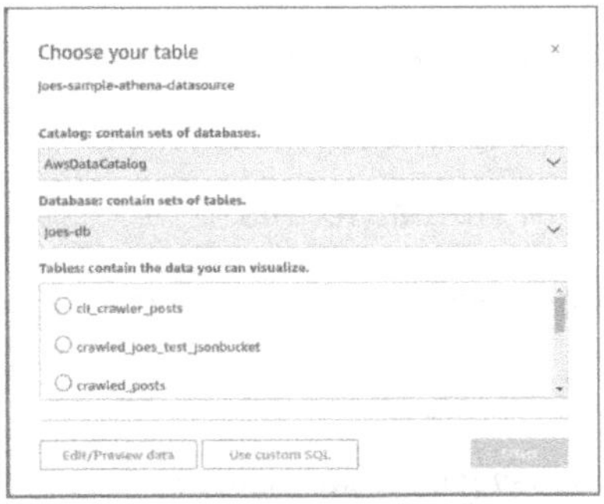

Figure 8.11: Choose Your Table

QuickSight automatically picks up the available databases and tables, and lets you choose them as the raw data for a dataset.

Once your table is selected, you have three choices:

- Simply click Select and create a dataset from the whole table.
- Click Edit/Preview Data to preview the data contained in the table and apply transformations such as data type change or add computed fields to the dataset.
- Click Use Custom SQL to create a dataset from a SQL query instead of the whole table.

We will explore the second and third options, since choosing the second without making any changes to the original data is the equivalent of the first option.

By clicking Edit/Preview Data, we are brought to QuickSight's data editor, a very powerful feature that allows us to manipulate data before it is used for visualization.

Creating a Dataset from a SQL Query

The process of creating a dataset from a query is nearly the same, but instead of picking a table from a drop-down list, you specify a SQL query that will generate a result set, which is then used as the base dataset.

All you need to do is click Use Custom SQL, and an editor opens where you can insert your SQL query, as shown in Figure 8.12. You can then click Edit/Preview Data to check the result of your query.

Figure 8.12: Enter Custom SQL Query

At this point, instead of the grid on the top pane you will have the SQL query you wrote, and you can run it to check what data it generates by clicking the Apply button, as shown in Figure 8.13.

Figure 8.13: Apply query to data source

Remember to change the default query name to something meaningful, especially if you want to join more datasets together. Otherwise, you will end up with a lot of New Custom SQL datasets on the screen.

After clicking Apply, you will see the data in the bottom pane. Let's explore the data editor to see how we can manipulate and prepare data for visualization.

Duplicating Datasets

One of the most common ways to create a dataset is to start from an existing one. Common use cases are enriching an existing dataset without unnecessarily increasing the size of the original one, or a version of an existing dataset with different filters applied on it.

In the QuickSight Console, go to Datasets and click the dataset you want to duplicate. A summary screen opens for that dataset. In the top right of the screen, you have an Edit Dataset drop-down menu. Clicking it gives you the option to duplicate the dataset, as shown in Figure 8.14.

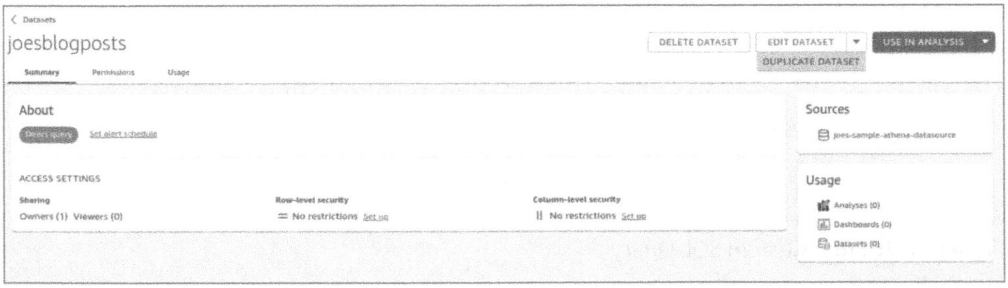

Figure 8.14: Duplicate Dataset

Note on Creating Datasets

From my experience, managing datasets can become extremely complex. Teams might strive to create reusability of datasets in the hope that once a few basic blocks are built, all other datasets can simply be derived. But this is more often than not just an illusion. Each analysis will have its own use cases, and manipulating data in QuickSight becomes a suboptimal place to do so.

So, complex datasets are better created as an Athena view. There you can put all sorts of conversion/cast operations and filters, and have data land in QuickSight already as clean as it possibly can be. I tend to see QuickSight as a place where data is manipulated for the sake of visualization only, and nothing else.

Also note that QuickSight supports autodiscovery of datasets within the AWS account running QuickSight, which is a nice way to obtain access to databases and data stores in your AWS account from QuickSight. For more information on this Enterprise plan feature, visit `https://docs.aws.amazon.com/quicksight/latest/user/autodiscover-aws-data-sources.html`.

QuickSight Favorites, Recent, and Folders

Clicking the star icon next to a dataset, analysis, or dashboard will mark it as a favorite, which will become easily accessible through the Favorites link in the QuickSight Console. The Recent link will store the 10 latest items you have worked on.

One very handy feature of QuickSight is the folders available in the QuickSight Console, as shown in Figure 8.15. Folders allow you to group datasets, analyses, and dashboards in a way that makes sense to you. Additionally, you can create shared folders across users and groups, making it easy for other users to find your work.

Figure 8.15: Available resource categories in the UI

SPICE

QuickSight allows you to import data in two ways: by direct query of data sources or with SPICE. SPICE (Super-fast, Parallel, In-memory Calculation Engine) is an in-memory calculation engine that allows QuickSight to perform super-fast calculations to render visuals almost instantaneously.

SPICE has two main benefits:

- It is orders of magnitude faster than direct querying.
- Data can be refreshed at a specified rate (maximum of 100 times per day). In my experience the vast majority of dashboards rely on a daily rate of data refresh.

Dashboards and analyses relying on direct queries get refreshed when you open them, which can be slow to load.

SPICE, however, is not free, having a price of 38 cents/month as of this writing.

Manage SPICE Capacity

The documentation suggests the following formula to calculate the SPICE capacity for a dataset:

```
Total logical row size in bytes =
   (Number of Numeric Fields *  8 bytes per field)
 + (Number of Date Fields    *  8 bytes per field)
 + (Number of Text Fields    * (8 bytes + UTF-8 encoded character length
per field) )

Total bytes of data = Number of rows * Total logical row size in bytes

GB of SPICE Capacity Needed = Total bytes of data / 1,073,741,824
```

This is important to keep in mind when planning the SPICE capacity for your datasets. Since I started using QuickSight I've only used direct queries for exploration work, but for any analysis underlying a dashboard destined for consumption, I always use SPICE, and that is also my recommendation to you.

At any point while working on an analysis or editing a dataset, you can always refresh the data imported in SPICE by clicking the Refresh Now button in the bottom-left corner of the data editor, as shown in Figure 8.16.

Figure 8.16: Refresh Now button

You can also refresh the dataset by selecting it from the list of datasets in the Web Console and choosing Refresh.

Refresh Schedule

When viewing the summary of a dataset (QuickSight ➢ Datasets, then clicking a dataset's name, *not* the three-dots icon), you can choose to refresh the data manually or add a refresh schedule, as shown in Figure 8.17.

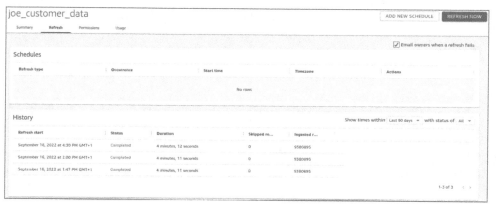

Figure 8.17: Refresh schedule and history of a dataset

This is certainly the option you will want to adopt when your dataset is used by live dashboards used for active consumption. In my experience, most pipelines, from import to visualization, run on a daily rate, but monthly and weekly are not uncommon.

To create the schedule, click Add New Schedule at the top right of the dataset summary.

QuickSight Data Editor

The graphical editor in QuickSight is a very powerful and intuitive tool. It features a grid in the top half of the screen, where it is possible to manipulate and join datasets, and a preview pane at the bottom, showing the result of the manipulations.

Upon creating your first dataset, you might encounter the error shown in Figure 8.18.

Figure 8.18: Common SQL error message

If you click Show Details, you will get an error indicating QuickSight has no permission to access the S3 bucket where the underlying data for your AWS Glue Catalog or Athena table resides.

To fix this, click the User icon and select Manage QuickSight ➤ Security & Permissions, and then click Manage in the QuickSight Access To AWS Services section. You will be presented with a menu similar to the one shown in Figure 8.19. Click Select S3 Buckets, add the bucket where your data is contained, and repeat the dataset creation operation.

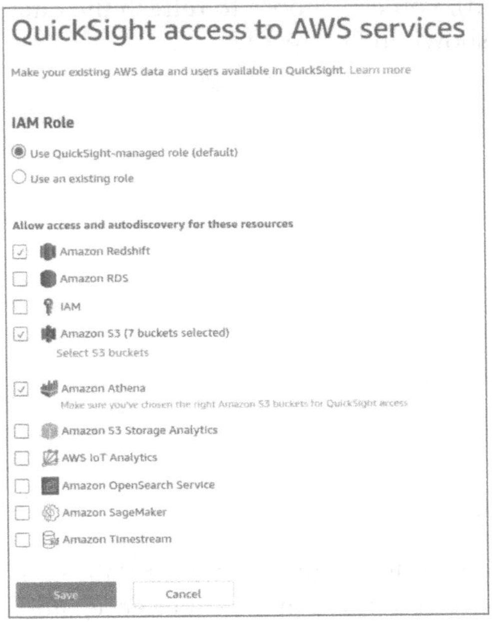

Figure 8.19: Available services in QuickSight

At this point, all should be looking good. At the top of the screen, you should have a grid diagram with the table you selected and, at the bottom, a table preview of the data, much like Figure 8.20.

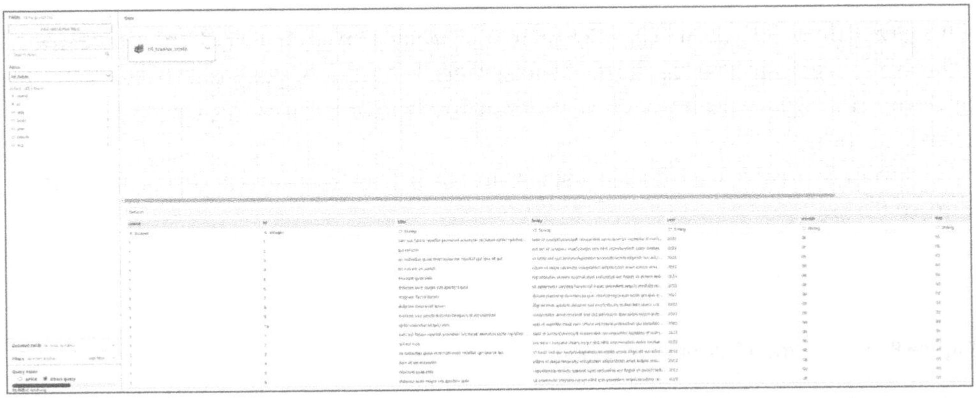

Figure 8.20: Editor view

In Figure 8.20, I have used the blog post data from previous chapters, taken straight from the table generated by the crawler we created through the AWS CLI tool.

If you are happy with the data that you want to visualize, then click Save And Publish, which will save the dataset in QuickSight. Be sure to give the dataset a meaningful name in the text-editing box in the top-left corner of the screen.

Return to the main screen and click Datasets to display the newly created dataset. You can also retrieve the complete list of datasets in the AWS CLI with this command:

```
$ aws quicksight list-data-sets -aws-account-id XXXXXXXXXXXX
```

which produces an output similar to this:

```
{
    "DataSetSummaries": [
        {
            "Arn": "arn:aws:quicksight:eu-west-1:972520707061:
dataset/2ae4f121-c447-478a-876a-0bd9a80d47f8",
            "DataSetId": "2ae4f121-c447-478a-876a-0bd9a80d47f8",
            "Name": "my dataset",
            "CreatedTime": "2021-02-04T13:32:52.547000+01:00",
            "LastUpdatedTime": "2021-02-04T13:32:52.547000+01:00",
            "ImportMode": "DIRECT_QUERY",
            "RowLevelPermissionTagConfigurationApplied": false,
            "ColumnLevelPermissionRulesApplied": false
        },
        {
            "Arn": "arn:aws:quicksight:eu-west-1:972520707061:dataset/
2ccea31f-6014-46e7-81a3-dfe36918b20d",
            "DataSetId": "2ccea31f-6014-46e7-81a3-dfe36918b20d",
            "Name": "my other dataset",
            "CreatedTime": "2021-07-01T14:11:26.973000+00:00",
            "LastUpdatedTime": "2021-07-13T08:20:53.146000+00:00",
            "ImportMode": "SPICE",
            "RowLevelPermissionTagConfigurationApplied": false,
            "ColumnLevelPermissionRulesApplied": false
        }, ...
```

Now that the dataset is ready for use, click the three-dots icon at the end of the row to open a menu with the options shown in Figure 8.21.

Figure 8.21: Dataset options

Let's click Edit Dataset to manipulate the data in the editor.

QuickSight Data Types

QuickSight supports a small number of data types: Integer, Decimal, Date, and String, as well as geo types such as Country, State, County, City, Postcode, Longitude, and Latitude.

Change Data Types

The first kind of manipulation operation you can perform is to change the data type of a field. Once the data is loaded in the editor, the fields will be listed on the right side. You click the three-dots icon next to a field to see the options in Figure 8.22.

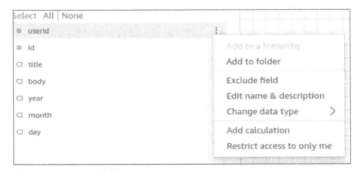

Figure 8.22: Field options

If you hover over the Change Data Type option, you will be offered the choice of any of the other types. In our example, the Integer option will not be offered since the field type is Integer. Every other type will be available for selection. Changing a data type is not necessarily a successful operation, especially when it comes to non-obvious conversions such as dates. The most common use case for a data type change is the conversion of strings to dates.

Calculated Fields

Another interesting option is calculated fields. Calculated fields add a field to the dataset whose value is derived from one or more of the other fields. The programming language to create calculated fields is a scripting language, with built-in functions provided by QuickSight. The full documentation for the available functions and operators is here: https://docs.aws.amazon.com/quicksight/latest/user/working-with-calculated-fields.html.

Calculation Scripting Language

QuickSight's scripting language looks a bit like JavaScript or Python, simplified. The value of a calculated field will be the result of the expression you entered, so there's no need for `return` statements.

For example, if you want to add a calculated field that is the concatenation of two string values, this is all you need to do:

```
concat(string1, string2)
```

There's no need for creating variables or including `return` statements. Indeed, QuickSight's calculated field feature is not suitable for long and complex calculations that may be better addressed at ETL time instead, so creating variables for reuse is not possible.

Conditional control is done through the `ifelse` function, whereby the first argument is the statement being computed (the `if` part), the second argument is the expression in case the `IF` statement is true, and the last argument is the `else` expression. Pairs of expressions preceding the `else` expression are to be considered `if-else` conditions followed by the final `else` statement. In other words:

```
ifelse(if-expression-1, then-expression-1 [, if-expression-n, then-
expression-n ...], else-expression)
```

In Chapter 6, "Processing Data," we added a field called `bodyLength` to the data at ETL time, so we'll perform a similar operation. Let's add a field called `bodyLength`, which is the numeric value of the length of the string of the `Body` field. To do this, click the three-dots icon next to a field and select Add Calculation, or click the big Add Calculated Field button that is at the top of the Fields list.

The calculated field interface has a field name box at the top, a code editor on the left, and a list of built-in functions that can be included in the code for the field calculation on the right. You can inspect what each function does, what arguments it takes, and what type it returns by selecting a function. The bottom-right corner of the interface will be populated with the information, as shown in Figure 8.23.

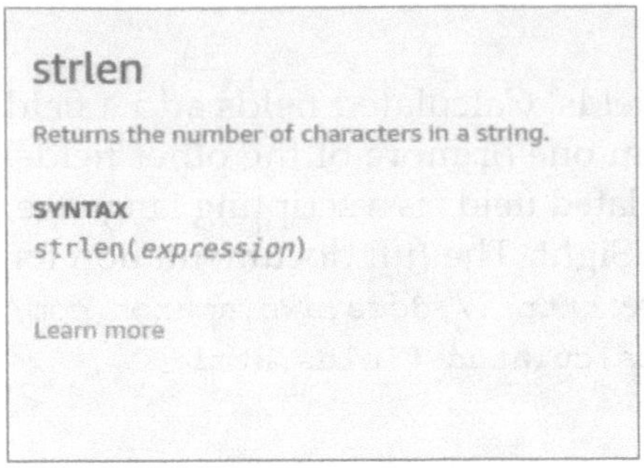

strlen
Returns the number of characters in a string.
SYNTAX
strlen(expression)
Learn more

Figure 8.23: Inspecting a script function

In our case, if you double-click the function `strlen` (string length), it will be automatically added into the editor where your cursor is, as shown in Figure 8.24.

bodyLength
strlen()
Fields
Functions

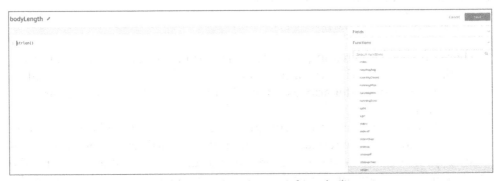

Figure 8.24: Placing a function in a script by selecting it from the list

Now we want to specify the field being processed, so place the cursor between the parentheses of the `strlen` function, collapse the Functions list, and expand the Fields list. Then, double-click `body`, and you should get the following code generated for you:

```
strlen({body})
```

Notice that fields are wrapped in curly brackets.

Clicking Save will add the field to your dataset. Now the new field will appear in the dataset, as shown in Figure 8.25.

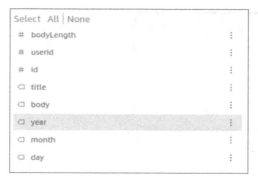

Figure 8.25: `bodyLength` field now available

As a second example of adding a calculated field, let's create a field called when that is a concatenation of the year, month, and day fields in a YYYY-MM-DD format and then parsed into a date, like this:

```
parseDate(concat({year},'-',{month},'-',{day}))
```

Now, under the list of fields in the dataset, you will have a new field, with the calendar icon representing the date type, as shown in Figure 8.26.

Figure 8.26: Data type icon changed

When you are finished adding fields, remember to click Save And Publish to save the edits you performed. This will trigger a background save operation, and you can keep modifying your data in the data editor.

Joining Data

Very often you will be in a position where you want to enrich data to create actionable Insights, so you may want to include multiple sources of data in your dataset. Once other tables/result sets have been included in the dataset that you are working on, you can join them to create an extended/enriched dataset. To do this, click the Add Data button at the top-right corner of the data editor interface.

After clicking the button, you will be able to bring more data in, effectively restarting the dataset creation from the start. However, whatever data you import will not be created as an independent dataset but will be included only in the one you are currently working on (Figure 8.27).

Add data   ×

Select   ⌄

    Dataset
    Data source
    Upload a file

Figure 8.27: Add data to current dataset

Select Dataset if you want to import a whole dataset, or select Data Source if you want to create a specific result set from a table or a SQL query (which is advisable, as you should always limit yourself to what you absolutely need) or upload a file. Once you have imported the new data, it will be added to the grid, as shown in Figure 8.28.

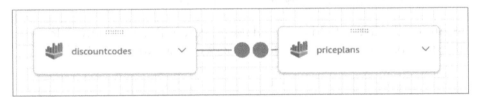

Figure 8.28: Newly added dataset

Note those red dots that signify the relationship between the two datasets. At first, no relationship at all is defined. To define it, we click the two dots, and a form that lets us select fields from each dataset to join them on will appear on the bottom half of the screen. As in actual SQL, you will be able to define OUTER, LEFT, RIGHT, and INNER joins, as shown in Figure 8.29.

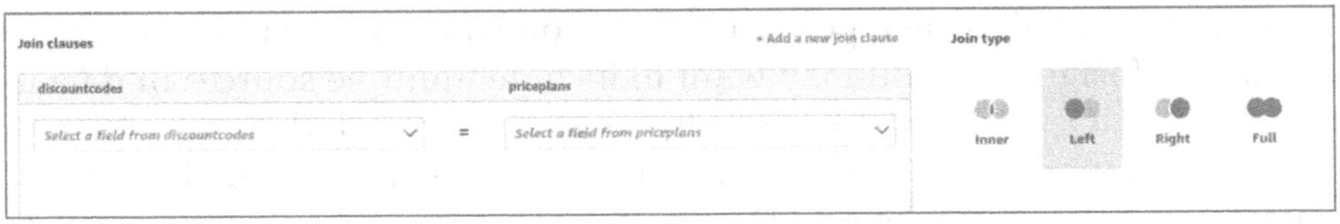

Join clauses		+ Add a new join clause	Join type			
discountcodes	priceplans					
Select a field from discountcodes ⌄	=	Select a field from priceplans ⌄	Inner	Left	Right	Full

Figure 8.29: Relationship UI

All you need to do is select one field from the left dataset and another from the right one, and define the join type. It's quite common to have to deal with tables with hundreds of fields, so you can also leverage the field search feature when you click on a drop-down list, as shown in Figure 8.30.

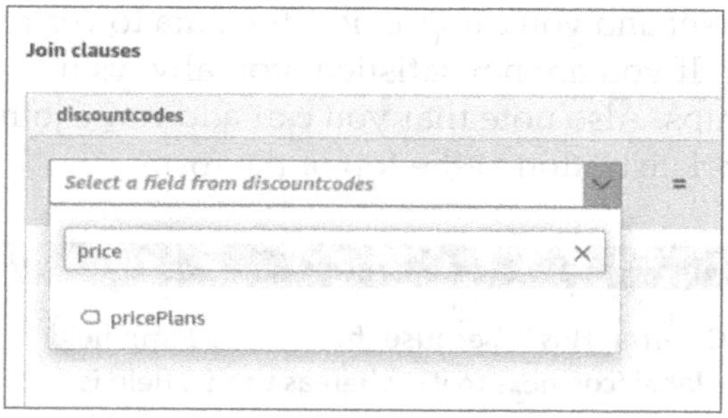

Figure 8.30: Field search

In this example, we use an INNER join (see Figure 8.31).

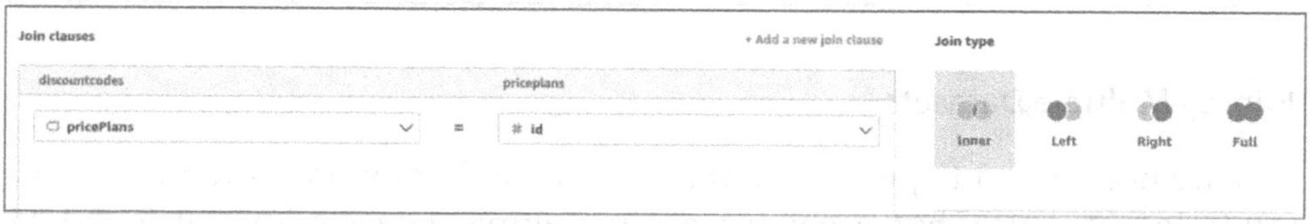

Figure 8.31: Specifying an INNER join

Note that, upon choosing the join type, you will also be asked if there is a unique key value in either dataset. QuickSight will recommend a join type based on that information (Figure 8.32).

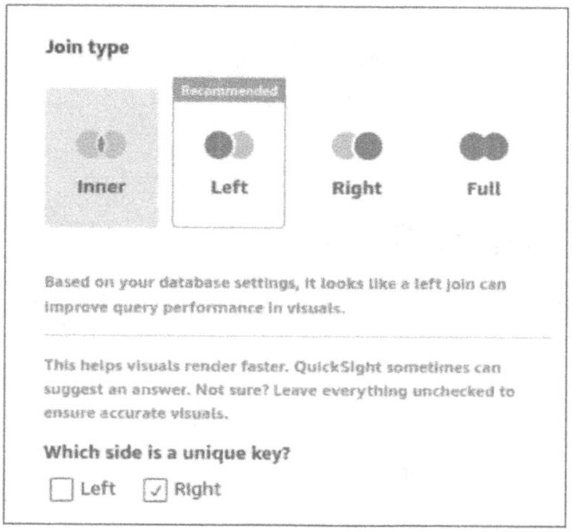

Figure 8.32: Recommended join

Click Apply to generate the result set and you can preview the data to verify that you are happy with the output. If you are not satisfied, you always have time to change fields and relationships. Also note that you can add more join relationships by clicking the appropriate button at the top of the form.

BEWARE DATA TYPES

Note that our example will generate a SQL error. This is because the `pricePlans` field is a `VARCHAR` (as symbolized by the blue label icon next to it), whereas the `id` field is an integer (as symbolized by the green hash icon). You cannot perform joins on fields with incompatible data types. So how would you perform that kind of join if you absolutely needed it? The quickest solution is to generate the dataset from a SQL query and perform a cast operation within the SQL, effectively casting a `VARCHAR` to an `int`, which will then be joined to an `int` field in the second table.

Joining Multiple Datasets

You are not limited to joining a dataset with another on one key. You can use multiple join clauses but also you can join multiple datasets. You can join dataset A to dataset B on some condition, and then you can join dataset C to either A or B. Indeed, you could end with a fairly large diagram of result sets joined on different fields.

For example, you could construct a dataset that is the result of a single table joining to two others, as shown in Figure 8.33, or chained linearly, with the third table joined to the second one (Figure 8.34).

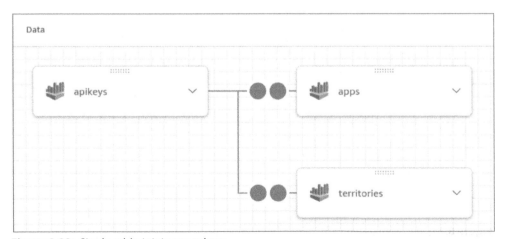

Figure 8.33: Single table joining to others

Figure 8.34: Complex relationship diagram

There is really no limit to the structure of your dataset.

Excluding Fields

Unless you are creating a dataset from a SQL query, chances are that all the fields you retrieved from a table are not of interest for your analysis. Therefore, it is good practice to exclude those fields since they take up space in your SPICE storage.

Excluding a field is as simple as clicking the three-dots icon next to a field on the list of fields and selecting Exclude Field. This will add the excluded field to the list of excluded fields, which is still available immediately below the field list, as shown in Figure 8.35.

Figure 8.35: Excluded fields at the bottom of the list

Filtering Data

Another option to keep data relevant and slim is to filter it. Under the list of fields, there is a Filters collapsible section that shows you the filters you have created and allows you to create new ones. Clicking Add Filter brings up the list of fields in the dataset. Select a field and immediately a filter with the condition `Equals - none` will be created, as shown in Figure 8.36.

Figure 8.36: Filter view

Now, click the three-dots icon and choose Edit, and you can specify whatever conditions satisfy your use case. The conditions available are like those shown in Figure 8.37.

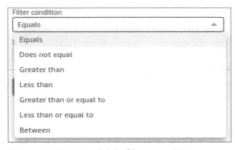

Figure 8.37: Available filter conditions

You will see a Value text box, where you enter the desired value, except for the Between condition, in which case you'll need to fill two text boxes, Minimum Value and Maximum Value. The menu also gives you the option to disable the filter without deleting it in case you want to observe how data changes in your result set. After you have created the filter, the data not satisfying the conditions of the filter will disappear.

Removing Data

At any point, clicking on the drop-down arrow of a dataset in the grid gives you the option to remove the dataset by selecting Remove. This will also (obviously) delete any join relationship that dataset might have had associated with other imported datasets.

Geospatial Hierarchies and Adding Fields to Hierarchies

When converting a field to geo data types such as Country or City, the option to add the field to a hierarchy becomes available from a field's menu. When you click Add To A Hierarchy, you are then offered the option to add the field to an existing hierarchy or to create one (Figure 8.38).

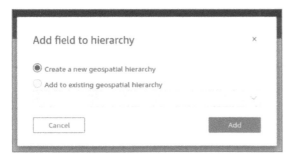

Figure 8.38: Add Field To Hierarchy

Clicking Add will then allow you to create the hierarchy. In my case I have a field, `signupCountry`, symbolizing a country, so I am going to create a geo-hierarchy called `geoInfo` and use the `signupCountry` field in it (Figure 8.39).

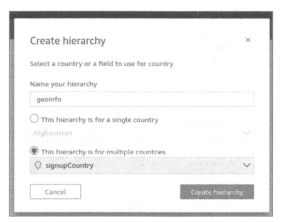

Figure 8.39: Adding to an existing hierarchy

Alternatively, choosing This Hierarchy Is For A Single Country lets you select a single country in the world and this newly created hierarchy will only apply to that country. The purpose of this option is to address the different ways of composing addresses in the different countries of the world. Hierarchies can then be used in analyses to create maps and geospatial data visualizations.

Unsupported Format Dates

If your fields are coming from a database query, it's likely QuickSight will be able to automatically infer the Date type on them. But if this does not happen, or if you have dates stored in unsupported formats, you can always instruct QuickSight to operate this transformation for you, and if all the values for that field adhere to the pattern you provided, then you should be able to convert the field to a Date. A prerequisite for this kind of type conversion is that the original field be of type String. If it's not, then you have to first convert the original field to a String, and then convert it to a Date.

When you click the menu to convert the field, after selecting the Date type, you'll see the Edit Date Format dialog box. Here you can enter the format of your dates. If, for example, the string 05202203 is your custom representation of the standard 2022-05-03, you would enter the format MMYYYYdd, following the convention of the Java `DateTime` class, which is as follows:

```
Symbol  Meaning                    Presentation  Examples
------  -------                    ------------  -------
G       era                        text          AD
C       century of era (>=0)       number        20
Y       year of era (>=0)          year          1996
```

x	weekyear	year	1996
w	week of weekyear	number	27
e	day of week	number	2
E	day of week	text	Tuesday; Tue
y	year	year	1996
D	day of year	number	189
M	month of year	month	July; Jul; 07
d	day of month	number	10
a	halfday of day	text	PM
K	hour of halfday (0~11)	number	0
h	clockhour of halfday (1~12)	number	12
H	hour of day (0~23)	number	0
k	clockhour of day (1~24)	number	24
m	minute of hour	number	30
s	second of minute	number	55
S	fraction of second	millis	978
z	time zone	text	Pacific Standard Time; PST
Z	time zone offset/id	zone	-0800; -08:00; America/Los_Angeles
'	escape for text	delimiter	
''	single quote	literal	'

You'll find supported QuickSight date formats here: `https://docs.aws.amazon.com/quicksight/latest/user/supported-date-formats.html`.

Visualizing Data: QuickSight Analysis

When you are satisfied with the data preparation, you can start creating visuals and Insights. The way to do this is to click Publish And Visualize in the data editor. This will immediately create an *analysis*, which is where you will create visuals and place them on the screen in the same layout that your final dashboard will have. Figure 8.40 shows how the newly created analysis looks.

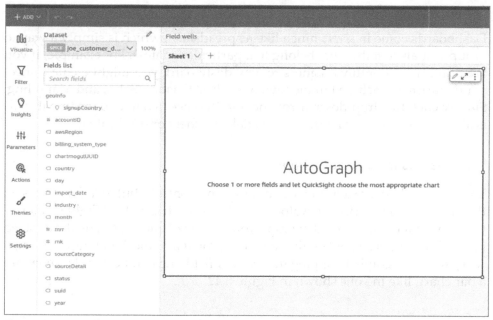

Figure 8.40: Newly created visual default view

That +Add button is your starting point for most actions when creating an analysis.

Adding a Title and a Description to Your Analysis

The first thing you will want to do is add a title to the analysis, so click the +Add button and select Add Title from the options shown in Figure 8.41. Clicking Add Title will add a text box at the top of the visualization. After that you can click + Add again and select Add Description, which will create a text box just under the title one you just added.

Figure 8.41: Add options

Renaming the Sheet

Dashboards come in *sheets* much like a spreadsheet, which is simply a way to group visuals together that belong to a particular context. For example, if you are building a monthly business review dashboard, you might create a sheet per department included in the review, such as Finance, Sales, and Marketing. Simply click the drop-down arrow next to the sheet's name to rename it. This is also where you click if you want to delete a sheet or duplicate it.

Your First Visual with AutoGraph

You can see there are a number of options and controls, but let's first focus on the visualization marked as AutoGraph. AutoGraph is a QuickSight visualization type that infers the kind of graph you want to display based on the data fed into it. If you select a field on the right and drop it into the AutoGraph visual, it will generate a graph. Dropping the country field into it, for example, generates a bar chart, like the one shown in Figure 8.42.

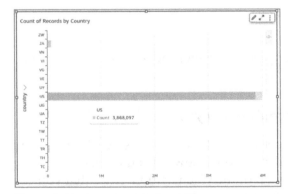

Figure 8.42: Autogenerated graph

If instead of a categorical dimension you drop a numerical field, AutoGraph outputs the sum of all the values in the field.

Field Wells

Once a value has been dropped into the AutoGraph, controls called *field wells* become available, although collapsed by default (and for this reason not immediately obvious), as shown in Figure 8.43. I am referring to the figure 8.44, where the field "mrr (Sum)" has a drop down arrow.

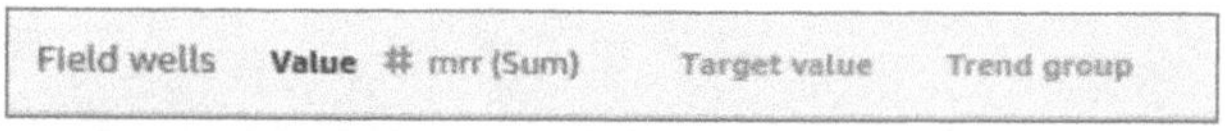

Field wells   **Value**   # mrr (Sum)   Target value   Trend group

Figure 8.43: Fields information bar

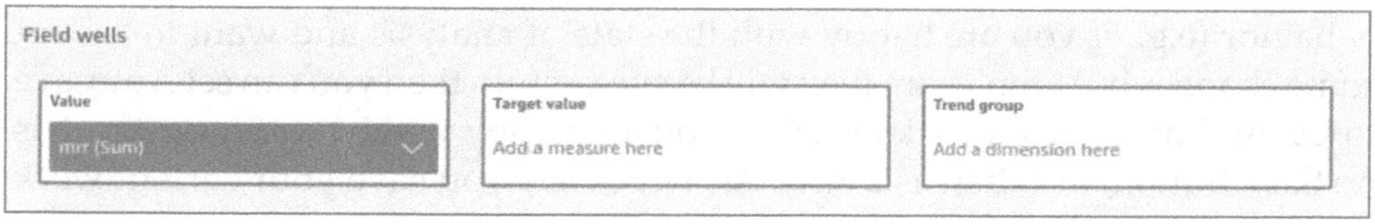

Field wells

Value	Target value	Trend group
mrr (Sum) ⌄	Add a measure here	Add a dimension here

Figure 8.44: Field wells

Field wells are how you control what data is visualized and how it is aggregated, binned, and so on. Depending on the type of graph, the field names will also change.

Visual Types

At any point you can change the type of visualization by selecting one of the symbols at the bottom-left corner of the interface. The various symbols represent the various types supported by QuickSight, which cover the most common types of visualizations for BI purposes. The options are shown in Figure 8.45.

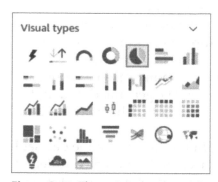

Figure 8.45: The various graph type icons

From the top right in order they are AutoGraph, KPI, Gauge, Donut Chart, Pie Chart, Horizontal Bar, Vertical Bar, Horizontal Stacked, Vertical Stacked, Horizontal Stacked 100%, Vertical Stacked 100%, Waterfall, Line, Area, Cluster Bar Combo, Stacked Bar Combo, Stacked Area, Box Plot, Pivot Table, Table, Heatmap, TreeMap, Scattered, Histogram, Funnel, Sankey, Points on Map, Map, Insight, Word Cloud, and Custom Visual (with the supplied URL).

Saving and Autosaving

When working on an analysis, you should leave the default option (Autosave) set to On. Whenever you apply a change to the analysis, the change is saved and you never have to worry about it. If, for any reason, you don't want this behavior (e.g., if you are happy with the state of analysis and want to try out some changes but aren't sure they will be successful), then you can set Autosave to Off and only turn it back on when you are happy with your work. There is no Save button, but there is a Save As, which lets you save your current work as a separate analysis.

A First Example: Pie Chart

A pie chart is one of the most common types of visuals you will probably generate, so it's a good starting place. To create a pie chart, select the AutoGraph visual and then the pie chart symbol, or click Add + ➤ Add Visual and then select the Pie Chart symbol.

For this example analysis, I will be working with a sample dataset that represents customer data. In this first pie chart, I want to gain an understanding of the geographical distribution of the customers, so the first thing I will do is drop the `account ID` field into the chart.

Clearly, one dimension isn't enough for the pie chart, and QuickSight will display the message "You need to add or remove fields," followed by the help message "pie chart requires 1 dimension in Group/Color."

Looking at the Group/Color field well, you will notice it's empty (QuickSight populates the Value field when you drop a field in the chart), so it's time we populate it. From the left side list of fields in your dataset, select a field and drop it into the Group/Color field well. In my case I am going to select the `geoInfo` field. Immediately a pie chart will be generated, and next to the `AccountID` field in the `Value` field well you will notice that data has been aggregated using a `Count` function.

This may be what you want to accomplish, but in the case of the dataset I have, there are multiple records for the same account imported on different dates. Therefore, I don't want a simple `Count`, but rather a `Count Distinct` (which will count how many distinct `AccountIDs` are present in the dataset and group them by `geoInfo`).

To change the aggregation function, click the drop-down arrow next to the field name, then hover over Aggregate, and you will be given more options like those shown in Figure 8.46.

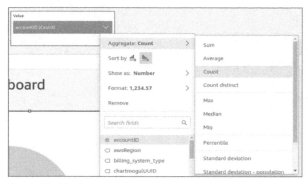

Figure 8.46: Aggregation options

Here I will select `Count Distinct` for the purpose I had in mind. Immediately the pie chart will re-compute and be redrawn on screen, with each segment of the pie chart using the `count-distinct` function as opposed to a single count. As Figure 8.46 shows, other options to aggregate data are Sum, Average, Max, Median, Min, Percentile, Standard Deviation, Standard Deviation – Population, Variance, and Variance – Population.

Renaming a Visual

QuickSight will generate the name of the visual based on the type of chart you are using and the data you provided (and how it's aggregated), but you may want to rename the visual itself to something more meaningful. The autogenerated name of a visual is something like `<aggregate>` of `<field>` by `<field>`, which in our example translates to `Count distinct of AccountID by SignupCountry`.

Double-clicking the title opens a window where you can edit the title of the visual with a rich-text editor, which includes some basic formatting options. I will rename the visual "Geographical distribution of Customers," with the word "Customers" in red bold font. Note that the maximum length of the title is 120 characters. Figure 8.47 gives a peek at what the sheet looks like at this point.

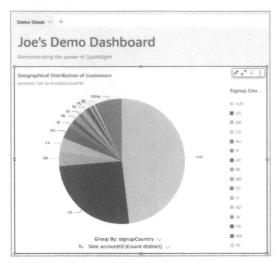

Figure 8.47: Example dashboard with one graph

You can see that the sheet's name is changed, the sheet's title is renamed, a description is added, the pie chart contains a geographical distribution of customers, and the title of the visual reflects that.

Filtering Data

When creating visuals, you may want to focus on a subset of the data for the single visual (or a group of them), but you don't necessarily want to filter that data out for the entire dashboard. QuickSight's filters have a customizable scope that you can apply to a single visual or to the entire sheet/dashboard.

If you take a look at Figure 8.47 you will notice that about half of the records do not contain geographical information. In a real-life situation, you would probably want a graphical representation of how much of the data contains geo information and, in a separate visual, the distribution of customers for which we possess geo information. So let's take out all those records with no `geoInfo` field populated.

There are two ways to accomplish this:

- Click the Null segment of the pie chart and select Exclude Null, which will automatically generate a filter.

- Manually create the filter by clicking the visual to select it, then choosing Filters ➢ Add Filter, selecting the relevant field in your visual (in our case `signupCountry`), and selecting Exclude in the condition and NULL in the value list, as shown in Figure 8.48. Then click Apply.

Figure 8.48: Filtering values

Note the scopes available to your filter:

- This Visual
- Some Visuals (manual selection)
- All Visuals Of This Dataset (it is possible to import more datasets in a single analysis, hence the distinction)
- All Applicable Visuals (all visuals that the filter can be applied to)

If you want an OR-type filter, then you can add another condition to the filter you just created. In QuickSight jargon, a filter with more conditions is called a filter group.

If you want an AND-type filter, you simply create another filter for the visual and apply it. The data will have to satisfy both to be included.

In the specific case of filtering null values (including them or excluding them), you can select Custom Filter List from the Filter Type drop-down list and select Exclude Nulls in the Null Options at the bottom of the form, as shown in Figure 8.49.

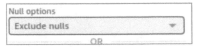

Figure 8.49: Null Options

Different data types can be filtered in different ways, so QuickSight intelligently adjusts the types of filters available according to the selected field to which the filter will be applied. You can create text filters, numeric filters, and date filters. Some filters are common (such as Equals and Does Not Equal) whereas others are type specific (such as Contains, Starts With, and Ends With for text filters; Greater Than and Greater Or Equal To for numeric filters; and Year To Date and X Months for date types). Each filter initially applies to the sheet in which it was created, but you can apply it to another sheet by selecting a sheet, then clicking the three-dots icon and selecting Apply To Sheet. Here you can also choose to edit or disable the filter, or even delete it altogether.

Adding Drill-Downs

Very often, once you have created a visualization that contains broken-down information you may want to select an element and drill down into it to discover its underlying components. For example, you may want to display sales data divided by territory, then select the territory to see what products generated sales in that geographical area. You can do so by dragging the field physically "under" the current field in the Group/Color field well, as shown in Figure 8.50.

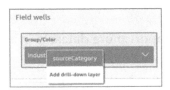

Figure 8.50: Group/Color field well

In Figure 8.51, I have created a pie chart illustrating the industry breakdown of customers. Once I click a particular industry segment, I can then drill down to its sourceCategory (that is, the Marketing source through which a customer was acquired) breakdown.

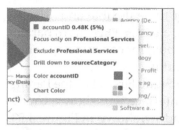

Figure 8.51: Drilling down

You can create as many levels in a hierarchy as you want, but it is important to understand that it is a hierarchy. If I added a third level in the example hierarchy, say `AWS Region`, I could only see that detail from the sourceCategory level. You cannot see the breakdown of `AWS Region` directly from `Industry`.

When you have drilled down a level, the top-right corner controls of the visual change to allow you to go up and down levels, or apply or disable filters, as shown in Figure 8.52.

Figure 8.52: Navigation between levels of drill-down

Parameters

One way to filter and control the content of the various visuals you create is through parameters. When you create a visual, you can apply filters that you create for that visual or for more visuals in the analysis. This is a good way to filter data but at the same time it's a bit inflexible, since you have to specify the values of the conditions in the filter. QuickSight comes to your aid by providing you with the option to create parameters and make filters use the value of a parameter as opposed to a manually specified value.

Why does this matter? Because you can then include parameter controls (text boxes, drop-down lists, and so on) that will allow end users to specify the value of a parameter. All those visuals containing filters configured to use the associated parameter will be re-computed and redrawn to reflect the change in parameter value. As an example, imagine you have a line chart representing the timeline of sales of 100 products, and that stakeholders asked for the graph to only represent the products that sold more than an X amount of money per month. The simplest solution is to create a filter on the `Sales Amount` field where `sales >= X`.

If, however, stakeholders wanted this parameter to be flexible and, ideally, supplied at data consumption time, you could create a `sales threshold` parameter, supply a default value, include a control (a text box) for consumers to enter a value, and then let users decide what the threshold is.

Let's see how these parameters are created in QuickSight. First, click the Parameters icon. If you don't have any parameters, the interface will show a Create One link to bring up the Create New Parameter window, shown in Figure 8.53. There are four types of parameters: integer, decimal, string, and datetime. In my case, I have created a `highsellers` Number (that is, decimal) parameter with a value of `200M`. As soon as you have created the parameter, QuickSight lets you create a filter, an action, a control, or a calculated field based on that parameter.

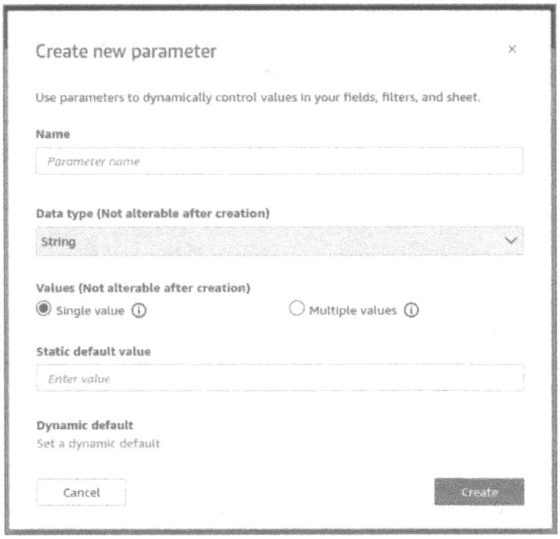

Figure 8.53: Create New Parameter

Let's create a control.

Parameter Controls

When creating a control, the first thing you need to supply is the name of the control and then the type of control you are going to use (text field, drop-down list, slider, and so on). See Figure 8.54.

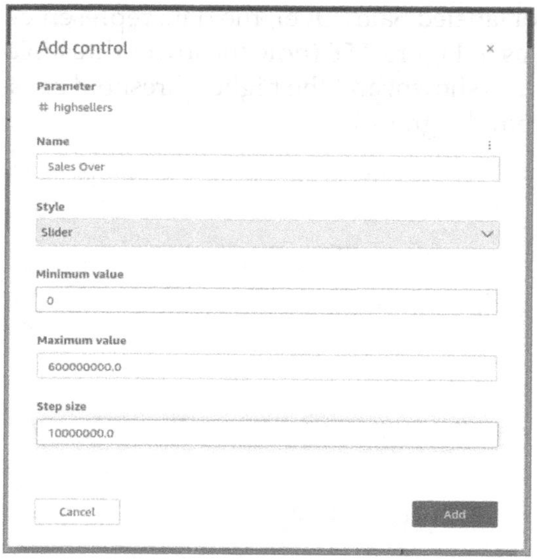

Figure 8.54: Add Control

If you specify Text Field, you can just create the control. If, however, you are choosing Slider as your control for the parameter, you have to specify a minimum and a maximum value for the slider and the step size, as in Figure 8.54. If you choose Dropdown, you will have to list all the possible values in the drop-down list.

To create a filter based on your parameter, choose Filter ➢ Create Filter and start filling in the form, as you've seen earlier. In the form, you will have the option to select Use Parameters, and if you do, you can specify which parameter to use, as shown in Figure 8.55.

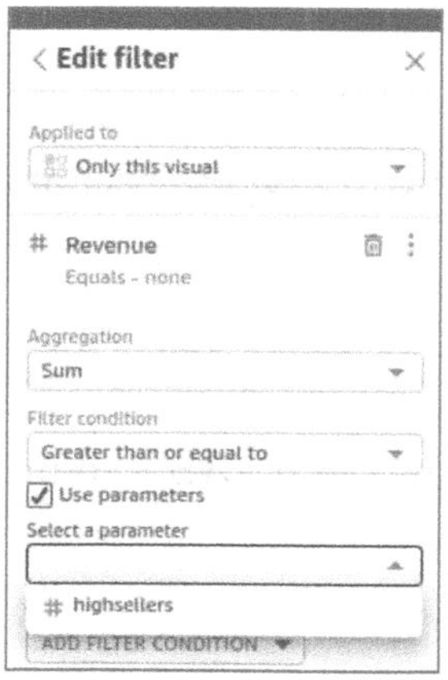

Figure 8.55: Using a parameter in a filter

Now, when you change the control labeled Sales Over, the data represented in the visual will adjust accordingly, as in Figure 8.56 (note the lower threshold specified on the left, with more products shown, and the higher threshold causing more products to be excluded from the graph).

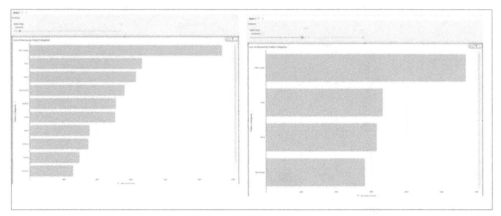

Figure 8.56: Application of parameters affecting graphs

Creating parameters is a perfect way to hand control over the data displayed in the visuals to the data consumers, and it is a nice way to handle several visuals. Figure 8.57 shows controls based on two parameters. The second control is based on a list of values dynamically retrieved from the field Product Categories in this sample dataset.

Figure 8.57: Gauge control

Actions

Another type of interaction with visuals is actions. There are five types of actions that can be configured on a visual:

- Apply a filter to the visual.
- Navigate to another sheet in the dashboard.
- Navigate to another sheet in another dashboard in the same AWS account.
- Open a URL in a browser.
- Send an email.

To create an action, select a visual and then click the Actions icon. In the resulting window, define a name for your custom action, an action type, and other options that depend on what action type you choose.

Filter Action

The default choice is Filter Action, which can be triggered by either selecting an element in the visual or by selecting Menu Option. Menu Option means that, upon selecting an element in a visual, a context menu will be displayed, and you can choose to trigger the action (which will appear in the context menu). The form for a filter action looks like Figure 8.58. As you can see ,you can select what visuals are going to get their content filtered accordingly. In my case, I have two visuals, one that has an action configured on it and another that will be redrawn upon triggering the action.

Figure 8.58: Edit Action

Selecting a bar in the bar chart on which the action is associated will bring up the context menu shown in Figure 8.59.

Figure 8.59: Action available in menu

As you can see, the My Filter Action option is available, and if I click it, the target visual will apply a filter to only display a particular field value, which in my example is the Books product category. Figure 8.60 and Figure 8.61 show a comparison of the dashboard before and after the triggering of the action.

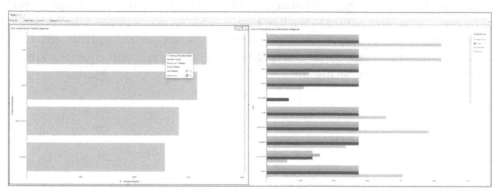

Figure 8.60: Before action trigger

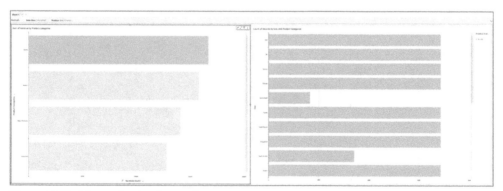

Figure 8.61: After action is triggered

Effectively, you can deem a visual to be the main controller on a sheet and filters triggered in the controller visual will cascade to all other visuals in the sheet (or specific ones, as you've seen).

Deactivating the Filter

Clicking the element that triggered the action removes the filter. There's no major visible change in the UI, so this change may not be obvious.

Navigation Actions

Navigation actions are quite simple: you give them a name, specify the select/menu option (I recommend the Menu Option, at least whenever you have more than one action configured on the same visual—otherwise you risk triggering filters and navigating away from the visual at the same time), then specify a sheet to navigate to, as shown in Figure 8.62.

Figure 8.62: New Action

Now, when you click an element in the visual, you will see all the actions you have configured in the context menu (Figure 8.63).

Figure 8.63: List of actions in context menu

Note the Go To Timeline and My Filter Action options. Clicking Go To Timeline will bring you to the selected dashboard sheet.

Navigating to a URL

If you choose URL Action, you can configure a URL that you can open in the same browser tab, another browser tab, or another browser window, as shown in Figure 8.64.

Figure 8.64: Specifying a destination URL for the action

If you specify a `mailto://` URL, you can send an email through the client configured on your machine.

Insights

QuickSight has a very powerful feature called Insights. Insights are snippets of information that QuickSight automatically calculates when importing a dataset and that can be included with your dashboard. Select a visual and see what Insights are available for you. Some of them will be simple calculations, whereas others may be Machine Learning Power (ML-powered) and will be marked as such.

In the case of the analysis I created from a sample dataset, there are lots of useful Insights and Autonarratives (natural language textual information automatically generated by QuickSight containing interesting statistics about your data) ready to be added to the analysis by simply clicking the + sign of each Insight, as shown in Figure 8.65.

Figure 8.65: Suggested Insights

If you click + (Add Insight), a new visual with the exact content of the preview will be added. You can then resize and relocate the Insight on the screen to look exactly how you want, as shown in Figure 8.66.

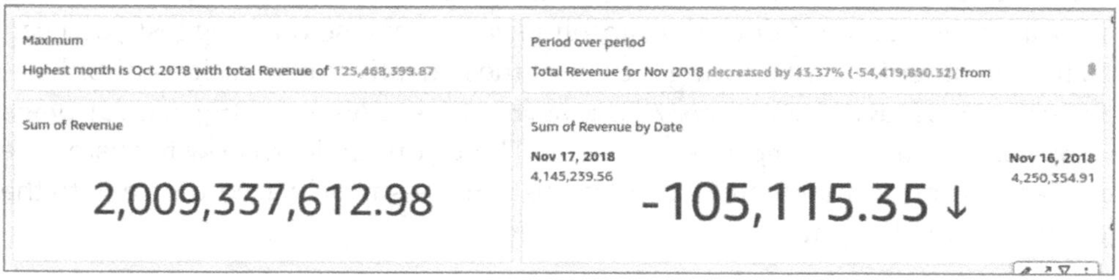

Figure 8.66: Example autonarratives

The Insights that QuickSight generates for you cover the vast majority of information snippets you would want to immediately see when creating a dashboard, and therefore I rarely had to resort to creating a customized Insight. However, doing so is a possibility, so here's a brief overview of this feature.

Customizing Insight Narratives

If you click the menu of an Insight visual, you will have the option Customize Narrative, as shown in Figure 8.67.

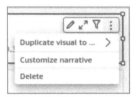

Figure 8.67: Narrative context menu

Customizing the narrative of an Insight allows you to change the text of the Insight and even what calculation is performed over what field. Not only that, but you can even apply conditional formatting to the narrative itself. For example, if I click Customize Narrative for the Insight showing the maximum revenue in Figure 8.67, the Narrative editor will show the content displayed in Figure 8.68.

Figure 8.68: Edit Narrative

Each of those fields can be edited. You can edit the time granularity of the calculation, the field being calculated, and its formatting. Exploring each of the possible alternatives would be unnecessarily tedious, since the type of calculations and functions available are standard math in an analytics context: max, min, average, standard deviation, absolute values, and so on. I suggest you head to the documentation exploring the use of the Narratives expression editor here: `https://docs.aws.amazon.com/quicksight/latest/user/using-narratives-expression-editor-step-by-step.html`. There you can learn how to customize narratives and format them to display custom messages in accordance with the content of the Insight.

ML-Powered Insights

QuickSight can automatically generate Insights that are powered by machine learning models. There are specific requirements for a dataset to be able to leverage this feature of QuickSight; check them out here: `https://docs.aws.amazon.com/quicksight/latest/user/ml-data-set-requirements.html`.

As of this writing, the requirements include:

- At least one metric (e.g., sales, orders, shipped units, sign-ups, and so on).
- At least one category dimension (e.g., product category, channel, segment, industry, and so on). Categories with NULL values are ignored.

Anomaly Detection

Anomaly detection requires a minimum of 15 data points for training (by training we refer to the process of feeding data to a machine learning model for the purpose of increasing its accuracy until a satisfactory level is achieved). For example, if your data has a daily frequency, you need at least 15 days of data. If the frequency is monthly, you need at least 15 months of data.

Forecasting

Following are the requirements for each time frequency:

- Years: 32 data points
- Quarters: 35 data points
- Months: 43 data points
- Weeks: 35 data points
- Days: 38 data points
- Hours: 39 data points
- Minutes: 46 data points
- Seconds: 46 data points

If you want to analyze anomalies or forecasts, you also need at least one date dimension.

When your dataset meets these requirements, QuickSight notifies you of the option to create ML-powered Insights in the Visuals menu at the top-right corner of the visual (Figure 8.69).

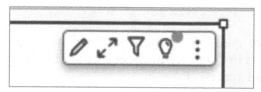

Figure 8.69: Dot indicating that ML-Insight is available

That dot next to the bulb means that you can include a forecast narrative or an anomaly detection. If you click the three-dot icon you can choose to add either a forecast or an anomaly detection, as shown in Figure 8.70.

Figure 8.70: Visual menu including

Clicking Add Forecast will create a 14-period forecast based on your data, and QuickSight will include it in the graph itself. Figure 8.71 shows the graph before and after the inclusion of a forecast.

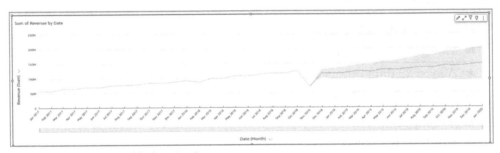

Figure 8.71: Forecast added to timeline

ML-Insights Sample Dataset

If you want to play around with QuickSight's forecasts and anomaly detection, you can download the sample dataset available at the bottom of the Dataset Requirements page, which is located here:

```
https://docs.aws.amazon.com/quicksight/latest/user/samples/
ml-insights.csv.zip
```

When you enter the URL in your browser, the zip file will download automatically. Extract the zip, go to Datasets in QuickSight, choose Upload A File, upload the extracted CSV, and create an analysis from it.

Augmenting Data with SageMaker Predictions

While QuickSight offers the option to generate single-metric forecasts and anomaly detections, you will most likely want to create other kinds of predictions (such as regressors and classifiers). One way to integrate ad hoc models into your QuickSight visuals is to use Amazon SageMaker integration.

Once your SageMaker model has been deployed, you can create a SageMaker integration in your data editor, which will need four details specified in order to work correctly:

1. The SageMaker model you are using for your predictions. This is a list prepopulated by QuickSight that queries SageMaker in your account and produces a list.

2. A name for the SageMaker integration (this is just so you can identify it—the name can be anything you want).

3. The schema's input.

4. The schema's output.

We will explore SageMaker in detail in the next chapter, so for now let's work under the assumption that you have developed a SageMaker model and deployed it, and that it correctly shows up in the model drop-down list.

In the QuickSight data editor, click Augment With SageMaker and then select your working model from the model drop-down. Assign a name to your integration, then specify the schema's inputs and outputs, as shown in Figure 8.72.

Figure 8.72: Integration with SageMaker

If you are familiar with machine learning, you will know that any trained model receives a specific data structure and produces an output. But input and output structures vary according to the model's features. A regressor produces a single numerical output, and so may a classifier, unless it is a deep learning neural network, in which case the output is normally an array of values.

QuickSight needs to be instructed on the values it needs to feed SageMaker to obtain the prediction as well as what values it is expected to receive back. The input and output are specified in JSON format, and as per the official documentation, it has a structure similar to this:

```
{
  "inputContentType": "CSV",
  "outputContentType": "CSV",  "input": [
    {
      "name": "petals",        "type": "INTEGER"
    },
    {
      "name": "petal_width",        "type": "DECIMAL"
    },
    {
    "name": "color",
    "type": "STRING"
    },
    {
                    "name": "sepal_width",
      "type": "DECIMAL"
    }
  ],
  "output": [    {
      "name": "FlowerType",
      "type": "STRING"
    }
  ],
  "description": "some description here…",
  "version": "1.0",
  "instanceCount": 1,
  "instanceTypes": [
    "ml.m4.xlarge",
    "ml.m4.4xlarge"
  ],
  "defaultInstanceType": "ml.m4.xlarge"
}
```

NOTE CSV is the only format supported for inputs and outputs.

When the integration is activated, the additional field with the value provided by SageMaker will be added to the fields.

Please refer to the full documentation for the SageMaker integration guidelines:

```
https://docs.aws.amazon.com/quicksight/latest/user/sagemaker-
integration.html#sagemaker-usage-guidelines
```

There are a few limitations:

- You cannot use output fields for a calculated field.
- You can only use SageMaker batch transform, not endpoints.
- Each dataset can be integrated with only one ML model.

Sharing an Analysis

At any point, you can share the analysis with other users in QuickSight, by clicking on the "Share" button on the top right corner of the screen. The window has a search field where you can enter usernames and retrieve the matching users. When sharing, you can set the role of a user to Reader, Author, or Co-owner. Reader can access the analysis without making changes, Author can make changes to the analysis but cannot perform administrative tasks such as inviting other users, and Co-owner enables the user to perform every possible action on your analysis.

Dashboards

Now that you know how to create visuals, you can organize them into a dashboard. In practice, this means creating an analysis, creating the sheets and the visuals in each sheet, laying out the various components in a way that makes sense, and then publishing the final result.

Dashboard Layouts and Themes

In the menu bar on the left side of the screen there's a Settings option. If you click it you will get a choice between three types of layout:

Tiled Dashboards   Visuals can be moved around, and they snap to a grid with standard spacing. This is the suggested option because it removes a lot of work in terms of aligning elements and displaying them on different devices, since it automatically handles mobile devices, too.

Free-Form   With this option you can place elements where you want, with no constraints and no snapping available. However, there is the option to fit the dashboard to the screen size.

Classic   Much like the Tiled option, the dashboards are not displayed as designed; rather, they adjust to screen size. In the Tiled option, visuals resize to keep the layout you defined.

Whenever you add a visual to the sheet you are working in, with the visual selected you drag corners or edges to resize it and move the cursor near the borders until you get a crosshair that allows you to move the visual into the desired position. New visuals can be resized to have the same height or width as existing visuals, promoting an orderly layout that is simple to organize. Figure 8.73 is an example of a dashboard containing various types of charts and visualizations, including Insights and a timeline forecast.

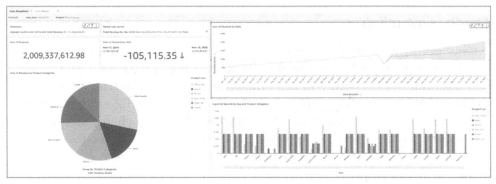

Figure 8.73: Example dashboard

Themes

QuickSight provides you with a number of color schemes for your visuals as well as the ability to create your own color schemes. If you click the menu options for any theme, you can select Save As, which will bring up the theme editor. Here you can select background and foreground colors for data, layout, and other UI elements. This is very useful because it allows you to create dashboards that adhere to your company's color palette, which makes for consistent aesthetics, especially in the context of embedded dashboards exposed on publicly accessible websites.

Publishing a Dashboard

At this point, with your data prepared, filtered, manipulated, and maybe even augmented with machine learning predictions, and with your visuals configured to respond to user interactions through actions, you can publish your dashboard and share your Insights. To publish a dashboard, you click on the Share icon at the top-right corner and select Publish Dashboard.

When the Publish Dashboard window appears, you can either publish the dashboard as new or overwrite an existing one. Pay careful attention to the advanced publishing options; there are several and they affect the dashboard behavior significantly (see Figure 8.74). These options are important because they enable the user to perform certain actions such as ad hoc filtering, without which the dashboard may not deliver its full value.

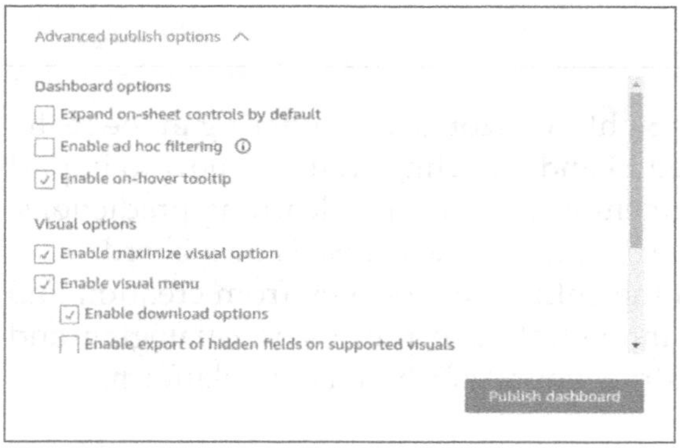

Figure 8.74: Publishing options

Embedding Visuals and Dashboards

For customers using the Enterprise Edition of QuickSight, it's possible to embed dashboards and visuals in websites with a feature called *1-click embed*. Provided you have turned on the public access option in Manage QuickSight for your dashboards, you can obtain the embedding code by clicking the Share icon in a dashboard and selecting Copy Embed Code. Then you can paste that code in the HTML of any website to include your dashboard in it. The full documentation for embedding analytics is available here: `https://docs.aws.amazon .com/quicksight/latest/user/embedded-analytics.html`.

Data Consumption: Not Only Dashboards

While QuickSight is probably the most common and intuitive way to deliver the majority of Insights, it's not the only solution available. Many people in management and leadership nowadays look for more personalized Insights that can be delivered as an attached spreadsheet in an email or as a rich text message or document, shared or sent through a messaging channel. One could argue that this kind of delivery is actually more automation-friendly than a QuickSight dashboard.

Thanks to technologies such as AWS EventBridge, AWS Lambda, and Amazon Athena, it's incredibly easy to set up a schedule for a simple pipeline that produces a report and sends it to a specific list of entities. QuickSight also allows you to send dashboards via email as PDF extracts, which may suit simpler use cases such as tabular outputs.

Summary

In this chapter, we explored QuickSight, Amazon's main offering in the realm of cloud-powered and cloud-scaled BI and reporting. You saw how to import data, manipulate it, enrich it, augment it with machine learning predictions, and then create Insights that can be organized in a shareable dashboard.

At this point we have covered the entire data journey from creation and ingestion to visualization, passing through storage, processing, cataloging, and search. Now you are ready to construct your AWS-based data platform.

Machine Learning at Scale

In this chapter, we'll explore the various solutions that AWS offers in the field of machine learning and artificial intelligence, with a strong focus on Amazon SageMaker, since it is a product that offers ultimate flexibility.

If you are reading this book, there is a good chance you are creating a data platform with large quantities of data (terabytes, petabytes, and beyond). Therefore, training ML models on large volumes of data on a personal development machine is neither practical nor ideal.

> **NOTE** Knowledge of Python will certainly result in an advantage, since all of the code in our examples is Python. Being a machine learning (ML) engineer or a data scientist is not a prerequisite because my intention is not to develop machine learning models (that would be the subject of a data science book), but to provide an understanding of the concepts of training, testing, and deployment of ML models. Moreover, the SageMaker API used in Python notebooks is a very large library, which possibly deserves am entire book.

Machine Learning and Artificial Intelligence

This book is not specifically about machine learning and artificial intelligence (ML/AI), so we are going to focus on the tools that enable you to train and deploy models, but we won't be discussing the details of algorithms or matters such as model optimization techniques that are more pertinent to data science. In this respect, the subject we are going to cover can be better defined as machine learning operations (MLOps) and its role in a data platform. That said, a brief introduction to ML/AI's use cases and types of ML models follows.

What Are ML/AI Use Cases?

ML has made remarkable progress in recent years in terms of speed of development and accuracy. There are several types of ML models; here are the most common ones:

- **Forecasting:** ML models can intelligently predict future trends of metrics, including elements such as seasonality that were previously harder to accurately forecast.

- **Regression:** ML models can be trained to predict a numeric outcome representing a metric of any kind, such as the likelihood of an event occurring.

- **Classification:** ML models can take an input and classify it with a high degree of accuracy, such as the case of computer vision models recognizing objects.

- **Recommendation:** ML-powered recommendation engines enable better decision-making at a business and an end-user level

This is not an exhaustive list, but it should give you a good idea of what ML is used for.

Types of ML Models

ML algorithms can be divided into a few families:

Supervised Learning   These are algorithms in which training data is "labeled" and the model learns to associate the correct label to data previously unseen by the model. This algorithm is commonly used for regression and classification models.

Unsupervised Learning   These are algorithms in which training data has no label, and the model learns to detect associations or commonalities among groups of data points. This algorithm is commonly used for "clustering" models.

Reinforcement Learning   These algorithms are used to reward correct choices by the model, and so it is particularly recommended for online models that learn in real time and keep learning as new data is fed to the model.

Overview of ML/AI AWS Solutions

Amazon, like most giants of the tech industry, has heavily invested in ML/AI in recent years, so the products relating to this area of development have multiplied at remarkable speed. The following list contains a few that have gained particular popularity, but this list is by no means comprehensive:

CodeGuru   Intelligent recommendations for building and running modern applications

Comprehend   Analyzes unstructured text

DevOps Guru   ML-powered cloud operations service used to improve application availability

Forecast   Fully managed service for accurate time-series forecasting

Fraud Detector   Detects online fraud using machine learning

Lex   Builds voice and text chatbots

Panorama   Enables computer vision applications at the edge

Personalize   Helps you easily add real-time recommendations to your apps

Polly   Turns text into lifelike speech

Rekognition   Searches and analyzes images

SageMaker   Builds, trains, and deploys machine learning models

Textract   Extracts text and data from virtually any document

Transcribe   Provides powerful speech recognition

Translate   Provides powerful neural machine translation

Amazon SageMaker

As mentioned, our focus in this chapter is primarily on SageMaker. Why? Because if you take a look at the previous list of Amazon products relating to ML/AI, most problems have been effectively resolved (speech recognition, keyword extraction, and so on) and there is little to no point to reinventing the wheel; for example, if you are trying to detect key words and phrases in a piece of text, I wholeheartedly recommend you use Comprehend rather than developing your own solution, and only resort to your own model development where existing products do not reach a satisfactory performance (which, in my experience, has never been the case).

Where your AI needs are limited to common tasks such as the aforementioned use cases, you can simply integrate those services in your own code work with simple API calls. For example, I do not recall the last time I developed a natural language processing (NLP) model; NLP is a truly resolved problem, and API calls to Comprehend have been fully sufficient to satisfy my needs. This means that your unsatisfied ML/AI needs will lie in problems and domains that are specific to your organization, and therefore you have little choice but to develop your own ML/AI solutions.

This is where SageMaker comes into play. With SageMaker, you can train and deploy models specifically addressing your unique use cases, monitor their performance and accuracy, and manage the entire pipeline, including CI/CD.

There are several parts to SageMaker, since ML is a complex subject, and its life-cycle management is an even more complicated task.

SageMaker Domains

Before you can produce an ML model and deploy it, you will need to create a *domain*, which will include your cloud development environment, complete with AutoPilot, debugger, monitoring, model versioning, and endpoint management (we will see what SageMaker endpoints are in the section "Inference"). There is one domain per AWS account, and you can bring users in either through SSO or IAM.

To set up the domain, go to SageMaker and you will be offered the option to create a domain with either a quick setup or a standard one (see Figure 9.1).

Figure 9.1: Domain creation form

The standard setup will configure the following details:

- Network security and data encryption
- SageMaker Studio and RStudio integration
- SageMaker Studio Projects and Jumpstart
- SageMaker Canvas and other services integration
- IAM or IAM Identity Center (successor to AWS SSO)

Proceeding with the domain creation will bring you to the network configuration form. In the Permission section, you have the ability to create a SageMaker execution role (or choose an existing one). If you choose to create one, this role will contain the timestamp of creation in the role's name, which is handy (see Figure 9.2).

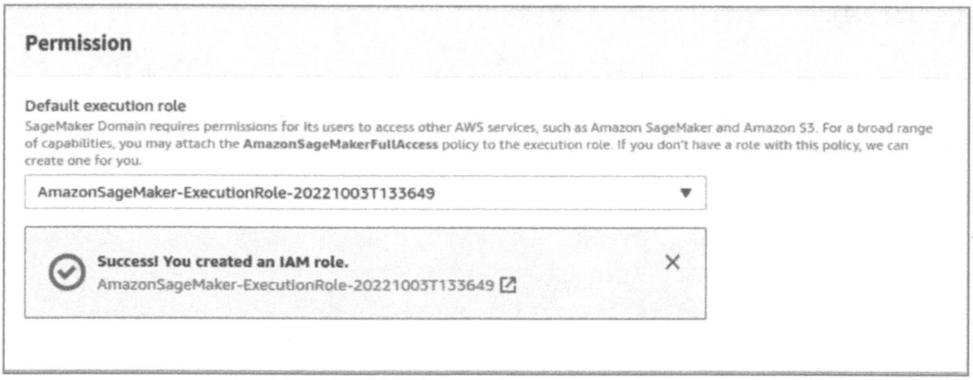

Permission

Default execution role
SageMaker Domain requires permissions for its users to access other AWS services, such as Amazon SageMaker and Amazon S3. For a broad range of capabilities, you may attach the **AmazonSageMakerFullAccess** policy to the execution role. If you don't have a role with this policy, we can create one for you.

AmazonSageMaker-ExecutionRole-20221003T133649 ▼

✓ **Success! You created an IAM role.** ✕
AmazonSageMaker-ExecutionRole-20221003T133649 ☑

Figure 9.2: IAM role for SageMaker execution

In the Network And Storage Selection section, you can choose the VPC, the subnet, and the security groups for your domain. You can always change this information later, so some default choices are enough at this point.

In the Studio Settings, RStudio Settings, and Canvas Settings, unless you have particular needs (in terms of encryption, storage buckets, or Jupyter Notebook version), you can leave everything as it is.

Note that in Canvas Settings, you can choose whether or not to allow the upload of local files—which I suggest you do. If you do, SageMaker shows the cross-origin resource sharing (CORS) policy that will be attached to the receiving bucket. The policy looks like this:

```
[
  {
    AllowedHeaders: [*],
    AllowedMethods: [POST],
    AllowedOrigins: [*],
    ExposeHeaders: []
  }
]
```

Clicking Next will start the creation of your SageMaker domain. which will take a few minutes. You will get a nice summary of your information, status, authentication method, domain ID, and execution role that's always available in the dashboard.

Adding a User to the Domain

The next thing to do is add a user. From the SageMaker menu, choose Studio, and you will see the Launch Studio window in Figure 9.3. Click Add User to open a screen where the username and execution role will be prepopulated (but you can change them if you want). I renamed the user's name to something less obscure, which, once created, will appear in the list of users in the dashboard (Figure 9.4).

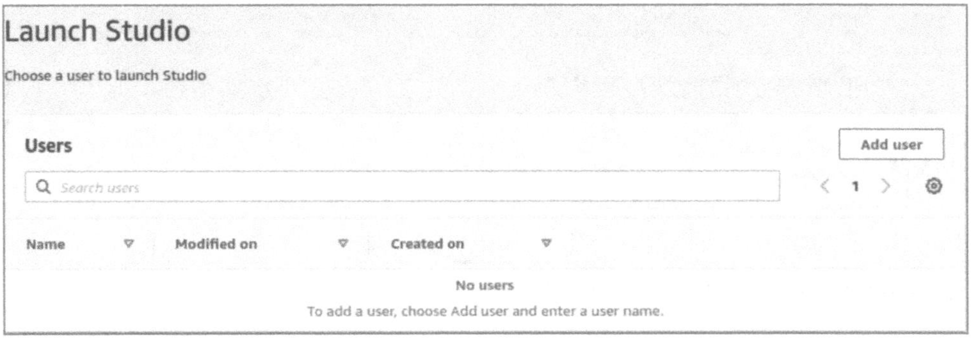

Launch Studio

Choose a user to launch Studio

Users   Add user

Q Search users   < 1 > ⚙

Name	▽	Modified on	▽	Created on	▽

No users

To add a user, choose Add user and enter a user name.

Figure 9.3: Launch Studio

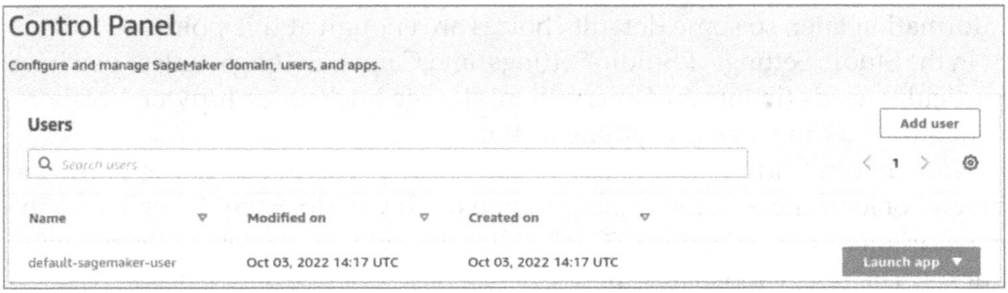

Control Panel

Configure and manage SageMaker domain, users, and apps.

Users   Add user

Q Search users   < 1 > ⚙

Name	▽	Modified on	▽	Created on	▽	
default-sagemaker-user		Oct 03, 2022 14:17 UTC		Oct 03, 2022 14:17 UTC		Launch app ▼

Figure 9.4: View user

SageMaker Studio

Now we can successfully launch SageMaker Studio. From the SageMaker menu choose Studio and (after a short loading time) you will be presented with a fully integrated development environment with the interface shown in Figure 9.5.

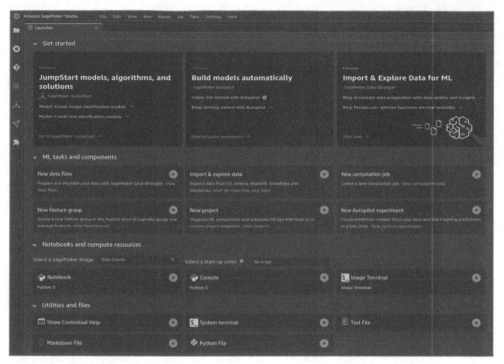

Figure 9.5: SageMaker Studio

SageMaker Studio is an extremely powerful tool. Some of its features are tools in their own right, such as Data Wrangler, Autopilot, and more. Therefore, it may at first look quite daunting, but fear not, because SageMaker Studio is very similar to any integrated environment you may have used in the past, especially Microsoft's VSCode, which it visually resembles in terms of layout and navigation.

To illustrate the power of SageMaker Studio, let's dive into the JumpStart models that the welcome page offers. To do that, click Go To SageMaker JumpStart. JumpStart has all sorts of scenarios with sample data provided for you, divided into the following categories: Solutions, Data Types, ML Tasks, Notebooks, Frameworks, Resources. Let's launch one of the example notebooks (as of this writing there are 44 sample notebooks you can use).

When you click any one of the notebooks available, it will be displayed in read-only mode on your screen. To modify the notebook and execute it, you must import it into your workspace. To do so, click the Import Notebook button at the top-right corner.

Let's use the very first example provided in the notebooks: the Linear Learner with the MNIST database. The MNIST database is a famous database of handwritten digits that is in the public domain. It can be used to train models that can recognize a handwritten digit. Each handwritten digit is contained in an image that's 28 × 28 pixels, which yields a matrix with 784 values in it.

After importing the notebook in our workspace, we can edit it. But before doing that let's take a look at the steps the notebook will be performing:

1. Introduction
2. Prerequisites and preprocessing
3. Permissions and environment variables
4. Data ingestion
5. Data inspection
6. Data conversion
7. Train the linear model
8. Set up hosting for the model
9. Validate the model for use

The reason why this list is important is that no matter how complicated your use case is and how complex the model you intend to develop is, these steps are standard and you will always perform them. For this reason, we will go through the notebook, paying particular attention to those code lines that represent standard steps that you will probably perform regardless of the task at hand.

SageMaker Example Notebook

Let's now dive into the actual notebook. This will serve as a template for your future work on notebooks. As was the case for ETL notebooks, always bear in mind that notebooks are the place where you conduct your prototyping and exploratory work. Once you reach a stage at which you are happy to deploy to production, you will be relying on SageMaker Model Building pipelines. Notebooks are not and should never be considered production artifacts.

Step 1: Prerequisites and Preprocessing

In this step, we establish a few important details, such as S3 bucket and key/prefix for objects we will work with. We'll also load a few required libraries. This is the first code block in the notebook:

```
import re
import boto3
import sagemaker
from sagemaker import get_execution_role

sess = sagemaker.Session()
```

```
region = boto3.Session().region_name

# S3 bucket where the original mnist data is downloaded and stored.
downloaded_data_bucket = f"jumpstart-cache-prod-{region}"
downloaded_data_prefix = "1p-notebooks-datasets/mnist"

# S3 bucket for saving code and model artifacts.
# Feel free to specify a different bucket and prefix
bucket = sess.default_bucket()
prefix = "sagemaker/DEMO-linear-mnist"

# Define IAM role
role = get_execution_role()
```

The first four lines import the libraries `re`, `sagemaker`, and `boto3` (which is the default AWS Python library). Then the `get_execution_role` function of the `sagemaker` library is explicitly imported so that it can be invoked without prefixing it with `sagemaker`. That's not a needed step but it certainly makes the code more explicit and readable.

Next, we create a session object. Every notebook interacting with AWS resources needs a session created, so we do that with the `sagemaker` library.

If in your notebook you need region information, you can derive that from the session object. Again, that's not a necessary step unless you intend to deploy the same code in different regions and potentially change the names of variables and resources in your script based on the region you are using.

At this point, we specify the bucket and prefix where the MNIST data is stored:

```
# S3 bucket where the original mnist data is downloaded and stored.
downloaded_data_bucket = f"jumpstart-cache-prod-{region}"
downloaded_data_prefix = "1p-notebooks-datasets/mnist"
```

You will need to change the bucket name, as you may remember that there cannot be two buckets named the same way (even cross accounts). S3 buckets have unique names all over the world. There are various sources where you can download the MNIST dataset in "pickled" format. I obtained it from `https://github.com/mnielsen/neural-networks-and-deep-learning/blob/master/data/mnist.pkl.gz`, which is a publicly available GitHub repository.

Step 2: Data Ingestion

Next, we need to download the data into the location we specified.

The block that performs this operation looks like this:

```
%%time
import pickle, gzip, numpy, urllib.request, json
```

```
# Load the dataset
s3 = boto3.client("s3")
s3.download_file(downloaded_data_bucket, f"{downloaded_data_prefix}/
mnist.pkl.gz", "mnist.pkl.gz")
with gzip.open("mnist.pkl.gz", "rb") as f:
    train_set, valid_set, test_set = pickle.load(f, encoding="latin1")
```

As you can see, bucket and prefix are used to locate the dataset, which is then loaded in memory split into the three conventional training, validation, and testing sets.

If all goes well, the cell will produce an output similar to this:

```
CPU times: user 838 ms, sys: 423 ms, total: 1.26 s
Wall time: 1.71 s
```

Step 3: Data Inspection

We want to make sure that data has been loaded correctly and inspect its distribution. This is normal in data science; you want to ensure that everything looks as you would expect it to. The block for this operation contains this code:

```
%matplotlib inline
import matplotlib.pyplot as plt

plt.rcParams["figure.figsize"] = (2, 10)

def show_digit(img, caption="", subplot=None):
    if subplot is None:
        _, (subplot) = plt.subplots(1, 1)
    imgr = img.reshape((28, 28))
    subplot.axis("off")
    subplot.imshow(imgr, cmap="gray")
    plt.title(caption)

show_digit(train_set[0][30], f"This is a {train_set[1][30]}")
```

which produces the output shown in Figure 9.6.

Figure 9.6: Example prediction

Essentially it verifies the correctness of labels with the associated images.

Step 4: Data Conversion

Original image data is provided in integers, but in this particular case data needs to be converted to `float32` types, so that's what this block is doing:

```
import io
import numpy as np
import sagemaker.amazon.common as smac

vectors = np.array([t.tolist() for t in train_set[0]]).astype("float32")
labels = np.where(np.array([t.tolist() for t in train_set[1]]) == 0, 1,
0).astype("float32")

buf = io.BytesIO()
smac.write_numpy_to_dense_tensor(buf, vectors, labels)
buf.seek(0)
```

At the end of the conversion, data is stored on disk, ready for upload to S3.

Step 5: Upload Training Data

SageMaker models read training data from S3, so once we have completed the data conversion, we need to re-upload the converted training data:

```
import boto3
import os

key = "recordio-pb-data"
boto3.resource("s3").Bucket(bucket).Object(os.path.join(prefix, "train",
key)).upload_fileobj(buf)
s3_train_data = f"s3://{bucket}/{prefix}/train/{key}"
print(f"uploaded training data location: {s3_train_data}")
```

Now we set up a destination for the model artifact to be stored once the model is trained:

```
output_location = f"s3://{bucket}/{prefix}/output"
print(f"training artifacts will be uploaded to: {output_location}")
```

Step 6: Train the Model

All the preparation work has been done, so we can now train the model. This is done with a ready-made SageMaker container for the "linear-learner" model, which is then passed as a parameter in the model constructor:

```
from sagemaker.amazon.amazon_estimator import get_image_uri

container = get_image_uri(boto3.Session().region_name, "linear-learner")
```

```
import boto3
import sagemaker
from time import gmtime, strftime

sess = sagemaker.Session()

linear = sagemaker.estimator.Estimator(
    container,
    role,
    instance_count=1,
    instance_type="ml.c4.xlarge",
    output_path=output_location,
    sagemaker_session=sess,
)
linear.set_hyperparameters(feature_dim=784, predictor_type="binary_
classifier", mini_batch_size=50)

job_name = f"jumpstart-example-linearlearner-binary-{strftime('%Y-%m-%d-
%H-%M-%S', gmtime())}"

linear.fit({"train": s3_train_data}, job_name = job_name)
```

Of particular note in this block are the following:

1. The need to specify a container and a role for the model training

2. The number of instances that will perform the training

3. The instance type

4. The hyperparameters, where `feature_dim` defines the array size of each training record (remember, this is the 28 × 28 pixel data of each image); the `predictor_type`, which is `binary_classifier` because we are only predicting whether or not a digit is a zero; and the `mini_batch_size`, which is the number of records processed at a time by the learner

5. The `linear.fit` call, which is how we practically start the training

After a little while, the notebook will produce an output similar to the following:

```
2022-08-21 09:32:43 Starting - Starting the training job..[2022-10-21
09:40:43.795] [tensorio] [info] epoch_stats={"data_pipeline": "/opt/ml/
input/data/train", "epoch": 15, "duration": 36320, "num_examples": 1000,
"num_bytes": 159200000}
#metrics {"StartTime": 1666345243.7957091, "EndTime":
1666345243.7957952, "Dimensions": {"Algorithm": "Linear Learner",
"Host": "algo-1", "Operation": "training", "epoch": 6, "model": 0},
"Metrics": {"train_binary_classification_cross_entropy_objective":
{"sum": 0.027115659337192774, "count": 1, "min": 0.027115659337192774,
"max": 0.027115659337192774}}}
```

with as many `#metrics` lines as learning iterations performed.

After a while (in my case roughly 13 minutes), the training will complete, and the model will be uploaded to the output location specified in the learner constructor. We can verify that the model is correctly uploaded and registered by going to the SageMaker dashboard and choosing Inference ➤ Models, and the model should appear in the list, as shown in Figure 9.7.

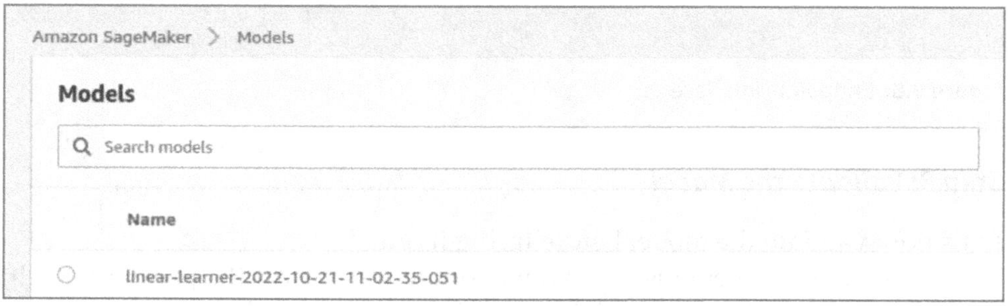

Figure 9.7: Models list

Step 7: Set Up Hosting and Deploy the Model

Now we can deploy the model with the following code:

```
endpoint_name = f"jumpstart-example-linearlearner-binary-{strftime('%Y-
%m-%d-%H-%M-%S', gmtime())}"

linear_predictor = linear.deploy(initial_instance_count=1,
instance_type="ml.m4.xlarge", endpoint_name=endpoint_name)
```

This operation will also take a few minutes. Note that you have to specify the number of instances and their type here, too.

This apparently minor operation underlines one of the most important aspects of SageMaker: the ability to decouple a model from its deployment resources. In other words, once you are happy with the performance of a model, the model is stored in S3 and can be used whenever you need it. You can have multiple deployments with different endpoints, you can change the instance count and type performing predictions, and generally you have all the flexibility you need to make the best use of your models.

I confess that I feel the output of this operation could be a little more informative:

```
--------!
```

You can verify that the endpoint is correctly deployed by going to the SageMaker dashboard and choosing Inference ➤ Endpoints. The model I just deployed appears in the Endpoints list, marked as In Service (Figure 9.8).

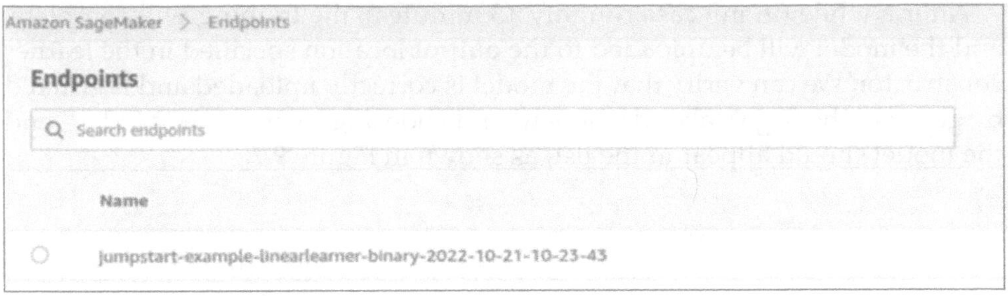

Figure 9.8: Endpoints interface

Step 8: Validate the Model

Let's now validate the model before trying it out.

The result of the previous deployment operation returns the predictor itself, which can be used to create serializers and deserializers, like so:

```
from sagemaker.serializers import CSVSerializer
from sagemaker.deserializers import JSONDeserializer

linear_predictor.serializer = CSVSerializer()
linear_predictor.deserializer = JSONDeserializer()
```

Upon successful execution of the block, the linear predictor will use CSV to serialize and JSON to deserialize.

Now we can try to perform a prediction:

```
result = linear_predictor.predict(train_set[0][30:31], initial_
args={"ContentType": "text/csv"})
print(result)
```

which outputs something like the following:

```
{'predictions': [{'score': 4.112601914834507e-13, 'predicted_label': 0}]}
```

Inference works, but how accurate is it? Let's try a mass prediction and compare it to the associated labels to get an idea of how well the model does:

```
import numpy as np

predictions = []
for array in np.array_split(test_set[0], 100):
    result = linear_predictor.predict(array)
    predictions += [r["predicted_label"] for r in result["predictions"]]

predictions = np.array(predictions)
import pandas as pd
```

```
pd.crosstab(
    np.where(test_set[1] == 0, 1, 0), predictions, rownames=["actuals"],
colnames=["predictions"]
)
```

In my case, the output was the following matrix:

	PREDICTED 0	PREDICTED 1
Actual 0	8980	40
Actual 1	41	939

This is quite an acceptable performance for a linear learner, especially considering this was not much of a linear problem.

Step 9: Use the Model

Now that everything is set up, we can start using the model through the endpoint that SageMaker created for us. In SageMaker Studio, all available resources can be found by clicking the SageMaker Resources icon.

In our case, when I select Endpoints from the drop-down list of resources, I can see the available endpoints (Figure 9.9).

Figure 9.9: Endpoints in SageMaker interface

Inference

Inference refers to the predictions made by a machine learning model. There are several ways to perform inference in SageMaker:

- Real time
- Asynchronous
- Serverless
- Batch transform

Real Time

Real-time inference refers to the inference performed by a model through its endpoint in real time—that is, sending a request and receiving a response that contains the ML model's prediction. This is a plausible use of a ML model but not one that is very common in a data analytics context or as part of a data platform. It is only suitable for payloads small enough that the prediction can be sent back to the requester in a matter of seconds or less.

Asynchronous

When dealing with payloads large enough that it would be unfeasible (or simply not convenient) to wait for a response from the ML model, you can use the asynchronous inference type.

The difference here is that upon completion of the request, the asynchronous inference will send a message with SNS, which can be processed by other components within the AWS cloud in a kind of "fire and forget" fashion.

Serverless

Another interesting option is serverless inference, which has reached general availability only recently. Models do not use a persistent instance but rather a Lambda-like infrastructure that allows you to run inference without having to provision the resources for it. The same advantages that are applicable to Lambdas are also applicable to serverless inference: pay-per-use model, auto-scaling, and high availability.

If you are not entirely sure of the traffic that your ML model will receive, then serverless inference is definitely an option to consider.

Batch Transform

When it comes to producing data for analytics, however, batch transform is the go-to method of integration of inference in a data platform.

Batch transform refers to an inference model that runs on a schedule, collects input data from an S3 location, and produces predictions that are stored in another S3 location. There are several advantages to batch transform:

- You don't need a persistent endpoint. You can create the endpoint before running the transform and shut it down when finished.
- You can process large datasets.

- You can run a notebook that performs data preprocessing and validation before inference.
- You can associate input records with predictions so that you can make the best possible use of the output of the inference.

To create a batch transform, go the SageMaker dashboard and select Inference ➢ Batch Transform to open the Batch Transform options. The first thing you will need to do is configure the job (see Figure 9.10).

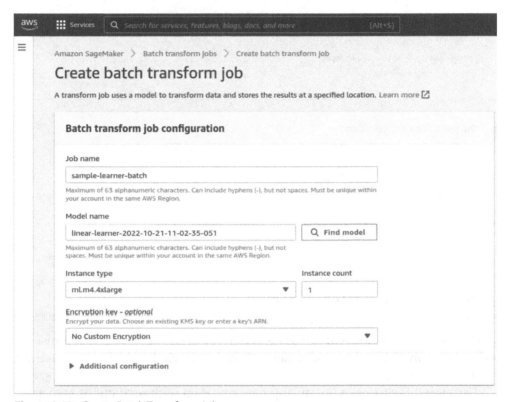

Figure 9.10: Create Batch Transform Job

Click Find Model and you will be prompted with the same list that you saw after deploying the model for the first time. Select your model from that list.

Next configure the location of inputs and outputs, which are S3 locations (Figure 9.11).

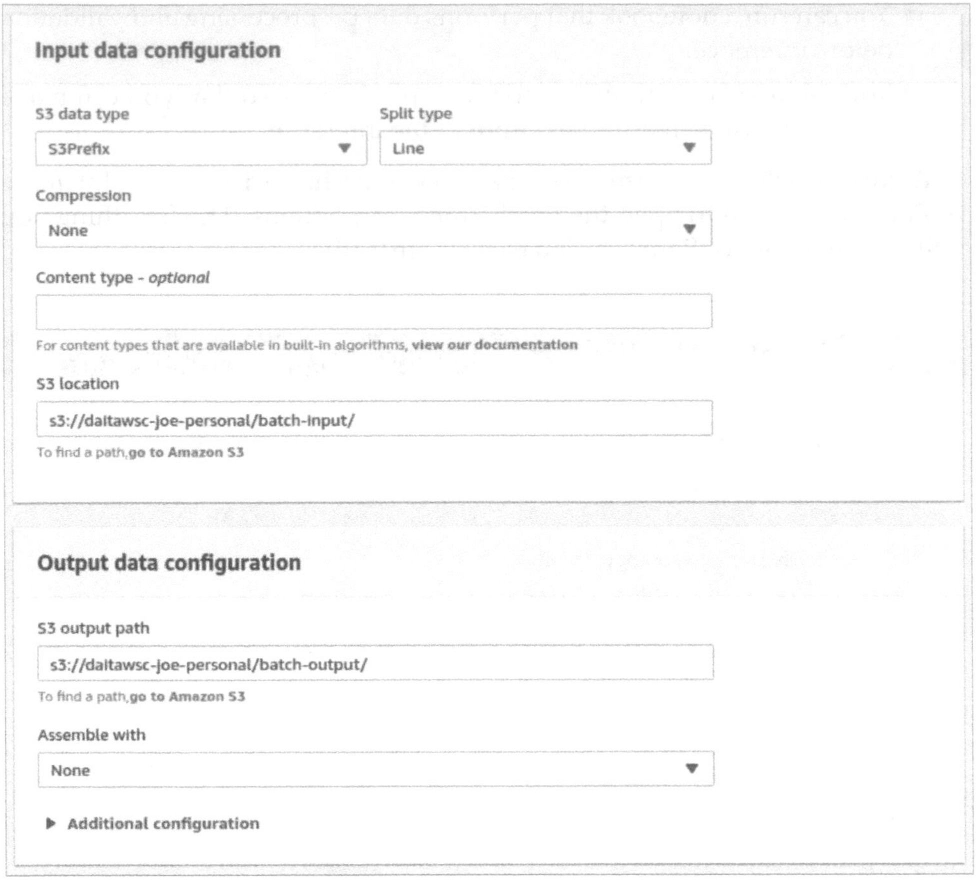

Input data configuration

S3 data type

S3Prefix ▼

Split type

Line ▼

Compression

None ▼

Content type - *optional*

For content types that are available in built-in algorithms, **view our documentation**

S3 location

s3://daitawsc-joe-personal/batch-input/

To find a path, **go to Amazon S3**

Output data configuration

S3 output path

s3://daitawsc-joe-personal/batch-output/

To find a path, **go to Amazon S3**

Assemble with

None ▼

▶ **Additional configuration**

Figure 9.11: Input and output data configuration

Once created, the job will run immediately. The output of the batch transform is stored in an S3 location, and as such, it can be crawled and cataloged like any other S3-based data.

Through this process, you can augment raw data with predictions associated with your original records and proceed with the creation of tables and views in the AWS Glue Catalog, and subsequently use these in dashboards, reports, and so forth.

Data Wrangler

One interesting feature of SageMaker is Data Wrangler, which allows you to prepare data for machine learning, conduct exploratory work, and train models and deploy them all through the use of a point-and-click UI and no code (unless you want to write your own custom data transformations).

The ease with which Data Wrangler allows you to prepare and deploy models is very impressive. However, as you can imagine there is a limit to the complexity of the scenarios you can address in no-code solutions, so I highly recommend trying Data Wrangler out if you have a fairly standard use case on your hands, such as simple regressions or classifications.

For more complex scenarios, Data Wrangler can still be of help for the following reasons:

- It allows you to create visualizations of your training data, giving you a clear idea of data distribution.

- It allows you to easily conduct exploratory work and feature engineering with simple drag-and-drop operations.

- The final output can be exported to a notebook, which you can then use as the starting point for further development, saving you the time it would take to write boilerplate code and implement the initial basic data transformations.

These aspects are very useful because they allow you to inspect data quality ahead of complex data science and feature engineering work. Use Data Wrangler as a production tool for simple use cases and a great prototyping tool for more complex ones.

SageMaker Canvas

The last feature of SageMaker that is worth mentioning is Canvas. Canvas is a web application that allows you to develop ML models by uploading training data (or connecting to stores containing the training data) and selecting a target variable (that is, the value you want to predict in your models), and quickly build a ML model that is ready for deployment.

As part of the model build, you can also choose to preview data, which will allow you to inspect column impact, and visualize correlations between columns with scatterplots and data distribution with bar charts. Once you are happy with your choices, you can simply click Build Model to create the machine-learning model.

When the model is ready, you can select a dataset (from either a file you uploaded to Canvas or a connected data store such as Redshift) and make predictions. The output will be saved into a file, which you can download as CSV.

SageMaker Canvas is extremely helpful for simple use cases such as time series forecasting and linear regressors (e.g., sample datasets to play around with Canvas allow you to make house price predictions based on location and size of the house).

I find Canvas to be suited for internal data science work that is not meant to be put into production or repeated over time. If you need a model built that also operates a periodic (normally, daily) prediction over S3-based data and outputs results to S3 for discoverability, then SageMaker Studio/Notebooks is the path to take and batch inference the way to perform such predictions.

Summary

In this chapter we have explored AWS's solution for the implementation of machine learning pipelines that process data at scale. We explored SageMaker, AWS's main offering in the realm of custom machine learning model development. You learned how to create a notebook and perform preprocessing, validation, and model training and deployment. We also explored the existing alternatives in terms of inference models, such as real time and batch-transform.

Finally, we explored how to integrate the result of your inferences in your data platform to augment the original data with artificial intelligence coming from your ML models' predictions.

Example Data Architectures in AWS

This appendix explores a few use cases and the architecture I recommend you put in place to implement them.

A good place to start for data architects in charge of designing AWS architectures is the AWS Well-Architected section of the AWS documentation at `https://aws.amazon.com/architecture/well-architected`.

Well-Architected is a tool that guides you toward the best possible implementation of your architecture according to the following principles, which in AWS Well-Architected jargon are called *pillars*:

- Performance
- Scalability
- Security
- Operational excellence
- Sustainability
- Cost

These are the principles you should keep in mind when designing your architectures.

There are a number of scenarios that AWS lists in "Data Analytics Lens," and we will focus on a few:

- Modern Data Lake Architecture (formerly Lake House)
- Batch processing
- Stream processing

At this point of your journey, you should be familiar enough with the terminology and the technologies used in each scenario, and this appendix will work as a quick reference for your design work.

Modern Data Lake Architecture

If you were to memorize only one of the scenarios listed in this appendix, I recommend the Modern Data Lake Architecture (formerly Lake House). This is because it is the most comprehensive architecture of all, and one that every modern organization should put in place if they want to expand a world of possibilities in their analytics data platform.

Let's take a look at Figure A.1 and then explore its parts.

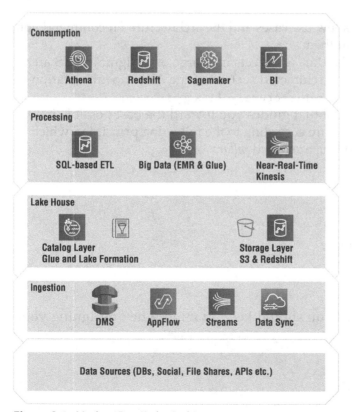

Figure A.1: Modern Data Lake Architecture

At first glance, this architecture should not be too different from the serverless data lake architecture we explored in this book. There are many formal definitions of Lake House, which, in my opinion, introduce confusion more than answer the question "What is a lake house?" To me a lake house is a transactional data lake that lets you query the data in a lake the same way you would query data in a warehouse.

And that is precisely the reason a warehousing solution like Redshift is added into this dual architecture—so that raw data in the data lake gets a schema enforced upon it that speeds up and optimizes queries.

A WORD ON HUDI

In recent times, a library called Hudi has appeared that enables you to maintain an index on data stored in S3 and "overwrite" (albeit maintaining historical versions of records) the current state of an S3-based table. This practically achieves the very arduous objective of maintaining a table in an OLTP or operational store in sync with an S3 representation of that same table. This is great for real-time updates and running analytical queries on the current state of datastores on a data lake.

ETL in a Lake House

At this point, whether you are implementing the lake house with Redshift or pure S3 with Hudi, your lake house can be accessed with SQL (Athena for S3, or Redshift MPP queries), which means that you are able to run ETL jobs using SQL. This approach is an advantage for a number of reasons, above all the simplicity of implementation of ETL jobs, which is now just a matter of selecting a data source (Athena tables or Redshift clusters), running a query, and storing the result in the desired target store.

Whatever manipulation is needed (filtering, joining, mapping, and so on) can all be done in SQL in the form of WHERE clauses or JOIN statements. You can also publish the changes received in the lake house on streaming channels and execute streaming analytics and streaming ETLs on that data.

Consuming Data in the Lake House

Lastly, once your data has been processed in the ETL phase, you can consume it much the same way you would in a traditional data lake, with Athena, Redshift, or QuickSight.

You can also use ETL jobs to create datasets that are then used by SageMaker for the continuous creation of machine learning models, or for SageMaker batch transforms that will take the result of your queries and augment it with ML predictions.

The Modern Data Lake Architecture

If we think back to the name of the architecture itself, we may realize that, in reality, all modern data lakes should be built with a Modern Data Lake Architecture. And I agree—this is most definitely my recommendation, too. The best part is that you can use your existing data lake as the foundation for your modern data lake, and incrementally transition.

It may not be an overnight process, but eventually it will yield many advantages that your organization will benefit from. So go ahead and build your data lake, and you can always take the next step when your organization and team are ready to do so.

Batch Processing

When you're dealing with large volumes of data, it may be ideal to generate datasets, including aggregate data, roll-ups, counts, and general statistics. To do so efficiently, it may be preferable to process data in batches (as opposed to real-time processing, or not processing at all, leaving aggregation computation to the BI layer).

Following the processing step, results can then be stored in the ideal data store for consumption, such as S3, OpenSearch (ElasticSearch), DocumentDB, DynamoDB, or whatever other store is suited for the purpose of retrieval of this data.

Let's take a look at the architecture, shown in Figure A.2.

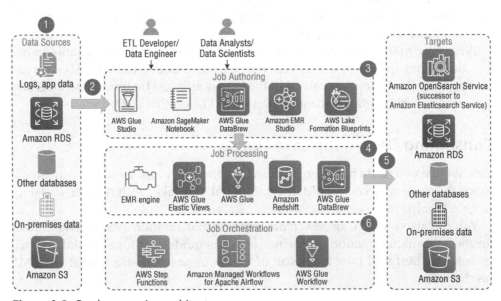

Figure A.2: Batch processing architecture

There are six distinct sections, some of which should, at this point, seem familiar to you. Data residing in a data source (1) will get ingested (2) in batches with an ETL job (3), processed (4), and stored in a destination of choice (5).

The Orchestration section of the diagram illustrates the technologies available in AWS for job orchestration should your use case necessitate that. Orchestration refers to the process of decomposing the entire data processing phase into steps that can be ordered in a sequence and (potentially) invoked on certain conditions, including the ability to iterate over a number of cycles of steps until some break condition is met. For this, AWS Step Functions and managed airflow are very useful and intuitive.

So, what are practical use cases for batch processing? One example is serving aggregate data and statistics to the front-end of a web or a mobile application. It would be unthinkable to compute those values over terabytes of data in the standard amount of time that a modern web user expects from a website or a mobile application. This kind of data has to be computed ahead of time and must be stored somewhere suitable for an application to retrieve it, such as an RDS database or OpenSearch.

Another common use case is business intelligence, where it would be impossible to delegate the computation of aggregates to the likes of QuickSight or another BI tool, as the amount of data to be processed far exceeds the tool's capacity (for example, refer to QuickSight's limitation of 250 million rows of data for a dataset). In this case you would most likely choose S3 as your target store and trigger a cycle of crawling and cataloging, using an Athena View to construct a base dataset for your visualizations.

Stream Processing

The last architecture we are going to explore in more detail is stream processing. Let's take the diagram in Figure A.3 as a starting point.

Stream processing is an architecture aimed at resolving the question of real-time processing. If real time is not needed, you can easily fall back to batch processing.

This kind of architecture is normally employed to resolve the real-time processing challenge that large volumes of data such as click-data, IoT and sensors, and server logs normally pose.

The AWS recommended way is to take this data (which would be coming from AWS sources such as CloudWatch events and logs, IoT Core or DMS, or from outside AWS in the form of custom applications and services) and publish it on a streaming channel. For this, there are three main solutions: Kinesis, Managed Kafka, and plain Kafka.

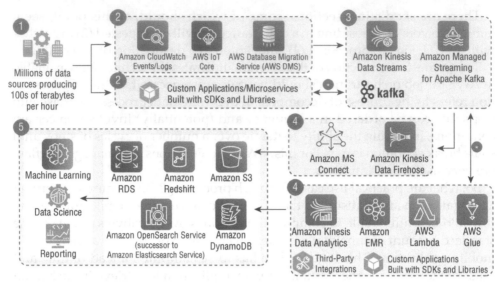

Figure A.3: Stream processing architecture

Kinesis is normally more manageable and requires very little operational overhead to be maintained, so it would always be my first port of call. However, if you need a latency smaller than 70ms, you will have to resort to Kafka. Once the data has been published on a streaming channel, you can deliver it to a target store (normally S3) while also sending it for processing to an ETL streaming job, a processing Lambda, or an EMR cluster, and even use the original stream as a source for a Kinesis Data Analytics stream, which queries a time window in the retained records of your stream and produces analytics stored in S3.

The output of your processing is then made available for standard consumption or use: S3 for storage and use with ML and OpenSearch and DynamoDB for consumption by applications, Redshift, and RDS for BI.

Architecture Design Recommendations

While we tried to cover the most common use cases, it is practically impossible to cover them all. The challenges that the real world throws at data architects are so varied that you will inevitably find yourself having to apply principles to your designs, rather than copy an architecture from some documentation.

For this reason, I list here the guiding principles that I use on a day-to-day basis, which I hope you will find useful.

Automate Everything

Dealing with terabytes of data makes it impossible to manually maintain a system. Strive to automate from the get-go. The idea is that you build maintenance tools for your data platform, and then it maintains itself.

Build on Events

If you use AWS EventBridge, and events in general, as the heartbeat of your pipelines and data platform, then you obtain true flexibility and extensibility. Do not couple your components tightly; let events be the backbone of your architecture.

Performance = Cost Savings

In AWS, especially when dealing with serverless technologies such as Lambda or Athena, optimizing performance will most likely translate into a cost saving. The better your system performs, the cheaper it is to run.

AWS Glue Catalog and Athena-Centric Workflow

The AWS Data Catalog and Athena are at the exact center of that data spectrum that goes from data ingestion to BI in a data platform. Be sure to leverage the centrality of the catalog for data access and data storage, and treat Athena as your data mart, where data personnel at all levels can access the data they need, already curated for their use case.

Design Flexible

I like to design architectures, not by naming the technology that will perform a certain job, but rather the technology type. For example, if you need data published for real-time consumption, simply include a "streaming technology" in that portion of the architecture. This way, you make your architecture adaptable to unforeseen constraints, such as having to deal with legacy technology, or having to leverage a preexisting in-house precise skill set. In general, resist the temptation to think of implementation details at the architecture design level.

Pick Your Battles

More often than not, there is a fully managed or serverless AWS technology that will resolve a problem for you without much fuss. If you build on events and design with flexibility in mind, you will always be able to swap out a fully managed solution like Kinesis for a manually maintained (but more performant) tool like Kafka.

Parquet

In the vast majority of cases, Parquet is the file format you will want to use.

Summary

This is the end of the book, and the beginning of your journey into building a data platform on AWS. I sincerely hope this book helped you learn how to accomplish the task of building a data platform on AWS from scratch, as well as teach you guiding principles for architecture design. I am very excited to know what you built using the knowledge I shared in this book and encourage every reader to get in touch to show me what they have done.

Happy architecting!

Index